The Physiocrats and the Wo

The Physiocrats believed that wealth came exclusively from the land, that nature was fecund, and that man could harness its reproductive forces. Capital investments in agriculture and hard work would create profits that circulated to other sectors and supported all social institutions. Physiocracy, which originated in late eighteenth-century France, is therefore widely considered a forerunner of modern economic theory. *The Physiocrats and the World of the Enlightenment* places the Physiocrats in context by inscribing economic theory within broader Enlightenment culture. Liana Vardi discusses three theorists – Francois Quesnay; Victor Riquetti, marquis de Mirabeau; and Pierre Samuel Du Pont de Nemours – and shows how their understanding of mental processes, science, politics, and the arts influenced their individual approach to economic writing. The difficulty in explaining the doctrine, combined with the expectation that the public would be persuaded by its arguments, mired physiocracy in endless contradictions. This work offers a framework for understanding physiocratic theory and its complicated relation to modern economics.

Liana Vardi is associate professor of history at the University at Buffalo, SUNY. Vardi specializes in French history and the eighteenth century. She is the author of *The Land and the Loom: Peasants and Profit in Northern France, 1680–1800* (1993). She contributed to a volume titled *Agrarian Studies: Synthetic Work at the Cutting Edge* (2001).

# The Physiocrats and the World of the Enlightenment

LIANA VARDI
*University at Buffalo,
State University of New York*

CAMBRIDGE UNIVERSITY PRESS
Cambridge, New York, Melbourne, Madrid, Cape Town,
Singapore, São Paulo, Delhi, Mexico City

Cambridge University Press
32 Avenue of the Americas, New York NY 10013-2473, USA

Published in the United States of America by Cambridge University Press, New York

www.cambridge.org
Information on this title: www.cambridge.org/9781107681408

© Liana Vardi 2012

This publication is in copyright. Subject to statutory exception
and to the provisions of relevant collective licensing agreements,
no reproduction of any part may take place without the written
permission of Cambridge University Press.

First published 2012
First paperback edition 2013

*A catalogue record for this publication is available from the British Library*

*Library of Congress Cataloguing in Publication Data*
Vardi, Liana.
The physiocrats and the world of the Enlightenment / Liana Vardi,
University at Buffalo, State University of New York.
p. cm.
Includes bibliographical references and index.
ISBN 978-1-107-02119-8
1. Physiocrats. 2. Economics. 3. Enlightenment. I. Title.
HB93.V375  2012
330.1–dc23    2011049373

ISBN 978-1-107-02119-8 Hardback
ISBN 978-1-107-68140-8 Paperback

Cambridge University Press has no responsibility for the persistence or
accuracy of URLs for external or third-party internet websites referred to in
this publication, and does not guarantee that any content on such websites is,
or will remain, accurate or appropriate.

*To Elise*

# Contents

| | | |
|---|---|---|
| *List of Figures* | | *page* viii |
| | Introduction | 1 |
| 1. | Art, Craft, and Court | 23 |
| 2. | The Ways of the Mind | 52 |
| 3. | The Ways of the Heart | 83 |
| 4. | A Delicate Balance | 113 |
| 5. | Representative Assemblies | 149 |
| 6. | The Journalist | 182 |
| 7. | The Education of Princes | 211 |
| 8. | Changing the World | 241 |
| *Acknowledgments* | | 279 |
| *Bibliography* | | 281 |
| *Index* | | 309 |

# Figures

1.1. *Portrait of François Quesnay* by J. Chevallier, engraved by Jean-Georges Wille (1747), Réunion des Musées Nationaux/Art Resource, New York. *page* 24
2.1. *Tableau économique*, in *l'Ami des hommes*, vol. VI (1760) (author's copy). 80
3.1. *Marquis de Mirabeau* by Jacques Aved (1743), Réunion des Musées Nationaux/Art Resource, New York. 84
6.1. *Portrait and Coat of Arms of Pierre Samuel Du Pont de Nemours* (1789), Hagley Museum and Archives. 183
8.1. "Hommage funèbre au maire d'Etampes," *Révolutions de Paris*, June 1792, General Research Division, The New York Public Library, Astor, Lenox and Tilden Foundations. 266

# Introduction

## Who were the Physiocrats?

The resurgence of interest in physiocratic ideas in the twenty-first century is nothing short of astonishing. New studies of pre-Revolutionary economic and political debates devote at least a section to them.[1] Young scholars, in particular, have been reexamining texts written by the major physiocrats, although in some instances *before* they became physiocrats, and linking them to Enlightenment debates on natural law, luxury, sentiment, sovereignty, or the national debt. At the same time, physiocracy increasingly features in more general surveys as shorthand for Old Regime reform projects or even for an interest in agriculture.[2]

---

[1] Michael Kwass, *Privilege and the Politics of Taxation in Eighteenth-Century France. Liberté, Egalité, Fiscalité* (Cambridge, 2000); David Bell, *The Cult of the Nation in France, Inventing Nationalism, 1680–1800* (Cambridge, Mass., 2001); Jay M. Smith, *Nobility Reimagined: The Patriotic Nation in Eighteenth-Century France* (Ithaca and London, 2005); John Shovlin, *The Political Economy of Virtue, Luxury, Patriotism, and the Origins of the French Revolution* (Ithaca and London, 2006); Michael Sonenscher, *Before the Deluge: Public Debt, Inequality, and the Intellectual Origins of the French Revolution* (Princeton, 2007); Amalia D. Kessler, *A Revolution in Commerce, The Parisian Merchant Court and the Rise of Commercial Society on Eighteenth-Century France* (New Haven, 2007); Dan Edelstein, *The Terror of Natural Right, Republicanism, the Cult of Nature, & the French Revolution* (Chicago, 2009); and, most recently, Paul Cheney, *Revolutionary Commerce, Globalization and the French Monarchy* (Cambridge, Mass., 2010).

[2] For example, in French scholarship, in the form of a "physiocratic current" [*courant physiocratique*] in several articles in Nadine Vivier, ed., *Elites et progrès agricole, XVIe–XXe siecle* (Rennes, 2009). T. J. Hochstrasser in "Physiocracy and the Politics of *Laissez-Faire*," in Mark Goldie and Robert Wokler, eds., *The Cambridge History of Eighteenth-Century Political Thought* (Cambridge, 2006), pp. 419–42, expands the group to include what he calls a "distinctive second wave of physiocratic thinkers" (p. 420). William Doyle uses

Since the physiocrats' practical suggestions for economic improvements overlapped with those of other reformers, especially within government circles, the temptation to disregard their important divergences has been greatest for scholars of French finances and ministerial projects.[3] There is a difference therefore between understanding the physiocratic movement as it developed internally and its strident and doctrinaire public face. The Economists, as physiocrats were then known, were useful for those high-ranking administrators who agreed with some of their ideas and could use them to test public response to liberalization of the economy. Opponents of such reforms were equally quick to focus on physiocratic writings whose "sectarian tone," as the *intendant* of Limousin remarked, won them more enemies than friends and could be used to undermine royal policies. For its true followers, physiocracy involved a psychological conversion that was more visible to contemporaries than to later generations and that needs to be restored to understand physiocracy's successes and failures.

Since it was more politic to subsume their peculiar beliefs within a broader program of economic reform, a conflation was consciously orchestrated by the movement's major popularizer, Pierre Samuel Du Pont de Nemours, and the confusion was sustained in mid-nineteenth century by Alexis de Tocqueville in his analysis of the origins of the French Revolution. Since then, it has served to bolster reinterpretations of the Revolution focused on the political culture of the late eighteenth century, where "physiocrats" are granted a particularly important role that must be addressed and corrected. In this study, I will argue that physiocracy must be defined very narrowly indeed, given the epistemological as well as economic tenets that its espousers had to accept. Extending membership to partial sympathisers masks the movement's peculiarities, why it so frustrated contemporaries and proved opaque and burdensome even

---

physiocracy to explain the freeing of the grain trade and treats Turgot as a physiocrat. *The Oxford History of the French Revolution*, 2nd edition (Oxford, 2002), pp. 57–8, 60. Jessica Riskin does the same in "The 'Spirit of System' and the Fortunes of Physiocracy," *History of Political Theory* 43 (annual supplement 2003), 42–73; Otto Mayr, *Authority, Liberty, and Automatic Machinery in Early Modern Europe* (Baltimore, 1986), p. 165. Mauro Ambrosoli, *The Wild and the Sown, Botany and Agriculture in Western Europe: 1350–1850* (Cambridge, 1997), takes physiocracy to mean agronomy (p. 360), as does Jeremy L. Caradonna, *The Enlightenment in Question, Academic Prize Competitions* (concours académiques) *and the Francophone Republic of Letters, 1670–1794* (PhD diss. Johns Hopkins, 2007), p. 324.

[3] For example, Joël Félix in his study of L'Averdy's ministry, *Finances et politique au siècle des Lumières, Le ministère L'Averdy 1763–1768* (Paris, 1999).

to its most devoted followers. Physiocracy was much more than an economic theory: It rested on a particular understanding of the human mind, of the role of reason and imagination so that, as well as expanding their doctrine into the social and political realms, physiocrats also tackled culture, attempting to define an aesthetic.

Such fine distinctions will no doubt surprise nonspecialists who, if they have heard of the movement at all, probably recall its central contention that only agriculture creates renewable wealth (renewable being the key term here). Some might even be familiar with its image of zigzagging exchanges known as the *Tableau économique*, or have tried – and commonly failed – to figure out how it works. The physiocracy I present here is more arcane, although it encompasses the standard description. Physiocrats believed that François Quesnay had pierced the mysteries of nature and understood the economic system that Providence had intended for mankind. He laid out a rule for the annual reproduction of a marketable surplus, based on nature's capacity to multiply itself, although this "law" was only truly comprehensible to those who took the trouble to study it carefully and let the evidence penetrate their minds. Once they had done so, its truths would become self-evident and cohere into the same set of relations that Quesnay had so clearly perceived. His "vision" was embodied or summarized (depending on the exegesis) in the *Tableau*, a representation that was more than the sum of its parts. Time and again physiocrats contended that Quesnay's sudden flash of insight could not be properly put into words. It had come to him through a chain of reasoning that culminated in an inner certainty. Evident truths were justified by God. Men had been created with the capacity for higher thought and granted occasional insights into his divine wisdom. In its less lofty embodiment, the doctrine explained why only agriculture could furnish the necessary surplus and assure societies of a steady income down the ages. But it came enveloped within a theory of knowledge that vacillated between Cartesian innateness and Lockean sensationalism, the role of the senses disappearing at times in a fog of divinely inspired intuition.

Once Quesnay had worked out his ideas, all he required from his collaborators was to find a way to disseminate them since he chose not to do this himself. He converted the marquis de Mirabeau, then at the height of his fame, to his system and the latter took on the role of chief exponent with alacrity. Yet Mirabeau was unable to explicate the mathematical arguments behind the *Tableau*, since he did not understand them himself, and Quesnay had no use, in any case, for anyone who questioned his conclusions. Physiocratic texts would lead the public to accept unassailable principles by asserting their material and moral necessity. Since they believed the physical and moral laws of the universe were one and the same, accepting physiocracy and living according to its teachings would occur simultaneously. No invisible hand was at work here. In order for the system of reproduction of profits "that nature intended" to work, the entire population had to collaborate and understand that individual self-interest lay in adhering to this necessary order. They had to be taught, persuaded, and perhaps even stirred emotionally to accept physiocratic ideas. The means differed, Quesnay believing that his scientific system demanded intellectual concentration, Mirabeau meaning to arouse men's better selves, and Du Pont invoking sentimental contagion. Disseminating the doctrine required particular agility in balancing "scientific" demonstration and moral persuasion, and hence relied greatly on the temperament and beliefs of the collaborators themselves. They shared a common faith in Quesnay but, based on their own appreciation of human motivation, veered in unexpected directions when publicizing his thought. This is the subject of this book.

Quesnay's economic "law" fitted within natural religion in the same ways as Newton's investigations (or as they were understood to have done), and he hoped that his theory would be similarly treated as a mathematically demonstrated phenomenon. Unlike gravity or light, however, Quesnay's outcomes depended on human decisions, on the *will* controlling the passions. Social institutions and political authorities would reinforce the right choices and monitor them, but the Achilles heel of Quesnay's system, as of all subsequent social theory, lay in its reductive human psychology. Quesnay's system faced the additional difficulty of requiring total adherence to work properly (rather than just a significant majority), since one could not opt out of nature's dictates. Calculating probabilities (which mathematicians such as Condorcet would endorse in this domain) was anathema to Quesnay because it introduced the element of chance which his entire system meant to overcome. Although Quesnay divided the population into large groups of landowners, farmers, and artisans and calculated aggregate exchanges, overall success nonetheless rested on millions of individuals making the right choices. Mirabeau would call this "fulfilling one's duties" and develop the doctrine's moral system around it.

As Pierre Samuel Du Pont, Quesnay's young acolyte, would later explain, Quesnay "had seen that man had only to look inside himself to find the indisputable rules that governed these laws, and had only to study the physical realm assiduously in order to grasp its precepts, foundation, and authority. He realized that this evidence and the authority of these sovereign laws would become irresistible once they became widely known and demonstrated."[4] To be a physiocrat was to share in these certainties. As a result, those who merely assented to the *consequences* of physiocratic principles (such as free trade in grain) were quickly ejected from the movement's inner circle or broke with the group, as happened with the inspector of trade and manufactures Louis-Paul Abeille or the philosopher Condillac.[5]

The physiocrats arrived on the scene in the late 1750s in the midst of the Seven Years War. New projects to bolster the nation's productivity had surfaced, been adopted, or rejected since Colbert's time, and planning and calculating were not new to the Control General (the Old Regime combination of Ministry of Finance and Ministry of the Interior). To be sure, Colbert's protectionist policies, his zeal in regulating artisanal production, and his subsidies to luxury industries would garner increasing criticisms.[6] Still, one must not forget the extent to which Louis XIV's minister had offered a positive vision. In a world subjected to ferocious international military and commercial rivalries, Colbert had told France that she would be able compete successfully

---

[4] Pierre Samuel Du Pont, *La Physiocratie ou constitution essentielle du gouvernement le plus avantageux au genre humain* (Paris, 1767).

[5] See Letter from Abeille to Du Pont, 28 February 1769, Hagley Museum and Library, [henceforth Hagley] Winterhtur Mss Group 2 Series A w2-17, complaining that he had been included in Du Pont's list of proto-physiocrats. Walter Eltis, "Le rejet de Condillac par les physiocrates: une occasion manquée," in B. Delmas, T. Demals, and Ph. Steiner, eds., *La diffusion internationale de la physiocratie (XVIIIe–XIXe siècles)* (Grenoble, 1995), pp. 177–93. Georges Weulersse, *La physiocratie sous les ministères de Turgot et de Necker* (Paris, 1950) pp. 22–3. For an alternate reading and a full list of collaborators, see Christine Théré and Loïc Charles, "The Writing Workshop of François Quesnay and the Making of Physiocracy," *History of Political Economy* 40:1 (2008), 1–42. On the English side, David Hume abhorred the Economists and wondered what could possibly drive Turgot to support them. See his letter to the abbé Morellet, dated 10 July 1769, in John Hill Burton, *Life and Correspondence of David Hume*, 2 vols. (Edinburgh, 1846), vol. II, pp. 427–8. Adam Smith was more generous. While he criticized the physiocrats for denying industry and trade a role in the creation of surplus wealth and calling them "barren or unproductive" (the physiocrats' actual term was *sterile*), "yet in representing the wealth of nations as consisting, not in the unconsumable riches of money, but in the consumable goods annually reproduced by the labour of the society; and in representing perfect liberty as the only effectual expedient for rendering this annual reproduction the greatest possible, its doctrine seems to be in every respect as just as it is generous and liberal." Adam Smith, *An Inquiry into the Nature and Causes of the Wealth of Nations*, Book IV, Chapter IX, in Kathryn Sutherland, ed. (Oxford, 1993), pp. 387, 388–9.

[6] For a more nuanced version of Colbertism, see Philippe Minard, *La Fortune du Colbertisme: état et industrie dans la France des Lumières* (Paris, 1998), chapter 1.

and prosper (or, optimally, conquer all). Economic prophets were less lucky thereafter. The Regent Philippe d'Orléans's advisor, John Law, might have exuded unbounded optimism, but his bank and his trading companies spiraled out-of-control in the early 1720s and ended in a massive collapse, convincing the French public to steer clear of visionary "systems." As the government scrambled to raise funds in the midst of the Seven Years War, physiocrats offered their own remedies to France's national debt and depleted resources.[7] Their solutions resonated favorably, initially at least, because they tapped into the era's romanticization of nature and celebrated France's underrated agricultural potential. While everything was on the verge of collapse, physiocrats showed how everything could be fixed.[8] Their ideas, far-fetched at times, nonetheless overlapped sufficiently with reforming currents within the royal administration, to create a superficial alliance that went a long way to secure physiocracy's initial success.

Georges Weulersse's masterly study of 1910 offers an excellent overview of the doctrine. Weulersse disentangled the various strands of physiocratic doctrine and described how, once the basic principles had been laid out, Quesnay and his collaborators set to propagating their ideas within reforming government circles. Weulersse's story of the rise and fall of the doctrine thus followed the arc of its administrative favor. The movement began auspiciously in the late 1750s, reached its apex with the 1763 and 1764 edicts freeing the grain trade, and collapsed in 1770 when those measures were rescinded. Weulersse extended this study to the Revolution over several volumes (published posthumously), without discerning a true revival of physiocratic ideas.[9] The temptation has been, however, to stretch physiocracy beyond these chronological and ideological boundaries. The aim of this study is to pull physiocracy out of the penumbra into which it has fallen, restore its peculiarities, and show how

---

[7] For excellent overviews of the financial crisis and solutions to it, see James C. Riley, *The Seven Years War and the Old Régime in France: The Economic and Financial Toll* (Princeton, 1986); Kwass, *Privilege and the Politics of Taxation*; David Stasavage, *Public Debt and the Birth of the Democratic State: France and Great Britain 1688–1789* (Cambridge, 2003); Michael Sonenscher, "The Nation's Debt and the Birth of the Modern Republic: the French Fiscal Deficit and the Politics of the Revolution of 1789," Parts I and II, *History of Political Thought* XVIII (1997), and *Before the Deluge*. I agree with Rosanvallon that the eighteenth century liked simple solutions. Pierre Rosanvallon, *Le libéralisme économique, Histoire de l'idée de marché* (Paris, 1989, orig, ed., *Le capitalisme utopique*, 1979), p. 29.

[8] Gustave Schelle also sees the Physiocrats as optimists. *Du Pont de Nemours et l'école physiocratique* (Paris, 1888), p. 65.

[9] Weulersse, *Le mouvement physiocratique en France*.

## Du Pont de Nemours

difficult it was, even for its most active supporters, to work out and disseminate Quesnay's ideas.

The longstanding blurring of the lines between physiocracy and promoters of laissez-faire can be traced back to 1768 when Pierre Samuel Du Pont published a selection of Quesnay's writings. He called the collection *Physiocratie*, a term meaning the "reign of nature," that became associated with the group initially known simply as the Economists.[10] At the same juncture, he penned a separate pamphlet *De l'origine et des progrès d'une science nouvelle*.[11] In the first, Du Pont praised Quesnay's principal associates the marquis de Mirabeau and Le Mercier de la Rivière. In the second, Du Pont interjected: "Three men truly deserved the friendship of the inventor of the Science and the Tableau économique, M. de Gournay, M. le marquis de Mirabeau, and M. Le Mercier de la Rivière, who became his intimates in this period [the late 1750s]." Jean Claude Marie Vincent de Gournay, the Intendant of Commerce who turned the phrase *laissez-faire, laissez-passer* into a commonplace,[12] died in 1759 and was hence unable to challenge Du Pont's move to ally physiocrats with top government reformers. Nor could he challenge Du Pont's other claim that he and Quesnay had reached the same conclusions, "although by different routes," unless this was confined to economic deregulation. The high administrators, Du Pont added, "with whom the nation's fate now rested," had been tutored by Quesnay. But Du Pont was overstepping. The riposte came two years later, from one of those very figures and Gournay's most prominent disciple,[13] the future Controller General of Finances Jacques Turgot. He was incensed by Du Pont's "corrections" of his text, *Réflexions sur la formation et distribution des richesses*, which he had allowed Du Pont to publish in the physiocratic monthly, *Les Éphémérides du citoyen*.[14] Du Pont had amended the text to make

---

[10] The term had been invented by the abbé Baudeau, the editor of the *Ephémérides du citoyen* but Du Pont popularized it through his collection of essays.

[11] Pierre Samuel Du Pont de Nemours, *La Physiocratie*, op. cit.; *De l'origine et des progrès d'une science nouvelle* (London, 1768).

[12] The phrase has been traced to a merchant François Legendre in the seventeenth century responding to Colbert. Georges Weulersse, *La physiocratie à la fin du règne de Louis XV* (Paris, 1959), p. 73.

[13] See his famous "Eloge de Vincent de Gournay" (1759), in Joel-Thomas Roux and Paul-Marie Romani, eds., *Turgot, Réflexions sur la formation et distribution des richesses* (Paris, 1997), pp. 123–53.

[14] Turgot had written the piece in 1766 and it appeared in three parts, in volumes XI and XII (1769) and volume I (1770) of the *Ephémérides du citoyen*.

Turgot's views conform more closely to Quesnay's, and Turgot demanded "he disavow all the additions which give the impression that I am an Economist, something I do not wish to be, just like I do not wish to be an Encyclopedist."[15] He had already reproached Du Pont, in 1765, of claiming he had approved of a report that he hadn't even read.[16]

Du Pont published a retraction but did not end his eclectic search for physiocratic precursors or prominent supporters. Citing C. Cusano's analysis of the *Éphémérides du citoyen* under Du Pont's editorship (1768–1772), Bernard Delmas, Thierry Demals, and Philippe Steiner describe the process whereby physiocrats, seeking publicity and validation, projected a physiocratic outlook onto all of Europe by praising any "laudable act" by foreign rulers or individuals that promoted agriculture.[17] Their ecstasy knew no bounds when they discovered a monarch engaging in symbolic ploughing (Joseph II or the future Louis XVI) or chatting with harvesters (Marie Antoinette).[18]

This enthusiasm wasn't matched on the ground. Historians have shown that those Spaniards, Portuguese, Italians, Germans, Austrians, or Swedes who showed any interest in physiocracy rarely did so because they believed in the doctrine (the Margrave of Baden being one notable exception). Rather, they drew from it a generic support for agricultural improvement, free trade in grains, or fiscal reform, while also rejecting the more arcane, rebarbative aspects of Quesnay's thought.[19] In France as well, government converts to laissez-faire found it expedient at times to ally themselves with the *économistes*. This conflation would backfire dramatically when Turgot's opponents used it to tar his ministry.[20] As their "prime representative," he was accused of enacting the program of the "dangerous sect" of Economists.[21] If this was not entirely false in matters

---

[15] Letter from Turgot to Du Pont, Limoges, 2 February 1770 in Gustave Schelle, ed., *Oeuvres de Turgot et documents le concernant*, 5 vols. (Paris, 1913–1923), III, p. 374.

[16] Letter from Turgot to Du Pont, Limoges, 10 May 1765. Hagley, W2-1522.

[17] "Présentation: les physiocrates, la science de l'économie politique et l'Europe," pp. 7–29, in B. Delmas, T. Demals, and Ph. Steiner, eds., *La diffusion internationale de la physiocratie (XVIIIe–XIXe)* (Grenoble, 1995), pp. 18–19.

[18] See "Suite d'augures heureux pour l'agriculture: Mme la Dauphine encourage les moissonneurs," *Éphémérides* (1770), V, pp. 246–8.

[19] See the articles by L. Argemi and E. Lluch, J. M. Pedreira, A. Alimento, K. Tribe, D. Klippel, C. Lebeau, and L. Magnusson in *La diffusion internationale de la physiocratie*. Also, Keith Tribe, *Governing Economy: The Reformation of German Economic Discourse, 1750–1840* (Cambridge, 1988), pp. 119–31.

[20] Edgar Faure, *La disgrâce de Turgot* (Paris, 1961), p. 486; Weulersse, *La physiocratie sous les ministères de Turgot et de Necker*, p. 15.

[21] Weulersse, *La physiocratie sous les ministères de Turgot et de Necker*, p. 29. Weulersse then states, on the following page, that relations between Turgot and the physiocrats were

of policy (or in the appraisal of the importance of agriculture), more perceptive contemporaries knew Turgot to be too independent of mind to be anyone's devotee.[22]

One should not forget that eighteenth-century agronomists were not pleased to be considered physiocrats either. Historian André Bourde thus differentiated between the agricultural "philosophers" of the physiocratic school, and those who thought of themselves as *"practitioners* of the agricultural arts." While seemingly joined by a common interest in agriculture, and often confused by outsiders who might refer to them interchangeably, most eighteenth-century agronomists had no wish to be associated with physiocracy, and historians should remember this.[23]

There is a further reason for all this confusion. The close personal ties that bound friends and foes alike made it sometimes hard to know where individual members of the French intelligentsia stood on various issues. They frequented the same salons, had mutual friends, did not wish to attack one another in print and preferred to let their displeasure be known in other ways.[24] This meant insiders knew what the general public could not, unless they kept up with gossip and those gazetteers who let the cat out of the bag. This is not to say that open breaks and disavowals did not occur from time to time, but rather that those who basically shared similar, but not identical, views often desisted from airing those differences in public. Correspondence and memoirs are therefore crucial to making finer distinctions between fellow-travelers and true believers.

Turgot's death in 1781 generated a string of testimonials, including a full-blown biography penned by Du Pont. He weaves an engaging narrative – his journalistic style serving him well here. Whereas Du Pont had once viewed Turgot as synthesizing Quesnay's and Gournay's

---

sometimes strained, despite what their opponents believed. On the ferocity of attacks on physiocratic ideas, see also Steven L. Kaplan, *Bread, Politics and Political Economy in the Reign of Louis XV*, 2 vols. (The Hague, 1976), for example, II, pp. 601–2.

[22] All those who challenged the status quo were furthermore accused of being "Encyclopedists," even if, in the case of Turgot and Quesnay, they ceased submitting entries after 1757, when the enterprise fell into disfavor. Moreover, whereas D'Alembert and Voltaire continued to support physiocratic ideas, Diderot, after his initial enthusiasm, grew increasingly skeptical of the movement in the late 1760s. See on this Weulersse, *La physiocratie sous les ministères de Turgot et de Necker*, pp. 23–4, 31.

[23] André J. Bourde, *Agronomie et agronomes en France au XVIIIe siècle*, 3 vols. (Paris, 1967), I, pp. 367–8.

[24] See Antoine Lilti, *Le monde des salons, sociabilité et mondanité à Paris au XVIIIe siècle* (Paris, 2005), and for a more conflictual version of this world, see Jonathan Israel's summary of his previous studies, *A Revolution of the Mind: Radical Enlightenment and the Intellectual Origins of Modern Democracy* (Princeton, 2009), and Guy Chaussinand-Nogaret, *Comment peut-on être intellectuel au siecle des lumières?* (Paris, 2011).

insights, Du Pont now regarded Turgot as surpassing both.[25] Still, Du Pont remained sufficiently faithful to Quesnay to lecture Jean-Baptiste Say, in response to the latter's denunciation of physiocracy and his praise of Adam Smith, to acknowledge his debt to Quesnay and Turgot. "I note that we don't merely have a pupil in you, but a strong emulator.... your fanciful attempt to disown us, which you do not hide sufficiently well, my dear Say, doesn't stop you from being, by way of Smith, a grandson of Quesnay and a nephew of the great Turgot."[26] Quesnay had "laid the foundations of the temple to this noble goddess [liberty]; built its thick walls. You and I then added the cornices, finials, astragals, and capitals to the columns that were already standing."

## Tocqueville, Marx, Foucault

Although some critics, like Edmund Burke, had immediately linked the events of the Revolution to the Economists' vile influence,[27] interest in their ideas withered in the early decades of the nineteenth century. The trend reversed in the 1840s when Eugène Daire and his associates published collections of economic texts that privileged a homegrown political economy to rival Britain's. Daire treated the physiocrats, Turgot and other French eighteenth-century economic reformers as the real progenitors of classical economics.[28] In making available these "classic texts," Daire moreover described Turgot as the most eminent physiocrat, thus becoming one of the main agents of the conflation that I have described.[29]

---

[25] Pierre Samuel Du Pont de Nemours, *Mémoires sur la vie et les ouvrages de M. Turgot, Ministre d'Etat* (Philadelphia, 1782), pp. 51 and 110 (that all that is worthwhile in Adam Smith can be found in Turgot's *Réflexions sur la formation et la distribution des richesses*). On the shifts in Du Pont's allegiances see, Schelle, *Du Pont de Nemours*, p. 183, and by 1809–1811, in his notes to his edition of Turgot's works, Du Pont restores the distinction between followers of Quesnay and those of Gournay, and Turgot and Smith are independent of either (pp. 375–6); Weulersse, *La physiocratie à l'aube de la Révolution*, pp. 20, 223–4.

[26] See the letter to Say, 22 April 1815, in Jean-Baptiste Say, *Cours d'économie politique pratique* (Brussels, 1833), vol. V, pp. 28, 30.

[27] Edmund Burke, *Reflections on the Revolution in France* (London, 1790), p. 113.

[28] Eugène Daire, *Economistes financiers du XVIIIe siècle* (Paris, 1843) with selections from Vauban, Boisguilbert, John Law, and Dutot, p. vi. Eugène Daire, *Physiocrates*, 2 vols. (Paris, 1846). Daire left out Mirabeau for overstating the importance of the *Tableau économique* which Daire deemed made physiocracy impenetrable ("les enveloppe des ténèbres les plus profondes" (I, p. xliv).

[29] Ibid., I, Preface, p. v, and Introduction, p. xxvi: "Condorcet, qui partageait les opinions économiques de Turgot, lesquelles n'étaient que celles des Physiocrates, dans les points essentiels de leur doctrine." Eugène Daire, *Oeuvres de Turgot*, 2 vols. (Paris, 1844); Daire followed with Condorcet's *Mélanges d'économie politique* in Eugène Daire and G. de Molinari, *Mélanges d'économie politique*; volume 2 included texts on luxury, trade,

His Turgot legitimates physiocratic thought. "No one is entitled to ascribe such nonsense to philosophers who include the likes of Turgot."[30] Whereas Daire's purpose was to validate physiocracy, Alexis de Tocqueville, who perused his volumes very carefully, drew a quite different conclusion from the rapprochement between the physiocrats and Turgot.[31]

Tocqueville struggled to understand "one of the most puzzling aspects of the French Revolution: the benignity of its theories and the violence of its acts."[32] Searching for the spirit that had inspired it, Tocqueville fastened on the Economists' dreams of a radical reordering of society, a view that he believed had come to infect the French intellectual climate as of the 1750s. Physiocrats had therefore convinced the future revolutionaries that they could remake the world by legislative fiat. They had placed little store in human freedom, whatever their advocacy of a free market, and Tocqueville feared, that like them, America would abandon its commitment to liberty in favour of the easier option of "equality before the law." If one wanted to understand the Revolution's drift, there was no better place to begin than physiocratic writings.[33]

According to Tocqueville, the revolutionaries had succeeded in enacting the Economists' vision of a rational state that oversaw every domain, a dream the monarchy itself had nursed since the days of Richelieu. By destroying all intermediary bodies and treating politics as the realization of a popular will whose nature they could never fully explain, the revolutionaries had brought into being an homogenizing equality where individuals became interchangeable units, like peas in a pod.

According to the Economists, the State's role was not just to govern the nation, but to fashion it in a specific direction; its duty was to shape the citizens' outlook based on a vision that had already been decided; its duty was to fill their minds with a set of ideas and to develop in their hearts the sentiments that they deemed necessary [to fulfill these exigencies].... They knew no bounds ... men were not merely to improve, they were to be transformed.... For the Economists this power does not come from God, it is not bound by tradition, it is impersonal, it no longer refers to the King, but the State.[34]

---

finances, and agriculture by Hume, Forbonnais, Condillac, Condorcet, and Benjamin Franklin.
[30] Daire, *Phyiocrates*, I, Introduction, p. xxxiii, and also p. xxxvii.
[31] See Alexis de Tocqueville, *L'ancien régime et la révolution,* in François Furet, ed. *Oeuvres* (Paris, 2004), p. 1066.
[32] Ibid., p. 227.
[33] Tocqueville, *L'ancien régime et la révolution* in *Oeuvres*, pp. 186, 447. "It is in their writings that one can best grasp [the Revolution's] essence (*dans son vrai naturel*")."
[34] Ibid., pp. 190, 194.

This utopianism, along with physiocratic advocacy of state-ownership of property (in fact, "co-ownership" or as we might put it, "eminent domain"), prefigured the socialist theories of his own day. Whether or not the physiocrats had this in mind is not the point here. Rather it is Tocqueville's insistence that his "economists" – principally Quesnay, Mirabeau, Let Trosne, and Turgot – had promoted an unrealistic, transcendent ethos that accounted for the Revolution's determination to remake the world in its image.

Moreover, Tocqueville blamed Turgot, whom he considered more liberal than the physiocrats, for suggesting the establishment of local assemblies, which, when they were implemented in 1787, so undermined the royal administration that they destroyed the Old Regime. No matter the strand of real humanism he accorded him, Tocqueville reduced Turgot to his physiocratic Übernensch.[35]

Karl Marx also examined very carefully Daire's selections from the physiocrats and Turgot, and revisited Quesnay's *Tableau économique* in spring and summer 1863.[36] He was amazed at Quesnay's ingenuity in devising a visual model that included both production and circulation, and, where, according to his own recalculations, the profit (or net product as Quesnay called it) in the form of an annual "rent" was *really* based on the capitalist appropriation of surplus labor. Quesnay's insights were groundbreaking; "in the second third of the eighteenth century, the period when political economy was in its infancy – this was an extremely brilliant conception, incontestably the most brilliant for which political economy had been up to then been responsible."[37] Despite feudal aspects, namely the privileging of agriculture and landownership rather than industry, "the Physiocrats transferred the inquiry into the origins of surplus-value from the sphere of circulation into the sphere of direct production, and thereby laid the foundation for the analysis of capitalist production." In Quesnay's rendering, "only the agricultural labourers, not the landowners, appear as a productive class. The importance of this class of landowners, which is not 'sterile', because it is the representative of 'surplus value', does not rest on its being the creator of surplus value, but exclusively on the fact that it appropriates surplus

---

[35] Tocqueville, *Old Regime and Revolution*, pp. 175, 188, 217–18, 206.
[36] On the dating of Marx's reading of the physiocrats, see the illuminating article by Christian Gherke and Heinz D. Kurz, "Karl Marx on Physiocracy," *The European Journal of the History of Economic Thought* 2:1 (1995), pp. 53–90, 80.
[37] Karl Marx, *Theories of Surplus Value* in *Economic Manuscript of 1861–63*, Karl Marx and Frederick Engels, *Collected Works*, vol. 31 (New York, 1989), pp. 239–40.

value."³⁸ Yet the *Tableau* itself, he concluded, after struggling with it both in 1863 and 1877, was unworkable. It offered an abstract representation of Quesnay's ideas rather than a means to calculate the extraction of profits.³⁹

Although physiocrats had depicted the landowner as the "true capitalist, that is the appropriator of surplus labour," they had done so within a feudal framework. Turgot, however, tore off the veil and revealed "bourgeois society as it breaks its way out of the feudal order."⁴⁰ While Quesnay had significantly advanced the understanding of economic processes, Turgot had offered the means to apply these concepts beyond agricultural productivity. Even if by moments Marx treated Turgot as a sophisticated apotheosis of physiocratic thought, he was equally alert to the differences between them.

This was also true of Michel Foucault, the only twentieth-century philosopher to have granted physiocracy a major place in his thought. He uses its theory of value as one of the three examples of a new intellectual outlook that he calls "the classical episteme," refusing the more common term of "Enlightenment." As of the late seventeenth century, concepts were pared down to their physical manifestations and then classified, all the symbolic elements that had once attached to them being treated as misleading mystifications. Quesnay's theory of value seemed to embody this new approach, and Foucault was therefore as keen as Marx had one been to examine how it "worked" in practice. Physiocrats began by assuming value lay in the earth's products and followed its translation into monetary equivalents that then circulated from hand to hand and finally looped back in the form of the rent that farmers paid to landowners. Foucault admired Quesnay's cleverness in restricting his analysis of circulation to a single year, from one harvest to the next, thus neatly combining spatial and temporal analysis.⁴¹ Foucault had also noted with interest that physiocracy reflected the classical age's fascination with "tableaux," be they tables, graphs, or paintings. Images played such an important role because they revealed immediately to the eye the location and relative importance of objects, something that language could only

---

³⁸ Ibid., p. 362.
³⁹ *Theories of Surplus Value*, pp. 204–40, which leads him to conclude: "Adam Smith in fact only took over the inheritance of the Physiocrats" (p. 240); in vol. 45 (New York, 1991), pp. 258–65 (August 1877).
⁴⁰ Ibid., vol. 30, pp. 358–9.
⁴¹ Michel Foucault, *Les mots et les choses, une archéologie des sciences humaines* (Paris, 1966) p. 198.

render sequentially.[42] The strength of Quesnay's *Tableau*, then, lay in its ability to depict circulation over time and space.[43] Foucault did not treat Turgot as a physiocrat but rather as an Utilitarian for whom the value of goods depended on consumer needs and preferences, rather than on its natural source.[44]

## Recent Trends

To understand the role assigned physiocratic texts in recent scholarship one needs to distinguish between those who focus on their economic ideas and those who peruse the same texts for the physiocrats' political platform. The first group examines the physiocrats' belief that only agriculture provides a surplus, as well as their presumption that man is (or should be) guided by his rational self-interest, in other words, the advent of *Homo economicus*. In the second, physiocrats are sometimes associated with government reform and sometimes viewed as presenting a totally new version of political authority based on natural law. As I will argue, not enough attention has been paid to the disagreements among physiocrats regarding political arrangements, but the temptation to tie physiocratic political ideas to Jacques Turgot and his ministry has proved altogether more subversive. Turning his ministry into the embodiment of the physiocratic project gives them more credit than they deserve and highly simplifies Turgot's intentions. Yet, with Tocqueville in the lead, such conflation has allowed physiocratic "political" ideas to extend into the Revolution.

In the specialized arena of the history of economic thought, physiocracy is generally treated as a step in the direction of classical economics, although it has also been ridiculed as obscure or elevated as more profound than Adam Smith.[45] No matter what the conclusions, the aim is to produce a clear genealogy of ideas which is why scholars of economic thought are careful to distinguish clearly between the tenets of physiocracy and those of rival schools.[46] Physiocracy has also been granted

---

[42] Ibid., p. 143.
[43] Ibid., p. 198.
[44] Ibid., pp. 195–214.
[45] For a critique of the "Whig" version of economic thought, see Cheney, *Revolutionary Commerce*, p. 8, and Catherine Larrère, *L'invention de l'économie au XVIIIe siècle. Du droit naturel à la physiocratie* (Paris, 1992), pp. 5–6.
[46] See for example, Joseph A. Schumpeter, *History of Economic Analysis* (Oxford, 1954, reprint 1994), "A. Smith's capital theory grew out of critical absorption of Quesnay's, which would in fact make the latter the ancestor of practically all the capital theorists down to J.S. Mill's" (pp. 236–7), although Schumpeter had an astute appraisal of

precursors such as Boisguilbert and Vauban in the seventeenth century and Montesquieu and Condillac in the eighteenth, all critics of mercantilist orthodoxy whose projects, presuppositions, and conclusions are carefully assessed.[47] Historians of the physiocratic *movement*, after spending so much time in the company of the Founding Fathers, also separate the "real" physiocrats from the mere supporters, such as Controllers general Henri Bertin and Jacques Turgot, who were sympathetic to some aspects of their doctrine but not all.[48] Corinne Beutler neatly summarized the difference in her introduction to a posthumous volume by Georges Weulersse, the august historian of the group: In order to do justice to physiocratic doctrine, one must separate it from practical reforms enacted alongside.[49] This was a refreshing departure from Ernest Labrousse, whose introduction to an earlier volume by Weulersse included Jacques Turgot and the marquis de Condorcet among the members of the school, a claim that scholars of physiocracy would surely contest, including Weulersse himself.[50]

In his study of the rise of capitalist rhetoric, *The Passions and the Interest,* Albert Hirschman presumed physiocracy's dependence on the discourse of self-interest. His overall argument was that self-interest acquired a positive tincture through a reappraisal of human sinfulness. Positive impulses (or passions) were balanced against destructive passions to neutralize them, and such calculations were then redeployed

---

physiocratic *aporia*. Also the more recent *Nouvelle histoire de la pensée économique* edited by Alain Béraud and Gilbert Faccarello, vol. I (Paris, 1992), with its chapter on Quesnay by Philippe Steiner and a separate one on Turgot by Gilbert Facarello.

[47] Lionel Rothkrug, *Opposition to Louis XIV, The Political and Social Origins of the French Enlightenment* (Princeton, 1970); Simone Meyssonier, *La Balance et l'horloge, la genèse de la pensée libérale en France au XVIIIe siècle* (Montreuil, 1989); Jean-Claude Perrot, *Une histoire intellectuelle de l'économie politique, XVIIe–XVIIIe siècle* (Paris, 1992); and Larrère, *L'Invention de l'économie*. This is of course also the case of economic historians such as Ronald L. Meek, *The Economics of Physiocracy* (London, 1962), or Gianni Vaggi, *The Economics of François Quesnay* (Basingstoke, 1987) who analyze physiocratic economics.

[48] Schelle, *Du Pont de Nemours*, despite a few oscillations; the numerous volumes produced by Georges Weulersse; Yves Citton, *Portrait de l'économiste en physiocrate: Critique littéraire de l'économie politique* (Paris, 2000).

[49] "Qu'en fut-il, par exemple, de la fameuse liberté du commerce des grains, à laquelle très tôt les contemporains avaient en quelque sorte identifié la doctrine physiocratique, confondant ses principes avec leur application." Corinne Beutler, "Introduction," p. 11, Georges Weulersse, *La Physiocratie à l'aube de la Révolution*.

[50] "Préface," p. viii, Georges Weulersse, *La Physiocratie à la fin du règne de Louis XV* (Paris, 1959). So prevalent had the confusion become that Claude Morilhat devoted an entire book to the differences between Turgot and the leading physiocrat François Quesnay. *La Prise de conscience du capitalisme, Economie et philosophie chez Turgot* (Paris, 1988).

in the eighteenth century in the guise of "enlightened" self-interest.[51] Physiocrats, Hirschman argued, relied on such motives both to stimulate the economy and to convince monarchs that they would benefit from adopting their policies.[52] Although this is not altogether false, it is hard to find straightforward invocations of self-interest in physiocratic writings themselves. Self-interest must be "enlightened," and it can only prove so when subsumed within nature's dictates. Recent scholarship, moreover, has demonstrated that the acceptance of the pursuit of self-interest was anything but straightforward in Enlightenment Europe and entailed protracted efforts to reconcile the drive toward accumulation with morality – "commerce and virtue" in the parlance of eighteenth-century civic humanists – despite optimistic philosophies, such as Montesquieu's, that argued that commerce was a civilizing force.[53]

This moral discourse engaged nobles and commoners alike.[54] One of the leading physiocrats, the marquis de Mirabeau, contributed directly to these discussions, demonstrating how "greed" could be offset by "sociability," honor allied to virtue, and the nobility regenerate itself and the kingdom. As we shall see, Quesnay subscribed to some of this moral discourse, but his indifference to the fate of the patricians and his mistrust of sentimental effusions stood in stark contrast to his erstwhile collaborator's cherished beliefs.

When the Revolution was treated primarily as a class struggle produced by socioeconomic forces, the physiocrats were often dismissed as feudal throwbacks and Turgot as the representative of a new bourgeois

---

[51] Albert O. Hirschmann, *The Passions and the Interests* (Princeton, 1977).
[52] Ibid., p. 97.
[53] See on this Hirschman himself, pp. 56–62, Meyssonier, *La balance et l'horloge*, pp. 13–41, Istvan Hont, *Jealousy of Trade, International Competition and the Nation-State in Historical Perspective* (Cambridge, Mass., 2005); Catherine Larrère, "Montesquieu's Paradoxical Economics," The Gimon Conference on French Political Economy 1650–1848, Stanford University, April 2004. Examination of how ideas were retooled in new contexts was boosted by British historians of political thought Quentin Skinner and J. G. A. Pocock, especially in the realm of eighteenth-century Republicanism. See the latter's *The Machiavellian Moment: Florentine Political Thought and the Atlantic Republican Tradition* (Princeton, 1975) and *Virtue, Commerce, and History: Essays on Political Thought and History, Chiefly in the Eighteenth Century* (Cambridge, 1985).
[54] For a thorough analysis of the French context, Jay M. Smith, *The Culture of Merit: Nobility, Royal Service, and the Making of Absolute Monarchy in France, 1600–1789* (Ann Arbor, 1996); *Nobility Reimagined*; and Jay M. Smith, ed., *The French Nobility in the Eighteenth Century: Reassessments and New Approaches* (College Park, 2006). Annelien de Dijn, *French Political Thought From Montesquieu to Tocqueville, Liberty in a Levelled Society?* (Cambridge, 2008), chapter 1, and continues the story into the nineteenth century.

Introduction

ideology.⁵⁵ The collapse of the Marxist paradigm gave a boost to alternative interpretations and approaches. The most successful entailed a new emphasis on "public opinion" and "political culture" to explain opposition to the existing system. If the Revolution could not be ascribed to the long-term rise of the bourgeoisie and consequent class struggles, resentments and hopes must have brewed within Old Regime institutions and the intellectual climate of the age.⁵⁶ The institutional approach demonstrated the contradictions that the state itself had engendered by selling offices and pitting groups against each other.⁵⁷ The cultural approach meanwhile stressed the subversive and liberating effects of texts and the proliferation of arenas in which to discuss them. Daniel Mornet famously argued that revolutionaries had been raised on a diet of the Ancients and contemporary literature, not on political theory. Revisiting this theme, Roger Chartier preferred to stress the role of an inchoate public sphere whose repeated criticisms of the existing regime prepared the ground for Revolution.⁵⁸ The political imaginary of the Old Regime grew into full-blown explanations for the Revolutionary dynamic.⁵⁹ This new analysis covered publications and social institutions (such as academies, Masonic lodges, or reading clubs) and more problematically (given the difficulty in interpreting them) ceremonies and festivities, and old and new symbols

---

[55] See for example Jean Cartelier, ed., Quesnay, *Physiocratie, Droit naturel, Tableau économique et autres textes* (Paris, 1991), p. 12. Elizabeth Fox-Genovese contested this consensus in *The Origins of Physiocracy* (Ithaca, 1976). For Turgot as bearer of the bourgeois ideology, see Morilhat, *La Prise de conscience du capitalisme*, p. 93.

[56] The historical literature is vast, but examples include David A. Bell, *Lawyers and Citizens: The Making of a Political Elite in Old Regime France* (Oxford, 1994) or Dale K. Van Kley, *The Religious Origins of the French Revolution from Calvin to the Civil Constitution, 1560-1791* (New Haven, 1999).

[57] See the summary of this literature in Thomas E. Kaiser and Dale K. Van Kley, eds., *From Deficit to Deluge, the Origins of the French Revolution* (Stanford, 2011).

[58] Daniel Mornet, *Les origines intellectuelles de la Révolution française* (Paris, 1933), and on this also Roger Chartier, *The Cultural Origins of the French Revolution* (Durham and London, 1991). Keith Baker made the study of public opinion central to the analysis of political culture. See Craig J. Calhoun, ed., *Habermas and the Public Sphere* (Cambridge, Mass., 1993) and also Daniel Roche, *La France des Lumières* (Paris, 1993).

[59] Challenging this approach, Timothy Tackett and Michael Fitzsimmons demonstrated how representatives to the Estates General were galvanized by unforeseen events. Timothy Tackett, *Becoming a Revolutionary: The Deputies of the French National Assembly and the Emergence of a Revolutionary Culture (1789-1790)* (Princeton, 1996); Michael Fitzsimmons, *The Night the Old Regime Ended: August 4, 1789, and the French Revolution* (University Park, 2003). See also Vivian Gruder, *The Notables and the Nation: The Political Schooling of the French, 1787-1788* (Cambridge, Mass., 2007), and for a combination of the two forces, Patrice Gueniffey, *La politique de la Terreur, Essai sur la violence révolutionnaire 1789-1794* (Paris, 2000).

that were deemed to have influenced public perceptions.⁶⁰ Whereas a previous generation had read political tracts for their "economic subtext," the opposite was now true as historians trawled economic texts for their "political message." In the process, the Marxists' totalizing socioeconomic analysis ran the risk of being replaced by an equally totalizing cultural analysis.

A major culprit was François Furet, who, like Tocqueville, sought to understand the violent destructiveness of the Revolution and traced the revolutionary tabula rasa to the physiocratic rejection of tradition and their belief that the world could be reordered without any reference to the past.⁶¹ Civil society challenged the monarchy in the late 1780s from a new commitment to change that fed on its own discourses rather than responding to social realities.⁶² Thus, Furet endorsed Tocqueville's view that the "great revolutionary goal was 'democratic despotism'." Physiocratic doctrine prefigured it: "it 'prepared' 1793 much more than it anticipated 1789."⁶³ The vehicle was Turgot.

The essence of Turgot's philosophy is that of the physiocratic school, for he is one of their most prominent thinkers. There exists a natural order that governs societies and that reason can grasp, so that it is the government's duty and wisdom to enact it: a mental outlook diametrically opposed to the notion so often upheld by the parlementaire opposition, that, lost in the mist of time, there existed a Constitution of the kingdom which contained the nation's original claims against the king. Turgot acknowledged no authority other than reason as the foundation of the true social order. Society becomes independent from its past, the idea of tradition is emptied of content, while the state is made to embody this reason, which is at one with the public interest, royal absolutism being only absolute to the extent that its role is to implement the natural order: productive agriculture, a flourishing land rent managed by landowners, and economic circulation animated through freedom of exchange.⁶⁴

Turgot explained the Revolution's hegemonic drive to remake the State and Man from scratch. Whatever happened in 1793–4, this is not only

---

⁶⁰ See, for example, Lynn Hunt, *Politics, Culture, and Class in the French Revolution* (Berkeley, 1984); Keith Michael Baker ed., *The Political Culture of the Old Regime* (Oxford, 1987).

⁶¹ François Furet, "L'Ancien régime et la Révolution" in Piere Nora, ed., *Lieux de mémoires*, vol. III (1992), reproduced in *La Révolution française* (Paris, 2007) pp. 828–54, see pp. 829, 834. In this, he says, they followed the Cartesian call to reject all prior authority.

⁶² Francois Furet, *Penser la Révolution française* (1978) pp. 7–220 in François Furet, *La Révolution française* (Paris, 2007) pp. 40 and 146.

⁶³ Ibid., p. 174.

⁶⁴ François Furet, *La Révolution de Turgot à Jules Ferry* (Paris, 1988), pp. 221–794 in *La Révolution française*, p. 245.

unfair to Turgot, who was deeply interested in history and the slow transformation of customs, but also grants too much authority and cogency to physiocratic ideas (and ideas altogether), a point to which I shall return throughout this book.[65]

The Terror as the fundamental quandary posed by the Revolution – and its authoritarian, genocidal sequels in the twentieth century – attracted much scholarly attention around the time of the Bicentennial.[66] Understanding totalitarian projects had led to renewed interest in Hannah Arendt's political theory but also in Carl Schmitt's ideas of sovereignty and the "state of exception" first penned in the 1920s to justify absolute state authority, and his interpretation of Bodin and Hobbes.[67] Rheinart Koselleck, for example, used this version of absolutism (and influenced other scholars in the process) and deemed it could only be countered by an equally totalizing ideology legitimized by a transcendent moral order. Turgot embodied this alternative. "Outwardly a defender of the Absolutist State, Turgot in fact sided with the new, emerging society. As a physiocrat and representative of society, he criticized the existing order by applying the yardstick of a natural, moral law above the State, and as a minister of that State sought to end the crisis that elicited his criticism by means of his physiocratic reforms."[68] Turgot was yet again one of the mainsprings of an illiberal, utopian *Enlightenment* that prefigured future dogmatisms and was the mirror image of its absolutist predecessor.[69] This view is echoed by Pierre Rosanvallon: "The physiocrats thus demonstrate the extent to which Liberal utopianism, by twisting reality, could potentially lead to

---

[65] Not least in the article "Etymologie" that he contributed to the Encyclopedia.
[66] Keith Baker, François Furet, and Colin Lucas, eds., *The French Revolution and the Creation of Modern Political Culture*, 4 vols. (Oxford and New York, 1987–1994).
[67] Hannah Arendt, *The Origins of Totalitarianism* (New York, 1951). Carl Schmitt, *Political Theology: Four Chapters on the Concept of Sovereignty* (Chicago, 2006; orig. German ed. 1922); *The Concept of the Political, Expanded Edition* (Chicago, 2007; orig. pub. 1927, 1932), *The Leviathan in the State Theory of Thomas Hobbes* (Chicago, 2008; orig. pub. 1938). See a contrario Quentin Skinner, *Reason and Rhetoric in the Philosophy of Hobbes* (Cambridge, 1997) and *Hobbes and Republican Liberty* (Cambridge, 2008). Despite similarities, J. L. Talmon's *The Origins of Totalitarian Democracy* (London, 1952) played little role in Furet's notion of revolutionary extremism according to Steven Kaplan, *Farewell Revolution: The Historians' Feud, France, 1789/1989* (Ithaca, 1996), p. 90.
[68] Reinhart Koselleck, *Critique and Crisis: Enlightenment and the Pathogenesis of Modern Society* (Cambridge, Mass., 1988) pp. 142, 155–6, in a chapter devoted to Turgot. The original German edition appeared in 1959.
[69] The best criticism of this approach remains Margaret C. Jacob's article, "The Mental Landscape of the Public Sphere: A European Perspective," *Eighteenth-Century Studies* 28 (1994), 95–113.

totalitarianism once the democratic impulse erased the figure of the legal despot."⁷⁰ Turgot "the physiocrat" offered a more visible and useful target than the genuine physiocrats because of his reputation as reforming minister and *philosophe*. Interestingly, the current I have just examined presumed that the physiocrats and Turgot endorsed representative assemblies, albeit of the unsatisfactory sort that would enact a Rousseaunian General Will.⁷¹ Yet other historians have describe how their advocacy of absolutism drove a wedge between physiocrats and the Patriot party in the Parlements (the sovereign lawcourts) by aligning them with high administrators in the royalist camp.⁷² Rather than placing physiocrats in one particular camp, I will argue that physiocrats were divided on this question, and that this compounded their difficulties in disseminating their doctrine.

Famous partnerships such as those between Marx and Engels, Darwin and Huxkey, Banting and Best, or Watson and Crick, have aroused the curiosity of scholars and popularizers alike. Recently a new genre has emerged in the history of science, philosophy, or literature, focused on fortuitous meetings, collaborations, or, even the disputes that opposed equally brilliant men.⁷³ Physiocracy would seem an obvious candidate, given the close-knit partnerships between Quesnay and Mirabeau or

---

⁷⁰ Rosanvallon, *Le libéralisme économique*, pp. 55–6. This position would then be restated by T. J. Hochstrasser, "Physiocracy and the Politics of *Laissez-Faire*," in Mark Goldie and Robert Wokler, eds., *The Cambridge History of Eighteenth-Century Political Thought* (Cambridge, 2006), pp. 419–42.

⁷¹ Or do away with government altogether. See Edelstein, *The Terror of Natural Right*. On physiocrats and enlightened despotism, see, for example, Derek Beales, *Enlightenment and Reform in Eighteenth-Century Europe* (London and New York, 2005), pp. 48–9, 264–71.

⁷² Kent Wright summarizes discussions of popular sovereignty, civic engagement, and the physiocrats in *A Classical Republican in Eighteenth-Century France, The Political Thought of Mably* (Stanford, 1997), pp. 109–21.

⁷³ For example, Laura J. Snyder, *The Philosophical Breakfast Club: Four Remarkable Friends Who Transformed Science and Changed the World* (New York, 2011); Richard Holmes, *The Age of Wonder: The Romantic Generation and the Discovery of the Beauty and Terror in Science* (New York, 2010); Jenny Uglow, *Lunar Men: Five Friends Whose Curiosity Changed the World* (New York, 2003); Matthew Stewart, *The Courtier and the Heretic: Leibniz, Spinoza, and the Fate of God in the Modern World* (New York, 2007); Robert Zaretsky, *The Philosophers' Quarrel: Rousseau, Hume, and the Limits of Human Understanding* (New Haven, 2010); Richard Davenport-Hines, *Proust at the Majestic: The Last Days of the Author Whose Book Changed Paris* (London, 2006); David Edmonds and John Eidinow, *Wittgenstein's Poker: The Study of a Ten-Minute Argument Between Two Great Philosophers* (New York, 2001); not to mention that old classic, by William Irvine, *Apes, Angels, and Victorians: A Joint Biography of Darwin and Huxley* (London, 1955).

between Quesnay and Du Pont, but the story I have to tell emphasizes the problems of collaborating in this particular endeavour. Quesnay's closest associates were literary men without "scientific" training, not even as dilettantes, and none became an economist in his own right, although Du Pont later served in the administration.

Quesnay framed his doctrine within a cognitive theory that began with sensation but allowed for "flashes of insight" that revealed "true essences" to the mind. Beyond this, imagination was treated as the source of error and the danger that physiocracy had to ward off. This insistence sat oddly – unless carefully explained – with the expectation that physiocratic tenets would become imprinted in the mind through an arduous process of cogitation that culminated in an inner vision or revelation. Despite attempts to keep imagination at bay and to create a purely "rational" system, imagination lay at the heart of the system, so that an alliance with the arts grew increasingly tempting.[74] One can see why generations of scholars have neglected this aspect of physiocratic writings and relegated it to footnotes, if they mentioned it at all. For the accepted wisdom is that physiocrats offered ways of approaching economic phenomena that spoke to contemporary concerns about French finances. They also "demonstrated" that seemingly random patterns of production and exchange yielded to rigorous analysis to reveal an underlying constancy. The rest is immaterial.

What is one to do then with the physiocrats' insistence that their conclusions arose from an "incommunicable" intuition? Despite all appearances, the physiocrats were not appealing to reason, per se, but to a very specific type of reason (that allowed sublime flashes of understanding). It is not that they "discovered the cure for cancer" but couched it in new-age mumbo-jumbo. It is rather that there were aspects of the cure that they simply could not explain and that had to be taken on faith. If one prepared one's mind properly, one *might* come to grasp these.

The physiocrats' "discovery" of the law of the "natural order" prodded contemporaries in two directions: (1) a more thorough inquiry into economic processes themselves, clarifying the nature of "profit," "prices," "value," and so on – which fortified the contours of an embryonic discipline of "economics"; (2) a more sustained governmental experimentation with new policies such as the deregulation of the grain trade and

---

[74] Schumpeter was especially lucid on this subject, see *History of Economic Analysis*, pp. 223–8. On physiocrats as a "sect" see for example M. Beer, *An Inquiry into Physiocracy* (London, 1939), pp. 179–81.

encouragement of agricultural improvements (as they were then understood, not least because of physiocratic writings). As for the physiocrats themselves, they continued to investigate agricultural productivity and state finances, redoubling their efforts to convince their opponents of the truth of their claims through articles, books, dinners, and poetry, any genre that would prepare readers to accept their ideas. Their mission fragmented along two lines. One drew them deeper into royal administration in the hopes of encouraging economic reforms. The second led them to reflect on education and how they might prepare the public "to think properly," invoking, that is, the very mental processes that lay behind their own acceptance of Quesnay's insights.[75] This led them to probe into the mysteries that Quesnay had initially posited beyond men's ken. The remainder of this book seeks to explain how they got there.

---

[75] For an interesting spin on the development of economic writing, see Mary Poovey, *Genres of the Credit Economy: Mediating Value in Eighteenth- and Nineteenth-Century Britain* (Chicago, 2008). My argument differs from Emma Rothschild's who underlines the importance of *conscious* sentiments, since physiocrats wished to tap both conscious *and* unconscious mental processes. *Economic Sentiments: Adam Smith, Condorcet, and the Enlightenment* (Cambridge, Mass., 2001), p. 9.

# I

# Art, Craft, and Court

## Visual Apprenticeship

The future economist, François Quesnay, was born the eighth of thirteen children in the village of Méré northeast of Paris in the Ile-de France to a family of *laboureurs*, those middling farmers who fought a losing battle against the encroachment of large-scale farming in the region.[1] Only four of the siblings survived to adulthood, two dying in their twenties, and François's last remaining sister in 1741. This might account for Quesnay's lifelong commitment to medical improvements, although, despite his own reputation as *accoucheur*, he was unable to save his own wife from the puerperal infection that followed the birth of their last child.

Little is known about Quesnay's early years except for the myths spread by his son-in-law Prudent Hévin (1715–89) who granted him a higher pedigree than he actually possessed. Quesnay's early biographers thus presumed that Quesnay's father had indeed been a lawyer at the local *bailliage* (bailliwick), promoting him out of the ranks of peasantry into that of the lower bourgeoisie.[2] It was commonly asserted, moreover, that

---

[1] On this see Jean-Marc Moriceau, *Les Fermiers de l'Île-de France* (Paris, 1994); Jean Meuvret, *Le Problème des subsistances à l'époque de Louis XIV*, 6 vols. (Paris, 1987–1995).

[2] This early evidence appears in contemporary *éloges*, for example, "Eloge de M. Quesnay par M. d'Alembert," *Mercure de France*, XXX (15 November 1778), 145–57, and those by Mirabeau, Fouchy, Albon, and Mesmon in Auguste Oncken, *Oeuvres économiques et philosophiques de F. Quesnay, fondateur du système physiocratique accompagnées des éloges et d'autres travaux biographiques sur Quesnay par différents auteurs*, 2 vols. (Frankfurt and Paris, 1888), I, pp. 3–114. The only other extant biographies are those of P. Lorin in the *Mémoires de la Société archéologique de Rambouillet* (Versailles, 1900),

FIGURE 1.1. *Portrait of François Quesnay* by J. Chevallier, engraved by Jean-Georges Wille (1747), Réunion des Musées Nationaux/Art Resource, New York.

he had been raised a "child of nature," still illiterate at the age of eleven, and that a gardener, using Etienne and Liébault's sixteenth-century husbandry manual *La maison rustique*, had taught him his letters. Stung by

XIV, pp. 63–236; Gustave Schelle, *Le Docteur Quesnay, Chirurgien, Médecin de Madame de Pompadour et de Louis XV, Physiocrate* (Paris, 1907); and Jacqueline Hecht, "La Vie de François Quesnay," in Jacqueline Hecht, ed., *François Quesnay et la Physiocratie*, 2 vols. (Paris, 1958), I, pp. 211–94, reproduced in Christine Théré, Loïc Charles and Jean-Claude Perrot, eds., *François Quesnay, Oeuvres économiques complètes et autres textes*, 2 vols. (Paris, 2005), II, pp. 1331–1420. See also Christine Théré and Loïc Charles, "François Quesnay: A 'Rural Socrates' in Versailles?," in E. Roy Weintraub and Evelyn L. Forget, eds., *Economists' Lives: Biography and Autobiography in the History of Economics* (Annual Supplement to Volume 39 of *History of Political Economy* (Durham and London, 2007), pp. 195–214. A novel about Quesnay's life, *Un Laboureur à Versailles* by Hélène Vergonjeanne embroiders on this received wisdom about his youth (Paris, 2008).

the reading bug, the young Quesnay, we are also told, would head for Paris returning that same evening laden with books, which, as one skeptical biographer remarked, was quite a feat given the ninety kilometers this journey entailed.[3] While archival research has shown that his father farmed, sold groceries, and collected taxes for the local abbey, no new evidence has emerged about Quesnay's early education. It seems safe to presume, however, that he was taught the three Rs and the rudiments of Latin by the local curé, for he would have been unable to obtain his master of arts degree without such a foundation. He seemingly demonstrated an early interest in surgery and trained briefly with a nearby country surgeon before departing for the capital. Widowed when François was thirteen and frustrated by his lack of interest in farming – not to mention his attraction toward the poorly remunerated post of village surgeon – his mother packed him off to Paris, four years later, to learn the highly fashionable craft of copper engraving.

His apprenticeship contract states[4]:

On the first of October 1711, Louise Giroux, the widow of Nicolas Quesnay, *laboureur* at Méré, for the benefit of her son, François Quesnay, aged seventeen, certifies that she has allotted [*alloué*] him for five years to the sieur Pierre de Rochefort, ordinary engraver of the king at the Academy of Sciences, so that he might teach and show him the aforementioned art of engraving in *taille-douce* and everything related to it, to feed, lodge, clean his clothes and treat him kindly [*humainement*] for the sum of 400 livres of which the said Rochefort received 100 livres on account ... Witnessed by Henri Desnoyers, prior at Gambaiseul and Nicolas Bardet, *procureur* at the balliwick of Montfort.

That they chose an accredited engraver to the Royal Academy of Sciences might indicate that they had more than engraving in mind, for François Quesnay spent the next five years in Paris, both as an apprentice and as a student earning a liberal arts degree from the university. He returned home briefly in 1716 to train with another neighborhood surgeon. Such practical experience was a prerequisite for obtaining a mastership. On 8 January 1717 he married the daughter of a Parisian *épicier* and moved with his bride to Mantes where he petitioned the local surgeons to admit him to their fold. Following their refusal, Quesnay went back to Paris to begin an eighteen-month course of study, since a degree from the Paris surgeons' Academy of Saint-Côme, allowed him to

---

[3] Schelle, *Le Docteur Quesnay*, p. 13.
[4] Maurion de Laroche, "Notice sur François Quesnay" in *Mémoires et documents publiés par la société archéologique de Rambouillet*, vol. 18 (1887–8), pp. 93–102, 95.

work anywhere in the country. Armed with his title of master-surgeon in August 1718, he opened a practice in Mantes, accruing fame for his skills as *accoucheur*.[5]

Biographers have paid scant attention to his various apprenticeships, given the dearth of concrete information. Gustave Schelle summarizes his growing accreditation thus: "He attended the lectures at the College of Surgery and was registered in those of the Faculty of Medicine; he studied pharmacy, took anatomy, chemistry, and botany classes at the Jardin du roi, visited hospitals ... and was allowed to 'work' at the Hôtel-Dieu, all this while performing his professional duties and acquiring a general education, including mathematics and philosophy."[6]

Ascribing to Quesnay a medical education from as early as the 1710s creates the impression of an unbroken commitment to physiology and deflects attention from his formal training in engraving. Yet Quesnay must have learned to draw somewhat credibly before being taken on as apprentice: Jean-Georges Wille (1715–1805) the great German engraver who worked for decades in Paris, asked applicants to send him samples of their work before taking them on, and his own son was an accomplished draughtsman by the time he began his apprenticeship with the fashionable painter Greuze.[7] Wille trained his students both to "draw and engrave." He himself had continued to perfect his skills as a young man freshly arrived from Germany in 1736, sketching tirelessly. Besides copying the old masters, he also studied anatomy "for I believed that both had to advance in tandem" so that the body might be accurately depicted.[8]

Quesnay's master, Pierre de Rochefort (1673–1728), features fleetingly in standard dictionaries of engravers, perhaps because his full name was Pierre de Massart "dit de Rochefort" and hence is somewhat difficult to trace. Research on the history of the Royal Academy of Sciences shows that he was one of the artists recruited by the Academy to produce plates for its *Description des Arts et Métiers*. We also know that he illustrated

---

[5] There is no sign of formal training in obstetrics, although his postmortem inventory shows that he owned standard texts on the subject.

[6] Schelle, *Le Docteur Quesnay*, pp. 17–18: paraphrasing here Grandjean de Fouchy one of the eulogists who used Hévin's notes.

[7] *Mémoires et Journal de J-G Wille, graveur du roi* edited by Georges Duplessis, 2 vols. (Paris, 1857), I, pp. 145–7, 169. Wille executed the engraving of Quesnay's portrait by J. Chevallier in 1747. Wille's journals on the period between 1743 and 1759 are missing, so that there is no record of the actual commission, but in 1764, Wille was sending a print of the portrait worth 6 livres along with the portrait of the Comte de Saint-Valentin, worth 30 livres, to a painter in Amsterdam via the printseller Basan. I, 272, 21 November 1764.

[8] Wille, *Mémoires et Journal*, I, pp. 7–14.

a series of knitting frames and architectural plans.[9] Besides this, he engraved paintings by Gillot, Watteau, and Rigaud.[10] He also collaborated with France's most celebrated engraver, Charles-Nicolas Cochin the Elder, on the *Nouveau livre des vases*.[11] Thus, the claim that Quesnay lodged with Cochin, which Gustave Schelle treated as spurious, seems perfectly plausible.[12] Around 1720, Rochefort left France for Portugal and died in Lisbon.[13]

Engravers, although successfully challenging incorporation in 1694, were nonetheless subject to official regulation, including the number of apprentices they could take on. They could however employ any number of journeymen, and few rose above that station.[14] Older than the norm of fifteen when he began his apprenticeship, Quesnay was training in a desirable trade, given increasing demand for illustrations in Enlightenment Europe.[15] By then Paris had become the unrivaled center of print production, surpassing both Italy and the Low Countries.[16]

At the workshop of an Academy of Sciences engraver, Quesnay would have acquired a specific set of manual and visual skills.[17] Copper

---

[9] Madeleine Pinault-Sorensen, "Les dessinateurs de l'Académie royale des sciences" in Christiane Demeulenaere-Douyère and Eric Brian, eds., *Réglement, usages et science dans la France de l'absolutisme (Actes du colloque international, Paris, 8–10 juin 1999)* (London, Paris, New York, 2002), pp. 147–67, 159, and Anne Chassagne, *La bibliothèque de l'Académie royale des sciences au XVIIIe siècle* (Paris, 2007), p. 132. Rochefort was also known for his engravings of P. Menant's *Views of the Palace and Gardens of Versailles*, and some pictures by J. B. Santerre. Michael Bryan, *Dictionary of Painters and Engravers*, II (London, 1889), p. 396. François Basan, *Dictionnaire des graveurs anciens et modernes* II (Paris, 1789), p. 123.

[10] Chassagne, *La bibliothèque de l'Académie*, p. 132; Bryan, *Dictionary of Painters and Engravers*, II, p. 396; Charles Le Blanc, *Manuel de l'amateur d'estampes* (Paris, 1971), II, p. 344; E. Bénézit, *Dictionnaire critique et documentaire des Peintres, Sculpteurs, Dessinateurs, et Graveurs*, vol. VII (Librairie Grund, 1966), p. 294.

[11] *Allegemunes Lexikon de bildenden Kunstler* (Leipzig, 1934), p. 449.

[12] Schelle, *Le Docteur Quesnay*, p. 17. A note in Lorin's biography of Quesnay, (" François Quesnay, " 75) states that Rochefort had resided rue des Cordiers, near the Sorbonne, and rue Saint-Jacques near rue de la Parcheminerie in 1712. It does not state whether these lodgings were large enough to house apprentices.

[13] Le Blanc, *Manuel*, II, p. 344. Evidence that Rochefort was still alive in 1728 rests on a letter auctioned by François Courboin and Marcel Roux, *La Gravure française, Essai de bibliographie* (Paris, 1927), II, p. 462.

[14] Peter France, *The French Renaissance in Prints from the Bibliothèque nationale de France* (Los Angeles and London, 1994), pp. 39–41.

[15] Some illustrations in the *Mémoires de l'Académie de médecine* might be by his hand, for they are unacknowledged (and once again Hévin claimed that he owned a whole series of engravings by Quesnay). Lorin, "François Quesnay," p. 79.

[16] Timothy Clayton, *The English Print 1688–1802* (New Haven and London, 1997), p. xi.

[17] See Hecht, "La vie de François Quesnay," pp. 1335–6.

engraving, although more expensive than woodcuts and more difficult to produce, was favored for its precision. Shortcuts, such as etching (or a combination of etching and engraving), might be employed as suggested by Abraham Bosse, who remained the standard authority.[18] Incisions were made on the plate by means of cutting tools (gravers or burins) whose lines, cross-hatchings, and dots produced the effects of brushwork.[19] To prevent the reversal of the image, engravers used mirrors, and relied on grids and protractors to adjust the size of their reproduction.[20] Each step demanded infinite care and attention: from polishing and smoothing of the blank plate to its final immersion in an acid bath to fix the grooves (which required some acquaintance with chemistry). Between each immersion, details on the plate could be rectified. Should the engraver also be the printer, he would then ink the plate (and this demanded yet another set of skills) and roll it through the press. Engravers copied original paintings when they were available. More commonly they relied on existing prints and sketches, or produced their own. Being able to draw was therefore a prerequisite.[21] Prints were the photographs of their day: offering reproductions of famous artworks, illustrations of exotic and everyday scenes, scientific specimens and instruments, cityscapes and architectural plans, portraits of monarchs and celebrities, religious and mythological scenes.

Copper engraving employed a sizable, highly trained workforce. Producing high-quality plates took time. The craft was therefore well remunerated.[22] The Academy of Sciences had specific requirements for scientific engravings, and their expectations would become second nature to Quesnay, even if he chose not to pursue the trade. Most significantly, he acquired a visual acuity that distinguished him from his fellow

---

[18] Abraham Bosse, *De la manière de graver à l'eau-forte et au burin et de la gravûre en manière noire* (Paris, 1745). Revised and expanded edition of Bosse's original 1645 text by Charles-Antoine Cochin.

[19] As Cochin explains in his addendum to Bosse's treatise, it was thanks to a 1730 invention based on Newton's *Optics* that separate applications of yellow, red, and blue on the plates were combined to produce color engravings, particularly suited to scientific depictions, artistic works proving trickier to render.

[20] Susan Lambert, *The Image Multiplied, Five Centuries of Printed Reproductions of Paintings and Drawings* (New York, 1987), pp. 61–3.

[21] On the prestige and difficulty of line engraving, see also, for example, Clayton, *English Print*, pp. 13–14.

[22] David T. Pottinger, *The French Book Trade in the Ancien Régime, 1500–1791* (Cambridge, Mass., 1958), p. 324: "the social and economic position of most engravers was an enviable one. They lived in great comfort and were considered as ornaments of the age."

economists, the most important being the capacity to extract a universal model from a defective specimen.[23]

The Academy had sponsored, since its creation in 1666, lavish illustrations for anatomical, botanical, and zoological texts.[24] In 1640 already Abraham Bosse had engraved dozens of plants for La Brosse, the first director of the Jardin du roi, and a special workshop had been set aside for him, enabling him to produce plates in situ, including for the Academy's *Histoire des plantes* of 1676.[25] This was the period when engravers strove to demonstrate a creativity that went beyond mere replication of existing works, culminating in their inclusion in the Royal Academy of Painting and Sculpture in the late seventeenth century.[26] Yet the very aestheticism that established their credentials among the liberal arts was reproved for scientific illustrations where even shading was deemed superfluous.[27] Whatever they produced for other clients, engravers were not called to demonstrate "genius" in their scientific imagery.[28] They copied real specimen and used microscopes to get at smaller detail,

---

[23] See also Alice Stroup, *A Company of Scientists, Botany, Patronage, and Community at the Seventeenth-Century Parisian Royal Academy of Sciences* (Berkeley and Los Angeles, 1990), pp. 58–9, 80–2. E. C. Sparry, "Rococo Readings of the Book of Nature" in Marina Frasca-Spada and Nick Jardine, eds., *Books and the Sciences in History* (Cambridge, 2000), pp. 255–75; Therese O'Malley and Amy R. W. Meyers, eds., *The Art of Natural History: Illustrated Treatises and Botanical Paintings, 1400–1850* (New Haven and London, 2008); James E. McClellan III, *Specialist Control: The Publications Committee of the Académie Royale des Sciences (Paris) 1700–1793* (Philadelphia, 2003), pp. 84–7. Brian J. Ford, "Scientific Illustration in the Eighteenth Century" in Roy Porter, ed., vol. 4, *Eighteenth-Century Science* (Cambridge, 2003), pp. 561–83; and Barbara Maria Stafford, *Body Criticism, Imaging the Unseen in Enlightenment Art and Medicine* (Cambridge, Mass., MIT Press, 1993). Jacqueline Hecht presumes Quesnay completed his apprenticeship and obtained his liberal arts degree afterwards. Quesnay's engraving contract does not appear to have been formally broken, and it is therefore unlikely that Quesnay reneged on the arrangement for which his mother had paid a substantial sum. What is more, the 400 livres paid over four years would have cost far less than registering either at the medical faculty or at one of the private academies that dispensed general or surgical training.
[24] Chassagne, *La bibliothèque de l'Académie*, pp. 99–100.
[25] José Lothe, "Les livres illustrés par Abraham Bosse," in Sophie Join-Lambert and Maxime Préaud, eds., *Abraham Bosse, savant graveur, Tours vers 1604–1676* (Paris, 2004), pp. 46–7.
[26] Susanne Anderson-Riedel, *Creativity and Reproduction: Nineteenth-Century Engraving and the Academy* (Newcastle upon Tyne, 2010), pp. 2–4.
[27] See Chassage, *La bibliothèque de l'Académie*, pp. 100 and 119 citing the French naturalist Michel Adanson. On the centrality of shading in engraving, see Bosse, *De la manière de graver*, p. 107: "De la façon de conduire les tailles."
[28] Chassagne, *La bibliothèque de l'Académie*, p. 105.

although such privileges were in theory restricted to the Academy of Painting and Sculpture's students.[29]

The Academy of Sciences meant to catalogue nature as accurately as possible, yet at the same time to provide prototypes that all viewers would recognize. Thus, even if the illustrator or engraver had before him a bird with a damaged wing or a flower with shrivelled petals, he was to recognize and offer a generic version. Observation yielded relevant detail but only those traits that enriched scientific understanding were to be included. This scientific imperative meshed with the period's dominant aesthetics that expected painters to portray nature as it "ought to be" (*belle nature*) rather than as it was. The visual, including scientific imagery – despite the latter's utilitarian avocation (showing what the text explained) – was granted special potency. Images, it was believed, possessed the inherent capacity to encapsulate phenomena more powerfully than words because they allowed immediate perception both of the whole and its parts.[30] This aspect would not be lost on Quesnay.[31]

Training with one of the Academy's engravers offered an ambitious young man like Quesnay a broad induction into the natural sciences and the processes of abstraction as well as firsthand awareness of the networks that supplied naturalists with specimens. In later years, he would solicit botanical samples from his correspondents to help him assess the earth's agricultural potential. The utility of such networks would have become all the more evident during his last years with Rochefort. The duc d'Orléans, Regent of France, had commissioned an inquiry into the natural resources of the kingdom in 1715: a vast information-gathering initiative that engaged all of France's administrators and local

[29] Alice Stroup, *Royal Funding of the Parisian Académie Royale des Sciences during the 1690s* (Philadelphia, 1987), pp. 40, 47–50, 87.
[30] Ulrich Lebem *Object Design in the Age of Enlightenment: The History of the Royal Free Drawing School in Paris* (Los Angeles, 2004), pp. 78, 84. The Free Drawing School was established in 1766 to teach 1,500 students at a time and its training began with geometry, to instill notions of symmetry "found in Nature," and followed by "the principles of drawing, applied geometry, mechanics, chemistry and natural history" (pp. 114–16). Patrons of the school were numerous, including Du Pont de Nemours and Turgot (pp. 132–3) but not Quesnay. Chassagne, *La bibliothèque de l'Académie*, pp. 118–19, citing the English naturalist George Edwards, and concluding: "L'illustration sert donc non seulement de justification aux thèses d'un auteur, mais constitue un instrument de connaissance autonome dont tout lecteur peut tirer parti pour se forger une idée des objets décrits" (p. 124).
[31] Quesnay thus embodied Foucault's classical episteme on more than one front. *Les mots et les choses* (Paris, 1966), see pp. 144–6 on words, visual, especially geometric, representation.

naturalists.[32] The Regent's inquiry (abandoned at his death) melded with the Academy's longstanding, although sometimes dormant, ambition to document all French arts and crafts, a mammoth enterprise initially launched by Louis XIV's finance minister Jean-Baptiste Colbert (1619–83) and still not completed at the outbreak of the Revolution. Quesnay's master, Rochefort, provided plates for both endeavors.[33]

As apprentice-engraver to the Academy of Sciences, Quesnay was entitled to attend scientific demonstrations to further his training. The Jardin, supervised by the King's First Physician, subsidized talented scientists to lecture and carry out public experiments.[34] During his first stay in the capital (1711–16), Quesnay would thus have acquired smatterings of botany, chemistry, and anatomy (which the Faculty of Medicine had also been required to demonstrate since the Edict of Marly of 1707).

As Quesnay contemplated pursuing a career in surgery, he was surely aware of the deep divisions between physicians and surgeons, which recalled similar frictions between engravers and artists. Medical practioners looked down on the surgeons, who had merged with the barbers' guild in 1656, as no better than manual workers who drew blood or amputated limbs and taught "through imitation like any other craftsmen." In the late seventeenth century, surgery experienced a number of significant breakthroughs, and their newfound status allowed them to separate from the barbers in 1691. By 1700, Parisian surgery was attracting students

---

[32] David J. Sturdy, "L'Académie royale des sciences et l'enquête du Régent de 1716–1718" in *Réglement, usages et science*, pp. 133–46. And also Christiane Demeulenaere-Douyère and David J. Sturdy, *L'enquête du Régent, 1716–1718, Sciences, techniques et politique dans la France pré-industrielle* (Paris, 2008).

[33] Demeuleneare-Douyère, "Introduction" in *L'enquête du Régent*, p. 25: "Le carton 18 des 'Enquêtes du régent' aux Archives de l'Académie des sciences, contient trente planches gravées entre 1716 et 1719 par Rochefort et Quineau pour servir aux *Descriptions des arts et métiers*." Articles on the engravings relating to the Arts et Métiers project have tended to focus less on the "Réaumur" period than on the subsequent "Duhamel du Monceau" revival of the project in the 1760s. See Madeleine Pinault-Sorensen, "La *Description des arts et métiers* et le rôle de Duhamel du Monceau" in *Duhamel du Monceau 1700–2000, un Européen du siècle des Lumières* (Orléans, 2001), pp. 133–55; Georges Huard, "Les planches de l'Encyclopédie et celles de la Description des arts et métiers de l'académie des sciences," *Revue d'histoire des sciences et de leur applications*, 4 (1951), 238–49; Maurice Daumas and René Tresse, "La description des arts et métiers de l'académie des sciences et le sort de ses planches gravées en taille-douce" *Revue d'histoire des sciences et de leurs applications* 7 (1954), 163–71; F. Gardey, "Quelques planches des Descriptions des Arts et Métiers de l'Académie royale des sciences au Cabinet des Estampes," *Nouvelles de l'estampe*, 5–6 (1964), 166–9.

[34] Alexandre Lunel, *La Maison médicale du roi, XVIe–XVIIIe siècles, le pouvoir royal et les professions de santé* (Paris, 2008), pp. 212–14.

from as far afield as Leiden (the most advanced medical center in Europe) who came to train privately with top Parisian surgeons since the medical faculty refused to allow surgeons to teach.[35]

Medicine meanwhile, involved four years of university lectures on the classics of "physiology, pathology, and therapeutics" with little contact with patients.[36] Doctors continued to insist that surgery was merely practice with no use for "theory." In the first half of the eighteenth century, the surgeons consequently engaged in fierce battles to win intellectual recognition, insisting that the principles of surgery be taught by accredited professors at their own college of surgeons, Saint-Côme.

Under new regulations in 1699, the Parisian surgeons' community at Saint-Côme had briefly revived its public lectures, and a new amphitheater was inaugurated in 1695 (at great cost to the surgeons' guild) to accommodate 750 observers. Quesnay might well have sat in their midst, although by 1714, when Jean-Louis Petit took over as provost, the endowments had been depleted and lecturing had all but ceased.[37] Preparing for the Paris guild exams at Saint-Côme was expensive and beyond the reach of most apprentice-surgeons, although far cheaper than medical school. Quesnay's marriage in January 1717 enabled him to cover the examination fees since, besides some landed property, he received 3,000 livres in coin from his mother and as his bride's dowry.[38] Moreover, Quesnay mastered enough grammar, rhetoric, philosophy, history, geography, physics, and mathematics to qualify for a Master of Arts degree in 1716.[39]

---

[35] The *éloge* of Jean-Louis Petit of 26 May 1750 states that he offered a few public courses on anatomy and operations at the medical faculty, but that "he then established in his own house an anatomical and surgical school and his disciples included the most famous doctors and surgeons of Europe." A. Louis, ed., *Eloges lus dans les séances publiques de l'Académie royale de chirurgie de 1750 à 1792* (Paris, 1859), pp. 4–5. That of Albrecht von Haller of 30 April 1778 recalls that, after two years in Leiden studying with Boerhaave, he came to train in Paris in 1727 with Ledran, "un des premiers practiciens de cette capitale, alors chirugien en chef de l'hôpital de la Charité, où il tenait une école d'anatomie et de chirurgie" (pp. 266, 268).

[36] Laurence Brockliss, *French Higher Education in the Seventeenth and Eighteenth Centuries, A Cultural History* (Oxford, 1987), p. 391.

[37] Toby Gelfand, *Professionalizing Modern Medicine, Paris Surgeons and Medical Science and Institutions in the 18th Century* (Westport, Conn. and London, 1980), pp. 32–5, 48–55. In theory, although not always in practice, the Hôtel-Dieu offered courses in surgical theory and anatomy beyond the observation of operations and dissections.

[38] Lorin, "François Quesnay," p. 82. The dowry was paid by 1721. Lorin, "François Quesnay," p. 84.

[39] A very clear overview of the Humanist curriculum and the requirements for admission to the Paris medical faculty can be found in Brockliss, *French Higher Education*: "On the whole elevation to the MA and to the degrees of bachelor and licentiate in any faculty

# Art, Craft, and Court 33

Engravers had already demonstrated to painters that they were more than mere imitators, and surgeons were about to demand that their craft also be raised to the status of a liberal art. Quesnay would be instrumental in that struggle. In both cases, he had entered crafts that were open to newcomers, but whose masters were actively fighting to raise the status both of admission and of accomplishment.

By 1716, it would seem that Quesnay had made his mind up to become a surgeon, to which he would add a medical degree in 1745 after a mandatory five weeks' residence at the medical faculty of Pont à Mousson, producing a brief thesis.[40] He later reflected on how little he had enjoyed his years as surgeon, complaining that its unceasing demands left little opportunity for useful reflection on his craft.[41]

The Academy of Sciences did not altogether forget its mission to catalogue French arts and crafts, and parallel activities were also initiated by private bodies.[42] The short-lived *Société des arts* established in 1728 under the patronage of the Comte de Clermont meant to bring artisans and scientists together to promote new techniques. In 1730 Quesnay was invited to join the Society as one of its three consultants on surgery.[43] It stands to reason that his familiarity with the Academy's ongoing endeavors played a role in this nomination.

His previous training came in handy when he edited the first series of *Mémoires de l'académie de chirurgie* in 1743.[44] Quite a few illustrations

---

was preceded by two examinations, elevation to the doctorate by one" (p. 73). See also Gelfand, *Professionalizing Modern Medicine*, p. 55.

[40] Except for Montpellier, provincial medical faculties had far more lax requirements than Paris. On the other hand, Quesnay was an established authority on physiology by 1745.

[41] The 1747 expanded edition of the *Essai physique sur l'oeconomie animale*, opens with a dedication to the duc de Noailles and gives thanks to the "Mycaenas" who freed him from the obligation of practicing medicine and hence enabled him to study and increase his knowledge, unlike practitioners who had no leisure to do so and so perpetuated dangerous practices (I, pp. xii–xiii).

[42] Quesnay owned a set of *Arts et métiers avec figures, Académie royales des sciences de près le commencement jusqu'à présent* at his death in December 1774. Postmortem inventory, January 1775. Archives départementales des Yvelines, 2Mi798, Etude de Pierre Thibault. item 51. He also had several editions of Batteux's *Les Beaux-arts réduits à un même principe* (Paris, 1746), and other texts on artistic theory such as de Piles'. (I thank Christine Théré for giving me a copy of the inventory.)

[43] Roger Hahn, *The Anatomy of a Scientific Institution, The Paris Academy of Sciences, 1666–1803* (Berkeley and Los Angeles, 1971), pp. 108–10. Irène Passeron, "La Société des arts, espace provisoire de reformulation des rapports entre théories scientifiques et pratiques instrumentales" in Demeulenaere-Douyère and Brian, eds., *Réglement, usages et science dans la France de l'absolutisme*, pp. 10–32.

[44] See his introduction to the *Mémoires de l'Académie royale de chirurgie*, vol. 1 (Paris, 1743).

are not attributed, including those of a pelvic bone and harelip, and were probably supplied by Quesnay. Antoine Louis, in his *éloge* of his colleague read on 27 April 1775 (four months after Quesnay's death), recorded that "we have etchings featuring all the bones of the human body that Quesnay drew and engraved when he gave his course on osteology."[45] Quite a few of the volume's engravings bear the signature of [Louis] Simonneau while the classical frontispiece was by Charles Nicolas Cochin, both highly reputed Parisian engravers.

## Surgeon and Doctor

In 1717, as mentioned earlier, Quesnay married the daughter of a Paris grocer, Jeanne-Catherine Dauphin, who gave him four children, two of whom survived beyond infancy. Widowed in 1728, Quesnay never remarried, and no whiff of scandal ever attached to him, despite decades at the licentious court at Versailles. Armed with his mastership, Quesnay established himself as surgeon and obstetrician in the town of Mantes. He gradually built up a reputation attracting the attention of the duc de Noailles, the powerful court aristocrat who owned a house nearby, and of François Gigot de la Peyronie (1678–1747), who would become First Surgeon in 1735, and who took Quesnay under his wing. On the publishing front, Quesnay made quite a stir by challenging the royal physician, Jean-Baptiste Silva's views on bloodletting.[46] Cleary he was making his mark, attending salons, and rising up the social ladder. In 1731, Louis XV had agreed to the creation of an Academy of Surgery and La Peyronie named Quesnay its secretary, a post he occupied from 1740 to 1751.[47] He also advanced Quesnay the money to buy the office of royal surgeon in 1737 so that he could teach at the College of Surgery and serve as secretary to the Academy.[48]

---

[45] In *Eloges lus dans les séances publiques* (p. 250), Louis believed that Quesnay had taken up drawing to amuse himself. He also stated that Quesnay was named chief surgeon at the Hôtel-Dieu in the 1720s.

[46] François Quesnay, *Observations sur les effets de la saignée* (Paris, 1730).

[47] In the notes to the "Eloge de Jean-Louis Petit," op. cit., pp. 18–19, we read: "Quesnay était un homme de beaucoup d'esprit, fin courtisan, savant économiste; presque toujours à Versailles, dans son entresol du palais et très rarement à Paris; il était constamment suppléé dans ses fonctions de secrétaire par son gendre, le laborieux Hévin; mais il fit ce qu'on attendait de lui, on ne l'avait nommé que pour publier le premier volume des Mémoires de la compagnie, et c'est ce qu'il fit en 1743. Les séances de l'Académie étaient, du reste, à cette époque, très peu fréquentées."

[48] Lorin, *Mémoires de la Société*, pp. 111–17. Three thousand livres in 1736 that La Peyronie forgave him in his will (1747), leaving him more money. See Hecht, "La Vie

*Art, Craft, and Court* 35

In the 1730s, the Mantes surgeon had therefore attracted the attention of important people.⁴⁹ Not everyone viewed him favorably: at Mantes he had insisted on his right of precedence, claiming that with "his title of surgeon and master of arts, he outranked his fellow churchwardens."⁵⁰ La Peyronie's heirs accused him of pressuring the dying surgeon to change his will in his favor.⁵¹ On the whole, however, Quesnay repaid La Peyronie's patronage handsomely through the rhetorical prowess he demonstrated in defending the surgeons against the Paris Faculty of Medicine.⁵² He shared La Peyronie's determination to elevate the place of surgeons mingled with personal animus: Quesnay had been deeply stung by the Paris medical faculty's refusal to give its imprimatur to two of his medical texts of the 1730s because he was a mere surgeon.⁵³

Doctors, Quesnay declared, jealous of the progress in surgical methods were trying to undermine its practitioners and usurp their knowledge. "But, we will cast them into the shadows in which they hoped to envelop us and they can wait there for the enlightenment that has eluded them for three millennia."⁵⁴ In 1744 Quesnay revisited these questions: Surgery

---

de François Quesnay," pp. 226 and 236, and Archives nationales, Paris (hereafter A.N.), V3 192 Prévôté de l'hostel, folio 138, in July or August 1727 recording the grant of the post of surgeon of the hôtel by royal decree of 8 November 1736.

[49] Michel Antoine, *Louis XV* (Paris, 1989) p. 129. Few historians mention the Quesnay of those years.

[50] Hecht, "Vie de François Quesnay," pp. 1340–1.

[51] The duc de Luynes in his chronicle of the court mentions four possible candidates for the post of First Physician (*premier médecin du roi*) in 1747, including "someone called Quenet, who belongs to the duc de Villeroy; they say that he contributed the most to the great brief on behalf of the surgeons." *Mémoires du duc de Luynes sur la cour de Louis XV (1735–1758)*, ed. L. Dussieux and E. Soulié (Paris, 1861), vol. VIII, p. 193, 24 April 1747. Diderot celebrated his briefs in support of the surgeons, *Lettre d'un citoyen zélé qui n'est ni chirurgien ni médecin A M. D. Maitre en chirurgie sut les troubles qui divisent la médecine et la chirurgie* (Paris, 1748), p. 2.

[52] See Gelfand, *Professionalizing Modern Medicine*; Laurence Brockliss and Colin Jones, *The Medical World of Early Modern France* (Oxford, 1997), pp. 446–7 and [Quesnay] *Lettres sur les disputes qui se sont élevées entre les médecins et chirurgiens sur le droit qu'a M. Astruc d'entrer dans ces disputes* (Paris, 1737–8).

[53] Quesnay, *L'art de guérir par la saignée* (Paris, 1736) and *Essai physique sur l'Oeconomie animale*. See the correpondence with Falconet reproduced in Théré et al., *Oeuvres*, II, pp. 1157–60.

[54] Letter I, pp. 3–4. "Jews have always figured in Medicine either by intrigue, smoothness, or prattle [*babil*]; secretly antagonistic to everything that is not Jewish, they have cunningly managed to raise themselves on the ashes of physicians from other nations, hiding the discoveries of their colleagues in order to feed on their carcasses; they have regarded this plunder as so many victories against the Infidel. M. Astruc has not deemed doctors from such origins and with such talents unworthy [*inutiles*]." *Lettres sur les disputes*, p. 58 (Letter VI).

rested, he insisted, on a "long chain of truths." The variety of illnesses and their countless manifestations necessitate careful diagnoses. "This art can therefore be said to be based in and consist of the application of intelligence and the most enlightened form of reason."[55] His defense of surgery became famous, and successfully inclined the King to recognize the surgeons' new status.

For the purposes of this book, it is interesting to note that one of Quesnay's major objections to medicine was its reliance on *analogy*, which "lay behind its most preposterous hypotheses," a reproach against the false workings of imagination that would dominate his later thinking.[56] When criticizing analogy, Quesnay was not just infusing common sense, proposing a more "scientific" method for medicine, or calling for a plain writing style, he was addressing one of the fundamental assumptions of medical science in his day. Analogy allowed physicians to compare the body to a machine and to apply hydraulic models to biological phenomena (iatromechanism). It also allowed the equation between cadaver and live body, between animals and men, the transfer of remedies from one disease to another, and the extension of known phenomena, such as the circulation of the blood, to other bodily fluids whose movement was presumed to be similar. Mechanists tended to favor analogy, although they were suspicious of chemical analogies that privileged heat and fermentation (the domain of iatrochemistry).[57] Vitalists rejected the body's equation to a machine while generating their own analogies among various forms of life.[58] Contesting analogy was not uncommon,[59] but Quesnay did not, like other surgeons, substitute what he considered *correct* comparisons for *incorrect* ones. Rather, he came to view the mental process that generated analogies as flawed. Analogy stemmed from the imagination – and "imagination" was Quesnay's shorthand for all that he disagreed with.[60] Inappropriate associations and analogies endangered the proper treatment of disease.

---

[55] Quesnay, *Recherches critiques et historiques sur les divers états et sur les progrès de la chirurgie en France* (Paris, 1744), pp. 23–4.

[56] Ibid., p. xxxiii.

[57] Kathleen Wellman, *La Mettrie: Medicine, Philosophy and Enlightenment* (Durham and London, 1992), pp. 69 and 117.

[58] Roselyne Rey, *Naissance et développement du vitalisme en France dans la deuxième moitié du 18e siècle à la fin du Premier Empire* (Oxford, 2000), chapter 1, pp. 24–56.

[59] On this, see also Brockliss and Jones, *Medical World of Early Modern France*, pp. 424–5.

[60] For Turgot, on the other hand, Jean Claude Perrot, "l'analogie est au fondement de toute absraction et de la connaissance" in *Une histoire intellectuelle*, p. 249.

The mind yielded too readily to the arts of persuasion, even if rhetoric might at times bolster a worthy cause.

His treatises (on suppuration and gangrene [1749], bloodletting [1750], and fevers [1753]) continually exhorted readers to be wary of erroneous sources. In 1736 he published a general physiological overview, the *Essai physique sur l'oeconomi animale*, followed by an expanded edition in 1747.[61] He had time to devote to these compositions because the duc de Noailles had introduced him to the duc de Villeroy, then Governor of Lyons, who invited him to join his household in 1734. Under Villeroy's sponsorship, Quesnay became a member of the Academy of Sciences and Belles-Lettres of Lyons in 1735 and perhaps also a Freemason like his patron. The comte de Clermont, who headed the *Société des arts*, was yet another member of the fraternal order and these overlapping networks would have furthered Quesnay's social ascension.[62] While in Villeroy's service, Quesnay was granted the "post" of war commissioner for the city of Lyons with a revenue of 900 livres a year and continued to draw this pension till his death in 1774.[63] Quesnay accompanied the duc de Villeroy to the front in 1744 (during the War of Austrian Succession) and used this opportunity to obtain a medical degree. It was also at this time that he served as intermediary in the project to translate and expand Chambers' *Cyclopedia*. The abbé de Gua (who had been a fellow member of the *Société des arts*) had been commissioned to oversee the work in 1745 and, in 1747, reported to the Academy of Lyons:

It is in the nature of great works to be written only slowly, and that is the reason why I could not send you any sooner the outline I made for the edition of the Encyclopedia, about which M. Quesnay had the kindness to ask the Academy of Lyons to offer me advice.[64]

Gua withdrew from the project, replaced by Diderot and d'Alembert. Quesnay contributed several entries to their famous endeavor.

---

[61] Oncken, *Oeures,* II, p. 747. These were not universally well received. Not a word about the intestines, sense organs, muscles, and "all the animated anatomy commonly known as physiology," the renowned Swiss physician Albrecht von Haller complained.
[62] Hahn, *The Anatomy of a Scientific Institution,* pp. 108–10; Passeron, "La Société des arts," pp. 109–32.
[63] A record at the AN P2736 Plumitif de la chambre des comptes, dated 20 February 1772, renews the letters of a François Quesnay, commissaire ordinaire de la Province du franc lyonnais granted on 25 December 1764.
[64] Cited by Elisabeth Badinter in *Les Passions intellectuelles*, vol. I, *Désirs de gloire (1735–1751)* (Paris, 1999), p. 324.

## The Medical Sciences

Between 1730 and 1753, Quesnay published a series of physiological treatises: *Observations sur les effets de la saignée* (1730), *Essai physique sur l'oeconomie animale* (1736), *L'art de guérir par la saignée* (1736), *Essai physique sur l'oeconomie animale* (expanded edition, 1747), *Traité de la suppuration* (1749), *Traité de la gangrène* (1749), *Traité des effets et de l'usage de la saignée* (1750), and *Traité des fièvres continues* (1753).[65] These were the disorders that surgeons were typically called on to treat, resulting as they did from wounds or blockages in bodily fluids. Such engorgements threatened the body's proper equilibrium and needed bleeding, purging, or cutting.[66] Quesnay's approach was eclectic.[67] The standard mechanist position was disseminated through the writings of the Leiden physician Hermann Boerhaave, whom Quesnay much admired. Boerhaave also accorded a prominent role to chemical reactions in the body such as the fermentation and distillation of acids and salts in the stomach.[68] Quesnay's physiology examined fluids and various acids and "other elements" to which he devoted considerable detail in his two medical textbooks of 1736 and 1747. Hippocratic and Galenic precepts, in which a healthy body maintained the various bodily fluids in equilibrium, were readily integrated into this vision, encouraging perception of the body as an organic whole, and rejecting the argument that organs could function independently. He objected both to Théophile Bordeu's focus on glands, and to automatic, independent responses of nerves posited by Albrecht von Haller which mid-eighteenth-century vitalists were gleefully endorsing.[69] This view of the body enclosing a series of circulatory flows might well have influenced his view of the economy but, as Catherine Larrère points out, Quesnay did *not* make a case for the "autonomy of

---

[65] A full list of Quesnay's publications by Jacqueline Hecht can be found in Théré et al., *Oeuvres*, II, pp. 1422–35 that covers both medical and economic writings, as well as the dates of reprint editions during Quesnay's lifetime.

[66] Quesnay believed in both the humors and the temperaments associated with them. See both the 1736 and 1747 versions of his *Essai physique sur l'oeconomie animale*.

[67] On medical eclecticism, see Brockliss and Jones, *Medical World of Early Modern France*, p. 424.

[68] Descartes had also included chemical processes in his analysis of food consumption, see Stephen Gaukroger, *Descartes' System of Natural Philosophy* (Cambridge, 2002), pp. 21–2.

[69] Thomas H. Broman, "The Medical Sciences," in Roy Porter, ed., *The Cambridge History of Science*, IV, *The Eighteenth Century* (Cambridge, 2003), pp. 474–5, 477, 483.

the economic," treating it as a feature of the body politic,[70] in the same way that fluids and acids interact within the human frame.

Pre-modern pathology's principal dilemma was its reliance on outward effects to gauge disturbances hidden inside the body. The relationship between the visible and invisible was often no better than a guessing-game. The human organism, Quesnay argued, had gradually yielded some of its secrets enabling physicians, for example, to infer how pus flowed under the skin before it broke to the surface.[71] Thomas Broman stresses that resolving the issue of causation was more pressing for pathologists (such as Quesnay) than for physiologists. When people's lives were at stake, sorting out symptoms and attaching them to the right diseases was an urgent priority.[72]

Quesnay demonstrated endless prudence. As a self-proclaimed "disciple of Hippocrates," he favored mild treatments over energetic intervention. Natural resolution, he claimed, sometimes occurred even without recourse to medication.[73] He bolstered such assertions with case studies drawn from top Parisian surgeons (like La Peyronie), although he did not disdain older examples if they proved relevant.[74] What mattered most was a surgeon's judgment. The wise surgeon always took into account the specific nature of the case and the patient's response.[75]

The more one practices medicine, the clearer it becomes, when one stops to reflect, what an untrustworthy art it is, and the more one feels how urgent it is to set it on firmer foundations, if at all possible. Yet the more one seeks, the clearer it becomes that in order to attain this goal, one must think deeply about the physiology of the human body, about diseases and remedies, to be able to evaluate the theories and experiences that the Masters of our Art have handed down to us.[76]

The best course was to study the particular causes, effects, and properties of various disorders and suggest potential cures. One might cautiously hazard observations such as the apparent different response of various temperaments (sanguine, bilious, melancholic) to bloodletting or

---

[70] Larrère, *Invention de l'économie*, p. 6.
[71] *Traité de la suppuration*, p. 31.
[72] Broman, "The Medical Sciences," p. 476.
[73] Quesnay, *Traité de la suppuration*, p. 25.
[74] Quesnay, *Traité de la suppuration*, pp. 24–8, compares La Peyronie to older authors, such as Paré, who also observed that abscesses were sometimes resolved through excretion.
[75] Quesnay, *Traité des effets et de l'usage de la saignée* (Paris, 1750), p. 479.
[76] Quesnay, *Traité des effets*, p. 480.

of women's "weaker constitutions." The bottom line remained that each particular case must guide the practitioner's ultimate decision.

The *Traité des fièvres continues* (1753) brought to a close Quesnay's multivolume examination of circulatory problems and proved to be his last medical publication (aside from two outlines, printed privately at Versailles in 1760, for books on vision and psychology that were never written). It was therefore fitting that Quesnay use this opportunity to summarize his accumulated wisdom. "No experimental science can be reduced to a true and correct system without the accumulation of all the information that can point us to the true principles of this science, for it is only in gathering this information that we can get at those principles."[77] Observations, however, should not be collected randomly and should be preceded by a thorough understanding of existing theories.[78] As he was about to embark on political economy, Quesnay remained wedded therefore to the experimental method and mistrustful of "systems."

## The Court

In 1749 Quesnay life changed and, although he completed his medical *oeuvre*, he abandoned his post as secretary of the Academy of surgery and his lectures at Saint-Côme. When her cousin the marquise de Pompadour was looking for a personal physician, the comtesse d'Estrades recommended François Quesnay whose discretion she had personally observed. Quesnay moved to Versailles that year.[79] He would remain in the marquise's household until her death in April 1764.[80] Her fragile health required that he be in constant attendance and this made it impossible for him to attend scientific gatherings in the capital or to have a private practice as other royal physicians commonly did. From what we know of his treatments, they consisted in prescribing drops and unguents, and recommending a sound diet to the favorite, as one might have predicted from reading his textbooks.[81]

---

[77] Quesnay, *Traité des fièvres continues* (Paris, 1753), p. 44.
[78] Quesnay, *Traité des fièvres continues*, p. 39.
[79] For a recent overview of the history and different aspects of the palace, see Joël Cornette, ed., *Versailles, le pouvoir de la pierre* (Paris, 2006).
[80] He was forbidden by Choiseul from treating her on her deathbed, leading to rumors that her enemies had poisoned her.
[81] Madame Du Hausset, *Mémoires sur Louis XV et Madame de Pompadour* (Paris, 1985), p. 54: Quesnay suggested that she keep a healthy regimen, exercise, and take care of her digestion so that she might overcome her "frigidity," rather than resort to hot drinks and potions. Du Hausset mentions using *gouttes d'Hoffmann* (or "liquide minérale anodyne

His new employer Jeanne-Antoinette Poisson was born in 1721 and rumored to be the illegitimate daughter of the farmer-general Le Normant de Tournehem who took a great interest in her upbringing and married her off to his nephew Le Normant d'Etiolles.[82] Exquisitely educated, talented, charming, clever, and ambitious, the young woman shone in the Parisian salons where the literati mingled with nobles and financiers. In 1745 Louis XV fell in love with her and took her to Versailles as his official mistress. He made her Marquise de Pompadour in 1745 and then a Duchess in 1752. Despite the loathing of nobles who resented her as a bourgeois interloper and "creature of the world of finance," the Marquise remained Louis's official mistress until her death. Mme de Pompadour looked favorably on new philosophical ideas, even if she could not support the Encyclopedists openly because of their challenge to established authority. She became an active patron of the arts, commissioning portraits, paintings, frescoes, furniture, plays, operas, sumptuous festivities, and especially refurbishing château after château for immense sums, some of which came out of her personal fortune (overseen by her Parisian sponsors Pâris-Duverney and Pâris-Montmartel, the richest financiers in the kingdom) and some out of Louis's purse.[83] She purchased the Elysée palace (now the official residence of French presidents) for 730,000 livres in 1753, had remodeled it lavishly, only to sell it to Louis XV several years later.[84]

This was where Quesnay stayed when the favorite came to the capital. At Versailles, he was lodged in an *entresol* or half-basement, underneath

---

d'Hoffman," a combination of wine spirits and oil of vitriol) [see Diderot, *Encyclopédie*, IX "Liqueurs"], to calm the king who had had a malaise in Mme de Pompadour's bed, while Quesnay, who arrived soon after, administered *gouttes du général de la Motte* a stimulant which did wonders (pp. 46–7). These drops were composed of "chlorure de fer dissous dans l'acool et l'éther sulfurique rectifié mêlés par parties égales" [Augustin Privat-Deschanel and Adolphe Jean Focillon, *Dictionnaire général des sciences théoriques et appliquées* (Paris, 1880), II, p. 1242]. When a portrait of the king fell on Mme de Pompadour's head, Quesnay prescribed sedatives and bleeding (p. 94).

[82] See Evelyn Lever, *Madame de Pompadour* (Paris, 2000).

[83] She had initially not been allocated a regular stipend as official mistress, and Pâris-Duverney advanced the monies she needed to the tune of 600,000 livres. When he called in the loan, the Controller general paid it off, and Mme de Pompadour was granted 50,000 livres a month pension from the royal treasury. Marcel Marion, *Machault d'Arnouville, Etude sur l'histoire du contrôle général des finances de 1749 à 1754* (Paris, 1891), p. 308.

[84] Lever, *Madame de Pompadour*, p. 216. On her artistic patronage and expenditures, see Colin Jones, *Madame de Pompadour, Images of a Mistress* (London, 2002) and Xavier Salmon, ed., *Madame de Pompadour et les arts* (Paris, Réunion des Musées nationaux, 2002).

her own suite, that looked onto an interior courtyard. It was tiny, dark, and cramped, like most of the palace's 364 lodgings.[85] Only a favored few among the three to four thousand courtiers with residences in the palace were assigned comfortable apartments or were fed at the royal table (or by the royal kitchens).[86] Others had to fend as best they could. Quesnay received visitors when Mme de Pompadour was in residence. The writer Marmontel described these gatherings:

While at the Court decisions were made about war, peace, the nomination of commanders and the sacking of ministers, we, in the entresol, pondered agriculture, calculated the net product, and sometimes dined merrily with Diderot, d'Alembert, Duclos, Helvétius, Turgot, Buffon; Mme de Pompadour, who could not invite this troop of philosophes to her salon, would drop in and join them at his table for a chat.[87]

This is hard to reconcile with Du Pont more sober version:

[Quesnay] had me come to Versailles, where Mme de Montmort, at his request, provided me with a lodging. I went to him at the crack of dawn; we worked with extreme ardor. His lodgings were very cramped; his bedroom served as his study; he left me there when he went to see Madame de Pompadour and the King. The rest of the time and especially after dinner, he was overwhelmed with visits, as are all people in favor; he then settled me at his desk, and often said [loudly] to me: *do not budge* – so that others would not disturb me.[88]

However attractive Marmontel's claim, it is therefore hard to imagine Mme de Pompadour ensconced in Quesnay's half-basement: there was

---

[85] See Hecht, "La Vie de François Quesnay," p. 1361. William R. Newton, *L'Espace du roi, La Cour de France au château de Versailles 1682–1789* (Paris, 2000) for the location of Quesnay's lodgings in Mme de Pompadour's large suite. He had ceded his lodgings in the Grand Commun to Hévin and the Dauphine asked that her surgeon be allowed to keep it and that Quesnay be assigned another in 1764. William R. Newton, *La Petite Cour: services et serviteurs à la Cour de Versailles au XVIIIe siècle* (Paris, 2006), p. 455. The King requested Marigny to find space for Quesnay in the Grand Commun (p. 455), and this took place at some point since the lodging he had occupied went to the Queen's confessor after his death (p. 455).

[86] Joël Cornette, "Le Versailles des historiens" in *Versailles, le pouvoir de la pierre* (Paris, 2006), p. 362 and in the same collection, Frédéric Garrigues, "Trois mille bouches à nourrir," in Joël Cornette, ed., *Versailles, le pouvoir de la pierre* (Paris, 2006), pp. 207–15, and William R. Newton, *Derrière la façade, Vivre au château de Versailles au XVIIIe siècle* (Paris, 2008), pp. 15–72.

[87] Jean-François Marmontel, *Mémoires* (Paris, 1999), p. 173.

[88] Pierre Samuel Du Pont de Nemours, *The Autobiography of Du Pont de Nemours*, translated by Elizabeth Fox-Genovese (Wilmington, Del., 1984) p. 251.

nothing "folksy" or Bohemian about her.[89] As Mme Du Hausset recalled: "I sometimes, albeit rarely, traveled in her carriage with doctor Quesnay, to whom she barely addressed four words, even though he was a very clever man."[90]

Quesnay was thrown in the midst of the very luxury he would later condemn in his writings. Besides buying and refurbishing châteaux, the marquise took a direct interest in the fortunes of the Sèvres porcelain manufacture. The factory was relocated at huge cost near the marquise's Bellevue estate in 1756. As of Christmas 1754, new designs were displayed in the king's *petits appartements* for the courtiers to view. In 1762, Mme de Pompadour spent 26,172 livres and the King 23,034 on exquisite pieces. To put this in perspective, an average artisan earned 250 livres a year.[91]

Historians disagree on how much power Mme de Pompadour wielded. Michel Antoine grants her none, but the current consensus is that Louis allowed her some say, partly to deflect attention from his private diplomacy and in order to test public response to his projects. She thus helped negotiate the reversal of alliances that brought about a rapprochement between Austria and France in 1756, and was instrumental in the choice of several ministers and military commanders during the Seven Years War.[92] She (and the public) probably imagined she had more influence over the king's choices and decisions than she did.[93] Quesnay, as part of her entourage, was careful not to interfere.

---

[89] Evelyne Lever takes this for granted in her biography of Madame de Pompadour: "On s'en souvient, la marquise rencontrait, chez le docteur Quesnay, Diderot et d'Alembert, qui n'avaient pas droit de cité à Versailles," in *Madame de Pompadour*, p. 226. Colin Jones says the same in *Madame de Pompadour*, p. 65.

[90] Du Hausset, *Mémoires*, p. 32. See also Argenson, *Mémoires et Journal inédit du Marquis d'Argenson, Ministre des affaires étrangères sous Louis XV*, vol. IV (Paris, 1858), p. 262. "Elle admettoit à sa conversation avec le roi le sieur Quesnel [sic], son médecin, homme de beacoup d'esprit, et qui se pique d'être esprit fort."

[91] Sven Eriksen and Geoffrey de Bellaigue, *Sèvres Porcelain. Vincennes and Sèvres 1740–1800* (London, 1987), pp. 37, 103. Nicole Blondel and Tamara Préaud, *La manufacture royale de Sèvres, parcours du blanc à l'or* (Charenton, 1996), pp. 18–20 and Marcelle Brunet and Tamara Préaud, *Sèvres des origines à nos jours* (Fribourg, 1978), p. 29.

[92] See Lever, *Madame du Pompadour*, pp. 183–4; Jones, *Pompadour*, pp. 122–37. Bernard Hours, *Louis XV et sa cour* (Paris, 1995) argues that Mme de Pompadour had the power that it suited Louis XV to grant her, leaving him freer for his own maneuvres. She clearly was someone to be reckoned with and flattering her was important to anyone seeking a position. Attempts to bring her down failed. Louis remained loyal to her till her death.

[93] Lever, *Madame du Pompadour*, p. 281.

Did Quesnay preach his economic ideas to the king? One of the physiocratic myths, peddled by Du Pont among others, was that the king himself had printed a version of the *Tableau* (1759) on the little printing press that Mme de Pompadour had bought to amuse him.[94] There is no corroborating evidence that the King ever saw, never mind set the image. It seems unlikely, given Quesnay's caution. He would have been loath to embarrass his patron with pointed critiques of the state's fiscal system.[95] Mme Du Hausset recounts an anecdote about perlimpimpin powder [a magical ingredient that he used as a metaphor for coin] that seems to capture the tone of Quesnay's exchanges with the monarch. It also reveals how well he understood the Court and the cultural capital it engendered.

"Tell me who is the most impressive of all the visitors who come here?" "I don't know," I replied. "Well! It is M. de Montmartel [one of the Pâris brothers], who comes four or five times a year. Why does he make such a sensation? Because his coffers are filled with perlimpinpin powder." He took some *louis* [gold coins] out of his pocket. "Everything that exists is contained in these little coins which will bear you most comfortably to the ends of the earth. All men obey those who have this powder and are keen to serve them. To despise money is to despise happiness, freedom, and every pleasure afforded to man." A blue ribbon [Order of Saint-Louis] walked under our window and I said: "Having this ribbon makes this nobleman happier than thousands and thousands of your coins". "When I ask the King for a pension," Quesnay replied, "it is as if I were saying: Give me the

---

[94] Ibid., p. 393, and, for example, repeated by Henri-Jacques Martin, *The History and Power of Printing* (Chicago, 1994), p. 327, who mentions that the tableau was printed on Mme de Pompadour's printing press in her "apartments at Versailles ... with the collaboration of her royal lover." Du Pont recounted this story in his memoirs (see the translation by Elizabeth Fox-Genovese, *The Autobiography of Du Pont de Nemours*, pp. 242–3). Perhaps this entertainment was more to the liking of the Marquise who had developed an interest in etching, under the guidance of Charles-Nicolas Cochin the Younger and François Boucher, both of whom corrected and retouched her plates. In 1755, fifty-two of her prints were gathered in a handsome edition and distributed to select courtiers. Quesnay at his death owned "*un carton de maroquin contenant soixante planches gravées par Mme de Pompadour*" including some of her later etchings. See on this, Pascal Torres Guardiola, "Remarques sur la suite d'estampes gravées par madame la marquise de Pompadour d'après les pièces gravées par Jacques Guay," in Xavier Salmon, ed., *Madame de Pompadour et les arts* (Paris, 2002) pp. 215–36. The bundle was item 136 in the probate inventory of Quesnay's library. His set of Mme de Pompadour's etchings included the *Frontispiece to Rodogune* of 1759 and reproductions of Boucher.

[95] Quesnay did at times engage in contentious causes: After an appeal from Voltaire, Quesnay supported Mme Calas; for Quesnay's relations to the "madman" Jean Danry (also known as Latude) who tried to kill Mme de Pompadour, see Claude Quétel, *Escape from the Bastille, The Life and Legend of Latude* (Cambridge, Mass., 1990) translated by Christopher Sharp.

means to get a better dinner, a warmer suit, a carriage to protect me from the rain, and to transport me without strain. But should the man who asks for this lovely ribbon dare to say what he thinks, he would proclaim: I am vain, and I would like when I stroll by, for the populace to stare at me in dumb admiration and let me pass, and I should also like, when I enter a room, to make an impression and to be noticed by people who might make fun of me after I've left; I would like the masses to address me as Your Lordship. Isn't all this just hot air? This ribbon will do him no good in most countries; it gives him no power: but my coins give you the means to help the needy wherever you happen to be. Hurray for the almighty power of perlimpimpin powder!" At these words, we heard bursts of laughter coming from the next room which was only separated by a doorway. The door opened and in came the King, Madame [de Pompadour] and M. de Gontault. He said: "Long live perlimpimpin powder! Doctor, can you get me some?" The King had entered, having taken a shine to what we were saying. Madame spoke warmly [*fit de grandes amitiés*] to the doctor, and the king left, laughing and praising the powder.[96]

Yet despite his famed "discretion," in later years Quesnay was rumored to be pushing his disciple, Le Mercier de La Rivière, for the post of controller general, unsuccessfully, we might add.[97] He also supported Louis-René de La Chalotais the embattled *procureur-général* of the Rennes Parlement, who dreamed of a ministerial post, and even took part in a sordid blackmail attempt to achieve this.[98] Louis gave Quesnay the benefit of the doubt as pawn in this affair and did not exile him from Versailles, but Michel Antoine traces Quesnay's gradual fall from grace to this incident. He retained his post at court as *médecin du roi* after Mme de Pompadour's death and, according to admirers such as the comte d'Angiviller (Superintendant of the King's Buildings from 1774 to 1789), led a stainless existence:

Surrounded by a whirlwind of intrigue, Quesnay took part in none and always told his mistress frankly and bravely all the truths he considered important for

---

[96] Du Hausset, *Mémoires*, pp. 38–40.
[97] Du Hausset, *Mémoires*, pp. 123, 77 recalls that Quesnay esteemed La Rivière above all others and thought him a man of great ability ("genius") and the best suited to oversee the kingdom's finances.
[98] Michel Antoine describes La Chalotais, rather hastily, as a committed physiocrat, when he recounts his visits to Quesnay in fall 1763 and spring of 1764 at the time of his famous quarrel with the governor of Brittany, the duc d'Aiguillon. After Mme de Pompadour's death, Quesnay was accused of engaging in a plot to blackmail Louis XV into naming La Chalotais his chief minister. He and Dereine (another alleged physiocratic fellow-traveler) had obtained a packet of the king's love letters to Mademoiselle de Romans, his current mistress, and were threatening to make them public. Dereine was arrested and the young woman was sent packing in August (pp. 827–32, 84–9, 850, 857).

the public good. He also took advantage of the position which granted access to her private quarters [*l'intérieur*] to draw the king's attention to important matters although this might have compromised him with the ministers of the day; but, since he feared nothing and wanted nothing for himself, it was no struggle for him to say what needed saying.[99]

The king, as we saw, would not have appreciated Quesnay's meddling in state affairs. The fact that the ambitious duc de Croÿ, whose diary is filled with his maneuvers to get positions for himself and his children, never mentions him, despite paying assiduous court to the "upstart" Mme de Pompadour, is a clear indication of the status accorded him at court.[100] The one exception to this aristocratic disdain appears to be the marquis de Mirabeau who agreed to meet Quesnay in summer 1757, at his brother's urging, to further their political ambitions. Rather cattily, Mirabeau and his brother mocked what they saw as Quesnay's servility, contrasting it to their own pugnacious and "manly" behavior.

### The Confucius of the West

Quesnay was lodged, fed, and housed in Mme de Pompadour's quarters and received a salary of 3,000 livres a year, augmented by a series of other perks that eventually added up to 20,000 livres a year.[101] Through the Marquise's patronage he had become *premier médecin ordinaire* in 1755 and consulting physician to the monarch in 1759 although the position of *premier médecin du roi* always eluded him.[102] In recompense for "saving the Dauphin from smallpox" in 1752, he and two other doctors were

---

[99] Angiviller, *Mémoires de Charles-Claude Flahaut Comte de la Billarderie d'Angiviller. Notes sur les Mémoires de Marmontel* (Copenhagen, 1933), p. 11.

[100] *Journal inédit du duc de Croÿ, 1718–1784*, 3 vols. (Paris, 1906), I, for example, p. 227. Marie-Pierre Diom, *Emmanuel de Croÿ (1718–1784) itinéraire intellectuel et réussite nobiliaire au siècle des lumière* (Brussels, 1987) claims, based on his library, that he read physiocratic works without approving of them, and supposes that he had met and chatted with Quesnay at the marquise's, pp. 165–6.

[101] The King's *premier médecin*, the *médecin ordinaire*, the *premier chirurgien*, and *chirurgien ordinaire* were all entitled to lodgings at Versailles, as were the *premiers apothicaires*. Newton, *La Petite Cour*, pp. 96–100. The Queen and the Princes each had their own medical entourage. See Lunel, *La maison médicale du roi*, pp. 304–14. On his income, see Hecht, "La Vie de François Quesnay," pp. 1361–2.

[102] Luynes, *Mémoires du duc de Luynes sur la cour de Louis XV*, VIII, p. 193, 24 April 1747. In subsequent volumes, Quesnay is mentioned twice again as candidate (IX, p. 384, 11 April 1749 and XI, p. 488, 16 April 1752) and twice as consultant (XI, p. 398, 10 February 1752 and XII, p. 83, 4 August 1752).

granted letters of nobility.¹⁰³ With the emoluments of the king's recent favor, Quesnay purchased a seigneurie in Nivernais where he ensconced his son Blaise-Guillaune so that mankind might benefit from his sound agricultural advice. His daughter, Marie-Jeanne, married the surgeon Prudent Hévin who became the Dauphine's *premier chirurgien* in 1747 and *chirurgien ordinaire* of the Dauphin in 1762.

No one has been able to pinpoint how and when Quesnay became interested in agriculture, and when he began to devise his system for reviving the French economy through landed investments. He perhaps whiled away his hours of attendance on Mme de Pompadour's reading political economy and works of philosophy, or discussing botany and gardening, Louis XV's favorite hobbies. Certainly the state of public finances was a constant concern both at court and in town.

As the playwright and moralist Jean-François Marmontel discovered to his surprise, Quesnay sought to convert literary men who might disseminate his ideas to a large audience. As Marmontel describes in his (not always reliable) *Memoirs,* he disappointed the doctor by pretending to be interested in his calculations, whereas all he sought was an entrée to Mme de Pompadour from whom he secured the editorship of the literary magazine Le Mercure de France. Following this debacle, Quesnay invited the marquis de Mirabeau to Versailles in the summer of 1757. Mirabeau's three-volume *L'Ami des hommes* had recently turned him into one of the most celebrated men in Europe. In this work, Mirabeau argued that a country's wealth lay in a large population and thriving agriculture. He peppered his work with moral exhortations and entertaining digressions. Quesnay explained to him that he had "put the cart before the horse" (as Mirabeau liked to repeat), and that population was the *result* and not the *cause* of national prosperity.¹⁰⁴ Quesnay converted him to his new economic doctrine after a series of stormy interviews that broke the

---

¹⁰³ AN P2594, Registre des Chartes, "annoblissement a François Quesnay, l'un des médecins consultans du Roy," folio 29–31 based on the *arrêt* from Fontainebleau in October 1752 and registered 5 April 1754; Z1a 603, No.139. "Arrêt d'enregistrement des lettres de noblesse du Sr. Quesnay, médecin, 5 mars 1755"; Z1a 604, "enquête de noblesse," 25 février 1755. See Du Pont's autobiography, chapter XIII, *Mémoires de Pierre Samuel Du Pont adressés à ses Enfans,* Hagley Museum and Library, Winterthur Manuscripts, Group 2, Series B, W2 – 4796, handwritten ms, and translated by Elizabeth Fox-Genovese.

¹⁰⁴ In the letter to Rousseau dated 30 July 1767. *Correspondance complète de Jean-Jacques Rousseau,* ed. R. A. Leigh 257, vol. XXXIII (Oxford, 1979), p. 26. One of the earliest public references to his conversion can be found *L'Ami des hommes,* vol. 6, Part II, p. 131.

Marquis's resistance.[105] By 1759, he was extolling Quesnay's genius[106]: "The Tableau économique, is, dare I say, the *nec plus ultra* of this most useful of Sciences, and perhaps the only human inquiry to have dug to the very bottom until it attained a sure and perfect foundation." Quesnay had been on the lookout for a spokesman and he found him in Mirabeau.

There is no doubt that Quesnay picked Mirabeau and that it proved a sorry bargain for the latter who, in return for "seeing the light," frittered away his credibility as broadminded "friend of humanity." Quesnay succeeded in harnessing the Marquis's energy and resounding popularity, and over the next ten years of their intense partnership, the new mentor would do his best to tame Mirabeau's anarchic, rambling style. They collaborated on four major projects, of which a treatise on monarchy was never published and a theory of taxation proved so controversial in its open critique of the French system that it landed the marquis in jail at Vincennes.[107] The duc de Nivernais, his close friend, appealed to the Dauphin for help, and Mirabeau was released and exiled to his estate at Le Bignon to stew for a few months.[108] Quesnay, meanwhile, did little to help his acolyte. Mme Du Hausset, the favorite's lady-in-waiting, reports that Mme de Pompadour questioned a "distressed Quesnay" on the contents of the work and that he replied that the author might have been a little careless but that his intentions were good.[109]

Quesnay and Mirabeau's association spawned a movement through a circle of committed followers. By 1767 they had their own periodical *Les Ephémérides du citoyen*, first under the aegis of the abbé Baudeau (its founder in 1765) and then the editorship of their most devoted acolyte

---

[105] Mirabeau described this meeting in the above-mentioned letter to Jean-Jacques Rousseau of 30 July 1767, pp. 255–64. Quesnay set him straight on the priorities of agriculture and he fell under his sway.

[106] *Mémoire pour concourir au prix annoncé et proposé par la très-louable Société d'Agriculture de Berne de 1759* in *L'Ami des hommes* (Paris, 1760), V, pp. ix–x. "C'est le tableau oeconomique, et l'on ose dire, le nec plus ultra de cette Science la plus utile de toutes, et la seule peut-être des notices humaines, qui ait été cavée jusqu'au fond et à la base certaine et infaillible." This sentence exemplifies Mirabeau's proclivity for neologisms.

[107] Marquis de Mirabeau and François Quesnay, *Traité de la monarchie* edited by Gino Longhitano (Paris, 1999) and *Théorie de l'impôt* (Paris, 1760). Du Hausset, *Mémoires*, p. 82: "Le roi est fort en colère contre Mirabeau."

[108] After a week's detention at Vincennes, the marquis was banished to his estates. Bibliothèque nationale, Paris (hereafter BN), ms occidentaux 3348, nouvelles acquisitions françaises, Librairie sous Malesherbes, dossier on Mirabeau and the *Théorie de l'impôt*. (I thank Loïc Charles for telling me about this dossier).

[109] Du Hausset, *Mémoires*, pp. 81–2.

Pierre Samuel Du Pont until 1772, when permission to publish was withdrawn. For several years in the 1770s Mirabeau hosted a "physiocratic salon" that met on Tuesday evenings during the season, where economic essays were circulated and discussed.[110]

On Louis XVI's ascension to the throne in May 1774, Quesnay was officially requested to relinquish his *entresol* in the palace (although other sources indicate he had already vacated it) and to move to new quarters in the Grand Commun nearby. Having attended on a detested royal favorite tarred Quesnay in the young monarch's eyes. Quesnay died peacefully at Versailles on 16 December 1774 destined to be remembered as one of the most famous economists of his age.

Quesnay was known as the "good doctor" to Physiocratic sympathizers like Georges Le Roy and Jacques Turgot, although both tired of the hectoring tone of his "sect." In his memoirs, the comte d'Angiviller portrayed him as disembodied brain, unmoved by the petty quarrels of the court, and always reading, even on horseback.[111] Mme Du Hausset saw him as an urbane and pleasant companion. She learned of his reputation in the outside world from others.[112] To Mirabeau he was nothing other than the "Confucius of the West who would change the face of history."[113] Louis XV and Mme de Pompadour appreciated his "services and silence."[114] Mme Du Hausset called him "monkey-face," and Mme de Pompadour referred to her two constant attendants as her "cat and dog."[115] Those who were most closely associated with him, saw his darker sides. Pierre Samuel Du Pont who "loved him like a son" found him severe.[116] The

---

[110] Carl Knies, *Carl Friedrichs von Baden, Brieflicher Verkher mit Mirabeau und Du Pont*, 2 vols. (Heidelberg, 1892), II, pp. 106–7, letter of 21 June 1773 from Du Pont to the Margrave of Baden, describing Mirabeau's "economic Tuesdays" as a sort of academy which included some of the greatest nobles of the nation along with forward-thinking writers. These meetings were suspended during the summer months when Mirabeau retired to his estates.

[111] Angiviller, *Mémoires d'Angiviller*, p. 10.

[112] Du Hausset, *Mémoires*, p. 40. "I have been told since that M. Quesnay was very knowledgeable about financial matters and that he was a great *Economist*, but I am not sure what that means. What I know for certain, is that he was very witty, jolly, very pleasant, and very gifted doctor."

[113] Mirabeau to Rousseau, 30 July 1767, *Correspondance*, XXXIII, p. 257. "La découverte du produit net ... due au vénérable Confucius de l'Europe changera un jour la face de l'univers."

[114] Du Hausset, *Mémoires*, p. 48.

[115] Du Hausset, *Mémoires*, pp. 32 and 89.

[116] *Autobiography*, p. 264: "To please M. Quesnay it was necessary to have intelligence and talent *good for something*. To be cherished by M. Turgot, it was enough to have a *good, honest, and sensitive heart*."

Marquis de Mirabeau, never shy of displaying the arrogance of his caste, marveled at his submission to the upstart doctor. While he paid constant homage to Quesnay's genius, the man he described to Rousseau was redoutable[117]:

Although the principles of my science are not mine and I was almost forty-four when I adopted them, and in so doing put my self-esteem to the test by renouncing the work to which I owed my fame and reputation, bowing my head under the crooked fist of the man the most antagonistic to my dear, native exuberance, the sourest of "debaters" the most unmoved by resistance, the most armed with sarcasms and disdain, even if, like all honest men, success has done much to civilize him; although I only yielded to the true and irresistible evidence that you negate and to which I have dedicated the last eight years, insofar as my health allowed, I do not come armed with fanatical or arrogant certainties.

We see Quesnay through the eyes of others because so little of his correspondence has survived. Aware of Court gossip and the maneuvering of its many cliques, the doctor was careful to put on a mask. He had ascended from humble beginnings to Court physician by hiding his feelings behind a gruff, jovial demeanor, keeping his mouth shut, and relying on powerful patrons. Was he trying to protect himself still in devising a system that did not address the court's profligacy head-on?[118] Mirabeau's brother certainly thought so.[119]

In constructing his abstract economic model, Quesnay certainly effaced his surroundings. Despite claims to transparency and self-evidence, physiocracy suppressed as much as it revealed.[120] Versailles was relegated to an invisible private sphere. There is no mention of the "cultural capital" that accrued to courtiers or of the Court's deleterious effects on the French economy, although Mirabeau had referred to this in his writings

---

[117] Mirabeau to Rousseau, 30 July 1767, pp. 255–6.
[118] Oncken was impressed by the contradictions between Quesnay's principles and his life at Court but later biographers have not addressed this.
[119] Letter cited in Louis de Loménie, *Les Mirabeau, nouvelles études sur la société française au XVIIIe siècle*, 2 vols. (Paris, 1889), II, p. 214. The bailli worried that Quesnay was manipulating Mirabeau for his own ends and was hypocritical. Mirabeau responded that his brother should have more faith in Quesnay's integrity.
[120] On the construction of models, see among others, Jean-Claude Perrot, *Une histoire intellectuelle,* passim; Jean-Yves Grenier, Claude Grignon, and Pierre-Michel Menger, *Le Modèle et le récit* (Paris, 2001); Peter Galison, Stephen R. Graubard, and Everett Mendelsohm, *Science in Culture* (New Brunswick and London, 2001); Lorraine Daston, ed., *Biographies of Scientific Objects* (Chicago and London, 2000); Michel Meyer, *Questionnement et historicité* (Paris, 2000); Thierry Martin, ed., *Arithmétique politique dans la France du XVIIIe siècle* (Paris, 2003); Cynthia Fleury, *Métaphysique de l'imagination* (Paris, 2000).

(like other moralists).[121] Yet the intention might well have been to draw attention away from standard complaints by shedding new light on the processes of economic exchange. The problems presented by Versailles would be resolved once the net product was properly constituted, taxation raised rationally, and the monarch regarded himself as the keeper of this system.

---

[121] See, for example, the analysis by Jean Ehrard, "'L'Ami des hommes', Paris et la capitale du royaume," in Albert Soboul, ed., *Les Mirabeau et leur temps, Actes du Colloque d'Aix-en-Provence* (Paris, 1968), pp. 37–43. For a full analysis of Mirabeau's views on luxury, see Michael Kwass, "Consumption and the World of Ideas: Consumer Revolution and the Moral Economy of the Marquis de Mirabeau," *Eighteenth-Century Studies*, 37:2 (2004), 187–213. I would, however, add this caveat: Mirabeau linked his discussion of luxury to decentralization.

# 2

# The Ways of the Mind

As he moved from physiology to the economy, Quesnay's approach to scientific inquiry changed.[1] Abandoning his earlier prudence, he extrapolated a theory of the reproduction of wealth from statistics on agricultural productivity and treated his conclusions as unassailable. Anyone who reflected deeply on the workings of nature, faced with the same evidence, could not fail to reach similar conclusions. His followers, the Marquis de Mirabeau in the lead, treated him as a seer and sage, never wavering in their conviction that he had been granted special insights into the workings of nature and reached indubitable truths about the reproduction of wealth.

These claims to self-evidence pervade the doctrine and were one of the chief stumbling blocks to its acceptance. No one addresses this dilemma better than Georges Weulersse in the opening lines to his chapter on the "Physiocratic philosophy of science."

There is hardly a word that Physiocrats used with greater affectation than the substantive evidence, the adjective evident, and the adverb evidently. Their entire moral philosophy rests indeed, just like their policies, on the notion of evidence. It is evidence that reconciles the individual to the general interest and allies it with justice; it is evidence that guarantees a community of interests between sovereign and nation; and it is evidence that orders man's submission to and cooperation with the natural order.[2]

---

[1] Quesnay should hence be excluded from Jean-Claude Perrot's conclusions about a basic Enlightenment scientific approach, "Quelques préliminaires à l'intelligence des textes économiques" in *Une histoire intellectuelle*, p. 32.
[2] Weulersse, *Le mouvement physiocratique en France*, vol. II, p. 120.

Whereas one might note that the French acceptance of the term "evidence" differs from the English in referring both to "evidence" and "self-evidence," physiocrats mostly used it in that second sense. Evidence was therefore a certainty in the mind rather than a demonstrable proof. This is not to deny that the Economists were keen on the constant accumulation of data to *substantiate* their theory. Thus, Ronald Meek, who must be credited as the most generous and most accessible explicator of the *Tableau économique*, concludes his analysis (rejecting a possible comparison with the Leontief input-output system) by stating that:

> The particular feature of the *tableau* which makes the comparison possible is the fact that Quesnay *gave specific values* to his aggregates – values which we have seen were by no means arbitrary, but based on a careful study of such statistics as were then available of national incomes, productivity, population, etc. The *tableau* is far from being the ideal and airy thing which it is sometimes made out to be: on the contrary, it is one of the most striking examples in the whole history of economic thought of the achievement of a harmonious unity between abstract theory and concrete investigation.[3]

The proof, nonetheless, always rested on the *économistes*' claim to have discovered a scientific law, summed up by the Marquis de Mirabeau[4]:

> It is in our era that the first real foundations of moral and political knowledge have finally been revealed and their effects systematically worked out, and that an exact science has emerged which is guided, like geometry, by evidence and mathematical demonstrations. The tableau économique is the basis, the algebra of this science.... The science of economics must be the beacon guiding all members of a society in their personal behaviour, in their patriotic endeavours, in all those branches of administration that they might oversee, in their allegiances [*suffrages*], in their discourses, in the challenges that honest souls set themselves on behalf of humanity.

Quesnay had displayed this new law of nature in a visual model, the *Tableau économique*, which demonstrated the circulation and recreation of capital, so that Mirabeau could assert:

> The *Tableau économique* is the first mathematical law that has been devised in accordance with fundamental principles and in perpetual fulfillment of God's dictum "you will earn your bread by the sweat of your brow" and expressed through

---

[3] Ronald L. Meek, "The Interpretation of the 'Tableau économique'," *Economica* NS XXVII (November 1960), 322–47, 347.
[4] Address to a Tuesday Physiocratic assembly where he publicizes a course in political economy to be offered by Court de Gébelin, n.d. A. N. Mirabeau papers, M 784 #7.

exact and precise calculations.... Calculation is to the science of economics what bones are to the human body.[5]

Yet the *Tableau*, just like the physiocratic treatment of evidence, proved anything but self-evident to the public. The fault lay with two sides of physiocracy that vied uncomfortably for supremacy. On the one hand, we find the experimental method of observation and calculation that Quesnay had endorsed as surgeon; on the other, a philosophy of mind that parted company with sensationalism in insisting on the power of "inner" visions. Physiocracy was underpinned by the conviction that Quesnay's mind had pierced nature's secrets with such acuity that societies could be built around these insights. Based on Descartes's depiction of the body's basic functions as a series of mechanical responses over which the mind had no control – the pressures on its fluids, the grinding motion of the stomach, or the receptivity of nerves – Quesnay accepted the usefulness of a mechanistic approach to the body, although he knew that the laws of physics did not suffice to explain living things, and that one had to gather evidence of "observed regularities" that lent themselves to mathematical formulation.[6] Wondering whether Quesnay was a Cartesian or a Newtonian is a *question mal posée* because Quesnay believed he approached the processes of nature in a "modern" way, whatever the source, because he sought overall explanations in regularities, and that these came from observation. Thus he noted that the evidence for attraction came from inanimate objects and that living things functioned instead through impulsion or contact, meaning, in effect, that the

---

[5] Mirabeau, *Philosophie rurale ou Economie générale de L'agriculture* (Paris, 1763), pp. xix–xx.

[6] On the strength of various theories, see Peter Hanns Reill, "The Legacy of the 'Scientific Revolution' Science and the Enlightenment" in Roy Porter, *The Cambridge History of Science*, vol. 4: *Eighteenth-Century Science* (Cambridge, 2003), pp. 23–43; Philippe Hamon, "Descartes, Newton et l'intelligibilité de la nature" in Pierre Wagner, *Les philosophes et la science* (Paris, 2002), pp. 110–65. Philippe Steiner in *La "science nouvelle" de l'économie politique* (Paris, 1998), pp. 33 and 43–8, argues that for Quesnay Physiocracy was not an "hypothesis" but a truth that transcended facts; moreover, he views him as milking Malebranche for Cartesian ideas, even though he ended by rejecting both Descartes and Malebranche in favor of Lockean empricism. See a contrario, Akiteru Kubota, "Quesnay, disciple de Malebranche" in Jacqueline Hecht, ed., *François Quesnay et la Physiocratie*, 2 vols. (Paris, 1958), I, pp. 69–96, and Michael Sonenscher, *Before the Deluge*, pp. 219–22. On medical thought see also Gilles Barroux, *Philosophie, maladie, et médecine au XVIIIe siècle* (Paris, 2008); Brockliss and Jones, *The Medical World of Early Modern France*; and Mirko D. Grmek, ed., *Histoire de la pensée médicale en Occident*, vol. 2: *De la Renaissance aux Lumières* (Paris, 1997).

jury was still out on Newtonian and Cartesian explanations.[7] However, skeptical of others' theories, Quesnay came to elevate his own "observed regularities" in the supply and pricing of cereals into a law, verifiable only within the parameters set by his insights. If one agreed with his premises, in other words, data would demonstrate that he had calculated relations among various economic branches properly.

We must be careful not to chide him too severely for this, since expectations of what constitutes proof have changed over time and historians of science argue over what it meant for seventeenth-century and early eighteenth-century natural philosophers. Thus, Descartes asserted that the clear and distinct ideas that formed in the mind did not need external proof since they represented their own proof guaranteed by God.[8] Leibniz, however, insisted that logical demonstrations were necessary if statements were to be taken as true.

Science and its practices have been the subject of critical scrutiny both by scholars who endorse a building-block approach to knowledge and those who regard it as a "social construct" that posseses, at best, only relative truth-value. Historians of economic thought have grappled with similar distinctions.[9] In a bold move, Deirdre McCloskey recently argued that the language and terminology of economic analysis are but "figures of speech – metaphors, analogies, and appeals to authority."[10]

---

[7] François Quesnay, Letter to a fellow physician, 16 January 1755, 4 pages, Pierpont Morgan Library, New York, literary and historical manuscripts, misc. French.

[8] I will have more to say on this later in the chapter. The positions are discussed in Jacques Bouveresse, *Essais V: Descartes, Leibniz, Kant* (Paris, 2005). See also Yvon Belaval, *Leibniz critique de Descartes* (Paris, 1960); François Duscheneau, *Leibniz et la méthode de la science* (Paris, 1993); Ian Hacking, "Leibniz and Descartes: Proof and Eternal Truths" in *Historical Ontology* (Cambridge, Mass., 2002), pp. 200-13; Donald Rutherford, *Leibniz and the Rational Order of Nature* (Cambridge, 1995); Gaukroger, *Descartes' System of Natural Philosophy*; Nicholas Jolley, *Leibniz and Locke: A Study of the News Essays on Human Understanding* (Oxford, 1984); Nicholas Jolley, ed., *The Cambridge Companion to Leibniz* (Cambridge, 1995): Lex Newman, ed., *The Cambridge Companion to Locke's Essay Concerning Human Understanding* (Cambridge, 2007); Steven Nadler, ed., *The Cambridge Companion to Malebranche* (Cambridge, 2000); Maria Rosa Antognazza, *Leibniz, An Intellectual Biography* (Cambridge, 2009): Quentin Skinner, *Reason and Rhetoric in the Philosophy of Hobbes*; and Dominique Weber, ed., *Hobbes, Descartes et la métaphysique* (Paris, 2005).

[9] For an excellent summary of the contending positions, see Stephan Boehm, Christian Gehrke, Heinz D. Kurtz et al., eds., *Is There Progress in Economics? Knowledge, Truth and the History of Economic Thought* (Cheltenham, UK, and Northampton, Mass., 2002), in particular the essays by Donald Winch, "Does Progress Matter" (pp. 3–20) and Mark Blaug, "Is There Really Progress in Economics?" (pp. 21–41).

[10] Deirdre N. McCloskey, *The Rhetoric of Economics* (Madison, 1998), p. xix.

The physiocrats, with their emphasis on terminology and their search for the most effective way to disseminate their ideas, fit this description, yet they also functioned within a society that had come to trust in science itself and this lent credibility and prestige to discourses and activities that were presented as scientific. This brings us back to Quesnay's methodology and his claims to have discovered a natural law.[11]

In Quesnay's time, physics and mathematics were the privileged models for "serious science."[12] Descartes's equating of the body to a machine reducible to mechanical laws had stimulated a new approach to medicine (iatromechanism) to which Quesnay mostly subscribed, hence his recourse to hydraulics to understand the circulation of bodily fluids. Not all natural processes could be reduced to mechanics, however; nor were all blockages easily resolved or all remedies effective Yet, despite uneven results, *regularities* in such outcomes suggested that nature worked uniformly in the biological realm[13] It is in that spirit that Quesnay argued that harvests (the most unpredictable of phenomena) evinced a logic that he had discovered.[14] Predictability was not yet integral to the natural sciences. Still, by positing ideal ratios in economic exchanges, Quesnay's model offered standards against which actual exchanges could be gauged. Should there be overinvestment in one sector, his *Tableau économique* would tip in that direction, hence into "disequilibrium," revealing where the obstruction to the desired flow lay.[15] In acting simultaneously as the prototype for economic exchanges and as a tool, the *Tableau économique* staked it claims to verifiability. As a consequence Quesnay had no interest in calculating "probabilities" *per se* since they distorted the *real* data on which

---

[11] Economists still debate appropriate methods. See Thomas A. Boylan and Paschal F. O'Gorman, *Beyond Rhetoric and Realism in Economics: Towards a Reformulation of Economic Methodology* (London and New York, 1995); E. Roy Weintraub, *How Economics Became a Mathematical Science* (Durham, 2002). For the continuing role of mathematics in the social sciences and criticisms, see Jean-Yves Grenier, Claude Grignon, and Pierre-Michel Menger, *Le modèle et le récit* (Paris, 2001).

[12] See Peter Dear, *Discipline and Experience, The Mathematical Way in the Scientific Revolution* (Chicago, 1995).

[13] A. C. Crombie, *Styles in Scientific Thinking in the European Tradition*, 3 vols. (London, 1994), II, p. 1166, on Albrecht von Haller and regularities in organic behavior. Lena Soler, *Introduction à l'épistémologie* (Paris, 2002), pp. 21, 24, 47–9, 55–62. The distinction between describing and explaining was important. The first showed how things worked, the second why they worked in this way. See also Reill, op. cit., pp. 25–7.

[14] Reill, "Legacy of the 'Scientific Revolution,'" p. 27, on, as he puts it, "the perceived horrors of the contingent."

[15] Victor Riquetti Mirabeau, "Tableau oeconomique et ses explications" in *Ami des hommes*, 7 vols. (Paris, 1759–1760), VI, part II.

state policy must rest.¹⁶ Of course, one should remember that the elimination of chance lay at the very heart of his system.

In making his "case for the Enlightenment," John Robertson ties modernity to the political economy of the second half of the eighteenth century. "Political economy was the key to what the Enlightenment explicitly thought of as 'the progress of society'." It was a "conscious attempt ... to render political economy a distinct systematic field of investigation ... whose goals were the wealth of nations (in the plural) and the improvement of the condition of all of society's members."¹⁷ The economists of the Scottish and Neapolitan Enlightenment with whom Robertson is concerned were offering broad conceptual analyses of economic processes while responding to the particular circumstances of their respective backwaters.

One might object, following Daniel Brewer's argument, that referring to distinctive Enlightenment practices becomes circular if one defines the Enlightenment as promoting "the autonomy of fundamentally rational individuals, the progressive function of the state to which individuals give up their freedom in return for increased collective well-being, the essential rationality of the natural order made accessible through scientific knowledge and its technological applications designed to better material existence, and the potentially just nature of collective social relations."¹⁸ The new political economy fits the bill since it displays all these protocols, especially if one brushes aside some of its more bizarre contentions. Although Brewer warns of the dangers of treating the Enlightenment as a radical break, like Robertson he ends up situating the Enlightenment in mid-eighteenth century, beginning with d'Alembert's conscious rupture with past practices announced in his preamble to the *Encyclopédie*.¹⁹ Yet open rejection of tradition goes at least as far back as Francis Bacon and Cartesian mid-seventeenth-century skepticism. Similarly the various Quarrels of the Ancients and the Moderns that preoccupied European

---

¹⁶ See Ian Hacking, *The Taming of Chance* (Cambridge, 1966); John Bender and Michael Marrinan, *The Culture of Diagram* (Stanford, 2010); Keith Michael Baker, *Condorcet, From Natural Philosophy to Social Mathematics* (Chicago, 1975).

¹⁷ John Robertson, *The Case for the Enlightenment, Scotland and Naples 1680–1760* (Cambridge, 2005), p. 29.

¹⁸ Daniel Brewer, *The Enlightenment Past, Reconstructing Eighteenth-Century French Thought* (Cambridge, 2008), pp. 1–2. Michael C. Carthart, *The Science of Culture in Enlightenment Germany* (Cambridge, Mass., 2007) demonstrates how rethinking tradition developed from arcane, erudite research into past cultures. There is no single, cookie-cutter Enlightenment (pp. 6–7, 22).

¹⁹ Ibid., pp. 2–6.

literati into the 1720s entailed mulling over the nature of modernity. Whatever side they took, Dan Edelstein has recently stressed that the participants in these quarrels displayed a common spirit of enquiry and were equally indebted to classical and modern authors.[20] Emma Rothschild has shown the importance of such questioning for eighteenth-century economists Jacques Turgot, Adam Smith, and the Marquis de Condorcet, rejecting the view that they were rigid rationalists.[21] She argues that their very notion of modernity entailed coping with uncertainties and that this was the price for the new freedoms they touted.

Such psychological niceties did not interest Quesnay, who eventually concluded that men would have to adjust to the dictates of nature through the use of their reason. Yet for much of his life Quesnay had exemplified eighteenth-century epistemological humility, doubting that man could get at the prime cause of disease. In his introductory essay to the first collection of Academy of Surgery articles, he had advised the good surgeon to start with observation and experimentation.[22]

Nature only reveals herself indistinctly to our eyes; we must therefore scrupulously observe her progress, follow all the twists and turns and note their effects. Yet as it observes, the mind is a spectator that only sees the surface of things; physical experimentation allows us to reach the deepest physical [*sensibles*] recesses of Nature, where we can surprise her, interrogate her, and force her to reveal herself.

Knowledge would increase so long as questions were properly framed and the results continually crosschecked.[23] For one had to resist the lure of false theories: "The mind, blinded by vanity, flatters itself that it can find answers to everything within itself. Philosophers have erected entire systems [*mécanisme*] to explain the workings of the universe on the strength of delusions that existed solely in their imagination."[24]

---

[20] Dan Edelstein, *The Enlightenment: A Genealogy* (Chicago, 2010), pp. 37–43.
[21] Rothschild, *Economic Sentiments,* for example, pp. 2, 14–15.
[22] "Préface," *Mémoires de l'académie de chirurgie* (Paris, 1743), p. 83. This essay had already appeared in the 1736 edition of the *Essai physique sur l'oeconomie animale.*
[23] "Experiments and observations carried out by a single person cannot offer real insights. We must check them against observations scattered in the writings of our predecessors and our contemporaries." Elsewhere, he says the opposite, approving of much of what the Ancients had to say about disease: "Their entire approach to the treatment of fevers was based on the operations of nature itself. The further we strayed from the teachings of these great masters, the more we erred; the more we credited false ideas, the more we fell into shameful ignorance, and the more medicine harmed mankind." Quesnay, *Traité des fièvres continues*, pp. 132–3.
[24] "Préface," op. cit., p. 92.

Consequently, the Academy of Surgery that Quesnay represented should promote observation and experimentation but warn of the dangers of *analogies*, in particular the inappropriate transfer of remedies (rather than the vitalists' bête noire of treating dead bodies as guides to live processes) from one disease to another (as had been attempted with mercury).[25] Medical knowledge remained uncertain. "[Some physicians] have imagined that they could attack the causes of fevers straightaway and, in this way, spare Nature a fight whose victory remains always uncertain."[26] This explained why most textbooks were just compendia of vague and imprecise claims, frequently in the form of aphorisms.[27] Yet nostalgia for the grand theory lurks in his writings, a hope that one day the governing principles of physiology might be revealed. He confessed such hubris regarding his *Traité des fièvres continues*:

I would not have embarked on this work, had I not hoped to advance knowledge, especially by separating features that others usually mix together and about which we remain too ignorant ... I tried to discover, insofar as it is possible, the root [*essence*] of illnesses, as distinct from their particular manifestations since, even in the event of complications, these are not dangerous in themselves. I admit that I failed to achieve this; that I put off the discussion of some diseases to a later work; and I also concede how difficult they are to treat, especially when they are spasmodic. We have heard a lot about spasms recently; but nothing very precise and rarely based on observation [*d'après nature*].[28]

Mindful of the precarious status of surgery within the medical canon that had so long rejected it, Quesnay was careful to offer examples of surgical practice while praising its intellectual distinction through references to a corpus of distinguished authorities. He does not cite his own findings,[29]

---

[25] The recent synthesis of eighteenth-century French medical thought by Gilles Barroux, *Philosophie, maladie et médecine* shows how common such stances were. Quesnay, *Essai physique sur l'oeconomie animale*, I, p. liv.

[26] Quesnay, "Mémoire sur le vice des humeurs" in *Mémoires de l'académie de chirurgie*, p. 153. In Quesnay, *Essai physique sur l'économie animale*, III, pp. 228–30: Physicians learn by observation and experience – and experience teaches men what is good or harmful to them. But experience is worthless without education and wisdom.

[27] Various editions, see for example, *Boerhaave's Aphorisms: Concerning the Knowledge and Cure of Diseases*, translated from the last edition printed in Latin at Leiden, 1722 (London, 1724).

[28] Quesnay to Tronchin, [n.d. 1753] in Henry Tronchin, *Un médecin du XVIIIe siècle: Théodore Tronchin (1709–1781) d'après des documents inédits* (Paris and Geneva, 1906), pp. 358–60.

[29] Except "I had fourteen ounces of the flesh of an ox macerated in lukewarm water for a fortnight. I was careful to use lukewarm water because hot water might have hardened the blood and lymph; I squeezed this flesh several times a day to draw out its juices [*sucs*]

and this differentiates him from other practitioners, such as Albrecht von Haller, the Swiss doctor who minutely described his neurological experiments on frogs, or, closer to home, his colleague Jean-Louis Petit, who compared his own results with those of fellow surgeons in his essay on tumors of the gallbladder.[30] In his article on trepanning in the same collection, Quesnay mentions thirty cases culled from other surgeons.[31] There is no "Quesnay" case. Yet in the *Traité de la gangrène* published in 1749, Quesnay recalled suggesting to another surgeon at the siege of Ypres in 1743 that he delay trepanning the head wound of an officer of the king's guards.[32]

> I advised him to put off the operation because the humors had barely coalesced and it would be premature and harmful to cut the tumor and that he should first attempt a resolution. To bring it about, we dissolved marine salt in water and spirits [*eau-de-vie*]; the tumor disappeared within three days and the patient completely recovered.

Quesnay's distancing from raw observation and his focus on others' experiments embodied the Academy's mission to describe "common

---

as soon as they were ready to ooze out of the fibres that enclosed them; I changed the water each time, in order to prevent rotting; I then took the flesh out of the water and let it dry slowly, and weighed it when it had totally dried. Its weight of fourteen ounces had been reduced to two ounces two *gros*, meaning that the liquids in this piece of flesh made up five sixths of its weight." Quesnay, *Essai physique sur l'oeconomie animale*, III, p. 91. Barroux raises the interesting possibility that it was by describing others' experiments that medical writers countered the charge of charlatanism (p. 33) and Mazzaloni in Grmek, *Histoire de la pensée médicale en Occident*, pp. 106–7, describes, on the other hand, the skepticism and "lassitude" of early eighteenth-century medicine vis-à-vis expensive, difficult, and rarely conclusive experiments.

[30] Albrecht von Haller, *Deux mémoires sur la circulation du sang et sur les effets de la saignée fondés sur des expériences faites sur des animaux*, trans. Tissot (Lausanne, 1756). There he related his mutilation of frogs in the service of a higher cause: severing limbs, watching them pulsate, placing them under the microscope, and sometimes even reattaching them to see how they responded to stimuli. Despite the popularity of his physiological textbooks, Haller's experimental method faced a new challenge in the form of vitalists who considered that experimentation induced unnatural states that offered no valuable insights into the healthy body. See Roselyne Rey in Gremk, *Histoire de la pensée médicale en Occident*, pp. 123–7. On Haller's views on science, see also *The correspondence between Albrecht von Haller and Charles Bonnet*, ed. Otto Sonntag (Bern, Stuttgart, Vienna, 1983); Petit, "Remarques sur les tumeurs formées par la bile retenue dans la véscicule du fiel, et qu'on a souvent prises pour des abcès au foie" in Quesnay, *Mémoires de l'académie de chirurgie*, pp. 168–83.

[31] "Précis de diverses observations sur le trépan dans des cas douteux, où l'on recherche les raisons qui peuvent en pareils cas déterminer à recourir au trépan, ou à éviter cette operation," ibid., pp. 183–205.

[32] Quesnay, *Traité de la gangrène*, p. 62.

practice," yet contravened its other stated intention to promote the "experimental method."[33] Quesnay maintained that experiments yielded very few discoveries on their own. Admittedly, dissection had demonstrated how the blood really circulates, but it had taken a genius to work it out.[34] Outstanding minds of this sort were rare. In fact, Quesnay found only three medical theorists worth praising: Hippocrates, Galen, and Boerhaave – thereby signaling his personal allegiance to the old humoral theory.[35] Quesnay's *forte* was critical acuity rather than familiarity with the laboratory.

## Physiocracy and Medicine

Eighteenth-century medical theory makes dull reading so it is perhaps not surprising that historians of economic thought have only paid scant attention to Quesnay's medical texts. Some, like Weulersse, argued that Quesnay's economics bore no relation to his earlier medical interests.[36] Others have taken the connection to physiocracy metaphorically presuming that, like other *médecins-philosophes* of his era, Quesnay moved from reflections on curing the body to healing the body politic.[37] The naturalist Buffon had already proposed this interpretation during Quesnay's lifetime, saying: "He once practiced medicine for individuals; this is medicine for governments, meaning for the entire species." Likewise Quesnay's

---

[33] See Gelfand, *Professionalizing Modern Medicine*, pp. 103–11. Quesnay suggested common practice with the frequent recourse to the indefinite article *on*.

[34] As Claire Salomon-Bayet has agued, Quesnay was instrumental in tipping the balance toward theoretically informed experimentation, distinguished from a highly disparaged, mindless empricism with which it has earlier been equated. *L'Institution de la science et l'expérience du vivant* (Paris, 2008), pp. 399–400.

[35] He is a prime example of what Brockliss and Jones call "eclectic iatromechanism." The recent synthesis of eighteenth-century French medical thought by Gilles Barroux, *Philosophie, maladie et médecine*, shows how common such stances were. Quesnay, *Essai physique sur l'oeconomie animale*, I, p. liv.

[36] Weulersse, Le *Mouvement physiocratique en France*, II, p. 128.

[37] See the latest speculations by Peter D. Groenewegen who argues that the 1740s are crucial to understanding Quesnay's switch from medicine to economics and the transfer of his new methodological conclusions grounded in sensationalism. "From Prominent Physician to Major Economist. Some Reflections on Quesnay's Switch to Economics in the 1750s" in Peter Groenewegen, ed., *Physicians and Political Economy: Six Studies of the Work of Doctor-Economists* (London and New York, 2001), pp. 93–115. Paul Christensen privileges the vivifying force of fire (or ether) in Quesnay's medical writings on matter and its transfer to the regenerative forces of agriculture. Paul Christenten, "Fire, Motion and Productivity: the Proto-energetics of Nature and Economy in François Quesnay" in Philip Mirowsky, ed., *Natural Images in Economic Thought, Markets Read in Tooth and Claw* (Cambridge, 1994), pp. 249–88.

protégé Du Pont remarked: "The *Science of Political Economy* seemed to him to be a kind of *Public Medicine*, as far above the *individual Medicine* that he had practiced up till then as the entire Nation is above each of the citizens that compose it."[38]

Elizabeth Fox-Genovese, who paid close attention to Quesnay's medical background, summarized his medical and economic pursuits as a common drive to place Man at the center of the analysis.[39] He was essentially a Newtonian who treated "Intelligence like Newton's original gravity, [as] a force from the outside."[40] But he retained elements of Cartesianism, with a special debt to Malebranche, in his belief that the human mind "partakes of the divine," so that he was no "doctrinaire sensualist."[41] Fox-Genovese believed Quesnay transferred these ideas to economics; however, Philippe Steiner in his little primer on the "new science of political economy" adopts a more eclectic approach, consonant with recent scholarship.[42] Quesnay does not appear as a *médecin-philosophe* and Steiner finds little resemblance between Quesnay's medical thought and his economics, which he views as resting principally on mathematics, aside from his early endorsement of observation and the "experimental method." Quesnay's reliance on mathematical analysis was his major innovation, raising "political arithmetic" (invented by the English in the late seventeenth century to estimate human longevity for actuarial projections and the calculation of annuities) to a new level.[43]

---

[38] Georges Louis Leclerc Buffon, *Correspondance générale*, ed. H. Nadault de Buffon, 2 vols. (Paris, 1885), I, pp. 165–6, letter to Guéneau de Montbeillard, 20 January 1768; Du Pont de Nemours, *The Autobiography of Du Pont de Nemours*, p. 238. "Il a fait autrefois de la médecine pour individus; ceci est la médecine du gouvernement, c'est -à-dire de l'espèce entière." On the *médecins philosophes*, see Anne C. Vila, *Medicine and Pathology* (Baltimore, 1998).

[39] Fox-Genovese, *The Origins of Physiocracy*. See also Michael Sonenscher, *Before the Deluge*, pp. 75–6, 202–3.

[40] Fox-Genovese, *Origins of Physiocracy*, p. 85. Newtonian association of this sort might at best fit Quesnay's "general ideas" before the mind disentangles them into simple and compound ideas, a view he held in 1747 rather than in 1756 in the article "Evidence" (in d'Alembert and Diderot, eds., *Encyclopédie ou Dictionnaire Raisonné des Sciences, des Arts et des Métiers*, 17 vols. [1751–1772] Volume VI on which Fox-Genovese bases her other conclusions. On the way Newtonian association would work, see Alexander Broadie, "The Human Mind and its Powers," pp. 60–78 in Broadie, ed., *The Cambridge Companion to the Scottish Enlightenment* (Cambridge, 2003), p. 67: "For Hume simple ideas are analogues of Newtonian particles – as particles attract each other, so also do ideas. There is, therefore, in the human mind an analogue of the law of gravity."

[41] Fox-Genovese, *Origins of Physiocracy*, p. 85.

[42] Steiner, *La "science nouvelle" de l'économie politique*.

[43] Crombie, *Styles in Scientific Thinking in the European Tradition*, p. 1424: "From the information for the natural increase of mankind, 'by a geometrical proportion', gathered

Quesnay bequeathed to future generations quantification and the use of models in economics embodied by the *Tableau économique*, his veritable "tour de force."[44] As a group, historians of economic thought view such contributions and the attendant project to rationalize the state apparatus positively.[45]

Whereas most postwar economic historians focused on the *Tableau*'s mathematics, some scholars have recently broadened the spectrum.[46] Loïc Charles, for example, makes the interesting suggestion that Quesnay's zigzagging flows were inspired by a display of mechanical clocks. Norton Wise treats the *Tableau économique* in terms of equilibrium between attraction and repulsion.[47] Paul Christensen and Spencer Banzhaf have instead pointed out the problematic infusions of vitalism in Quesnay's argumentation and his eventual recourse to the "mysterious" action of "the Ether" (animating matter) to explain nature's reproductive capacities.[48] As Banzhaf explains, Quesnay was adept at constructing abstract models of the circulation of the blood based on mechanical laws. Despite this, he resorted to Nature's mysterious force to activate his economic system. Exchanges depicted in the *Tableau économique* consequently required Nature's continual gift of "new goods." Banzhaf does not regard this as

---

by Graunt and others." See also Ted McCorrmick, *William Petty and the Ambitions of Political Arithmetic* (Oxford, 2010).

[44] Steiner, *La "science nouvelle" de l'économie politique*, pp. 19, 74, 123.

[45] See Thierry Martin, ed., *Arithmétique politique dans la France du XVIIIe siècle* and Theodore Porter, *Trust in Numbers, the Pursuit of Objectivity in Science and Public Life* (Princeton, 1995).

[46] Loïc Charles, "The Visual History of the Tableau économique," *The European Journal of the History of Economic Thought*, 10:4 (2003), 527–50; Albert E. Steenage and Richard Van Den Berg, "Transcribing the Tableau Économique: Input-Output Analysis a la Quesnay," *Journal of the History of Economic Thought* 29:3 (2007), 331–58. R. Sureau, *Les représentations figurées des physiocrates* (Paris, 1958); Richard Van Den Berg, "Contemporary Responses to the Tableau économique" in Stephan Boehm, Christian Gehrke, Heinz D. Kurtz et al., *Is There Progress in Economics? Knowledge, Truth, and the History of Economic Thought* (Cheltenham, UK, and Northampton, Mass., 2002), pp. 295–316. Margaret Schabas, *The Natural Origins of Economics* (Chicago, 2005) does not offer an interpretation but summarizes those of recent historians of economic thought and historians of science (pp. 42–57).

[47] M. Norton Wise, "Mediations: Enlightenment Balancing Acts, or the Technologies of Rationalism" in Paul Horwich, ed., *World Changes, Thomas Kuhn and the Nature of Science* (Cambridge, Mass., 1993), pp. 207–56. Here it is the balance between attraction and repulsion and models of equilibrium that inform the *Tableau économique*, yet vitalism lurks in the background, without much elaboration (see p. 242).

[48] Christensen, "Fire, Motion, and Productivity," pp. 249–88, (pp. 259 and 271). For the conclusion on the role of ether, see p. 277. H. Spencer Banzhaf, "Productive Nature and the Net Product: Quesnay's Economies Animal and Political," *History of Political Economy* 32:3 (2000), pp. 517–51

an infusion of *capital* (which Quesnay implies and Turgot then made explicit), meaning rather to stress to his fellow historians of economic thought that nature played a primal role in physiocratic economics.

Although Quesnay appears at times to be flirting with vitalism to account for the mysterious forces of nature, he actually watched with misgivings the increasing popularity of this approach. *Vitalism* is the umbrella term given to theories that attributed the body's motion and nature's generative powers to an irreducible force inherent to organic matter.[49] Quesnay defended the mechanist approach insisting that the body was passive, like all matter, and had to be stimulated by an external force. This safeguarded him from accusations of materialism or animism.[50] Yet he waxed so eloquently about this "mysterious force" that one understands why scholars have difficulty situating his ideas.

> All true physicians must acknowledge an invisible force everywhere ... whose effects largely exceed those of determining causes. I say everywhere because it is present in fire, electricity, magnetism, and the organic incompatibilities of animated bodies. It causes everything, we cannot define its power, it is subject neither to mechanical laws, nor to the laws of the communication of motion, nor to the calculation of effects from causes or causes from effects, as you yourself have demonstrated.[51]

There were no contradictions, from Quesnay's perspective, between his belief that the body functioned according to mechanical laws and the infusion of a life-giving force. In stressing the body's dependence on mechanical laws, he meant to refute the old medical canards about the

---

[49] Quesnay acknowledged involuntary reflexes such as sneezing or yawning but pointedly refused the vitalist theories offered "by Stahl and his followers," as he put it. See Quesnay, *Traité des fièvres continues*, pp. 66–7, 196–7, 205. On vitalism, see Joselyne Rey, *Naissance et développement du vitalisme*; Jacques Roger, *The Life Sciences in Eighteenth-Century French Thought* (Stanford, 1998, original French edition, Paris, 1963); Peter Hanns Reill, *Vitalizing Nature in the Enlightenment* (Berkeley and Los Angeles, 2005); Shirley Roe, *Matter, Life, and Generation: Eighteenth-Century Embryology and the Haller-Wolff Debate* (Cambridge, 1981); André Pichot, *Histoire de la notion de vie* (Paris, 1993).

[50] Quesnay, *Essai physique sur l'oeconomie animale*, III, pp. 133–6: Quesnay on his suspicion of animism and any theory that ascribed independent action to organs. On his relationship to La Mettrie, see Kathleen Wellman, *La Mettrie*, and his correspondence with Tronchin about *La Mettrie* in Quesnay, *Oeuvres économiques complètes et autres textes*, ed. Christime Théré, Loïc Charles, and Jean-Claude Perrot, 2 vols. (Paris, 2005), II, pp. 1160–3, Letter of 21 October 1746.

[51] Quesnay, letter to Tronchin of 16 January 1755, possibly addressed to François Boissier de Sauvages de la Croix, [n.d. 1753–57] in Quesnay, *Oeuvres économiques*, II, pp. 1169–70.

autonomy of organs, be it the liver or heart, each with its own power and logic. The body was an entity, not a compendium of parts, and one had to account for its overall functioning – an argument that would reappear in his economic analysis. He rejected vitalist arguments about the importance of reflexes on the same ground.

Jessica Riskin has approached physiocracy from yet a different angle, arguing that physiocratic flows (or circulation) were influenced by Benjamin Franklin's physics.[52] Mechanistic and hydraulic explanations did not serve Quesnay's purpose, but Franklin's electrical currents did.

> The natural purposes guiding the flow of wealth through Quesnay's Tableau were the same as those directing Franklin's electrical economy: conservation and the maintenance of balance.... When Physiocratic authors did call upon hydraulic and mechanical analogies to explain such principles, as when Franklin did so, it was not to reduce the economy to a machine, but, on the contrary, to invoke the hidden operation of natural purpose even in mechanical arrangements.

Even if Franklin himself only endorsed some physiocratic ideas, his model proposed "an organic, balance-seeking process whose flow must be left unimpeded; [and] that good administration was a matter of sensitivity to this organic process."[53] It is at this juncture that Riskin applies the terms "sentimental empiricism" to denote the physiocrats' justification of their ideas, "bringing in the language of sensibility from natural philosophy into political economy," most prominently through Turgot, although she does not view him as a full-fledged physiocrat.[54] Riskin has astutely fastened on aspects of sensibility in physiocratic thought, and this has allowed her to extend the discussion of physiocracy beyond its traditional boundaries. There are, however, distinctions that she elides by including Turgot and Lavoisier in her analysis. The recourse to sensibility was "contested terrain" among physiocrats. The Marquis de Mirabeau's recourse to sentiment retained its seventeenth-century religious and aesthetic dimensions, and Quesnay rejected it for those very reasons.[55] The eighteenth-century sensibility that Riskin refers to entered physiocratic discourse only with Du Pont de Nemours (as we shall see in later chapters), and other physiocrats did not adopt it. Moreover, physiocracy

---

[52] Jessica Riskin, *Science in the Age of Sensibility, The Sentimental Empiricists of the French Enlightenment* (Chicago, 2002), p. 112.
[53] Riskin, *Science in the Age of Sensibility*, p. 120.
[54] Ibid., p. 131.
[55] See the discussion, for example, in Annie Becq, *Genèse de l'esthétique moderne, 1680–1814* (Paris, 1994), Part I.

had no self-righting mechanism. Equilibrium was restored from the outside by those who observed the outcomes of economic exchanges.

Physiology certainly offered analogies that Quesnay did not disdain, such as the longstanding comparison between the circulation of the blood and the circulation of money.[56] In a related fashion, Quesnay's surgical work revolved around the internal *blockages* to the circulation of fluids (or humors as they were known) that resulted in inflammations, abscesses, and rot that could be fatal if not treated in time. In Hippocratic-Galenic *and* iatromechanical fashion, he advised the surgeon to remove the obstruction and then let the body heal itself.[57] Laissez-faire functioned the same way by permitting goods to circulate freely, removing harmful impediments to economic circulation (tolls, customs duties, and excise taxes). The ultimate purpose of the *Tableau économique* was to diagnose "blockages" or misdirection in economic exchanges.

In his approach to healing, Quesnay had repeatedly urged caution, observation, and careful crosschecking since human bodies responded in unpredictable, and hence contingent, ways despite their overall subjection to mechanical processes. We sense Quesnay's frustrations with contingency as he turns to discussions of the "fate of humanity." The origins of inequality, he explained in the *Essai physique* of 1747, lay in the human race's requirements for survival, based on "the designs of a supreme intelligence" that secured the welfare of the species.[58] Inequality, Quesnay stated, was neither just nor unjust: The Supreme Being had inscribed it within the laws of nature for reasons that man would never understand.

> A thousand natural causes contribute inevitably and necessarily to produce this inequality; these causes are not subject to the moral order, they belong to a far greater realm where human beings who have existed, exist, and will exist form only a tiny part; they work toward the conservation of the whole, and their activity is regulated by the goals and intention of the supreme intelligence who built the universe and who ensures its continuation; it is within this order, or general system, that one must look for patterns [*la régularité*] and not on the equal or unequal distribution to individual men; it is for men to adjust themselves to this

---

[56] See Chantal Beauchamp, *Le sang et l'imaginaire médical, histoire de la saignée aux XVIIIe et XIX siècles* (Paris, 2000), and Jean Nagle, *La Civilisation du coeur, histoire du sentiment politique en France du XIIe au XIXe siècle* (Paris, 1998), p. 244: Mirabeau writes in *L'Ami des hommes* that Paris needs to be "bled."

[57] Richard Olson, "The Human Sciences" in Roy Porter, ed., *Cambridge History of Science*, vol. IV (Cambridge, 2003), pp. 436–62, 452: Olson straightforwardly equates this approach with political economy.

[58] Quesnay, *Essai physique sur l'oeconomie animale*, III, pp. 364–71.

order and not to question it or to look pointlessly and unfairly [*injustemment*] to free themselves from it.[59]

Such sentiments would feature in his essay on "Natural Law" that his follower Du Pont turned into a pivot of the doctrine.[60]

Quesnay's economic theory rested on men's necessary subjection to the natural order and their aggregate efforts to reproduce agricultural profits. Societies rested on such overall results so that it made perfect sense to subsume individuals within blocks of "landowners," "farmers," or "artisans." Yet despite Quesnay's marginalization of individual *experience* (it mattered not whether individuals suffered from drought one year as long as the government could take remedial action to ensure better results), individual *behavior* remained problematic because his system required *everyone* to make the right economic choices. The peculiarity of Quesnay's natural law is that, unlike gravity which functions outside of human control, *his* law is predicated on human action.

Transgression of natural laws is the most widespread and common source of man's physical distress [*maux physiques*] even for the rich, who are better able to avoid them. By their ambition, passions and even their pleasures, they bring harm to themselves which they can only blame on their own misconduct [*déréglements*]. This leads us to another source of physical and moral ills: men's poor use of their freedom.... its blind and irresponsible use can lead to poor choices; by means of his intelligence, man can reach better decisions, behave wisely, insofar as the laws of the physical order that control the universe allow.[61]

Having adopted aggregation as a reprieve from contingency, Quesnay investigated other means of achieving certainty. He had once compared medical researchers to wanderers in the dark, without a map, who "perceived [the] objects [of research] under the false accoutrements furnished by their imagination."[62] This oft-repeated observation had pushed him to query how one might acquire "sure and luminous principles." He would trace imagination's hold over the human psyche to its physiological and psychological roots by delving into the processes of cognition.

---

[59] Ibid., pp. 370–1.
[60] "Observations sur le droit naturel des hommes réunis en société," first published in *Journal de l'Agriculture, du Commerce, et des Finances* in September 1765, and republished in *Physiocratie* (1767–8), I, pp. 1–38, see Quesnay, *Oeuvres économiques complètes et autres textes*, I, pp. 97, 123.
[61] "Droit naturel" in Quesnay, *Oeuvres économiques complètes et autres textes*, I, p. 116.
[62] Letter to Tronchin, [n.d., end 1752-early 1753] in Quesnay, *Oeuvres économiques complètes et autres textes*, II, p. 1168.

## Processes of Mind

Quesnay was a sensationalist insofar as he rejected the existence of innate ideas. Ideas originated in impressions received through the nerve-ends, although thinking differed from the body's mechanical responses to stimuli. Loïc Charles remarked that, based on his sensationalist epistemology, Quesnay hoped that the *Tableau économique* would be imprinted on the mind, especially Louis XV's, whom Charles credits with printing the third version of the *Tableau*, endorsing Du Pont's story.[63] Although he summarizes Quesnay's ideas on cognition, Charles does not explain how this "imprinting" might take place. I see Quesnay's endeavor differently. He believed his ideas would only be understood through a proper chain of reasoning, precisely because ideas could not be imprinted or transmitted from one person to another.

As Quesnay explained in his third volume of the *Essai physique* (added in 1747), a vital principle intervened at birth to set in motion the "animal spirits," activating the vegetative and sensitive "souls." It evaporated at the moment of death, as the body dissolved into its elementary particles (Quesnay restored the Aristotelian tripartite division of the soul abandoned by Descartes). The higher 'rational soul' *had* to be immortal, on the other hand, to account for mankind's ingrained capacity to grasp right from wrong and for divine judgment to make any sense.[64] The material world was governed by laws that man might eventually understand but the realm of the divine in which our soul partakes was beyond human comprehension.[65]

The Vital Principle is nothing other than Ether itself, and it is located inside the fluid that flows through the same Nerves.... This compound mass is known as *animal spirits* ... and to gain a more precise idea of this most subtle and active fluid, one must separate the Vital principle, or Ether, which animates it, from the other parts [*parties*] that compose it; because it is only to this principle that one

---

[63] Loïc Charles, "The Tableau économique as Rational Recreation," *History of Political Economy* 36:3 (2004), 445–74, 466, 469.
[64] See on this the section "Immortalité de l'âme" in Quesnay, *Essai physique sur l'oeconomie animale*, III, pp. 373–82. Quesnay refused to engage in "theological" debates, declaring God's nature to be "incomprehensible ... his attributes ... impenetrable, [but] such questions are not decided on the basis of evidence." See Ann Thomson's illuminating, *Bodies of Thought, Science, Religion, and the Soul in the Early Enlightenment* (Oxford, 2008).
[65] Christa Mercer and R. C. Sleigh, Jr., "Metaphysics: The Early Period to the Discourse on Metaphysics" in Nicholas Jolley, ed., *The Cambridge Companion to Leibniz* (Cambridge, 1995), pp. 67–123, 73: each philosopher has some way of making God the source of motion.

must attribute the tremendous activity of the Animal Spirits, which grants us all our sensations and moves all of our organs.[66]

The animal spirits circulate inside the pulpy substance of the nerves vibrating to the impressions they have received from various stimuli, which they then transmit to the brain through a process we might equate to Morse code.[67] The nerves terminate in the *sensorium commune* in the lower brain.[68] The mind receives clumps of sensations simultaneously from the animal spirits and proceeds to sort them both individually and collectively by what we call "imagination." This imaginative faculty is able to "retain the precise representations of objects it wishes to examine and know exactly." It performs the basic physiological functions hard-wired in our brains, but it is also able to recall a whole array of details, through the use of memory. This process entails a second kind of "imagination" by which the mind recombines information to create new patterns, images, or fantasies. The products of imaginative reconstructions are sometimes regarded as art, but they are the source of errors, not least when they arouse the passions by instilling fictitious needs. This occurs when the mind recombines its *initial* – and as yet unsorted – perceptions rather than waiting for the later, more focused images that it has separated from the mass. Locke's mistake, according to Quesnay, was to presume that our general ideas arise from these undigested impressions, despite Malebranche's insights.[69] The mind's superior activities arose from *attention* as Malebranche predicated.[70]

The accuracy of perceptions has been debated since the days of Plato when objects were thought to be imprinted on the retina, like wax impressions, either "captured" directly by a beam leaving the eye or "exuded" from the objects into the eye.[71] By Quesnay's time, the eye's operation as a *camera obscura* was well understood, and the effects of light had been investigated for over a century. Such discoveries exacerbated earlier debates by denying the possibility of direct

---

[66] Quesnay, *Essai physique sur l'oeconomie animale*, III, pp. 111–13.
[67] Ibid., III, pp. 173–83.
[68] Whereas the Ancients had attributed this capacity to various parts of the body – the Stoics to the chest – and Descartes to the pineal gland, Quesnay was following current practice in the attribution of the body's nerve center. Margaret R. Graver, *Stoicism and Emotion* (Chicago, 2007), p. 22.
[69] Quesnay, *Essai physique physique sur l'oeconomie animale*, III, pp. 249–50.
[70] Ibid., III, p. 261.
[71] See Richard L. Gregory, *Eye and Brain, The Psychology of Seeing*, 5th edition (Princeton, 1997); Krysztof Pomian "Vision and Cognition" in Caroline A. Jones and Peter Galison, eds., *Picturing Science, Producing Art* (London and New York, 1998), pp. 21–31.

imprints. To what extent could sensations then be trusted to render the world accurately?

Descartes argued that all we experience is the motion created through the stimulation of our nerve-ends, so we can never be sure that the animal spirits convey "true" information to the brain, yet the abstract patterns that our minds form as a consequence allow us to form ideas. The mind, then, through its God-given capacities, is able to translate perceptions and hone them into "clear and distinct" ideas. When the mind reaches such a point, these ideas necessarily become self-evident. We cannot doubt or deny these ideas because God guarantees the products of our reason. With this insistence Descartes switched the debate from perception to cognition, placing the emphasis on how the mind works.[72]

The reliability of the senses would be debated throughout the eighteenth century, but the sensationalism to which Quesnay basically adhered treated sensations transmitted to the brain as the source of knowledge.[73] We are born as blank slates and learn by accruing sensations.[74] Ideas – as described previously – arise as the mind sorts out the sensations it receives and focuses on individual components, picking and choosing to form relevant patterns (e.g., connecting the color red to a rose but not to the rain or the sound of the horn that accompanied this perception). Once the proper elements have been aligned and stored in its memory bank, the mind can recall them and cogitate further to create general ideas.[75]

The capacity of *attention*, which grants them accurate judgments, separates men from animals. Human beings *concentrate* and separate strands of sensory information from each other. Moreover, men's judgments transcend the mere responses to pain and pleasure that govern animals because men can distinguish a higher self-interest. This is what is meant by judgment.[76] Attention also accounts for our individuality. We concentrate on things we find appealing and establish personal preferences. All humans have the capacity to enjoy fruit, but we might like blueberries more than bananas. Individuation is tied to such personal experiences and hence cannot be reduced to automatic responses of pain

---

[72] Gaukroger, *Descartes' System of Natural Philosophy*, pp. 204–8, and Bouveresse, *Essais V*, p. 264.
[73] Pomian, "Vision and Cognition," pp. 218–21.
[74] Quesnay, *Essai physique sur l'oeconomie animale*, III, p. 249.
[75] Quesnay was not especially interested in primary and secondary qualities, or in Locke's simple and compound ideas – he was more concerned with how we get at truth than how we build up complex ideas.
[76] Quesnay, *Essai physique sur l'oeconomie animale*, III, pp. 312–13.

and pleasure. Judgment allows us to test our recollections and sensations against each other.[77] This means we have the capacity to choose and consequently possess free will.[78] Reason and free will allow human beings to *plan* and make decisions regarding their long-term survival, and this is how Quesnay approaches economic rationality. Reason is able to control passions aroused by poorly processed sensations.[79]

So that proper decision be reached, it was imperative to separate "good" imagination from its evil twin. Artists might welcome untutored inspiration, but a rational mind analyzed problems.[80]

All that genius and industry produce depend on the soul's ability to create *factitious Ideas;* this is how poets and painters arrive at the fictions that they represent; how orators get the imagery which embellishes their speeches, and architects the ornaments with which they decorate buildings; how mechanics conceive of their technological innovations and how workmen are able to execute them; this is also how hardworking physicians obtain the know-how from which they concoct the fables which they use to explain the operations and structure of the universe and the impenetrable workings of Nature.[81]

Mental training and proper concentration yield true insights. If one makes the proper connections, the road will be easy. Attention, Quesnay holds, reveals different possibilities to the mind but also shows it the right path to follow. One might have thought that delusions always lurked in the shadows, but Quesnay argues that with the proper use of attention, the mind will continually make the right connections as though its path were illuminated. "The mind will perceive the advantages presented to it and will know what direction to follow."[82] The more attention it applies, the more clearly and distinctly it sees.

All human beings are born with the (God-given) faculty to think clearly, but few have the discipline or inclination to exercise it.[83]

The truths [that the mind has perceived] can be verified through an examination of evidence, in other words by the strong and distinct impression that it makes

[77] Ibid., III, pp. 278, 312.
[78] Ibid., III, p. 360.
[79] See Susan James, *The Passion and Action, The Emotions in Seventeenth-Century Philosophy* (Oxford, 1997).
[80] For example Fleury, *Métaphysique de l'imagination*, pp. 17–24, 41.
[81] Quesnay, *Essai physique sur l'oeconomie animale*, III, pp. 286–7.
[82] Ibid., III, pp. 336–7.
[83] Becq, *Genèse de l'esthétique*, p. 268, argues that by the middle decades of the eighteenth century the power accorded to sentiment became such that even rationalists argued that only a minority of privileged souls had the temperament to pursue "true knowledge."

on the mind; but it is not enough to know such truths, they must be weighed, examined, evaluated, counted, measured. We gauge them by their degree of perfection and imperfection, the nature of their qualities, the worthiness of actions, by their causes and effects, the extent and precision in their relations, etc. We count by means of the axiomatic [self-evident] rules of arithmetic; we compare their attributes and their quantity to known and fixed attributes. Logic merely entails the use of comparison and measurement to assess and evaluate truths, and the Logician who weighs the truthfulness of evidence, and a Merchant who weighs a bundle of goods or measures a piece of cloth proceeds and thinks in the same manner.[84]

When judgment isn't called into play in this fashion, the mind remains mired in desires and fallacies. Education can instill the necessary mental discipline, and this is why physiocrats were such ardent advocates of universal schooling.

Quesnay defined evidence as "nothing other than a clear and distinct discernment of our sensations [*sentiments*] and of all the perceptions that they entail: Evidence therefore carries with it a certainty which we cannot refuse, because we cannot doubt the existence and diversity of the sensations [*sentiments*] which affect us distinctly."[85] Sensations are the source of our ideas, and their reliability is tested through repetition of similar sensations.[86] Locke accepted the constraints of our sensory experiences and limited knowledge. An inner restlessness ensured that men would seek further enlightenment.[87] Certainty was only possible in a few domains, and the remainder had to be treated as probable or as subject to

---

[84] Quesnay, *Essai physique*, III, p. 344.
[85] See Lex Newman, "Locke on Knowledge" in Lex Newman, ed., *The Cambridge Companion to Locke's* Essay Concerning Human Understanding (Cambridge, 2007), pp. 313–51, 349, quoting the *Essay Concerning Human Understanding,* IV, iv. And Quesnay, *Essai physique sur l'oeconomie animale*, III, pp. 291–2. See Thomas M. Lennon, "Malebranche and Method" in Steven Nadler, ed., *The Cambridge Companion to Malebranche* (Cambridge, 2000), pp. 8–30, 18. See Susan James, *Passion and Action*, p. 273.
[86] See Lorraine Daston, "On Scientific Observation," *Isis* 99 (2008), 97–110, on habit of seeing (p. 99).
[87] Paul Wood, "Science, Philosophy, and the Mind" in Roy Porter, ed., *Cambridge History of Science*, vol. 4: *Eighteenth-Century Science* (Cambridge, 2003), pp. 800–24, 805. I am drawing my understanding of Locke's epistemology from Lex Newman, ed., *The Cambridge Companion to Locke's* Essay Concerning Human Understanding (Cambridge, 2007), in particular, G. A. J. Rogers, "The Intellectual Setting and the Aims of the *Essay*," pp. 7–32; Samuel C. Rickless, "Locke's Polemic Against Nativism," pp. 33–66; Martha Brandt Bolton, "The Taxonomy of Ideas in Locke's *Essay*," pp. 67–100; Thomas M. Lennon, "Locke on Ideas and Representation," pp. 231–57; Michael Losonsky, "Language, Meaning, and Mind in Locke's *Essay*," pp. 286–312; and David Own, "Locke on Judgment," pp. 406–37.

further enquiry. Evidence becomes akin to testimony: We decide whether it is probable or not.[88] Certainty is psychological: It expresses the extent to which we feel persuaded.[89] Such indeterminacy was distasteful to Quesnay whose aim was to discover how our most trusted beliefs can be shown to be true.[90] In sensationalist fashion, he described the accumulation of sensations as a necessary first step, after which the mind "estimates, determines, evaluates, counts and measures" the value of what it had perceived.[91] Used in proper sequence mental processes lead to certainties, which can be trusted because God means for us to assent to clear and distinct ideas.[92] The process is internal: It takes place within individual brains. Clarity and certainty rest on an orderly sequence, meaning that we can only truly learn by making similar connections. Demonstration might clarify some steps, but proof rests inside the mind.[93] Physiocracy might be observed in nature but would truly be understood once one had acquiesced to its self-evident propositions.

Quesnay made an additional, very important point. Properly honed, ideas "present themselves to the mind through the relations that exist among them, and the mind takes in this pattern and yields to its evidence. Everything coheres as in a Picture, and upon seeing it, our mind becomes certain of the truth that it has been intent on finding; however, once we seek to convey this truth to others with the same self-evidence to which we yielded, we need to spell out [*énoncer*] the chain of ideas which led us to this certitude."[94] As with a painting, Quesnay had explained, the eye

---

[88] John Locke, *An Essay Concerning Human Understanding* (London, 1690), Book IV, Chapter I, subsection 1; Wood, "Science, Philosophy, and the Mind," p. 805.

[89] Newman, "Locke on Knowledge," p. 324.

[90] Locke looked for conformity between current impressions and past ideas, believing the mind assesses whether these are right or wrong, rather than true or false. Lennon, "Locke on Ideas," pp. 25–1.

[91] Quesnay, *Essai physique sur l'oeconomie animale*, III, p. 344.

[92] See Rickless, "Locke's Polemic Against Nativism," p. 47, and Bouveresse, *Essais V*, p. 67.

[93] On the differences between Descartes and Leibniz on demonstration, see Bouveresse, Belaval, Duscheneau, Hacking, "Leibniz and Descartes," and also Ian Hacking, *The Emergence of Probability* (Cambridge, 1975), p. 137. In other words, we adhere to ideas internally rather than because they have been demonstrated. Leibniz would argue that we accept our ideas as truthful, for example that a triangle has three sides, because the very definition of a triangle involves three sides. We are convinced by logic, which entails, as Ian Hacking puts it "internal consistency." "Leibniz was the first modern to understand that proof is a formal matter, attaching to the form of sentences, not to their content. He defined 'necessarily true' as provable from identities in a finite number of steps. Possibility, then, is freedom from contradiction."

[94] Quesnay, *Essai physique sur l'oeconomie animale*, III, p. 335: "Tout lui es présent comme dans un Tableau." On the contemporary debates on how far the eye captured the external

first sees the whole canvas, then studies its individual details, and finally takes in the whole image once more with deeper insights.[95]

Seventeenth-century theories of cognition referred to mental images without meaning that actual pictures formed in the mind, although Voltaire would make that very claim in mid-eighteenth century.[96] Images for Descartes and Locke referred to the product of initial sensations, which, in Descartes's case, did not need to resemble the object at all, but merely leave some trace of the object. Locke fastened on the distinguishing characteristics that cohered in the mind, through "archetypes" that allowed us, for instance, to distinguish a cat from a dog. Some sensationalists like Thomas Hobbes or Condillac focused on the human capacity to create signs (for Condillac this was a function of human imagination). It was language that enabled further thought, however arbitrary the terminology.[97] Quesnay acknowledged that human beings use signs (verbal, visual, written) to communicate and that these were established by convention but he did not make it central to his version of cognition. He was closer to those contemporaries who fretted about the inaccuracy of words, and he would insist on defining terms very clearly in his economic theory.

Malebranche came in handy for Quesnay because he was interested in images and the imagination, whereas Descartes had privileged pure thought and Locke focused on memory.[98] The Cartesian "eye" can do no more than perceive relations among objects since they only possess extension (they take up space). Malebranche proposed that once the mind has properly analyzed these relations, it proceeds to configure them into geometrical patterns. He too claims that clear and distinct ideas are indisputable because, through the use of its reason, the mind

---

world, see Carl Havelange, *De l'oeil et du monde: Une histoire du regard au seuil de la modernité* (Fayard, 1998), pp. 147–65. I thank Alain Guéry for pointing out this book to me.

[95] Quesnay, *Essai physique sur l'oeconomie animale*, III, p. 249.
[96] Becq, *Genèse de l'esthétique*, p. 157.
[97] See Lennon, "Locke on Ideas," pp. 247–54; Michael Losonsky, "Language, Meaning, and Mind in Locke's *Essay*" in Lex Newman, ed., *The Cambridge Companion to Locke's Essay Concerning Human Understanding* (Cambridge, 2007), pp. 286–312 (p. 303). In the mid eighteenth century Condillac would address this question more closely: André Charrak, *Empirisme et métaphysique, L'Essai sur les Origines des connaissances humaines de Condillac* (Paris, 2003) and *Contingence et nécessité des lois de la nature au XVIIIe siècle* (Paris, 2006); Aliénor Bertrand, ed., *Condillac, l'origine du langage* (Paris, 2002); Jean Sgard, ed., *Condillac et les problèms du langage* (Paris, 1982).
[98] Quesnay, *Essai physique sur l'oeconomie animale*, III, p. 256.

gains a glimmer of divine insight.[99] "I can clearly see the relations of size [*rapports de grandeur*] which exist between the intelligible ideas which it [the Word] encloses; and these relations are the same eternal truths that God sees, for God sees as does man, that two times two makes four."[100] The mind is led into error when it is over-hasty and fantasizes connections.[101] Geometry and mathematics trained it to conceptualize relations accurately.[102]

This geometric approach appealed to Quesnay who mistrusted words more than images. He had been trained as a draughtsman. Engravers created grids; used rulers and protractors to situate objects correctly on a plane; and drew in "black and white," adhering to a more cerebral aesthetic. In the latter part of the seventeenth century, the Academy of Painting upheld this orderly, intellectual conception of art, where drawing was granted primacy over color, although a few insisted that the latter presented a truer representation of nature, especially in its sensual appeal.[103] For the first, art's role was to get at "essences" and render the deeper truths of nature – not to strive for realism through vulgar imitation – whereas the second saw no purpose to rules that throttled creativity and turned art into a smooth, predictable product. Viewers would get bored and their attention had to be captivated by something unusual, enthralling, and even disturbing.[104] Such theories would privilege reception, emphasizing the power of images and words, and also presume the contagion of sentiment, which the real artist or performer brought out as well as embodied.

Whatever the power of images, Quesnay recognized that language was necessary to convey our ideas and "reliance on such artifices is a constant admission ... of the incommunicability of sensations and of the separateness of their souls."[105] Like Descartes and Locke, Quesnay believed that even the clearest thoughts are difficult to render into words because the

---

[99] Nicolas de Malebranche, *De la recherche de la vérité* in *Oeuvres*, 2 vols. (Paris, 1979), I, pp. 54–7.
[100] Malebranche, *Traité de morale*, cited by Patrick Riley, "Malebranche's Moral Philosophy" in Steven Nadler, ed., *The Cambridge Companion to Malebranche* (Cambridge, 2000), pp. 220–261, 240.
[101] Malebranche, *De la recherche de la vérité*, p. 594.
[102] Ibid., pp. 34, 44–54, 593, 619.
[103] Becq, *Genèse de l'esthétique*, pp. 75 and 187 on how color came into favor after Le Brun's death in 1690.
[104] See Annie Becq on de Piles (*Genèse de l'esthétique*, pp. 55, 62, 86–8).
[105] Quesnay, "Evidence" p. 81.

ideas in one's head are essentially incommunicable.[106] They are produced by our individual thought processes, and the only way to ensure that we have been understood is to induce people to follow the same steps so that they might obtain the same results. "The soul must prepare and then follow a type of discourse that awakens in others the same ideas with the same degree of conviction."[107] Truths can only become self-evident if they result from individual processes of cognition. Once they are established as true in the mind, they require no other "proof," although some validation might be in order, for example showing how investing in luxury prevents the recreation of the net product.[108]

Like Locke, Quesnay believed that we learn about cause and effect by noting their recurrence, in other words, through experience. Malebranche, who did not trust experience, believed that God had established cause and effect in the physical world and that they therefore functioned (as did our knowledge of them) "in God."[109] Leibniz stated this differently by positing a "pre-established harmony." Quesnay rejected Malebranche's occasionalism, although he was sympathetic to his general approach to cognition and the way the mind forms images.

Quesnay gathered up his thoughts once more for the entry "Evidence" he wrote for the Encyclopedia (in 1756). D'Alembert would later remark in his eulogy of the doctor (as fellow member of the Academy of Sciences):

He busied himself at the same time with his dear old friend Metaphysics, and wrote the article *Evidence* for the Encyclopedia, which met the fate of almost all such works: of hardly being read, even less understood, and much criticized. This abstruse Metaphysics led him naturally where it was meant to, toward Theology, on which he also wrote a great deal.[110]

Quesnay began by defining "evidence" as "a certainty so clear and manifest on its own that the mind cannot but yield to it," basing much of his

---

[106] Newman, "Locke on Knowledge," p. 316. "Like Descartes, Locke is committed to an 'epistemological individualism' that prevents knowledge from transferring from one person to another." Quoting Locke on this: "[the mind] hath no other immediate Object but its own *Ideas*, which it alone does or can contemplate, it is evident, that our knowledge is only conversant about them."
[107] Quesnay, *Essai physique sur l'oeconomie animale*, III, p. 356.
[108] Locke distinguished between intuitive, demonstrative, and sensitive knowledge. See Newman, "Locke on Knowledge," pp. 320–3.
[109] See Tad M. Schmaltz, "Malebranche on Ideas and the Vision in God" in Stephen Nadler, ed., *The Cambridge Companion to Malebranche* (Cambridge, 2000), pp. 59–86, 68.
[110] Jean Le Rond d'Alembert, "Eloge de M. Quesnay par M. d'Alembert," *Mercure de France* XXX (15 November 1778), 152.

subsequent analysis on Locke (to whom he had grown more sympathetic over the past decade). He now endorsed Locke's concept of consciousness, which causes us to be aware that we have feelings and perceptions, and the faculty of memory which demonstrates a continuity in our selves.[111] Memory tests old and new evidence, comparing it to our storehouse of previous perceptions, and permitting us to make a sound "judgment."

> My senses therefore assure me of the faithfulness of my memory, and nothing other than the exercise of my senses can convince me of this; hence the use of our senses is the source [*principe*] of all certainty, and the foundation of all our knowledge.... Indeed, it is memory that informs us of our continued existence, and the recurrence of sensations that we get from sensory objects, of the actual use of our senses, assures us of the faithfulness of our memory. Such objects are therefore the source of all *evidence*.

When we know things for certain, we cannot refuse this evidence. The brain's capacity for *attention*, which played such an important role in Quesnay's previous analysis of cognition (as it had for Descartes, Malebranche, and recently for Condillac), is here often equated with *discernment*, in Lockean fashion (although the reason for this shift is unclear). More significantly Quesnay renounced the proposition that the mind first formed inchoate general ideas before honing in on particulars. Memory now performed such functions. Having described sensory perception as the basis of our ideas, Quesnay moved on to the unique ability of humans to intuit higher truths, through a gift from "the Supreme Being who operates on our soul."[112] God has instilled in men the notions of right and wrong and of good and evil so that they might adhere to his higher justice and accept their ultimate rewards and punishments.[113] For

---

[111] "Le terme évidence signifie une certitude si claire et manifeste par elle-même que l'esprit ne peut s'y refuser." "Evidence" in *Oeuvres économiques complètes et autres textes* (Paris, 2005), I, pp. 61–90. All the following quotations come from this edition. Condillac also made this the cornerstone of his system. See *Essai sur l'origine des connaissances humaines* (1746), Part 1, Section 1, Chapter 1, Subsection 8; and his *Traité des sensations* (1754). See Charrak, *Empirisme et métaphysique*, for a discussion of Condillac's normative conception of his depiction of the mind's basic processes. Descartes and Malebranche, of course, offered "methods" to gain certainty. See on this Condillac, *Traité des sensations*. Lennon, "Malebranche and Method," p. 18.

[112] Quesnay makes no reference to Leibniz in his writings, perhaps because he denied any inherent activity to matter and did not approve of the imagination, which Leibniz saw as necessary to creative thought. See Maria Rosa Antognazza, *Leibniz: An Intellectual Biography* (Cambridge, 2009), p. 420.

[113] This is why Michael Sonenscher equates Physiocracy and Theodicy. "Physiocracy as Theodicy," in *History of Political Thought* XXIII:2 (2002), 326–39. On Leibniz's Theodicy, see for example, Jolley, *Leibniz and Locke*, p. 33.

besides the evidence of our senses, we also possess a completely different sort of evidence provided by faith. Our flashes of insight are therefore a manifestation of God's Grace.[114] Quesnay was voicing a version of the "sublime" that had long been a feature of Catholicism and his reliance on this phenomenon lent a spiritual aura to his otherwise worldly endeavors.[115] We begin to see why the theological apotheosis of the entry perturbed d'Alembert sufficiently for him to refer to Quesnay's derailment by his "*chère métaphysique.*"[116]

Quesnay conceded that man, being a social animal, created societies with customs and rules that rewarded and punished their members, but he insisted on the imprint of a universal God-given morality. We are born with an awareness of right and wrong and our freedom consists in weighing what course to follow. As he stated in "Evidence": "By acting freely and calmly, the soul almost always decides how to behave without needing to consider or reflect because it knows the rules that it must follow without hesitation." The will could override the passions and this capacity defined what it means to be human.

The cognitive processes that Quesnay outlined in "Evidence" inflected the whole physiocratic enterprise. The *Tableau économique* attempted to express the series of regular, proportional, and *necessary* exchanges that he had perceived in his mind.[117] He never explained how he had come by them, and the doctrine's central presumption was that he couldn't. Efforts would be concentrated instead on inducing a similar "vision" in others.

---

[114] Lord Shaftsbury, *An Inquiry into Virtue or Merit* in *Characteristics of Men, Manners, Opinions, Times* (London, 1711), and Francis Hutcheson, *An Inquiry into the Original of Our Ideas of Beauty and Virtue* (London, 1725). See Luigi Turco, "Moral Sense and the Foundations of Morals" in Alexander Broadie, ed., *The Cambridge Companion to the Scottish Enlightenment* (Cambridge, 2003), pp. 136–56.

[115] Nicolas Boileau had translated Longinus's treatise on the sublime, which describes the process as "feeling that a discourse gives us much to think about, that had at first seemed difficult if not impossible to resist, and which lingered in our memory and is erased only with some effort." *Traité du sublime ou du merveilleux dans le discours traduit du Grec de Longin* in N. Boileau-Despréaux, *Oeuvres diverses* (Paris, 1674), p. 15.

[116] In 1760, Quesnay printed privately the outline for a book on psychology (which is how "processes of mind" or "functions of the soul" were coming to be known) that he failed to pursue. François Quesnay, *Aspect de la psychologie: l'âme est une substance qui a la propriété de sentir*, 4 pages [Versailles], 1760. Kress Collection # 9648. "The copy that belonged to Adam Smith." For a recent summary on the emergence of psychology, see Fernando Vidal, *Les sciences de l'âme: XVIe–XVIIIe siècles* (Paris, 2006).

[117] Peter Reill summarizes this drive in natural philosophy most eloquently: "a mathematical description of reality was seen as the way to escape from the perceived horrors of the contigent, – and, hence, unsure – knowledge," "The Legacy of the 'Scientific Revolution' Science and the Enlightenment," p. 27.

## Tableau Économique

In later years, the writer Marmontel recalled: "Evenings I would go visit Quesnay at the appointed hour and find him busy drawing the *zigzag* of the *net profit*."[118]

Quesnay was lodged in small quarters in Mme de Pompadour's *entresol* and immersed himself day and night in political and rural economy. He believed he had reduced the system to calculations and axioms whose evidence was irresistible; and, since he was then forming a school, he took the trouble to explain his new doctrine to me so that he might turn me into a disciple and proselyte. Since I wished him to intercede with Mme de Pompadour on my behalf, I applied all my wits to understanding the truths he treated as self-evident, but which seemed vague and murky to me. It was beyond my powers to convince him that I understood what I in fact did not, but I listened to him with utmost patience and led him to believe that he might one day enlighten me and inculcate his doctrine. This would have sufficed to gain his goodwill, but I did more. I applauded an enterprise that I indeed deemed worthy for he meant to promote agriculture in a country where it was unduly disdained and to get intelligent men to study it.

Marmontel's condescending remarks about Quesnay infuriated the Comte d'Angiviller – as did most of Marmontel's recollections – and he composed his own memoirs to set the record straight.[119] "I have never known a sounder and simpler philosophy than [Quesnay's]." As for the *zigzag*: "It was a very correct, wise, exact, profound idea, expressed very simply, and to use Quesnay's expression: in notarial style," adding this proviso:

After delving into metaphysical questions and losing his way as many before him, he threw himself into political and rural economy, and did so with an inquisitive, penetrating, fine, profound, and persistent spirit, determined to pursue ideas to their finest ramifications. This turn of mind is conducive to creating systems where everything is made to fit and bend to its dictates and hence rarely gets at the truth, but it is nonetheless a unique ability [*l'esprit le plus rare*] for even if it almost always leads to error, a great deal of truth can be gleaned along the way.

Giving up on the moralist, Quesnay found a better prospect. The Marquis de Mirabeau, bestselling author of *L'Ami des hommes*, was a moralist in his own right, with the added advantage that he paid particular attention

---

[118] Marmontel, *Mémoires*, pp. 179 and 172. For similar sentiments, see Du Hausset, *Mémoires*, p. 80: "M. de Mirabeau arrived and the conversation got quite boring, focused on nothing but the net product."
[119] Angiviller, *Mémoires d'Angiviller*, pp. 11–17.

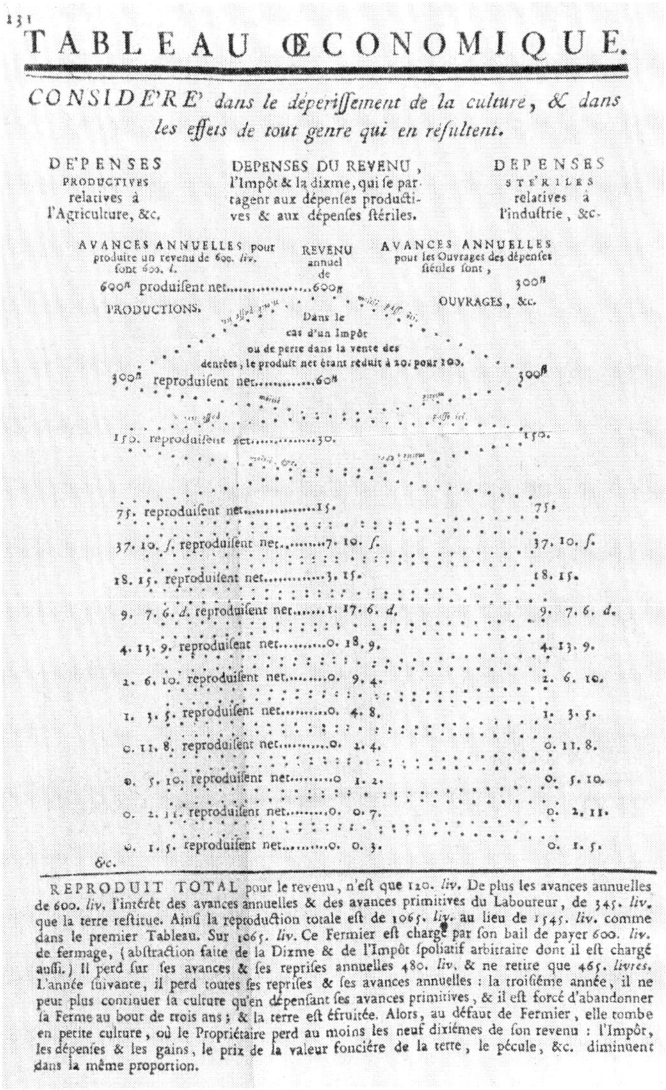

FIGURE 2.1. *Tableau économique*, in *l'Ami des hommes*, vol. VI (1760) (author's copy).

to agriculture and social relations. After a stormy meeting, Quesnay "converted" the Marquis to his analysis, and he became his most ardent follower and the first guinea pig of his epistemological theory.

Quesnay first presented the rough draft of his diagram (or *Tableau*) to the mystified Marquis de Mirabeau in 1758: "I have attempted to draw an image of the fundamental economic order that displays its expenditures and its products in a way easy to grasp and that enables one to assess clearly the order and disorder that governments can cause; you will see for yourself whether I have succeeded."[120]

The early *Tableau* was too schematic to be of use to anyone. A few days later, the doctor had to concede that the diagram was not as self-evident as he would have liked. "Madame de Pailly tells me that you are still mired in the Zizac. It is true that it touches on so many aspects that it becomes difficult to grasp its coherence or rather to grasp it with certainty. The Zizac shows what is, without showing how it comes about, which is not enough for you." He reiterated his exposition and concluded with further remarks on the *Tableau*:

It lets us apprehend in a single glance the source and product of earthly riches, the links and interactions among its various parts, and the principles behind the "economic governance" of agricultural nations; thus the zigzag, once properly grasped, condenses a great deal of details and paints to the eye complicated processes that are difficult to grasp by mere intellect, or decipher and make sense by means of discourse; such ideas would soon disappear, but by means of the *Tableau* these relations are verified [*apurées*] and fixed in the imagination and will not fade away, or at least they will be easy to conjure up again in their proper order and correspondence, to be meditated upon at leisure without losing sight of anything and without the mind having to organize this material. I will send you a second revised and amplified version.... I am having three copies printed to sort things out more easily, but I do believe that it belongs at the end of your essay for the Bern competition.

The *Tableau* was therefore the product of Quesnay's rigorous thinking and of the mind's geometric patterning of essential relations.[121] However detailed the surrounding discourse, the *Tableau* would truly be understood by embarking on the right cognitive steps and letting the chain of evidence resolve itself into the same patterns. Once the image was constituted in one's mind and affixed there, no confusion was possible: The brain would retain the necessary ratios among economic exchanges. Mirabeau eventually grasped the meaning of the *Tableau* and how it accorded with Quesnay's inner vision:

Having stored the result of his cogitations in his head, he felt that it was impossible to describe it intelligibly with mere words and that it was necessary to paint it. This realization led him to produce the *Tableau économique*.[122]

[120] A.N. M784/70/1 and 2, letter from Quesnay to Mirabeau, n.d. [1759].
[121] Note the emphasis on "all-at-once-ness" in Daston, "On Scientific Observation," p. 106.
[122] Victor Riquetti, marquis de Mirabeau, *Tableau oeconomique et ses explications*, p. 12. In Part II of Volume VI of *L'Ami des hommes* (Paris, 1760).

Quesnay could not put into words the relation between the statistical evidence on agricultural productivity he had collected and the proper exchanges that he had intuited, nor did he explain how he had arrived at the *Tableau*'s ratios. The belief that the *Tableau* embodied a higher truth demarcated Quesnay's disciples from those who merely accepted some of his conclusions about the future of the French economy. Fellow-travelers failed to "see" what the doctrine entailed and what the inner core claimed (at least) to have fully grasped.

Quesnay continued to privilege the visual[123] and to deem it the key to his economic analysis. He rebuked Mirabeau, in his comments on the draft of the *Philosophie rurale* (1763), for his heavy-handed discussion of sociability and mutual help: "This is somewhat abstract and metaphysical, of the genre that your readers call obscure. It reduces what belongs to sight into ideas. This mental chemistry is more distressful to readers than the mathematical hieroglyphics that you dislike more than they."[124] "Call on your readers to look more closely," he told Mirabeau.[125] This same admonition appears several years later, regarding Mirabeau's *Économiques*: "one must stay within the sphere of sight and the senses which at this point [of human development] grant us a rough perception of material objects. First one must show and then one can explain."[126]

---

[123] It is possible, although unlikely, that Quesnay used a visual model to differentiate himself from Richard Cantillon's version of economic circulation; see Anthony Brewer, "Cantillon, Quesnay, and the *Tableau Economique*," Discussion Paper No. 05/577, October 2005, Department of Economics, University of Bristol.

[124] Georges Weulersse, *Les manuscrits économiques de François Quesnay et du marquis de Mirabeau aux Archives nationales (M. 778 à M. 785)* (Paris, 1910), p. 81.

[125] Ibid., p. 82. "Sommez vos lecteurs de bien regarder."

[126] Ibid., p. 81.

# 3

# The Ways of the Heart

### Life of the Marquis de Mirabeau

Before delving into Quesnay and Mirabeau's collaboration, it is important to understand the outlook and experiences that Mirabeau brought to the enterprise. Quesnay was an upwardly mobile commoner; the Marquis de Mirabeau was a noble of the sword, albeit of relatively recent vintage. Quesnay took his destiny in hand by championing the surgeons' rights and cultivating powerful contacts. Mirabeau, too, was a spokesman but, in his case, for the privileges of the nobility and the moral regeneration of the nation. The physiocratic movement was created out of this combination of pragmatism and idealism.

Victor Riquetti, comte and then marquis de Mirabeau, was born at Pertuis, near Mirabeau in Provence, in 1715, second (surviving) son of Jean Antoine Riquetti and Françoise de Castellane-Norente. His father, a decorated war hero, was known as *col d'argent* from the collar he wore to support a neck shot through at the battle of Cassano in 1705 – an ordeal he miraculously survived.[1] The Riquettis had come from Italy, although perhaps not from Florence in the thirteenth century as they claimed, and figure on Marseilles city rolls as merchants in the sixteenth century. They purchased the seigneurie of Mirabeau in 1570, which, as a reward for military services and loyalty to the crown, was turned into a

---

[1] The best biography of the marquis de Mirabeau remains that of Louis de Loménie, *Les Mirabeau*, which he composed himself (the volumes on Gabriel-Honoré that followed were penned by his son Charles). Twentieth-century versions have not yet superseded it, for example Gilles Henry, *Mirabeau père, 5 octobre 1715–11 juillet 1789* (Paris, 1989), or Hubert de Montlaur, *Mirabeau."L'Ami des hommes"* (Paris, 1992).

FIGURE 3.1. *Marquis de Mirabeau* by Jacques Aved (1743), Réunion des Musées Nationaux/Art Resource, New York.

*marquisat* in 1685. Jean-Antoine, the second Marquis, a soldier like his own father, was a dour authoritarian, and Victor and his brothers were raised in an austere atmosphere imbued with martial values.[2] All three boys were made Knights of Malta and were destined for military careers: The youngest, Louis-Alexandre (born in 1724), disgraced himself by marrying an actress of ill-repute and remained cut off from the family until the Margrave of Bayreuth took a fancy to him and he entered his service in the mid-1750s. A second marriage to a German noblewoman in 1760 sealed the comte's reconciliation with the Mirabeau clan. He died soon

---

[2] Mirabeau confided to his friend Saint-Georges the toll his father's mistreatment took on him. AN M784/63/6 16 November 1724 [sic]. The letter was sent from Moron (near Bordeaux) suggesting the year might have been 1742.

after, and his widow, known as the *petite comtesse*, spent the remainder of her brief life in her brother-in-law's house, dying in 1772.³

Victor was extremely close, on the other hand, to his second brother Jean-Antoine, born in 1717, to whom he wrote almost daily, and who survived him by five years.⁴ The Chevalier de Mirabeau, better known as the *bailli* from the rank he attained in the Order of Malta, made his career in the navy, served as governor of Guadeloupe in 1753–5, and with the Marquis's help, obtained the post of general of the galleys (which required him to take religious vows) and, soon afterwards, the revenues of one of the order's richest properties in Provence.⁵ He was as calm and practical as his older brother was fiery and flighty. His sober lifestyle, moreover, contrasted with his older brother's extravagance.

After a few years at a Jesuit College in Marseilles, in 1728 Victor joined the regiment his father had once commanded and took part in the campaign to restore Stanislas Leszczynski to the throne of Poland, but saw no action. He was in Paris between 1735 and 1737, borrowing and especially spending money, going into society – where he was introduced to the duc de Nivernais who became a friend and patron (until they quarreled in 1787) and to Jean-Jacques Le Franc de Pompignan, the poet and magistrate.⁶ Less glamorous days were spent in garrison in Besançon and later Bordeaux (where he met Montesquieu and composed verses). It was from Bordeaux in 1739 and 1740 that he exchanged thoughts on life and literature with his childhood friend, Luc de Clapiers, marquis de Vauvenargues, himself garrisoned at Arras, Rheims, and Verdun.

Upon his father's death in 1737, Victor inherited a small fortune and bought a house in the capital and a barren estate near Nemours, Le Bignon.⁷ He moved there semipermanently in 1746. "He renovated the château, changed the course of the river that surrounded it, turned the sheep pastures into meadows, planted trees, dug ditches, all at huge expense."⁸ Thwarted in his attempt to purchase his own regiment,

---

³ Loménie, *Les Mirabeau*, I, pp. 142–3.
⁴ He died in Malta in 1794. Four thousand letters survive from the period 4 December 1753 to 8 July 1789. Loménie, *Les Mirabeau* I, p. 172.
⁵ Loménie, *Les Mirabeau*, I, pp. 300–15, 329. His two-year generalate term began in January 1763, although he left for Malta in July 1761.
⁶ Louis de Loménie, *La comtesse de Rochefort et ses amis. Etude sur les moeurs en France au XVIIIe siècle* (Paris, 1870), p. 224; Theodore E. D. Braun, *Un ennemi de Voltaire, Le Franc de Pompignan* (Paris, 1972), p. 25.
⁷ Loménie, *Les Mirabeau*, I, pp. 437–40.
⁸ Ibid., p. 446.

Mirabeau rejoined his old one and took part in the Bavarian campaign of the War of Austrian Succession, nearly making it to Prague. Tired of military life since it seemed to offer no immediate rewards, he resigned his commission in 1743, leaving the army with the rank of captain and the Cross of Saint-Louis on his breast.[9]

It was at this juncture that he made the surprising (and unfortunate) decision to marry. Despite what everyone around him deemed a poor dowry, he and Geneviève de Bassan were wed on 20 April 1743. He barely knew the bride or her family whom he had met through his friend Saint-Georges. Most alluring to Mirabeau was her future inheritance of properties in the Limousin, Périgord, and Poitou, that would one day, he reckoned, add luster to the Mirabeau name. As he told his brother, he meant "to turn a Provençal House into a French House."[10] The union produced eleven children, five of whom survived to adulthood. His famous son, the revolutionary orator Honoré Gabriel, was born in 1749. In 1752, the child caught smallpox, which left him disfigured, and his sight repelled his father ever after. Their relations would be stormy. More than once Mirabeau asked for *lettres de cachet* [royal writs] to have his son confined.[11]

Although he had written occasional salon entertainments, the marquis now began to consider a career in letters. This ambition was stimulated by his friendship with Jean-Jacques Le Franc de Pompignan whom he had met in Paris in 1737 and with whom he traveled across Provence in 1740, and whom he liked to address as his "master." He composed a *Testament politique* (intended for his offspring) in 1747 of which only fragments survive, and began to reflect on politics, stimulated by the publication of Montesquieu's *Esprit des lois* in 1748, and the remonstrances against the new *vingtième* tax (5 percent on revenue) in 1749. The latter resulted in a pamphlet, published anonymously in 1750, the *Mémoire concernant l'utilité des Etats provinciaux* where he extolled representative bodies and the nobility's leadership in local affairs.[12] He expanded the work a year later, worried that all provincial

---

[9] Henry, *Mirabeau père*, p. 57.

[10] Loménie, *Les Mirabeau*, I, p. 430.

[11] Such arrests of troublesome or insane family members could be requested and accorded directly by the King. See Arlette Farge and Michel Foucault, *Le désordre des familles. Lettres de cachet des archives de la Bastille au XVIIIe siècle* (Paris, 1982).

[12] The exact publication date remains unclear. It might have been as early as 1751; another possible date is 1755. See Marcel Marion, *Machault d'Arnouville*, p. 114 and Quesnay, *Oeuvres économiques complètes et autres textes*, II, pp. 1233–4. The longer version is reproduced in Part IV of Mirabeau, *L'Ami des hommes*.

estates would be dissolved following the suspension of the Languedoc Estates in 1750.[13]

His newfound role as spokesman for nobiliar interests might have precipitated his decision, in 1752, to purchase the duchy of Roquelaure in Armagnac from the Rohan family for 450,000 livres, in the hopes of acquiring a dukedom. This proved a fiasco salvaged only by sheer luck. Part of the seigneurie was reclaimed by *retrait lignagier* by a Rohan heir. The intendant of Auch then had the idea of establishing a stud farm at Roquelaure, allowing the Marquis to sell the remainder of the property to the king for 310,000 livres in 1761. All in all, the adventure left him with a deficit of 50,000 livres.[14]

He had been busy in the meantime. The book that would make him famous, *L'Ami des hommes*, appeared in summer 1756, with new editions in 1757, 1759, and 1760. His first encounter with Quesnay took place in summer 1757 and began their long collaboration to improve French finances and reorder the French economy. Mirabeau, dazzled by Quesnay's analysis, became his most ardent supporter. This is the Mirabeau known to posterity: the disseminator of physiocratic ideas and author (under Quesnay's keen eye) of the doctrine's major texts such as *La Théorie de l'impôt* in 1760, which landed him briefly in jail (from which the duc de Nivernais rescued him)[15] and the *Philosophie rurale* of 1763. In 1767 he began to host Tuesday soirées in his Parisian residence for those interested in the new economic doctrine. His engagement with political economy did not still other ambitions.

Old friends had died: Vauvenargues in 1747, Saint-Georges in 1754, and in 1763 Pompignan returned to Montauban in disgrace after a public spat with the philosophes. Provençal friends were equally in trouble.[16]

---

[13] Marcel Marion, *Histoire financière de la France depuis 1715*, 2 vols. (Paris, 1914) I, pp. 173–4. They were reinstated with fewer powers in December 1752.

[14] Ibid., pp. 447–62. On Roquelaure under Mirabeau, see Peter Jones, *Liberty and Locality in Revolutionary France, Six Villages Compared, 1760–1820* (Cambridge, 2003), pp. 23–5, 65.

[15] See Chapter 5. Melchior Grimm rather wickedly implied that Mirabeau's speedy release was due to his *dévôt* position, demonstrated by his support of Le Franc de Pompignan against the Philosophes. Grimm et al., *Correspondance littéraire, philosophique et critique* (Paris, 1879), IV, January 1761, p. 339.

[16] The battles between the Président d'Eguilles and Ripert de Monclar at the Parlement d'Aix over the dissolution of the Jesuit order in 1762, led to d'Eguilles's exile from France for five years. See Paul Cottin, *Un Protégé de Bachaumont, Correspondance du marquis d'Eguilles (1745–1748)* (Paris, 1887). Monique Cubells, *La Provence des Lumières, Les parlementaires d'Aix au 18eme siècle* (Paris, 1984), pp. 278–83. We know of the Marquis de Mirabeau's friendship with d'Eguilles through correspondence on his *Art of War*.

Mirabeau drew closer to the duc de Nivernais and especially to Nivernais's beloved mistress, Mme de Rochefort, and her literary côterie. His own personal life was in shambles. Both he and his wife were high-strung, and financial difficulties did not help matters. The couple began to live apart in 1762. Geneviève's infidelity having become patent, they reached an agreement whereby she would stay away from Paris in return for a pension of 2,000 livres a year. Mirabeau did not lack for female companionship. He first met the elegant Swiss matron Mme de Pailly in 1755. By 1760 she was a regular visitor at Le Bignon and became his lifelong companion. Mme de Rochefort took an immediate shine to her and she suited Mirabeau's aristocratic friends far better than his wife.

Mirabeau's mother died in 1769 followed a year later by his mother-in-law Mme de Vassan. Although this meant that Mirabeau's wife at last came into her inheritance, their troubles were only beginning. Mirabeau refused to pay the 18,000-livre pension which Geneviève now demanded, and she threatened a lawsuit, which Mirabeau could ill afford. Their children took sides and the marquise de Saillant paid her mother's legal fees in return for the promise of a 60,000-livre inheritance.[17] In December 1773, flouting the 1766 agreement, Geneviève came to Paris. Fearing that she would claim her right to coresidence, Mirabeau fled to the countryside while his brother guarded his Paris lodgings (rue de Vaugirard). Wrangling over properties and pensions followed, and the Marquis, anxious to avoid a formal *séparation de corps* that would threaten his income, bent over backwards to meet his wife's demands. Geneviève returned to the Limousin, but new trouble was brewing as Gabriel had by now accumulated debts of some 200,000 livres of his own, spent in part on remodeling the château de Mirabeau.[18]

In May 1775, Geneviève sought an official separation. Nothing would deter her, despite Mirabeau's renewed efforts at conciliation. Their children once again supported her. The Mirabeau seniors' separation had now come before the Châtelet Court in Paris, and, when it was upheld in January 1776, Mirabeau appealed to the Parlement of Paris. Gabriel had by then begun a liaison with Sophie de Ruffey, Marquise de Monnier, causing a public scandal. Her irate husband and father had Gabriel arrested in Dijon for seduction and kidnapping. He escaped to Holland

---

To confuse matters, one of the magistrates at the Aix Parlement who sided with d'Eguilles in 1762 was "Mirabeau père" who is *not* the Marquis, but André-Bruno Deydier, seigneur de Mirabeau and Beauveset.

[17] Loménie, *Les Mirabeau*, I, p. 476.

[18] Henry, *Mirabeau père*, pp. 229–31.

where Sophie soon joined him.[19] The disorders in the Mirabeau family had become common knowledge and the staff of pamphlets, including several penned by Gabriel denouncing his father.[20] Irritated by this turmoil, Louis XVI's minister Maurepas had the marquise de Mirabeau locked up in a convent. This did not deter her from launching further lawsuits against her husband. Meanwhile, Gabriel, who had been extradited from Holland, was locked up at Vincennes (while the very pregnant Sophie was allowed to retire to a convent) from which he addressed to her the celebrated *Lettres à Sophie*. Frustrated by his youngest daughter Mme de Cabris's support for her mother, the marquis de Mirabeau had *her* confined to a convent by *lettre de cachet*. His high-handedness toward his family had by then seriously tarnished Mirabau's reputation.[21] The contrast between his claims to love humanity as *L'Ami des hommes* and his mistreatment of his own flesh and blood made him appear the worst of hypocrites.[22]

Despite his lofty ambitions, the Marquis's plans had come to nothing. Familial squabbles had turned to ridicule a name he had sought to elevate. He continued to publish the odd physiocratic text and to keep up a voluminous correspondence. He died on 11 July 1789, saddened and embittered, having lived long enough to see Honoré Gabriel elected to the Estates General as member for the Third Estate and to witness his rise as one of the Revolution's great orators. "This is glory, real glory!"[23] At last.

If Mirabeau's writings suggest a single-minded devotion to physiocracy and its realization, his life reveals a quite different pattern. Mirabeau was a noble of the sword who, although he gave up his commission in his late twenties, was convinced that the "old nobility" had been granted a special historical role. This was in keeping with current justifications of the second order's role within the polity.[24] He had sworn to further the

---

[19] Montlaur, *Mirabeau*, pp. 248–9.
[20] See for example the printed brief *Mémoire pour la marquise de Mirabeau, intimée contre le marquis de Mirabeau, appellant* (Paris, 1777), 58 pages.
[21] Montlaur, *Mirabeau*, p. 256.
[22] "Le mémoire que Me Beau-Séjour vient de donner contre messire Victor de Riquetti, marquis de Mirabeau, premier apôtre de l'évangile du grand Quesnay" on behalf of Geneviève de Vassan. Citing from Mirabeau's correspondence, he concluded that Mirabeau was the world's greatest hypocrite. Grimm et al., *Correspondance littéraire*, September 1776, XI, p. 349.
[23] "Voilà de la gloire, de la vraie gloire!" he is said to have shouted on learning that Gabriel Honoré had been elected to the Third Estate. Cited in Georges Guibal, *Mirabeau et la Provence* (Paris, 1901) I, p. 422.
[24] Smith, *Nobility Reimagined*, p.16.

name and glory of his "race." This meant expanding his domains, raising his title, and ensuring that the nobility would recover its historic claims to participate in state governance.

"I am consumed with ambition," Mirabeau wrote Vauvenargues in April 1738, "but a peculiar one: I do not seek honours, or money, or favors, but a name, and to be somebody at last."[25] As biographers point out, he pursued such glory recklessly, making a disastrous marriage for properties that proved worthless, buying an overpriced fiefdom in the hopes of gaining a peerage, investing in mines and other failed commercial ventures, with manic impetuosity. "You are ardent, bilious, more agitated, more superb, more uneven than the sea, and supremely avid for pleasures, knowledge, and honours," Vauvenargues had told him.[26] Mme de Pailly, he reported to his brother, had echoed such sentiments. "From what I have seen of you, I detect one flaw in your education which is that you always see things from a single perspective rather than choosing from among a number." This explained his inconstancy: He had tried the army, belles-lettres, "philosophical and domestic" projects, augmented his patrimony, and developed political ambitions. Despite a lack of tenacity and easy discouragement, she hoped that he would realize the "risk of disgrace if [he] gave up the public course on which [he] had embarked."[27] The nobility of the sword might possess an innate capacity for virtue,[28] but could the flesh-and-blood Victor Riquetti fulfill such ambitions? Mme de Rochefort seemed to think so:

You ask me to tell you what sort of character you have. It seems to me that your dominant trait is chivalric. In the age of Bayard, you would have righted wrongs, sword in hand, in the age of philosophy the same urge makes you take up the pen. I have not yet read your book [*L'Ami des hommes*], but I am certain that in its pages you protect the widow and orphan, fight all your homeland's enemies, in other words, combat every wrong and prejudice. You live in your Paris hôtel as in the good old days one used to live in one's castle. You show hospitality, you see to your domestic affairs, and only go out to fulfill other duties and not frivolous obligations. In brief, my dear master [*maître*], you are gothic and will always remain so.[29]

---

[25] Vauvenargues, *Correspondance* in *Oeuvres posthumes et oeuvres inédites de Vauvenargues*, ed. D.-L. Gilbert (Paris, 1857), p. 98. Letter from Paris, 30 April 1738.

[26] Vauvenargues, *Oeuvres posthumes et inédites*, p. 166. Letter from Vauvenargues to Mirabeau from Verdun dated 16 January 1740.

[27] Letter to the bailli, Paris, 8 August 1758 in Ch. Laurent, *Les voyages en Bretagne du Chevalier de Mirabeau, 1758–1760* (Mayenne, 1983), p. 120.

[28] Smith, *Nobility Reimagined*, p. 10.

[29] Letter from Mme de Rochefort to Mirabeau, 26 March 1757, cited in Loménie, *La comtesse de Rochefort*, p. 90.

Friends engaged in such minute, character-analyses because the burning question for these nobles was whether they could live up to the role that destiny had imposed on them, both as an order and as individuals.[30] It is not for nothing that Vauvenargues suggested that Mirabeau had been the source of his own failures at Court:

You went into society without any experience; you wanted to reign there before you were known; a young man is filled with dreams but lacks the means to see them realized; the heart responds faster than the mind [*l'esprit vient plus tard que le coeur*]. You likely made mistakes; you make it a point of honour to bend before no one, not to compromise your morals or your character, and not to analyse events from various perspectives; you insist on approaching them only through the dictates of your heart and education.[31]

### A Man of Letters

Mirabeau meant to dazzle the public even while still a soldier and thought initially that he might do so by writing tragedies and epic poetry. Historians and biographers alike usually skip over this interlude because it seems immaterial to his later writings and because the phenomenon itself was so widespread among members of his class. Of course, the vast majority pursued this as a pastime rather than a "career." Mirabeau, however, claimed to be contemplating this second possibility in all seriousness, breaking with the more usual pattern.[32] His friend the duc de Nivernais was elected to the Académie française at age 27 in 1742. His fables, poems, and translations were circulated privately during his lifetime and were only published after his death by François de Neufchâteau.[33] This was a prime example of the successful and highly regarded dilettante, appreciated by his peers. But Mirabeau was drawn to another model, that of Le Franc de Pompignan, magistrate and successful playwright, of

---

[30] I therefore would argue that a strong sense of selfhood was evident in these discussions, whereas Jan Goldstein contends that it only emerged after the French Revolution. *The Post-Revolutionary Self, Politics and Psyche in France, 1750–1850* (Cambridge, Mass., 2005), pp. 8–9.

[31] Vauvenargues to Mirabeau from Verdun, 16 January 1740, Correspondence in *Oeuvres posthumes et inédites*, p. 171.

[32] See Alain Viala, *Naissance de l'écrivain* (Paris, 1985), pp. 180–83. On the separation of dilettantism from professional writing, see also Elena Russo, *Styles of Enlightenment, Taste, Politics, and Authorship in Eighteenth-Century France* (Baltimore, 2007), p. 7. Jean Starobinski, *L'Oeil vivant: La relation critique*, revised edition (Paris, 1999) also raises the issue of literary doubts.

[33] Nivernais, *Oeuvres posthumes du duc de Nivernois*, edited with an *éloge* by François de Neufchâteau, 10 vols. (Paris, 1807).

a lower social rank. In seeking public acclaim, Mirabeau would attempt to compose more serious pieces than the conventional entertainments (those that include his delightful poem "If" often attributed to Le Franc de Pompignan) produced for social occasions and to ponder the message he wished to convey to the public.[34] For a man determined to serve his country and his order, seeking literary renown required some justification whatever the content of the work. We can follow his soul-searching in his letters to his friend, the budding moral philosopher Vauvenargues, who was his exact contemporary, and whose ancestral properties lay close to Mirabeau's in Provence. Like Mirabeau, he was a military officer and spent many months in provincial garrisons, bored out of his mind. He eventually attracted the attention of Voltaire and moved to Paris in 1745 where, despite debilitating ill-health, he managed to compose his philosophical maxims, even seeing some to print. He died there in May 1747. Mirabeau had long urged him to publish his reflections, telling him in 1739:

> I have never received, my dear Vauvenargues, anything more striking than your letter; someone who thinks and expresses himself this way has no excuse for his lack of ambition.... What pleasant prospects your talents open to you in what is called the *Republic of Letters*! If you only realized what pleasures a reputation established in this way can offer! We no longer live in an age when a man of quality need blush about the talents that a nobody might try to deny him. I doubt that this was ever the case except with fools; and, without going into details, the Académie française now consists almost entirely of men of our class (*du bon ordre*), who have allowed a number of works to appear under their name.[35]

[34] "Nous fûmes donc au château d'If / C'est un lieu peu récréatif, / Défendu par le fer oisif / De plus d'un soldat maladif, / Qui, de guerrier jadis actif, / Est devenu garde passif. / Sur ce roc taillé dans le vif, / Par bon ordre on retient captif, / Dans l'enceinte d'un mur massif, / Esprit libertin, coeur rétif / Au salutaire correctif / D'un parent peu persuasif. / Le pauvre prisonnier pensif, / A la triste lueur du suif, / Jouait, pour seul soporatif, / Du murmure non lénitif, / Dont l'élément rébarbatif / Frappe son organe attentif. / Or, pour être mémoratif / De ce domicile afflictif, / Je jurai, d'un ton expressif, / De vous peindre la rime en if. / Ce fait, du roc désolatif / Nous sortîmes d'un pas hâtif, / Et rentrâmes dans notre esquif, /En répétant d'un ton plaintif: / Dieu nous garde du château d'If." A manuscript copy of the voyage in fall 1740 (with the abbé de Monville as third traveling companion) is in Mirabeau's papers at the Archives nationales. It was published by Le Franc de Pompignan as *Voyage de Languedoc et Provence*, and can be found in *Le voyage sentimental en France* (Paris, 1788) and the poem on page 308.

[35] Vauvenargues, *Correspondance*, p. 124. Mirabeau to Vauvenargues, from Bordeaux, 24 April 1739. In a letter to the comte de P ... of 21 September 1739 Mirabeau attacks the prejudice whereby "par un propos perpétué depuis Charles VII vous font entendre qu'un homme de qualité ne doit point être autheur." AN M 791, "Poésies du marquis de Mirabeau."

Mirabeau refuted the common conceit that a career in letters per se was unseemly for a nobleman and that, consequently, venturing into the world of commercial publication tarnished a man's reputation – which is why so many works circulated privately or appeared anonymously.[36] Quite the contrary, we learn from the same letter, dabbling in literature had lent him a new aura, opening up a fresh arena of contacts beyond his immediate circle.[37] "Talented men of science and learning form their own republic. Once you are asked to join them, you are set. They talk about you; wine and dine you, they recommend you to others; you feel at home everywhere."[38] Such was Mirabeau's entrée into the provincial literary world (he was writing from Bordeaux where his regiment was then garrisoned), and he would repeat this experience when he created his own physiocratic salon in Paris, in 1767, bringing together men of all ranks interested in agrarian reform.

Vauvenargues, on the other hand, found most writers trite and tasteless and saw no reason to emulate them, and he responded to Mirabeau's prodding by contrasting his "lazy" and somewhat melancholy disposition to his friend's fiery temperament.[39] Mirabeau, who never nursed undue illusions about his character, however grandiose his plans, replied: "I am aware that, having more imagination than judgment, I am drawn to many activities, and that the worthiest are the least likely to be realized.... I am getting quite skilled in all literary genres. Let me add this about you: you bury, if you do not work, one of the greatest talents in the world!"[40] We might note, in passing, the opposition between imagination and judgment that Mirabeau takes for granted. The irony is, of course that Vauvenargues eventually published his philosophical meditations, whereas Mirabeau's poems never saw the light of day.[41]

---

[36] Viala, *Naissance de l'écrivain*, p. 243. The nobility was actually quite prominent in the world of letters by then.

[37] The importance of the "semi-private" realm of talk, writing, and correspondence is addressed by Dena Goodman, *The Republic of Letters, A Cultural History of the French Enlightenment* (Ithaca, 1994) and Antoine Lilti, *Le monde des salons*. See also Paul Bénichou, *Morales du grand siècle* (Paris, 1948), pp. 99–100, 133, 203; Dougald Lane Patey, "The Institutions of Criticism in the Eighteenth Century" in H. B. Nisbet and Claude Rawson, eds., *Cambridge History of Literary Criticism*, vol. IV: *The Eighteenth Century* (Cambridge, 1997), pp. 3–31.

[38] Letter from Mirabeau to Vauvenargues from Bordeaux, 24 April 1739, *Correspondance*, p. 124.

[39] Vauvenargues to Mirabeau from Arras, 4 May 1739, *Correspondance*, pp. 127–8.

[40] Mirabeau to Vauvenargues, from Bordeaux, 16 May 1739. *Correspondance*, p. 132.

[41] In time Vauvenargues would urge everyone to write in order to clarify their thoughts and see what ties them together. This was both useful and permissible. *Réflexions sur divers sujets* in *Oeuvres complètes*, p. 99.

Mirabeau's play did not hinge on the torments of love, and Vauvenargues applauded this decision. "This type of intrigue has grown stale and seems often out-of-place on stage. It rarely arouses terror – which is the soul of tragedy. One must do violence to oneself to believe that it lies behind great events or drives great men; furthermore, tender and delicate feelings are no longer fashionable."[42] He looked forward to Mirabeau's tragedy. "I am distraught not to be in Paris to see your play performed. I have made arrangements to have it sent to me as soon as it is published. I have no doubt it will succeed and look forward to it, but have no fear that I will reveal your name."[43] Mirabeau confessed: "I am not sure whether my play will be performed this summer; I had relied on one of my friends and he no longer thinks it likely; I have no definite news yet."[44] The play crops up in another letter: "one of my most astute critics, who goes over my work with a fine-tooth comb, exclaimed, after hearing how quickly I had composed it: "yet another flaw!" ... for I am ardent and proof that the passions that agitate the soul keep the body in motion, and far from calming it, engender the quandary that the body can only do one thing at a time, whereas the soul demands a thousand."[45] And he reproaches himself for his self-indulgence: "Writing is even worse for me than reading, for I do not believe anyone else in the world scribbles as much as I."[46]

The play that Vauvenargues expected to be performed (but wasn't) might have been *Zéangir*, an adaptation of Racine's *Bajazet* that Mirabeau was composing in this period.[47] We know of its progress from his response to his friend Mme de Vouvray's comments. "If a plot must be complicated in order for a play to be successful in France, would you not advise me to publish [the play] instead? I aimed for simplicity, that idol of the Ancients ... Actions that are hurried along only agitate us: ... we

---

[42] Vauvenargues to Mirabeau, from Arras, 30 May 1739, *Correspondance*, p. 135.
[43] Anonymity still mattered, apparently.
[44] Mirabeau to Vauvenargues, Bordeaux, 14 June 1739, *Correspondance*, p. 137. This might have been Le Franc de Pompignan whose plays were performed in Paris to great acclaim in the 1730s but who gave up writing tragedies in 1739 after the Comédie française put off a production of his *Zoraïde* in favor of Voltaire's *Alzire*. Theodore E. D. Braun et Guillaume Robichez, eds., *Lumières voilées. Oeuvres choisies d'un magistrat chrétien du XVIIIe siècle* (Saint-Etienne, 2007), p. 12. Daniel Acke, *Vauvenargues moraliste, la synthèse impossible de l'idée de nature et de la pensée de la diversité* (Cologne, 1993).
[45] Mirabeau to Vauvenargues, Bordeaux, 31 July 1739, *Correspondance*, p. 144.
[46] Mirabeau to Vauvenargues, Bordeaux, 7 September 1739, *Correspondance*, p. 149.
[47] On 2 May 1739, he dedicates a poem to "Madame la comtesse de C [Caumont?]" who had asked him to read her his tragedy *Mustapha* [AN, M791 second notebook], so that he was, indeed, busy scribbling.

leave the theatre as empty as from an opera performance. Dare I tell you that this simplicity cost me more than any ploys of the imagination ever could?"[48] She urged more verisimilitude: His hero whined too much and this clashed with his apparent readiness to die for his beliefs. Mirabeau seemed to be aiming for the more "sublime" form of heroism associated with Corneille, depicting conflicts between love and duty in "manly" fashion, rather than the subjection to the passions associated with Racine.[49] His friend (and no doubt inspiration) Pompignan had shown him the way with his highly successful tragedy *Didon*, which had turned Aeneas into such a figure.[50]

Mirabeau was situating himself within a complex set of artistic expectations. Classical ideals of simple, restrained (cerebral) elegance clashed with the equally strong expectations of flowery expression and elevated feelings demanded by the high style.[51] The arts were meant to offer moral examples and rouse the soul but whether this was achieved by appealing to reason or the emotions incited heated debates. As of the middle of the seventeenth century, scholars have argued, nobles used the language of the heart in preference to the discourses of reason and will (that Quesnay so favoured) to bolster their claims of their selfless devotion to the nation's welfare.[52]

Mirabeau did not give up, despite the failure to get his play(s) performed, having a go at other genres including a didactic poem on the art of war, composed in 1744, commemorating the campaign in which his father had been wounded. "As for the battle of Cassano, I wrote about it, in episodes, in the first canto of the *Art of War*, a poem I composed at the

---

[48] AN, Mirabeau manuscripts, M 784/62/6.
[49] See Bénichou, *Morales du grand siècle* pp. 190 and 199–201; Jean Starobinski, "Sur Corneille" pp. 31–70 in *L'Oeil vivant*, Jean Nagle, *La civilisation du coeur*, pp. 200–5. Vauvenargues comes to prefer Racine. "Corneille et Racine" in *Réflexions critiques sur quelques poètes*, in Vauvenargues, *Oeuvres complètes*, Jean-Pierre Jackson, ed. (Paris, 1999), pp. 211–12. Bénichou treats Vauvenargues' perceptions of Racine as typical of the period, pp. 197–8. For Roland Barthes, however, Racine's plays are not about love but use love as a vehicle for power relations. *Sur Racine* in *Oeuvres complètes*, 5 vols. (Paris, 2002), II, pp. 76–7.
[50] Lefranc analyzes each of Racine's tragedies and divides them into three categories: those in which love plays too great a role; those where it can serve as a dangerous example; and those where it seems utterly out of place. He adds: "Yet Corneille makes worse mistakes.... Of the 22 tragedies that he composed, there isn't one that doesn't address love. Racine is the first French poet to write tragedies without that foolish passion [referring to *Esther* and *Athalie*]" cited in abbé Fr.-Albert Duffo, *J-J Lefranc, marquis de Pompignan, poète et magistrat (1709 1784)* (Paris, 1913), p. 263.
[51] Annie Becq, *Genèse de l'esthétique moderne, 1680–1814* (Paris, 1994), pp. 62–3.
[52] Ibid., pp. 216–17. Nagle, *La Civilisation du coeur*, pp. 222–6.

time when it was my *métier*."⁵³ Although the poem was never published, it circulated in manuscript, earning both praise and criticism from Le Franc de Pompignan, the Président d'Eguilles (of the Parlement of Aix), and the comte de Caumont. By this choice of subject Mirabeau demonstrated yet again that he meant to celebrate manly qualities and to stay clear of the "effeminate" genres of chivalric literature and romances he deplored in the culture of his day. He would guide the nobility toward elevated principles by appealing to its finer instincts and deriding the frivolities of *bel esprit* that sought merely to please.⁵⁴ Mirabeau's ideal warrior therefore displays the Stoic values of "utter simplicity and honor devoid of vanity. Since honor is his goal, he never interferes with another's. He must be feared as a warrior, be loved as a citizen, know military theory, and study both history and men; he must not display false valor or temerity (except in the first stages of battle), keep his cool and train himself to assess situations *(se former le coup d'oeil).*"⁵⁵ Endorsing this enterprise, his friends urged Mirabeau to use "noble and sublime imagery" but also to imbue the poem with warmth, "engaging the reader's attention through a pleasing style that cannot fail to earn you universal acclaim."⁵⁶

Unable perhaps to meet this arduous double requirement, Mirabeau never published the work and perhaps never finished it, but it demonstrates a continued ambition to extol the military nobility's special calling (despite abandoning the army himself). He confessed to Vauvenargues that he was unsure which way to turn.⁵⁷ Vauvenargues had no doubts about the nobility's martial role, and he sincerely lamented the century's

---

⁵³ Gabriel Lucas de Montigny, ed., *Mémoires biographiques, littéraires et politiques de Mirabeau écrits par lui-même, par son père, son oncle et son fils adoptif*, 8 vols. (1834–1835) III, p. 423, citing from the unpublished *Mémoires domestiques du marquis de Mirabeau*.
⁵⁴ See on this Russo, *Styles of Enlightenment*, p. 43.
⁵⁵ M784/34. The document summarizes each of the poem's nine songs. They described tactics and training, military organization, campaigning and strategy, with examples from great sieges and outstanding commanders.
⁵⁶ Archives nationales, M 784/16 "Pensées." Unsigned letter dispatched from Caumont, 1744. His friends also disagreed about whether or not he should introduce the work with a translation of Sallust.
⁵⁷ Letter to Vauvenargues, Paris 30 April 1738, in Vauvenargues, *Correspondance*, p. 98. He had been briefly engaged in spring 1738 to Mademoiselle de Nesle (Pauline Félicité de Mailly, soon to be marquise de Vintimille, who would die in 1741 after bearing Louis XV a son). Letters to Vauvenargues of 20 May and 6 June 1638. Letters from Bordeaux, 24 April and 16 May 1739, Vauvenargues, *Correspondance*, pp. 125, 132.

contempt for the profession of arms that deterred noblemen from pursuing their destiny.[58] "Propriety (*bienséance*) demands that our talents be suited to our rank [*état*]."[59] Nobles must defend this legacy as if it were a "precious heirloom" against the claims of "merit," which Vauvenargues dismissed as euphemism for a large fortune.[60] Nobility had existed since the dawn of society. "The distinction among the orders of the kingdom is one of the fundamental laws of the State."[61] Inequality was inscribed in nature. Man's lot was to be subordinate and dependent, first on God and second on social superiors.[62] Glory and virtue were intertwined: "To teach a Prince to love his people and glory was to inspire in him every virtue."[63] Mirabeau would soon himself insist on the "love" that circulated between the king and his subjects.[64]

Poetry, Vauvenargues told Mirabeau, "is one of heaven's greatest gifts ... because this genius entails, by definition, a very vivid imagination, or put another way, a fertile capacity to infuse expression with life and soul, lending a natural eloquence to our language, it is the one talent that seems useful in every position, occupation, and nearly every enjoyment."[65] But he worried that Mirabeau's literary ambitions were interfering with worthier aspirations: "I fear that your taste for literature is clouding your thinking. Fame from belles-lettres is either evanescent or comes when one is no longer around to enjoy it." It was the nobility's mission to strive for glory, and Mirabeau should not evade public responsibilities by staying away from the Court, whatever his disappointments. Mirabeau responded that Versailles was a cesspit: "You would blush at your vision, if you only knew Versailles; those who are forced to be there, weep. One spends one's time gambling, never hearing an ounce of sense; everyone agrees that the worst characters in the kingdom rule and hold the dice. What nonsense to court vice and the utter abasement of feeling

---

[58] Vauvenargues, "Sur les armées d'à-présent" in *Réflexions sur divers sujets* in *Oeuvres complètes*, p. 96.
[59] Letter from Vauvenargues to Mirabeau, Verdun, 16 January 1740, Vauvenargues *Correspondance*, p. 168.
[60] "Sur la noblesse" in *Oeuvres complètes*, pp. 67–8.
[61] [Posthumous] maxims 364 and 365, *Oeuvres complètes*, p. 373.
[62] Maxim 227, *Oeuvres complètes*, p. 348.
[63] [Posthumous] Maxim 694, *Oeuvres complètes*, p. 412.
[64] Jean Nagle refers to Mirabeau as a critic of the cold-hearted, self-seeking noble. *La civilisation du coeur*, p. 228. See also Kwass, *Privilege and the Politics of Taxation*, pp. 231–38.
[65] On the importance of serious civic oratory, see Vauvenargues, "Sur les Anciens et les Modernes" in *Oeuvres complètes*, p. 95.

in order to seem virtuous by contrast!"⁶⁶ The philosopher pooh-poohed Mirabeau's criticisms of the Court:

> To me it is rather the capital of taste, of society, of manners, the heart and head of the State to which all roads lead and where all gets agitated (*tout fermente*), from which all movement emanates, and, to top it all, within the most sumptuous, varied and lively spectacle to be found anywhere on earth. Its inhabitants, it is true, are not the best of men, vice is rampant: too bad for those who have these vices!⁶⁷

To flee the Court was cowardly; to prefer retreat to action, unworthy. Vauvenargues became famous for his insistence on action and the *élan* or inner fire that drove men to excel.⁶⁸ In the process he rehabilitated enthusiasm as a positive force and granted the irrational a place in human motivations.⁶⁹ Having transcendent goals spurred men to virtue, and it also granted them the fortitude to bear up with disappointments and bide their time.⁷⁰ They learned, in fact, to navigate the very obstacles that Mirabeau had encountered at Versailles.⁷¹ In his reflections and maxims, Vauvenargues tied this impulse to human restlessness: "the passion for glory and the passion for the sciences resemble each other in that both arise from our feelings of emptiness and imperfection."⁷²

Mirabeau was too extreme, ploughing ahead mindless of consequences, pursuing his obsession of the moment and then relinquishing it in disgust for something new.⁷³ Vauvenargues, despite his nods toward vitalism, remained wary of fervor, upholding moderation as befitted a moralist, always sensitive to men's shortcomings, starting with his

---

⁶⁶ Vauvenargues, *Oeuvres complètes*, p. 172 Mirabeau to Vauvenargues, Paris, February 1740, These exchanges reveal their authors' commitment to a renewed civic humanism, popular among the eighteenth-century nobility.

⁶⁷ Letter from Verdun, 16 January 1740, Vauvenargues, *Correspondance*, p. 163.

⁶⁸ Robert Mauzi calls him the philosopher of action, *L'Idée du bonheur dans la littérature et la pensée française au XVIIIe siècle* (Paris, 1994), pp. 137, 435, 488.

⁶⁹ Becq, *Genèse de l'esthétique*, pp. 432–3 and Acke, *Vauvenargues moraliste*, pp. 153–6.

⁷⁰ "Discours sur la Gloire" in *Oeuvres complètes*, p. 121.

⁷¹ Letter of 16 January 1640, Vauvenargues, *Correspondance*, pp. 166–7; letter from Mirabeau to Vauvenargues, Paris, February 1740, p. 172, where he recognizes that he is indeed too impetuous and unruly. Letter from Mirabeau to Vauvenargues, Versailles, 7 January 1740, p. 161, where he assures him that he understands that "a man of quality ought not to bury himself; he owes himself to the State."

⁷² "Vauvenargues, "De l'amour des sciences et des lettres" in *Introduction à la connaissance de l'esprit humain* in *Oeuvres complètes*, p. 36.

⁷³ See Daniel Acke, "Les moralistes européens entre 1680 et 1780," in Peter-Eckhard Knabe, Roland Mortier, and François Moureau, eds., *L'aube de la modernité 1680–1760* (Amsterdam and Philadelphia, 2002), pp. 441–69.

own.⁷⁴ "My reason is useless: it is like a mirror that reflects my weaknesses but does nothing to correct them.... We look at things from the perspective that suits our passions. Reason can do nothing, it is too weak to fight the impulses of the heart."⁷⁵ His ideas arose from his heart, and, as he told another friend, the mind just follows the path that the heart has already chosen.⁷⁶ And yet, he did not dismiss reason altogether, unlike Pascal. It was, he told Mirabeau, "among nature's fruits, the slowest, most delicate, rarest, most easily corrupted and hardest to nurture, but also the best." Man's true achievement [*grandeur*] lay in striving to be reasonable. But nature had imbued us with "*amour-propre* and *volupté*," the two foundations of our earthly pleasures, for a reason: They ensured our survival, and we could not simply pretend to do without them.⁷⁷

Mirabeau was more typical perhaps in professing the Stoic precepts of mastery of the self and, thus, to Vauvenargues' "take man as you find him," Mirabeau opposed a stricter code, even if he found it difficult *personally* to live up to such ideals. Vauvenargues's rejoinder was that, in giving too much weight to reason, Mirabeau was adhering to the bland aspirations of the "*honnête homme*."⁷⁸ He doubted that one could alter one's character, each person possessing his own natural inclinations.⁷⁹ Mirabeau dismissed this as sophistry.⁸⁰ He continued to believe that one might yet surmount one's passions, although he knew that he himself fell far short of that goal (and would therefore admire Quesnay's *sang-froid*).

Contemplating the fate of the nobility in the eighteenth century, its apologists still argued that nobles possessed innate qualities and were therefore a *race*, but they were just as likely to justify the nobility's

---

[74] Letter from Aix, 23 January 1739, Vauvenargues, *Correspondance*, p. 112.
[75] Letter from Arras, 9 April 1739, Vauvenargues, *Correspondance*, pp. 122–3.
[76] Letter from Aix, 1 March 1739, Vauvenargues, *Correspondance*, p. 115. Maxim 127 would affirm that "all great thoughts arose from the heart." Letter from Verdun, 10 October 1739, *Correspondance*, p. 154 and letter from Vauvenargues to Saint-Vincens, from Rheims, 8 August 1739, Vauvenargues, *Correspondance*, pp. 146–7.
[77] However important to other contemporary debates, they do not linger on self-love and self-esteem (*amour-de-soi* and *amour-propre* in contemporary parlance).
[78] See Nagle, *La Civilisation du coeur,* who described the position of the "honnête homme" as "allowing intelligence to open the heart to God" (p. 213). See also his discussion of Vauvenargues and Mirabeau whom he views as promoting action as the attribute of nobility whose thirst for glory comes from the heart (p. 225). See also Viala, *Naissance de l'écrivain*, pp. 147–50.
[79] Letter from Metz, 10 May 1740 in response to Mirabeau's letter from Paris of 14 April 1740. Vauvenargues, *Correspondance*, pp. 203–7.
[80] Letter from Mirabeau to Vauvenargues, Aix, 8 July 1740, in response to Vauvenargues' letter of 3 July 1740 from Metz, Vauvenargues, *Correspondance*, pp. 211–15.

primacy historically (by tracing its origins to the Franks or Gallo-Romans) and to insist on its demonstrated leadership.[81] By invoking Republican virtue (which defined a moral rather than a political system) as a noble attribute, as recent scholarship has established, the nobility placed itself at the forefront of public debates on the fate of the nation.[82] If public service and civic spirit spoke to these "Republican" ideals,[83] nobles' moral claims were also expressed through their cultural preferences and taste. Vauvenargues and Mirabeau were both champions of the Ancients, associating them with a purposeful eloquence and noble simplicity that ought to inspire the Moderns – since French culture was going to the dogs.[84] Readers must be elevated, nay, enraptured. "Great thoughts must rise up from the soul."[85] The vehicle could not be purely intellectual because readers were moved by example and hence through emotional responses.[86] It is therefore worth noting that Mirabeau found Boulainvilliers "boring," although he had his younger brother copy whole passages from his work.[87] Even moral argumentation required eloquence and stylistic sophistication. The personal anxieties strewn among their discussions of the value of literature or the nature of action reveal the extent to which thinking about the self was closely intertwined with thinking about the "aristocratic" self.[88] They did not separate the one from the other.

---

[81] Jay Smith in *Nobility Reimagined* discusses Vauvenargues within the larger context of the nobility's reassessment of virtue.

[82] David Bell, *The Cult of the Nation in France*, pp. 70–4 and Michael Sonenscher in *Before the Deluge*.

[83] Kwass, *Privilege and the Politics of Taxation*, p. 234 offers an excellent summary of its use in eighteenth-century discourse.

[84] Russo, *Styles of Enlightenment*, pp. 25–7. See Vauvenargues's letter to Voltaire, 4 April 1743 in Vauvenargues, *Correspondance*, p. 246

[85] Vauvenargues, on "Jean-Baptiste Rousseau" in *Oeuvres complètes*, pp. 215–17. He applauds Racine's "tenderness and vehemence" and Voltaire's "sublime simplicity," while decrying Corneille's ponderousness and the grandiloquent self-importance of his heroes, which some mistake for nobility of soul. See "Réflexions et maximes, # 265" and "Réflexions critiques sur quelques poètes" in *Oeuvres complètes*, pp. 222–3, 353.

[86] Emotions per se (as opposed to the emotional response to the arts) have only recently become a subject of historical investigation. William R. Reddy, *The Navigation of Feeling, A Framework for the History of Emotions* (Cambridge, 2001), Part I, and Philip Stewart, *L'invention du sentiment: roman et économie affective au XVIIIe siècle* (Oxford, 2010), chapter 1 summarizes recent literature on this.

[87] Letter from Mirabeau to Vauvenargues, 19 August 1740, Vauvenargues, *Correspondance*, p. 221.

[88] Elena Russo, *La cour et la ville de la littérature classique aux Lumières* (Paris, 2002) pp. 20–1, argues for the development of an urbane openness to others and questioning of self that she contrasts to physiocratic quests for the absolute.

The decision to resign from the army was a turning point in Mirabeau's life, leaving him formally "unemployed" except for self-imposed literary pursuits, the oversight of his estates, and maneuvers to obtain official posts (until he eventually gave up). Unlike his aristocratic friends with military commands, ambassadorships, governorships, or ministerial positions, Mirabeau staked his hopes on his pen. In 1743, he had his portrait painted surrounded by books, displaying to the world his new identity.[89] Yet he soon tired of this new pastime.

Abandoning serious versifying was a symbolic rite of passage and acknowledgment of adult status. A typical example is provided by one of Mirabeau's contemporaries, Pierre-Michel Hennin, the sometimes physiocratic fellow-traveler, who wrote his friends in Paris in fall 1749: "Yes, I have abandoned the Muses; they did not yield what they had promised. I will no longer write poems, so don't expect any." He made botany his hobby instead, pursuing it actively during his diplomatic postings. Not long after, his cousin Georges Le Roy, *garde des chasses* at Versailles and admirer of Quesnay, remonstrated with him: "Poetry is a pleasing garb for the feelings of the heart, it allows them to disport themselves gracefully.... Despite your attempts to deny nature, I know that she has favored you in this fashion."[90] The young Turgot exchanged similar pleasantries with the abbé Fargès about their mutual poetic gifts, worthy of Voltaire.

To be both a philosopher and pleasing poet combines two very rare talents.... Voltaire, is perhaps the only person who has been hailed both at the theatre and at the Academy of Sciences. Worthy pupil of such a master, you follow in his path and you show that wit [*bel esprit*] balances out philosophy.[91]

To which Turgot replied:

I am not fooled by your compliments, my dear abbé. I might have believed you, had you been less insistent. Are you aware that you profane the name of Voltaire? I do not lack in self-esteem and it takes only a little to give me too much, but I submit to you that he is at least more refined that you suppose.[92]

---

[89] The painting [which one can see at the start of the chapter] is by Jacques Aved, and Daniel Roche treats it as Mirabeau's assertion of the power of books, "Les Lectures de la noblesse" in *Les Républicains des lettres, gens de culture et lumières au XVIIIe siècle* (Paris, 1988), p. 85. It was displayed at the 1743 salon.
[90] I thank Loïc Charles for telling me about this correspondence located in the Bibliothèque de l'Institut, Manuscrits 1266, 1268.
[91] 12 October 1749, in Gustave Schelle, *Oeuvres de Turgot*, I, p. 513.
[92] Ibid., pp. 153–4.

Mirabeau later disparaged those salad days when he had taken such ambitions seriously. "My affairs and the study that fills my brief moments of leisure," he wrote in his defense of Le Franc de Pompignan's *Poésies sacrés*, in the early 1750s, "have for quite some time now distanced me from the literature in which I delighted ten years ago; all I have retained from my once-keen taste for poetry and eloquence are a happy and lively appreciation for first-rate works and a great deal of indulgence for those that fall short of that."[93] He was more candid with the interlocutor of his old age, Marquis Longo[94]: "I loved literature passionately and devoted myself to this endeavour in the flower of my youth, meaning from the ages of 23 to 28 under an excellent master [Le Franc de Pompignan]. I composed verses, as all hot-headed, lively youths do, but, what is more, I became familiar with the art and refinements of our true poetry." But he had come to understand, he added, that "whoever received much from society must appear to give something in return; that our own education must be the result and not the object of our labors. I therefore staked my reputation on politics, believing it to be the science and duty of notables, and I did well; I relegated my versifying to my chambers and did not lose by the exchange."[95] Although he kept even his "juvenalia," he would come to regard them as superficial and regrettable flirtations with *bel esprit*.[96] This included all the occasional poetry, love poems, and satires that had once earned him a reputation for wickedness.[97]

[93] AN, Mirabeau manuscripts, M 783/16/2. "Lettre à M. de S ... sur les poésies de M. Le Franc de Pompignan," published as *Examen des poésies sacrées de M. Lefranc de Pompignan* (Paris, 1755).
[94] Professor of political economy in Milan.
[95] Letter to Longo from Le Bignon, 25 November 1777, in *Mémoires biographiques, littéraires et politiques de Mirabeau*, III, pp. 448–9 (letter 4).
[96] M791 Premier cahier, January and February 1739 "This is a collection of my occasional verses, for my own use – although this would render this foreword pointless. But, no, I will no doubt lend it to my friends, and I hope I might escape their censure for the sloppiness and childishness of the contents. Should I ever offer it to the public, I will strive to make it more acceptable and only include those poems whose subject matter might be appealing." A second covered the period February and March 1739; a third, began in July 1739; a fourth in November 1741.
[97] Letter from Mirabeau to Vauvenargues written at Mirabeau, 14 October 1737. "I paint men; they find me nasty (*méchant*)." Vauvenargues, *Correspondance*, p. 95. He refers to this again in his third notebook of poetry, in the entry for 21 September 1739: "One of my mistresses of whom I was very fond ... asked me to compose a satire of a man; this was something new for me, but I did it with surprising liveliness, and some of his traits were priceless." AN, M 791 "Poésies du marquis de Mirabeau," troisième cahier. In a letter to "Madame la marquise des M, ce 23 décembre 1739," from Versailles Mirabeau asks her to "keep my miserable verses secret, for I detest what they call *bel esprit* and you know how easy it is to get that reputation with a few lines of doggerel" [AN 791]. On

In the early 1750s, Mirabeau would express his ideas in two new forms. The first was a pamphlet on provincial estates and the second a long commentary on Le Franc de Pompignan's translations of Hebrew hymns. In the one, he would address the specific problems of the nobility (and hence of the state); in the second, the nature of humanity as a whole: its longings, its history, its strivings, and its limitations. The voice of the heart was frequently invoked. Vauvenargues had wondered whether reason and emotion might ever be reconciled. A similar concern would now pervade Mirabeau's writings.

## Pompignan

The abbé Raynal (1713–1790), editor of *Le Mercure de France* commissioned Mirabeau to review his friend Le Franc's translations of the Psalms, the *Poésies sacrées,* published in 1751. His brief was to assess whether Pompignan had equaled or surpassed France's reigning religious poet, Jean-Baptiste Rousseau. Mirabeau expanded the review into a multipart, 200-page study.[98]

"I have for twenty years revered the talent of M. Le Franc," he confided, "and regarded him, from the time of *Didon* [1734] when I myself was very young, as the *magnae spes altera Roma* [second hope of great Rome]."[99] This was his opportunity to repay Le Franc's tutelage in the poetic arts and to express his gratitude. This panegyric would, unfortunately, come to haunt Mirabeau when Le Franc turned into the philosophes' *bête noire.*[100]

Jean-Jacques Le Franc de Pompignan, born in 1709 to a Languedoc noble family, became magistrate at the Montauban *cour des aides* (fiscal court) in 1730, resigning from his office as its *premier président* in 1755

---

the turn against *bel esprit*, see Russo, *Styles of Enlightenment,* and Alain Viala, *La France galante* (Paris, 2008).

[98] Mirabeau's commentary on the poems was published anonymously in 1755 but included as a separately paginated addendum to the new expanded edition of the poems in 1763. Loménie who devotes all of one page to this, believes it was to help Pompignan who had become the philosophes' bête noire. On the other hand, Mirabeau stayed out of the actual disputes that broke out in 1760 over Pompignan's attack of the philosophes at the Académie française. Braun, *Un ennemi de Voltaire,* p. 233.

[99] *Examen des Poésies sacrées* appended to *Poésies sacrées et philosophiques tirées des livres saints* par M. Le Franc de Pompignan, nouvelle édition considérablement augmentée, et enrichie de gravures (Paris, 1763), p. 3. *Didon,* Le Franc's one tragedy was performed at the Théâtre français in 1734 and again in 1745 to great acclaim (Braun, *Un ennemi de Voltaire,* p. 70). The citation is from Virgil's *Aeneid.*

[100] The relationship appalled Loménie, *Les Mirabeau,* II, pp. 133–4.

after a highly advantageous marriage. He was named honorary member of the Parlement of Toulouse that same year. His attack on fiscal policy earned him a six-month exile in 1738, and he penned remonstrances against the imposition of the *vingtième* tax in his province (in both 1749 and 1755).[101] He was better known, however, as of the early 1730s, as the author of light operas, comedies, and a single tragedy, *Didon,* which had entered the *Théâtre français'* repertory and enjoyed a revival in 1745. In response to a squabble over precedence with Voltaire who insisted that the company put on his play before his rival's, Le Franc gave up writing tragedies, although he still produced light entertainments and was among the first to compose a moralising opera in 1750. In the 1730s, Le Franc had also embarked on translations of religious poetry from the Latin, Greek, and Hebrew, publishing his first collection from the Old Testament in 1751. Expanded editions followed in 1763, 1771, and 1784.[102] In 1740 he had also translated Alexander Pope's Deist *Universal Prayer* (1738), and, once his poetry grew increasingly pious, his enemies used this fact to mock him, displaying the characteristic incomprehension of the Republic of Letters. He had been a Freemason at one time but the anti-religious tone of contemporary writings unsettled him, and he drew increasingly closer to the highly conservative *dévot* party. His attack on the philosophes in his inaugural address to the Académie française (1760) caused a scandal. In response, Voltaire, who already disliked him, launched a vicious campaign. The endless stream of satirical pamphlets flowing from Voltaire and the abbé Morellet's pen drove Le Franc back to the provinces, never to return to the capital.[103] He lived happily among his fields and peasants in quite comfortable circumstances, and in 1765 Louis XV granted him a marquisate. Mirabeau visited him in his country retreat and swore to destroy any "unsuitable" (meaning pornographic) manuscripts found after his death, a promise he fulfilled in 1784.[104]

[101] Duffo, *Pompignan,* pp. 109, 325, and Braun and Guillaume Robichez, *Lumières voilées,* pp. 7–9.
[102] He translated Hesiod, Virgil, Pythagoras, Ovid, Horace, and most notably Eschylus. Braun and Robichez, p. 19 and Claire Chevalier, *L'Invention d'une origine, Traduire Eschyle en France de Lefranc de Pompignan à Mazon: le* Prométhée enchaîné (Paris, 2007).
[103] The satirical pamphlets: *Pourquoi, Qui, Quoi, Que, Oui, Non, Car* and *Ah!ah!,* Braun and Robichez, *Lumières voilées,* pp. 9, 15–16. See also Olivier Ferret, *La Fureur de nuire: échanges pamphlétaires entre philosophes et antiphilosophes (1750–1770)* (Oxford, 2007), pp. 120–34, which deal specifically with Pompignan.
[104] Duffo, *Pompignan,* pp. 448–9. Pompignan dedicated three poems to Mirabeau, including two epistles on the joys of retreat and the hardships of political economy. See Pompignan, *Oeuvres complètes de Jean-Georges Lefranc de Pompignan suivies des*

Quesnay himself had denounced Le Franc (and his brother, bishop of Le Puy, later archbishop of Vienne), as Mme Du Hausset recorded. "I approve of Voltaire's campaign against the Pompignans (*la chasse aux Pompignan*): the bourgeois Marquis, without the ridicule heaped on him, would have become tutor to the royal children; and, along with his brother Georges, would no doubt have reinstated burning at the stake."[105] The doctor was worried that the deeply devout Dauphin might succeed an aging Louis XV and give religious fanatics a free hand. Mirabeau responded: "We must draw comfort from the way the Dauphin has been ridiculing Pompignan, despite his shows of piety. Someone who ran into him recently, found him puffed up with pride, and told someone else who then reported to me: Our friend Pompignan thinks he has become a somebody!"

Only a year earlier Mirabeau had urged Etienne de Silhouette, then Controller general and sympathetic to economic reform, to sponsor the Fine Arts (to occupy the idle) as an acknowledged patron (alluding to Silhouette's popular literary translations) and suggesting he name Pompignan Director of Libraries.[106] The latter, he maintained, was talented, pious, and highly knowledgeable about antiquity, clinching this praise with: "He loathes modern philosophy and holds it as much in contempt as he does its sects."[107]

Pompignan endorsed the manly virtues that Mirabeau meant to celebrate and his poems exuded the moral message and "sublime simplicity" he so admired.[108] In his play, *Didon*, Pompignan had transformed one of literature's most famous cads, Aeneas, into a Corneillian hero torn

---

*Oeuvres religieuses de J.-J. Lefranc marquis de Pompignan*, ed. M. Emery, 2 vols. (Paris, 1855), II, pp. 1307–17.

[105] Du Hausset, *Mémoires*, p. 81. Quesnay agreed that the Parlements were going too far in their attacks on religion. Their friend Duclos, the royal historiographer, also felt that the philosophes were overly ferocious (p. 80). The anecdote apparently made the rounds, eventually reaching the ears of a delighted Voltaire. Duffo, *Pompignan*, p. 378.

[106] Archives nationales M 784/2. Reproduced in Weulersse, *Manuscrits*, pp. 39–46. Etienne de Silhouette, *Mélanges de littérature et de philosophie* 2 vols. (London, 1742).

[107] AN, M784/12. Silhouette's ministry lasted only from 4 March to 21 November 1759. In the same letter, Mirabeau described what he considered proper literature. "True literature is virile, strong, noble and wise, and it is not from Plato and Homer, Bacon and Milton, Pascal, Bossuet, Corneille or Despréaux that the pygmies [*avortons*] of our day sucked the milk that gave them that shiny, bloated, taut complexion, always on the verge of explosion. But this race of insects comes in an age when dictionaries, newspapers and laziness have killed off good education."

[108] See the discussion by Caumont in a letter to Mirabeau of 15 August 1744, AN, M784/16.

between love and duty, surmounting his lust and leaving Dido only after routing her enemies in battle.[109] The magistrate's religious poetry meant to restore the sense of the divine experienced in earliest antiquity, a project that Mirabeau fully supported, and, in his commentary, digressed on the origins of language and the arts, primitive religion, the rise of civilization, urbanity, morality, and sociability.[110]

Mirabeau vaunted Le Franc's erudition. The magistrate had learned Hebrew to translate the Psalms and had consulted theologians about obscure passages. He had found equivalents for the vivid, overwrought "Oriental" imagery of the Hebrew tongue.[111] Ancient peoples "lent religious meaning and noble aspirations to everything, seeing the hand of the Creator behind all things, especially the majesty of nature," because they had been closer to the moment of Creation.[112] Like many contemporaries, Mirabeau had transferred his admiration of the Ancients to a search for the "primitive" force they embodied – the earlier the better. Retrieving this energy might rouse modern literature out of its "effete" doldrums. The older the arts, it was thought, the closer to the "voice of nature," the more recent, the more artificial and weaker its echoes.[113] Mirabeau feared the cycles of rise and decline to which civilizations were doomed and hoped that his own culture could be salvaged through an infusion of ancient vitality.[114] Thus, Mirabeau lauded Le Franc's "uncanny" ability to deploy the high style, arousing emotions as ably as he painted them.[115] "The sublime elevates the soul, feeling moves it, and style flatters the ears and taste," Mirabeau added.[116] The Scriptures were

[109] Braun and Robichez, *Lumières voilées*, p. 129.
[110] What Theodore Braun calls Pompignan's "muscularity" resonated as well. Braun, "Truth, Beauty, Harmony, Order, and Muscularity in Le Franc de Pompignan's *Poésies Sacrées*," *1650–1850: Ideas, Aesthetics, and Inquiries in the Early Modern Era*, vol. 3 (1996), pp. 99–116 Jean Starobinski, *Le remède dans le mal* (Paris, 1989), p. 14, who notes that Mirabeau's notion of civilization possessed a moral dimension (p. 21) so that societies could fail to rise to a truly "civilized" state (p. 53).
[111] Mirabeau, *Examen des poésies sacrées*, p. 55.
[112] Ibid., pp. 52–3.
[113] See Chatal Grell and Christian Michel, eds., *Primitivisme et mythes des origines dans la France des Lumières 1680 –1820* (Paris, 1989), and Nicholas Hudson, "Theories of Language" in H. B. Nisbet and Claude Rawson, eds., *The Cambridge History of Literary Criticism*, vol. IV: *The Eighteenth Century* (Cambridge, 2005), pp. 335–64. We find this also in Condillac, *Essai sur l'origine des connaissances humaines* (Paris, 1749), Part II, Sec. I, chap. VII, s.75.
[114] Mirabeau, *Examen des poésies sacrées*, p. 65.
[115] The excessive praise that Mirabeau lavished on Pompignan turned off reviewers.
[116] Mirabeau, *Examen des poésies sacrées*, pp. 4–5. His references are Longinus, Boileau, and Horace.

not only perfect, "their prime characteristic was their capacity to move, interest, and always speak to the heart."[117]

Mirabeau was probably merely expressing the standard rhetorical position, taught at school, in which the "high style" or literary sublime was the highest manifestation of human creativity.[118] But the interpretation of art had been evolving over the past half century, questioning the degree to which the arts were "mirrors of the world" and hence merely imitative, or whether they tapped into some inexpressible force, creating something altogether new. Behind this debate lay the age-old fear that the arts, so powerful at inducing responses, also distort and mislead, based on the Platonic belief that the terrestrial world itself was already a corrupt version of Ideal Forms, a view favored by Christian theology. Man should not waste his time on representations of representations and focus instead on true salvation. Yet the arts might be redeemed if they "imitated" ideal Nature (nature as it existed ideally or nature as it ought to look), a concept rendered as *belle nature* as of 1687.[119] Only then might it hope to fulfill lofty educational and moral goals. Even rationalists allowed for flashes of insight (an infusion of Grace) that allowed glimpses of higher truths, opening the door to an irreducible element of the irrational – or imagination – behind artistic creation (also known as "genius") and audience response. Hence, Malebranche and Fénelon's mystical Christianity proved important to the development of aesthetics, as Annie Becq has demonstrated, and Mirabeau supported their insights.[120] There could be no moral uplift if audiences were bored, and the early eighteenth century witnessed renewed efforts to reconcile the intellectual and sensory approach to the arts.[121]

The abbé Du Bos, in his influential *Réflexions critiques sur la poésie et sur la peinture* of 1719, proposed that the arts possessed the power to stimulate the same responses as the ones invoked by actual events.[122] Du

---

[117] Braun and Robichez, *Lumières voilées*, p. 25, "Extraits du *Discours préliminaire*" of the *Poésies sacrées*.
[118] L.W. Brockliss, *French Higher Education*, p. 127. See on the countercurrent, Russo, *Styles of Enlightenment*, and Marian Hobson, *The Object of Art. The Theory of Illusion in Eighteenth-Century France* (Cambridge, 1982). See also Gilles Declercq, "La rhétorique classique entre évidence et sublime (1650–1675)," pp. 629–706, and Jean-Paul Sermain, "Le code du bon goût (1725–1759)," pp. 879–943 in Marc Fumaroli, ed., *Histoire de la rhétorique moderne 1450–1950* (Paris, 1999).
[119] Becq, *Genèse de l'esthétique*, p. 79.
[120] Ibid., pp. 99–105.
[121] See ibid., pp. 34, 55.
[122] abbé Du Bos, Jean Baptiste, *Rélexions critiques sur la poësie et sur la peinture* (Paris, 1770), p. 52.

Bos's public was weak, bored, and in need of powerful stimulation.[123] Emotions were contagious. Good acting moved us, so that "repeated appeal to our [positive] passions renders us capable of virtue and brave actions that the mind, unaided, could never induce us to undertake otherwise."[124] And so it appeared that the arts tapped into a "sixth sense" that resonated to such surrogate emotions.[125]

Bishop Fénelon had asserted that "music, dance, eloquence, and poetry were invented to express the passions and in turn to stimulate these same passions by imprinting lofty sentiments on the soul, painting vivid and touching pictures of the beauty of virtue and the deformity of vice."[126] His hero Télémaque (in one of the most popular novels of the eighteenth century) was advised to follow the dictates of his heart in his search for wisdom.[127] As Mirabeau saw it, Pompignan was treading along the same path in arguing that the heart "has the imprint of the Divinity that made man in his image."[128] Mirabeau was positioning himself within cultural debates about the arts, man's spiritual aspirations, and his creative potential, and validating sublime impulses.

By contending that the heart was a true guide to action in 1752, whatever his earlier misgivings, Mirabeau was granting it the power that Quesnay attributed to the rational mind.[129] Quesnay did not believe in the communicability of emotions. His economic program entailed, as we saw, endorsing his interpretation of sensationalist psychology. Although Mirabeau would claim that he had absorbed Quesnay's teachings, it is unclear which organ he used. In fact the encounter with Quesnay would

---

[123] On the ways that Du Bos's theories about audience "reception" influenced French political discourse, see Thomas Kaiser, "Rhetoric in the Service of the King: The abbé Du Bos and the Concept of Public Judgment," *Eighteenth-Century Studies*, 23:2 (1989–90), 182–99.

[124] Du Bos, *Réflexions*, p. 49. Du Bos adds, moreover, that the heart is easier to touch than the mind ("l'esprit est d'un commerce plus difficile que le coeur," p. 65).

[125] See on this Becq, *Genèse de l'esthétique*, pp. 113 and 253.

[126] François de Salignac de la Motte Fénelon, "Sur l'éloquence" in M. Saucier ed., *Oeuvres choisies de Fénelon* (Tours, 1859), p. 193. Mirabeau would compose his panegyric of Fénelon and *Télémaque* in 1773. AN, M783/7. He exculpated Fénelon of every possible error of judgment, including his flirtation with mysticism, lauded him for teaching monarchs virtue and stressing the values of love, self-control, merit, and emulation, and for offering infallible moral axioms. He denied, however, that Fénelon was a precursor of the *économistes* because he viewed Quesnay as the sole inventor of this new science.

[127] Fénelon, *Les aventures de Télémaque* (Paris, 1968). Speaking to the heart was one of the book's important messages, see for example, p. 113 (book 3), which explains how to win over hearts.

[128] Mirabeau, *Examen des poésies sacrées*, p. 152.

[129] Ibid., pp. 159–60. This is what separates men from beasts.

call into question not just his stances on agriculture, populationism, or the nobility, but deeper conclusions regarding human motivation and the human condition.

### Later Literary Criticism

The arts featured in several places in *L'Ami des hommes* (1756–1757) – the book that turned Mirabeau into a household name – and reaffirmed their importance. "Poetry, Eloquence, Painting, Sculpture, Architecture and even Music ... demand a loftiness of soul [*âme*] that strives to attain the perfection of Greece, of Rome under Augustus, or of France under Louis XIV."[130] "True beauty moreover is not merely simple and noble, it is also confident and proud, its influence agitates us, it irritates the nerves out of their lethargy, as if scaring and repelling this inclination."[131] Mirabeau was also endorsing the vitalist notions that Quesnay rejected. Mirabeau had reached these conclusions through his aesthetics and moral reflections, not through training in physiology as had Quesnay. Like Jean-Jacques Rousseau, he could refer to enervation and treat invigoration in relation to primitive modes of being, rather than as medical states,[132] loyal to the "anthropology" that had permeated analysis of the *Poésies sacrées*. Mankind had been at it strongest, most vigorous, and most spiritual at the dawn of civilization. "Let us examine the nature of each phenomenon at its birth, in its original purity and nobility," he thus intoned, so that modern culture might recover its potency by abandoning its feminine affectations.[133] Nonetheless, one should not dismiss history altogether because "the storehouse of great events" could serve as "a school for virtue," once one realized that "only noble deeds make a lasting impression."[134]

There was little in Mirabeau's approach to the arts to interest Quesnay, at least initially. As far as he was concerned, society answered man's material needs and protected his hard-earned property; it did not exist to provide emotional bonding or entertainment.[135] The "laws" of the natural

---

[130] Mirabeau, *L'Ami des hommes*, II, p. 316.
[131] Ibid., p. 329.
[132] Jean-Jacques Rousseau, *Discours sur l'origine et les fondements de l'inégalité parmi les hommes* (1755) in *Du contrat social* (Paris, 1962). Yet these would soon be reduced to pathology. See Rey, *Naissance et développement du vitalisme*, and Anne Vila, *Enlightenment and Pathology*.
[133] Mirabeau, *L'Ami des hommes*, III, pp. 89–90.
[134] Ibid., pp. 88–90.
[135] Quesnay expressed this in his "Observations sur le droit naturel," see Quesnay, *Oeuvres économiques complètes et autres textes*, I, pp. 97–123.

order had been designed by God for man's benefit and could only be conveyed to his reason. Moral precepts therefore devolved from the needs of the species and resulted from man's regeneration rather than caused it. Yet, as their collaboration advanced, the need to discuss the foundations of society grew unavoidable. Their more analytically inclined readership would wonder about the historical development of societies and their failure to follow nature's "evident" dictates. Addressing such issues would naturally fall to Mirabeau and become imbued with his primitivism.[136]

Mirabeau never renounced his love of poetry and became, at the height of his fame, an arbiter of taste – at least in rustic/pastoral genres – a position he seemed to relish. He revised Madame de Bontems's introduction to her prose translation of James Thomson's *The Seasons*, which he had been instrumental in commissioning.[137] The French translation of Hans Caspar Hirzel's (1725–1803) *Rustic Socrates,* a series of sketches of a Swiss peasant named "Kliougg" [*Kleinjogg* in German] had been dedicated to *l'ami des hommes* in 1762.[138] The volumes dispensed some farming advice, endorsed simple mores and obedience to the dictates of nature, while offering a blueprint for a revitalized peasant economy. Mirabeau thanked its author, J. Frey des Landres, with a display of *noblesse oblige*[139]:

> More than anyone else, I feel how little I deserve the distinguished title [of man's friend] by which I have been honoured ... [but I] will tell you how happy I was with the *Rustic Socrates*. Its reputation is already sufficiently established here that it is enough for me to express my personal response. I can assure you that I find it one of the most useful texts I have come across. That sublime attribute supposes of course that it must also be enjoyable, for one must first keep readers interested if one wishes to indoctrinate them effectively [*les endoctriner solidement*].

The Marquis used this opportunity to criticize agricultural societies whose armchair agronomists had nothing useful to convey to farmers and to vaunt instead the peasantry's common sense. France's new craze for agriculture, he feared, was "but a Georgic romance, leading a benighted

---

[136] See also the discussion in Guillaume-François Le Trosne, *De l'ordre social* (Paris, 1777).
[137] A.N. M784/29 (1). Her prose translation stimulated a rash of poems on the seasons. Margaret M. Cameron, *L'influence des* Saisons *de Thomson sur la poésie descriptive en France (1759–1810)* (Paris, 1927).
[138] On Hirzel and Kleinjogg, see Paul H. Johnstone, "The Rural Socrates," *Journal of the History of Ideas*, 5 (1944), 151–75.
[139] A.N. M 784/ 42. "Lettre de Mirabeau à M. Frey, auteur du 'Socrate rustique' (1762)." Further French editions appeared in 1764, 1768, and 1777.

nation down a false path." Quesnay, who was looking over his shoulder, queried whether the arts and sciences would have existed at all had the world been left to storytellers and rhetoricians. "Let them at least use their talent to bring us back to the right path," Quesnay demanded.[140] Mirabeau approved of Hirzel's depictions of country ways, having searched high and low for "cheerful, edifying portrayals, and, since [he] could not find them elsewhere, had urged the translation of Thomson's poems of the *Seasons*, despite [his] awareness that they merely painted ... imaginary landscapes. [He] had yearned for something truer to life with more realistic depictions, and the *Rustic Socrates* offered more than [he] could ever have hoped for. It abounded with sound advice about the most beneficial and enlightened agricultural practices, the noblest philosophy and the most admirable piety. Kliougg was [his] hero." Once again Mirabeau was expressing the primitivist, "bardic" sensibilities of the age, although the rustic sage he promoted here was fully committed to making his farm [modestly] profitable.[141] The line between sentimental primitivism and a physiocratically virtuous lifestyle had to be carefully monitored to avoid the allures of the former that undermined the master plan of the latter. Physiocrats, by discussing rustic mores, had to contend with the pastoral tradition that had been so successfully revived during the Renaissance. The more robust Georgic genre with its actual depictions of farming methods had far fewer takers. In looking for poets to celebrate both simplicity *and* profit, physiocrats would encourage didactic poetry. Jacques Turgot would support the poets Jacques Delille and Antoine Roucher, but the second proved even less talented than the first.[142]

They had to make do with what was on offer, and in 1768 Mirabeau regaled Rousseau with the rumor that the Economists had packed the loges at performances of Charles-Simon Favart's comic opera *Les Moissonneurs* (The Harvesters). Given the subject, he wished this had been so. Anything that celebrated the countryside was a boon. "This, along with the success of the books I have written in a different genre,

---

[140] Quesnay had added "qu'on nous ramène au moins au vrai." Hirzel had raised the question of the role of the arts and sciences in the improvement of mankind in his original text, seeing agriculture as the mother of all arts, and presenting Kliouug as a pure "product of nature." Johnstone, "The Rural Socrates," pp. 167–8.

[141] McPherson's transcriptions of "Ossian's" Celtic tales had swept France by storm once Turgot translated a few fragments in 1761. See Paul van Thiegen, *Ossian en France*, 2 vols. (Paris, 1920).

[142] See on this my article "Imagining the Harvest in Early Modern Europe," *The American Historical Review*, 101 (1996), 1357–97.

tells me that men cannot deny their natures as easily as they think."[143] In other words, even light opera could strike a real chord:

> I have just seen *Les Moissonneurs*, which has two or three pleasant scenes, a bit of music, some pretty songs, much wit and many maxims, but no drama. The public applauds the maxims without enthusiasm, but sheds many tears at the scenes and pictures of rustic life filled with benevolence and gratified devotion. And when I think of what is offered to the public and what appeals to it today compared to years ago, what with the parodies, *dancourades*, even high comedy and especially tragedy [*le cothurne*], I conclude that men are civilized first through their hearts and only later through their minds.

One might conclude from this that Mirabeau remained faithful to the credo that one must "move the heart and touch the soul." Yet when it came to spreading economics, he yielded, telling Quesnay in 1761 that he had finally "understood" the doctor's approach to the sciences.[144] Only they offered guidance to mankind, not the "actor or singer" [*l'histrion ou le chanteur*] who enjoyed "ephemeral success."[145] "Mathematics, not moral philosophy, can correct harmful errors."[146] Mirabeau's surrender thus seemed to be complete. Melchior Grimm confidently asserted in 1767: "My last grievance against the Tuesdays of these économiste-farmers is that they are the enemies of the fine arts. They consider anyone who does not lead a plough as useless or even harmful, unless he happens to attend M. de Mirabeau's Tuesday assemblies."[147] Yet this was not quite the case. While the aged Quesnay took to geometry in his last years, trying to square the circle, Mirabeau turned to parables and moral exemplars to incite the public to heed the physiocratic message. This suited his temperament much better than appeals to mathematical evidence, recalling his inner conviction that if one wanted to reach the mind, one had to touch the soul.

---

[143] Jean-Jacques Rousseau, *Correspondance complète*, XXXV, Letter 6235, 3 February 1768, p. 84. The fragment from the next day follows on pages 84–5. When he wrote Rousseau: "Je trouve que les hommes se civilisent par le coeur en attendant qu'ils le soyent par l'esprit," he knew he was speaking to a kindred spirit, perhaps to convince him that not all of physiocracy was glumly rationalist.

[144] AN M784/41, letter of 13 June 1761, reproduced in Quesnay, *Oeuvres économiques complètes et autres textes*, I, pp. 753–64.

[145] This was a reference to the Latin *histrio*, which Quitilian used to denigrated "comedians" and separate them from the "actors" who performed tragedies. See Marc Fumaroli, *Héros et orateurs: Rhétorique et dramaturgie cornélienne* (Paris, 1996), p. 291.

[146] M784/46, letter of 13 June 1761, also in Quesnay, *Oeuvres économiques complètes et autres textes*, I, p. 763.

[147] Grimm et al., *Correspondance littéraire*, VII, p. 436.

# 4

# A Delicate Balance

The intellectual partnership between François Quesnay and Victor Riquetti, marquis de Mirabeau, is one of the most mystifying of all time. They make an unlikely pair as should be clear to the reader by now. One was a *parvenu* physician of peasant origins, self-controlled and ingratiating. The other, a scion of a Provençal military nobility, determined to maintain its historic role, was artless and volatile. Their first encounter in summer 1757 had been stormy and foddered a series of myths.

Never has a Goliath gone to battle with so much self-confidence as I did when I sought out the man who had, I was told, scribbled in the margin of my book these bold comments: "The child has sucked bad milk, his strength of character often leads him to the right conclusions, but he lacks the underlying principles." My critic showed no indulgence and told me straight out that I had put the cart before the horse and that Cantillon was but a fool and no guide to politics. Such heresies convinced me that I was dealing with a madman but I told myself that people treat arguments like jousting matches and held my peace, put an end to the conversation and, to my everlasting joy, went back that same evening to pursue the discussion with more equanimity (*à tête reposée*). That is when he cracked Goliath's skull.[1]

Mirabeau saw the light. "[I] begged my master to explain himself and to enlighten me, for I was but a child of forty-two." After his tempestuous interview with Quesnay, Mirabeau conceded that he had indeed got the wrong end of the stick. He had been endeavoring to promote population growth while he ought to have realized that a felicitous increase in

---

[1] Letter from Mirabeau to Rousseau, Rousseau, *Correspondance complète*, XXXIII, pp. 26–72.

population rested on steady investments in agriculture. As Yves Citton has pointed out, this was a dramatic change in orientation. Where once the nation's welfare had rested in its "people," this same felicity now lay in "capital-formation."[2]

## Farm, Field, And Finance

In the 1750s, while ministers scrambled to negotiate new loans and to obtain more taxes from the recalcitrant *parlements* (sovereign courts) that registered them into law, Quesnay was informing himself on the country's economic performance, reading broadly and talking to visitors. Like high administrators in this period, he looked to the successes of England and the Dutch Republic as examples to emulate. He classified them as commercial states but wished France to boost its agricultural production by imitating their cutting-edge husbandry and to adopt English-style large enclosed farms. By borrowing their methods, France would revive its agrarian vocation and leave its competitors to sail the seas.

Quesnay's first public foray into this new field took the form of articles for the *Encyclopédie,* "Farmers" and "Grains," which appeared in 1756 and 1757 respectively.[3] These articles summarized Quesnay's conclusions regarding the French economy and his contention that agriculture was central to the creation of a renewable wealth upon which a kingdom could safely rely. Only Nature, by its fecundity, enabled real as opposed to fictitious wealth. Its inherent capacity to multiply itself fed the nation, provided raw materials for artisanal goods, and generated monetary surpluses that were returned to landowners in the form of rent and to the government as taxes. "Farmers" and "Grains" offer the clearest guide to his economic ideas. Their style is straightforward and the argument deft. Quesnay convinces his reader that his conclusions rest on thorough research on the performance of various economic sectors. Physiocracy's claims to empirical verification were never better formulated.[4] The articles include statistics and charts and explain the use of "typical" farm budgets to calculate national averages.[5]

[2] Yves Citton, *Portrait de l'économiste en physiocrate*, p. 119.
[3] Two others had been drafted, on population (*Hommes*) and taxation (*Impôts*) but were withdrawn once the King blamed the attempt on his life on the Encyclopedists' challenge to the traditional order.
[4] The arguments were expanded in Patullo's *Essai sur l'amélioration des terres* (Paris, 1758) dedicated to Mme de Pompadour, and written in 1757, if not by Quesnay himself then certainly with a great deal of his input, it is now thought.
[5] On this, see, among other analyses, that of Jean-Claude Perrot, "La comptabilité des entreprises agricoles dans l'économie physiocratique" in *Une histoire intellectuelle*, pp. 217–36.

The entries did more than describe the current situation of farmers or of grain production. They also prescribed remedies. Quesnay called for greater investments in agriculture and demanded changes in governmental policy, such as free train in grain. In doing so, he adopted the parlance of political economy and the statistical methods developed by the English in the late seventeenth century known as "Political Arithmetic." He compared prices, reviewed the expenditures of farmers and sharecroppers, and calculated the type and extent of arable land in France. He also established a series of contrasts. On the one side we find the six million acres (*arpents*) of productive and prosperous large farms, run by tenant-farmers, ploughed with horses, using triennial crop rotation. On the other lie the thirty million acres of poorer small farms, many sharecropped, relying on oxen and biennial rotation.[6] Although covering less total acreage, the large farms produced the bulk of marketable cereals, especially wheat, and represented therefore both the breadbasket and fiscal hopes of the kingdom. Given this, the state must do all it can to support its farmers. It must rationalize taxation, free the grain trade from duties, tolls, and market controls, and encourage landowners to invest more in farming. Despite the common belief that physiocrats pushed for the clearance of wasteland, Quesnay, in fact, insisted that only certain soils were fit for wheat – and hence deserved sizable investments –whereas poorer soils might be reserved for minor crops or turned into pastures.

Quesnay's article on "Farmers (political economy)" is ten times the length of Charles-Georges Le Roy's companion piece on "Farmers (rural economy)," which offers a brief overview of farming techniques.[7] "Grains" (cereals) published in 1757 allowed Quesnay to revisit these questions in even greater depth. The data are ordered in yet another series of contrasts to great rhetorical effect. The activities of farmers are contrasted to those of artisans and merchants. Agriculture is truly productive, whereas industry and trade are "sterile"; the one yields the essentials of life, the second gets mired in useless luxury and frivolities. Lurking not

---

[6] Sizable farms, owned by absentee landlords, were leased as a block to well-to-do farmers usually for a nine-year term, which Quesnay compared unfavorably to far longer English leases. Sharecropping contracts in France were the resort of poor regions, where landlords advanced tools and seeds annually in return for 50 percent of the crop. See Jonathan Dewald and Liana Vardi, "The French Peasants, 1400–1789" in Tom Scott, ed., *The Peasantries of Europe* (London, 1998), pp. 20–47.

[7] "Fermiers [*économie rustique*]" in d'Alembert and Diderot, eds, *Encyclopédie ou Dictionnaire Raisonné des Sciences, des Arts et des Métiers*, vol. VI, pp. 527–8. Quesnay's article "Fermiers (économie politique)" followed pp. 528–40.

far from the surface is a contrast between "reason" and "imagination," each battling for supremacy. A misguided approach to wealth has endangered the French economy and risks destroying the kingdom completely. Population had already fallen from 24 million in 1650 to a mere 16 million a century later (Quesnay repeated this common misconception). True wealth did not rest on the export of luxury products and the accumulation of coin in the kingdom, but in land. In a final rhetorical touch, Quesnay attached names to these incompatible approaches. Henry IV's minister Sully (famed for "putting a chicken in every pot" and for engineering French reconstruction after the Wars of Religion) was a great supporter of agriculture and is the good guy, whereas Louis XIV's minister, Colbert, who brought the country to rack and ruin by his support of manufacture, is a very bad guy indeed.

Unlike medicine, where each body responded in its own unique fashion, Quesnay's analysis here rests on *aggregating, simplifying, and generalizing*.[8] Regions, soil types, and the peculiarities of each hill, dale, and farmstead are homogenized into prototypes. Ideal agricultural productivity, outlays, profits, and state revenue are compared to actual figures and are found sorely wanting. This is the final contrast: between what "is" and what "ought to be."

Through his new insights, Quesnay had satisfied himself that nature was far less volatile than his medical experience had suggested. Nature had a plan and an order, and if one tended to its needs through investment of effort and capital, it would yield its bounty despite caprices like hailstorms and other natural disasters.[9] This nature did not need to be pacified with prayers, offerings, and blood sacrifices. It responded to redoubled activity and could be turned into a sophisticated profit-oriented sector. The rules were simple: Invest more, consolidate large properties, use the best tools available. The reader's doubts about the efficacy of such measures were allayed.

Quesnay predicated his analysis on the price of cereals from one harvest to the next, although other crops were included in his calculations. But whenever he called for improvements in *agriculture*, he had cereals in mind, and it was their productivity and markets that he meant to secure. As Steven Kaplan has demonstrated, the economic centrality of cereals

---

[8] See also on this Catherine Larrère, "L'arithmétique des physiocrates: la mesure de l'évidence," *Histoire et mesure* 7:1 (1992), 5–24.
[9] Mirabeau expressed it thus: "The earth is a grateful mother, who returns, with interest, what is loaned to her, and in an infinite progression." *Tableau oeconomique et ses explications*, in Mirabeau, *L'Ami des hommes*, VI, p. 27.

made provisioning the prime political issue.[10] Quesnay was interested in cereals as the motor of wealth, but food itself or individual consumers were not his concern. His formula measured profits, not human outcomes. In theory, everyone's interests would be served through nature's munificence. This was no mere pious wish: in rendering Quesnay's ineffable inner vision, the *Tableau* reminded viewers that he was expressing Providence's plans.

## L'Ami des hommes

In looking for someone to disseminate his ideas to a broad public, Quesnay chanced on the marquis de Mirabeau's recently published *L'Ami des hommes*. The first limited edition of August 1756 had been followed by a more widely distributed version in 1757 that became an instant bestseller.[11] Even a cursory look at the three volumes demonstrates why Quesnay was intrigued by their author. A few examples should suffice. Mother nature wants to be respected and cared for (I, 63); agriculture is the primary activity and was honoured in early society but disdained ever since (I, 67); agriculture is not only the most necessary art, it is the most complex (I, 78), the most sociable, the noblest, the most hospitable and most generous (I, 80); the most useful (I, 82); to counter the flow of riches toward the cities and avoid wasteful luxury one should "cherish and love agriculture" (I, 157); one should praise the tillers of the field (I, 169); all orders and people in a State survive at the expense of the landowners (I, 183); wherever you find a happy and peaceful population, the countryside will be bright, populated, lush, brimming with fodder and animals (I, 257); prosperity leads to excess, riches lead to pride, luxury, refinement in the arts, neglect of public issues; the same obsession with artifice and novelty comes to infect all discourses (I, 279); everything must circulate or else the head becomes engorged (I, 286); we are heading to our doom with such policies (I, 296); free trade is key (I, 303); the king is the supreme authority, the three orders (the clergy, the military, the magistrates) are consultative, the duty of the rest is to work and obey (I, 352); our first resource is agriculture which provides all of our raw materials,

---

[10] This is the central contention of the work. Steven Kaplan, *Bread, Politics and Political Economy*.
[11] The first edition was published in Avignon, subsequent ones in Paris. The original edition had several runs in 1757. A revised edition followed in 1759 and additional volumes in 1760. Its twenty editions made an 80,000-livre profit. Louis de Loménie, *Les Mirabeau*, I, pp. 338–9.

the second is labour (I, p. 361); man is born only to work, reproduce, suffer and die (I, 379); social bonds show us how much we depend on each other (I, p.380). Books II and III continue in the same vein. We should remember that such sentiments, however resonant of Quesnay's own views, did *not* make Mirabeau a "physiocrat" in Quesnay's mold, *as yet*. The work not only lacked Quesnay's analysis of the reproduction of wealth, its celebration of the countryside was subsumed within a larger moral project.

Although Mirabeau looked to a moral reform of the kingdom, he only addressed this directly in Chapter IV of Book II because, as he put it, he meant to impress on his readers that everything began with man's physical needs. Mores were nonetheless of utmost significance because they were the mirror of a society as well as its foundation (*ressort*), as "the mothers, the tutors and the protectors of the Laws."[12] Within a revitalized body politic, local self-management and sound agricultural policies would secure the nation's economic welfare – for throughout the work, Mirabeau calls on the French government to "support and honour" agriculture to stimulate population growth (the source of national power), something he deemed impossible under the existing system. Free trade and improved husbandry would strengthen France's economy, but the nation must also address its moral woes. The remedy lay in emulation and the king must set an example by granting deserving subjects marks of prestige and recognition rather than rewarding them with pensions.[13] Handouts created a vicious cycle of competition, ultimately ruining the state through unbridled luxury.[14] "Let me attempt, therefore, to define luxury – without condemning all expenditures – in more cumbersome yet more accurate way as ... *excessive wealth.*"[15]

Emulation would stimulate sociability and counter a natural bent toward cupidity.[16] In florid tones, Mirabeau exhorted his readers to "love

---

[12] Mirabeau, *L'Ami des hommes*, II, p. 141. In all three cases, the reference is feminine in the original.

[13] Ibid., II, pp. 120–3.

[14] Ibid., II, pp. 259–60, 263, 268.

[15] Ibid., II, p. 246. "Let us define luxury without proscribing expenditures, more precisely as the abuse of wealth." To stimulate virtue, government had to oversee mores more closely (II, p. 141). For a full analysis of Mirabeau's views on luxury, see Kwass, "Consumption and the World of Ideas."

[16] See Sonenscher, *Before the Deluge*, pp. 194–6; Smith, *Nobility Reimagined*, pp. 90–9, and Michael Kwass, "Economies of Consumption: Political Economy and Noble Display in Eighteenth-Century France" in Jay M. Smith, ed., *The French Nobility in the Eighteenth Century, Reassessments and New Approaches* (University Park, Pa., 2006), pp. 19–41, 29.

each other. Religion, virtue, honour, true philosophy, all laws, arts and sciences work to this end and display it in turn."[17] An entire moral system had to be built to ensure human cooperation. The nation's mores had been corrupted and would be regenerated by the nobility's selfless service and the self-restraint and performance of their duties by all members of society. In granting the nobility this role, like Vauvenargues and other eighteenth-century aristocratic apologists in the mold of Boulainvilliers, Mirabeau stressed their honor and disinterest.[18] He went even further by endorsing traditional feudal arrangements.[19]

What harm to commerce if fiefs remain in the hands of noble lineages [*dans les races*]? I have already explained how this perpetuates old dynasties [*vieilles souches*] by encouraging younger sons to marry, and a spirit of subordination and unity among the rural population by inspiring its age-old respect for seigneurial bloodlines, and by encouraging landholding in families and munificence in those most likely to be led by family example to earn the gratitude of the nation [*patrie*].[20]

The nobleman must be "proud, brave, poor, and glad of it"; the magistrate "serious, just, austere, prudent, and glad of it"; the merchant "hard-working, enterprising, honest, independent, simple, and proud of it"; the artisan "industrious, vigilant, of sound morals, and restrained in his consumption [*borné dans sa consommation*]"; the farmer "that most precious of men," "tireless, honoured, loved, protected, aided, encouraged so that other envy his happiness, freedom, joy, peace, and the stern patriarchal morality that only exists in the countryside."[21] Every order, class, or group in society was confined to its own sphere and immutable role. Luxury's most damaging effect was indeed to blur social distinctions.[22] Mirabeau's reification of social groups bore a vague resemblance to Quesnay's distinctions between "landowners, farmers, and artisans" but went deeper insofar as he presented them as essences rather than division of labor. Despite this static social hierarchy, everything else in the

---

[17] Mirabeau, *L'Ami des hommes*, III, p. 516.
[18] See Smith, *Nobility Reimagined*, pp. 98–9. Cubells, *La Provence des Lumières*, pp. 98–104, shows how the Provençal nobility shared this outlook; Paul H. Beik, *A Judgment of the Old Regime* (New York, 1944), pp. 83, 107–8.
[19] Mirabeau, *L'Ami des hommes*, I, p. 217.
[20] Ibid., I, pp. 231–2.
[21] Ibid., I, pp. 248–9.
[22] See Mirabeau's manuscript "Sisteme politique sur l'intérest présent de la France," M 783/1, section on Luxury. The document is undated, but Théré et al. *Oeuvres économiques complètes et autres textes par François Quesnay* date it to 1748–9 (II, p. 1254).

kingdom must circulate: goods, political power, news, virtue. Resources must move to and from outlying regions and Paris should not develop at the expense of the periphery.[23]

Like his earlier work, *L'Ami des hommes* contained long digressions from the main points as Mirabeau himself admitted in the preface, "apologizing" for his lack of discipline. But the anecdotes were amusing; Mirabeau conveyed his basic sympathy for his fellow man, and sometimes managed the catchy phrase. "What is wealth? It is the possession of earthly goods achieved through social collaboration and never through greed. Necessity, abundance and superfluity are to goods what the positive, the comparative, and the superlative are to grammar."[24] He did not have the breadth or acuity of a Montesquieu or Rousseau but he established a chatty rapport with his readers that put them at ease, and readers responded by the thousands.[25] All in all he sent an engagingly positive message: The French were inherently virtuous, hardworking, and sociable. Something has gone awry but remedies were readily at hand since the "foundations remained sound." This sanguine line of argument goes a long way to explain the popularity of the text. Unlike the alarmists that surrounded him, Mirabeau offered a seemingly attainable level of "virtue," one that already existed "deep down" within his readers. Indeed, except for occasional testiness, Mirabeau continued to believe that man was perfectible. His sermons were built on that supposition.[26] In later years, he would compose a series of portraits of worthies such as Sully, Fénelon, and Boisguilbert to encourage public spirit.[27]

Quesnay too sought regeneration for the kingdom, but he had no special commitment to the nobility and was more interested in getting

---

[23] Mirabeau acknowledged his debt to Cantillon's notion of circulation. See also P. Chanier, "Le Dilemme de Mirabeau: Cantillon ou Quesnay?," pp. 23–35, and Jean Ehrard, "'L'Ami des hommes', Paris et la capitale du royaume," pp. 37–43, in Albert Soboul, ed., *Les Mirabeau et leur temps. Actes du Colloque d'Aix-en-Provence* (Paris, 1968).

[24] Mirabeau, *L'Ami des hommes*, I, p. 15.

[25] See for example the Marquis' response to a fan in 1757 in AN M784/21.

[26] Ibid., pp. iii–iv.

[27] Quesnay suggested this to him as early as summer 1760. See Letter from Quesnay, n.d., in Quesnay, *Oeuvres économiques complètes et autres textes*, II, 1189. See also Mirabeau's letter to Carl Friedrich von Baden, 20 August 1772, in Knies, *Carl Friedrichs von Baden*, I, p. 65. Catherine Jacques suggested that Mirabeau found his voice in such praise of great men. "Pratiques mondaines au travers de textes inédits" les "Assemblées économiques du Marquis de Mirabeau (1770–1777)," paper presented at the international conference on Quesnay, Versailles, 1994. I thank Loïc Charles for sending me a copy of this unpublished paper. Drafts of his planned *Éloges* of Fénelon and the abbé de Saint-Pierre can be found at the AN M783/7, F12 1096/5.

landowners to see the value of agricultural investments and to control their expenditures. His "agrarian capitalism" was not freewheeling, however. The physiocratic system rested on the proper allocation and circulation of resources, and a preordained pattern of consumption which presumed that the population was imbued with the right values.[28] A fixed percentage of profits had to be returned in the form of rent to landowners and they, in turn, had to allocate a certain portion to the state (as a tax on land). The sovereign and his magistrates monitored the overall outcomes, but success depended on the participation of the laity and its conscious abstinence. Mirabeau expressed this necessity to the Margrave of Baden: "My awareness and understanding that this pattern had to be universal led me to state and repeat many times in my *Letters on legislation*, that in order to ensure that a single field would be ploughed in perpetuity, the entire world would have to be converted."[29]

The stress on moral virtue that Mirabeau shared with other aristocratic reformers of his day could therefore mesh with Quesnay's demand that landowners, and the rest of the population, grasp that salvation for themselves and society lay in reproducing the "net product." In both versions, the public, high and low, was urged to look inward to tap their better qualities. Quesnay's system, as Michael Sonenscher concludes, offered Mirabeau the best possibility of regenerating the moral order.[30] But, for that, he had to adopt Quesnay's scientific approach.

Quesnay, meanwhile, had to confront the problem that Mirabeau was not as committed to economics as he was. The *Bailli* reported to his brother that Quesnay had told him when they met "that you must deepen your knowledge of agriculture so that you can then explain its principles."[31] Quesnay had to set Mirabeau straight about the origins of wealth and convince him that championing provincial estates (as he had been doing) was less important than obeying the simple dictates of nature. An additional hurdle was that the Marquis had no head for mathematics and felt that too many figures overwhelmed readers. One thus reads in *L'Ami des hommes* that "the author of the *Réflexions politiques sur les Finances et le Commerce* [Dutot] ... reasons too mathematically.

---

[28] *Leçons économiques* (Amsterdam, 1769), pp. 156–7 on proper and improper spending.
[29] Letter of 9 June 1774 in Carl Knies, *Carl Friedrichs von Baden*, I, p. 83.
[30] Sonenscher, *Before the Deluge*, p. 216.
[31] Loménie, *Les Mirabeau* (Paris, 1879), I, p. 231. Letter from the chevalier de Mirabeau to his brother the marquis of 31 July 1757. "I dined yesterday with your conquest (Quesnay) who is full of wit (*esprit*).... He said you should expand the chapter on agriculture and show from what it springs."

This very fine work, drowned me in its millions and billions until they swam before my eyes; my brain seemed to be dining with King Midas the day when he first realized he could turn everything into gold," adding "This is what I call politics overly dependent on the science of numbers, as if the earth were a field sown with *livres, sols, and deniers* whose harvest one appropriated as one extended its empire."[32]

Quesnay had to bring him round. Years later, explaining his conversion to Rousseau, Mirabeau remarked that Quesnay had not yet created the *Tableau* when they met, which was a lucky break, because Quesnay would have made him study it, "sensing its importance and utility the way Genesis tells us that God saw the beauty of his creations" and this would have turned him off since he hated mathematics and balked at the required technical operations. Quesnay had no alternative but to explain his system, "or, more correctly, nature's" more fully.[33]

After their meeting, Quesnay encouraged Mirabeau to enter the Bern Agricultural Society essay competition.[34] Focus on the *Tableau* followed and, even if he did not understand its mathematics, Mirabeau was certainly up to the task of describing the various states of disequilibrium into which the *Tableau* might fall if expenditures were misdirected.[35] Repetition would become common, and Quesnay explained why: "You will be aware that we are basically saying here what we have said elsewhere; but we say it more explicitly; present it from different perspectives; tie it to different variables which enhance the description, and this involves reworking it. On the scientific side, these different versions will display the essence from different perspectives and make readers cogitate as they work through them until they clear all the cobwebs [*leur tête se débrouille*]: this is why sciences are slow to spread."[36]

It was only once Mirabeau was on board that the public received lengthier explanations of the doctrine. This was the role that Quesnay had assigned him. Mirabeau certainly had his heart in the right place, especially once he bowed to Quesnay's brilliance. On the other hand, he was unable to challenge, or even refine, any of the *Tableau*'s features, and

---

[32] Mirabeau, *L'Ami des hommes*, II, pp. 68–9.
[33] *Correspondance complète*, XXXIII, letter from Mirabeau, 30 July 1767, pp. 256–64.
[34] Published as part V of *L'Ami des hommes* in 1760. On the role of physiocrats in such agronomic essay competitions, see Jeremy Caradonna, "The Enlightenment in Question: Academic Prize Competitions (concours académiques) and the Francophone Republic of Letters 1670–1794," PhD. Diss., Johns Hopkins, 2007, pp. 326–30.
[35] *Tableau économique et ses explications* in *L'Ami des hommes*, VI, part II, pp. 98–9.
[36] A.N., M 784/41, letter from Mirabeau to Quesnay and Quesnay's response in the margins, Paris, 13 June 1761.

while Quesnay expected this acquiescence, it did the doctrine no good. Mirabeau was reduced to pointing out the "elemental truths" depicted in the *Tableau*, explaining its principles and consequences, but not its mathematical underpinnings, underlining thereby the obscurities he could not decipher.

As a consequence, the *Tableau*'s exegesis came accompanied with normative guidance on how to approach the *diagram*: Initially, the eye will absorb the entire image. "You will grasp it quickly or, rather, you will think you have grasped it."[37] But "we would not have presented it so often, and with all its ramifications, if it could be appropriated at a single glance. Make the effort to read the entire explanation; rest assured that the more you read, the more its importance will become clear, and the better you will grasp its broad connections." In other words, true understanding would emerge from cognitive training. The more one read physiocratic texts, the more the mind would grow accustomed to the Economists' chain of reasoning. It would then be ready to pursue the evidence on its own and acknowledge its necessity in a final apotheosis.

Meanwhile, Quesnay's other associates regularly updated data on French economic performance in their various writings.[38] The base figures used in the *Tableau* rose with each new version, although the method and underlying principles remained the same (the farmers always reproduced the net product). Statistics were crucial to the *Tableau*'s "diagnostic" function, that is, its capacity to pinpoint overinvestment in industry or insufficient advances whenever the "zigzag" tipped in one direction. The physiocrats called this phenomenon "disequilibrium" rather than overspending, and this has led to false assumption that their system was "self-regulating."[39] The physiocrats utilized the statistics gathered by the French administration but would have preferred having at their fingertips assessments of "real" productivity through farm leases whose rising or falling values better expressed the farm's worth, once the necessary upkeep had been deducted. Quesnay encouraged his young follower, Pierre Samuel Du Pont, to gather farm accounts for the Intendant of Soissons in the mid-1760s, and he enlisted the services of the mathematician Charles de

---

[37] Mirabeau, *L'Ami des hommes*, VI, Part II, p. 13.
[38] See on this Christine Théré and Loïc Charles, "The Writing Workshop of François Quesnay and the Making of Physiocracy," *History of Political Economy* 40:1 (2008), 1–42.
[39] As explicated by uses of different out-of-kilter tableaux by Mirabeau in Part II of Book VI of *L'Ami des hommes*, "Tableaux économiques considérés dans leurs dépradations."

Butré to assist him in his own calculations.[40] The *Tableau* nonetheless remained the crucible for these appraisals:

> Hence to figure out precise relations in specific instances, it is enough to understand how the organization of expenditures represented in the *Tableau* might change, and then to calculate the results of the change, depending on the disruption whose effects one seeks to understand; the mathematical result will show the degree to which the overall amount increased or decreased, based on the effects of the change that has taken place.[41]

The message was that anyone doing the math would figure out that physiocracy corresponded to the natural order. Nonetheless, with Mirabeau in charge of the composition, God's plan and the moral benefits of a simple lifestyle surfaced repeatedly and this distinguished physiocratic discourse from "drier" scientific treatises and administrative memoirs of the times.[42]

## Writing Physiocracy

In 1759 Mirabeau was busy composing a treatise on monarchy to explain why it was the best – and most natural – of political systems.[43] Gino Longhitano, who recently published one of the many versions of the manuscript with Quesnay's comments, stresses that the resemblance between Mirabeau's agrarian philosophy and Quesnay's was superficial. They disagreed on fundamentals: Mirabeau wanted a monarchy that

---

[40] Butré helped Quesnay work out the figures in the tableaux in disequilibrium as well as the numbers he presented for various types of land, produce, taxation, etc. See Quesnay, *Oeuvres économiques complètes et autres textes*, I, pp. 394–5. So did François Véron de Forbonnais who was then *inspecteur général des monnaies* and author of *Recherches sur les finances* (1758). The collaboration would be short-lived since Forbonnais was the foremost supporter of mercantilism. See "Lettres de Quesnay à Forbonnais," 1 and 14 September 1758, Quesnay, *Oeuvres économiques complètes et autres textes*, II, pp.1373–80.

[41] The guiding principle is expressed in *Second Problème Economique* published in Du Pont's *La Physiocratie ou constitution essentielle du gouvernement le plus avantageux au genre humain* (Leiden, 1767) in Quesnay, *Oeuvres économiques complètes et autres textes*, I, pp. 619–35, 622.

[42] See the work on the Gournay School by Loïc Charles and his collaborators, *Commerce, population et société autour de Vincent de Gournay, 1748–1758, La Genèse d'un vocabulaire des sciences sociales en France* (Conference held at INED, Paris, 19–21 February, 2004). Yves Citton remarks on the fairytale structure of the physiocratic narrative, op. cit., pp. 56–7.

[43] Gino Longhitano believes that Mirabeau had begun this work before meeting Quesnay and that this precipitated their encounter in July 1757. Mirabeau and Quesnay, *Traité de la monarchie*, ed. Gino Longhitano (Paris, 1999), p. xxxv.

maintained the hierarchical order of an agrarian, seigneurial society, whereas Quesnay looked to dismantle the corporate bodies that that "the state had inappropriately created and that interfered with the natural reproduction of wealth."[44] Quesnay demolished Mirabeau's position, point by point, so that Mirabeau had to abandon the project.

The evidence that survives at the French National Archives shows how Quesnay influenced the writing of Mirabeau's texts.[45] Quesnay proved a hard taskmaster: "The fundamental principles underlying this section have not been properly expressed. It meanders needlessly and is riddled with metaphors."[46] This was a frequent complaint.

The development of this chapter is convoluted and grueling for the reader: make your ideas more tangible. Familiar, concrete examples are a great help to abstract subject matter, and they force the author to develop his thoughts fully and to express them clearly. By examples I do not mean metaphors or allegories, but specific aspects of the overall topic; use examples that get to the heart of the matter. Be sure to be clear.[47]

Mirabeau did not always appreciate the Doctor's meddling.[48] In joining forces with him, Mirabeau was fully aware of what he offered the venerable doctor: "I sent him those whom I had won over by the brotherly warmth of my writings."[49] Quesnay was not without resenting this, and would occasionally jab at Mirabeau, mocking his *nom de plume*. Thus, while they were composing the *Théorie de l'impôt*, Quesnay urged Mirabeau once again to be brief. "There have been complaints about the cost of the last book, even complaints that the *Ami des hommes* had not

---

[44] Ibid., Longhitano, p. xxxv.
[45] A.N. M784/41 (Letter from Quesnay to Mirabeau 13 June 1761) also in Quesnay, *Oeuvres économiques complètes et autres textes*, II, pp. 761–4. Quesnay could be abstruse himself. He demonstrated his famed quick-wittedness in conversation rather than print as in his tussles over luxury with Controller general Bertin: "[Bertin] claims people argue that ... luxury cannot be harmful to a nation.... I said ... one must calculate. But isn't this calculation hazardous, he replied; this hazard, I responded, has ... served most admirably to predict eclipses. This clinched it and he asked me to measure different returns and expenses, in the same way one measures the deviations of eclipses, so that he might respond to the opposition he would encounter; and I promised him victory."
[46] Letter from Quesnay, AN, M784/70/3.
[47] Notes on the *Grand Tableau économique*, the original title of the *Philosophie rurale*, in M 782, in Georges Weulersse, *Les manuscrits économiques*, p. 82.
[48] Letter from Quesnay to Mirabeau, n.d. [end 1768–1769] where he apologizes for referring to Mirabeau as puerile.
[49] Mirabeau to Rousseau, from Saint-Maur, 30 July 1770, Rousseau, *Correspondance complète*, XXXIII, p. 264.

spared a thought for his readers' purse. It would be good if they did not feel the same this time."[50]

Since physiocracy was an apprenticeship not just in a particular economic system but also in a way of thinking – its texts were meant to induce proper reasoning – Quesnay demanded "clarity" above all.[51] In June 1761 Quesnay was therefore compelled to articulate distinctions that came naturally to him but were foreign to his acolyte:

Sciences can be both theoretical and practical. Speculative sciences are either true or hypothetical and the latter deserve our greatest contempt.... true speculative sciences, on the other hand, illuminate all the operations of the mind whether they deal with civil and political matters, or applied sciences and arts that demand clear precepts.[52]

He then divided human knowledge into broad categories, each of which was subdivided in turn. The major divisions were mathematics, physics, natural law, metaphysics, grammar, and history. The last category, embracing logic, rhetoric, and poetry, featured the arts and not sciences. The location of logic is highly significant since Quesnay demoted it to a variant of rhetoric (in Cartesian fashion he dismissed syllogistic reasoning as palaver). Grammar on the other deserved its own category (making Quesnay indeed the prototype of Foucault's classical mindset)[53]:

Grammar, which is the elaboration, enunciation, communication, and transmission of our ideas, is the science which scrutinizes, analyses, generalizes, specifies, combines, organizes, and copies ideas; ... without the expression and methodical ordering of ideas by means of elocution or writing, there would be no metaphysics, no ideas, no distinct knowledge of the operations of the mind; so that grammar is not just an art with rules and precepts, it is ... essential to the perfection of human intelligence, the medium for all other sciences, for the communication of ideas among men, their organization, and mutual instruction. Logic, rhetoric, and poetry are arts and not sciences because their aim is not knowledge but skillful reasoning and persuasive or agreable presentation.

---

[50] Comments on *La théorie de l'impôt* from M. 784, in Weulersse, *Le mouvement physiocratique en France*, pp. 72–3.

[51] A.N. M 784 (the correspondence with Mirabeau has been reproduced in Quesnay, *Oeuvres économiques complètes et autres textes*, II. The degree of success is reflected in Melchior Grimm's comments in February 1767: "M. Quesnay is not only naturally obscure, he is also obscure by dint of his system for he claims that truth should never be expressed clearly." And he adds a few lines later: "At bottom, Quesnay is a decided cynic." Grimm et al., *Correspondance littéraire*, VII, p. 235.

[52] M 784/41.

[53] Physiocracy is one of the examples that Foucault used to substantiate his hypothesis of a classical *episteme*. Foucault, *Les mots et les choses*, for example pp. 137–8.

The breakdown of disciplines that Quesnay outlined to Mirabeau differs form the tree of knowledge presented in the *Preliminary Discourse to the Encyclopedia* (1751) where d'Alembert placed logic under the heading of reason and subsumed grammar under logic.[54] Quesnay wrote d'Alembert that the Prospectus delighted him, praising "its depth of knowledge, organization, beautiful style, and freedom from prejudice."[55] What is more, "Truth, probability, and error are clearly differentiated, and the overall aim of the enterprise is presented in the most sagacious, advantageous, and pleasing manner." What distinguished Quesnay's overall approach from d'Alembert's was not just a different sorting of knowledge. The *Encyclopédie* might have possessed an overweening structure but it did not require a leap of faith. Its own categories were subverted by cross-references to other entries.[56] There was nothing playful about physiocracy.

Quesnay meant to distance physiocracy from the realms of fiction by keeping imagination firmly at bay.[57]

The beautiful, the sublime, the prodigious, the magnificent, the terrible, the pleasant, are ably deployed to astonish, shake, and overpower our imagination; the interesting, pathetic, virtuous, vicious, heroic, craven, tender, voluptuous, ambitious and violent passions are forcefully arrayed so as to touch and move our hearts, arouse our passions, inspire respect, contempt, love, hatred, fear, or bravery, to excite the most pleasant and most vivid emotions, or to cause disgust and horror. These acts of genius are meant only to affect and move our hearts, startle, captivate, fix, and govern our imaginations. As much as this faculty is valuable to orators, poets, painters, sculptors, and musicians, so it is harmful to philosophers, lawyers, doctors, and all those whose duties [*fonctions*] demand that they rigorously adhere to the most exact truth which is the hardest to discover with certitude and precision.[58]

Moving the heart, as we can see, served only to encourage the imagination, and Mirabeau had to bow to that proposition, although the extent to which his own inclinations could be stifled remains unclear. Thus, as we saw, he conceded that one could only redress "regrettable errors with mathematics, not moral philosophy."[59] Yet his observation to

---

[54] Jean Le Rond d'Alembert, *Preliminary Discourse to the Encyclopedia of Diderot* (Chicago and London, 1995), pp. 144–5.
[55] Letter from Quesnay to d'Alembert [November or December 1751], in Quesnay, *Oeuvres économiques complètes et autres textes*, II, p. 1165.
[56] See for example Jacques Proust, *Diderot et l'Encyclopédie* (Paris, 1967).
[57] Quesnay, *Essai physique sur l'oeconomie animale*, III, pp. 394–5.
[58] Ibid., pp. 394–5.
[59] M784/46, letter of 13 June 1761, see also Quesnay, *Oeuvres économiques complètes et autres textes*, I, p. 763.

Rousseau that "men are civilized first through their hearts and only later through their minds," kept alive the notion that people learned through "contagion," as emotions flowed from the artist to the audience, or one person to the next. For Quesnay, such interactions could only be superficial and ephemeral, incapable of transmitting truths that were the result of individual reflection. He therefore offered two strategies to ward off imagination in the dissemination of his doctrine. The mind must teach itself to reason, and his followers must adopt a strict terminology. Elegant variation had no place in texts that meant to convey precise concepts. Like the Academy of Sciences' guidelines regarding scientific illustrations, aesthetics should be set aside in the service of clarity.

Quesnay expected his followers to use the plain style in their writing and to define terms precisely: Everyday words like "net," "product," "advances," "productive," and "sterile" that he had chosen to express his economic ideas.[60] Critics pointed out the dreary repetitiveness of their texts. For physiocrats, this was the necessary starting point to imbibing the doctrine's logic, a form of spiritual exercise that reiterated basic tenets and put the mind into gear. Repetition, however, would also come to imbue their vocabulary with the same unquestioned "self-evidence" they conferred on their doctrine. Property is the obvious example: Physiocrats would treat it as an emanation of nature.

Be that as it may, words still failed to render Quesnay's ineffable vision. Physiocrats kept repeating that language could not properly translate his mental image.[61] The fundamental relations it displayed had come to Quesnay in a flash, and the only real way to understand his insights was through a similar vision. This entailed looking inward into one's psyche rather than outward to the world, and this contradiction would haunt the new "economic science."

---

[60] Du Pont, *The Autobiography of Du Pont de Nemours*, p. 272. Quesnay also disliked Cicero's brand of eloquence, which rested on "words" as opposed to Demosthenes who based his on "things." Du Pont disagreed with Quesnay and from the vantage point of 1792, went on to explain that "Thoughts are certainly the foundation of any good writing, as invention and drawing are to any good painting; but thoughts gain tremendously from being expressed with force, with elegance, with harmony."

[61] Mirabeau and Quesnay, *Philosophie rurale* (Paris, 1763), p. i. "A man imagined and explained the *tableau* which paints to the eye, the source, progress, and effects of circulation, and he made it the précis and basis of his economic science and the compass that must guide governments." Mirabeau described it on the next page as "a shaft of light that appears first confusedly to the soul, and is then nourished and developed by study."

Quesnay's followers were typical Enlightenment wordsmiths whose natural medium was language and not images.[62] No educated person in the eighteenth century could fail to be self-conscious about style. In fact, they thought incessantly about it. For if there was a great chain of being, so was there a great chain of writing and both were being rattled in the eighteenth century. Physiocrats, persuaded that they had discovered important truths, fiddled endlessly with ways to get them across. They could have used natural philosophy as a model, with its mix of practical data, logical demonstration, and divine commandment but, although they invoked Providence, they did not want to come across as naïve providentialists.[63] They were, after all, asking people to "open their minds" to nature, rather than their hearts, and this sounded as odd then as it does today, like asking people to "open their hearts to mathematics." In the eighteenth century, one might use one's mind to dissect natural phenomena, but nature's irreducible powers induced a sense of awe, an emotional disquiet, that demanded expressive language. Quesnay was asking his followers to describe agricultural productivity as precisely as possible while at the same time vaunting the immense forces of nature, forcing a mixture of genres without proper balance, so that their texts fell, as it were, into their own disequilibrium. They could not avoid flights of eloquence when addressing Providence or nature's fecundity. When this was not their natural medium, they courted ridicule, yet were reproached for their dryness when they did not. Quesnay occasionally conceded that point.[64]

Before he met Quesnay, Mirabeau saw himself guiding the nobility and the nation-at-large to regenerated mores and revived prosperity. He had painted seigneurs' relations with their peasants in the syrupy tones

---

[62] The one exception appears to be his son, who engraved the doctrine's tenets in later years much to Grimm's amusement. "Such a bright and altruistic project was recently carried out by Quesnay the Younger. He has commissioned a very beautiful panel festooned with garlands and vignettes illustrating the subject in question: the *Maximes générales du gouvernment agricole le plus avantageux au genre humain,* by M. Quesnay, of the Academy of Science.... This engraving is sold under glass and in a gilded frame at the Palais Royal and Tuileries." Grimm et al., *Correspondance littéraire*, XI, September 1775, p. 128.

[63] Most expressly they wished to avoid sounding like Abbé Noël-Antoine Pluche's *Spectacle de la nature*, 8 vols. (Paris, 1732–51).

[64] On rhetoric, see for example Fernand Hallyn, "Dialectique et rhétorique devant la 'nouvelle science' du XVIIe siècle," pp. 601–28, and Peter France, "Lumières, politesse, et énergie (1750–1775)," pp. 945–99, in Marc Fumaroli, ed. *Histoire de la rhétorique dans l'Europe moderne 1450–1950* (Paris, 1999). See also Norman Bryson on Diderot's thoughts on speech and images in *Word and Image, French Painting of the Ancien Régime* (Cambridge, 1981), pp. 179–80.

then in vogue, and sighed nostalgically at the touching harmony that had once reigned in the countryside.[65] Rural idylls had already been revived in modern garb, and rural society had been turned into the counterweight of a corrupt urban culture and decadent royal court, and therefore a source of spiritual renewal. Jean-Jacques Rousseau stated this most forcefully, but also argued that man's downfall could be traced to the invention of agriculture.[66] Quesnay and Mirabeau held the opposite view: Far from a disaster, agriculture had been man's salvation and would continue to confer benefits as long as man devoted his energies to proper cultivation and obeyed nature's dictates. "Natural laws" and "natural rights" predated society, but there had never been a "state of nature." Theirs was not a stagial theory of human development (from primitive hunter-gatherers to modern commercial societies).[67] Physiocrats only conceded two epochs: before the discovery of agriculture and after.[68] To be sure, the *économistes* believed that progress in science and philosophy had been necessary for humankind (or rather for Quesnay) to grasp, at last, nature's true message, but nature's message had always been there for man to see, and the Chinese had, so the physiocrats argued, heeded it from the first.[69]

Historical speculations were important to Mirabeau who was keen to naturalize class distinctions and therefore trace their roots to the dawn of human societies. He shared Rousseau's quasi-anthropological approach but rejected the Genevan's belief that social differences were the result of oppression.[70] Mirabeau imagined an original patriarchal community

---

[65] Jean Ehrard, *L'Idée de nature en France dans la première partie du XVIIIe siècle* (Paris, 1963), and other classic works such as Daniel Mornet, *Le sentiment de la nature en France de J.-J. Rousseau à Bernardin de Saint-Pierre* (Paris, 1907); Donald G. Charlton, *New Images of the Natural in France* (Cambridge, 1984); and Raymond Williams, *The Country and the City* (Oxford, 1975).

[66] Rousseau, *Discours sur les origines de l'inégalité parmi les hommes*, p. 73.

[67] See Jean-Marie Goulemot, *Le Règne de l'histoire, Discours historiques et révolutions XVIIe et XVIIIe siècles* (Paris, 1996).

[68] Florence Gauthier suggests that this could only have come from Le Mercier de la Rivière's experience as governor of Martinique (1759–1764) in "Le Mercier de la Rivière et les colonies d'Amérique," pp. 261–83, in *Revue française d'histoire des idées politiques*, 20:2 (2004), p. 276.

[69] See Quesnay, *Despotisme de la Chine* in Quesnay, *Oeuvres économiques complètes et autres texts*, II, pp. 1009–114. Guillaume-François Le Trosne, *De l'ordre social*, whose third discourse explained the ways in which so-called advanced societies had turned their backs on nature and the guidance it offered. In *Lettres sur la législation* (Bern, 1775), p. ii, Mirabeau argued that it took a genius like Quesnay to decide to research what men in all previous centuries had disdained, and to discover at last nature's true principles.

[70] See Jay Smith, *Nobility Reimagined*, p. 36, and Cubells, *La Provence des Lumières*, p. 103, on the aristocracy's recourse to the past.

formed through the union of Woman, the nurturer, and Man, the source of authority, from which social groups (orders, estates, classes) had emerged. Sons of the original patriarch had formed their own clans, giving birth to an aristocracy, and it was from their midst that rulers had chosen their warriors. Religion had arisen to explain nature's mysteries. More complex needs had given birth to specialized trades, and they had contributed to the general welfare as long as they did not abandon their original functions. Quesnay had queried this preordained specialization, but Mirabeau needed it to bolster his argument that provincial assemblies represented clearly demarcated social orders and interests. Monarchy too was naturalized as a logical emanation of male authority and "descent" from the first patriarch.[71] Quesnay had to point out, however, that while the existence of "sovereignty" might be divinely ordained, monarchy itself was but a form of such sovereignty and Mirabeau could not support divine monarchy in this way.[72]

These wrangles convinced Mirabeau to abandon the manuscript. A new project, *La théorie de l'impôt* redirected their energies to criticizing the fiscal system whose inequities they both lamented. The arguments came wrapped inside a moral discourse. The work opened with a long disquisition on virtue and natural justice. Justice was "the invincible, irresistible sentiment, embedded in our very being [*la pâte de notre existence*], that stirs from the very first bubble of the divine flame that warms our hearts and nourishes our souls, and whose vapors stimulate our minds."[73] Emulation, honor, and duty were vaunted in similarly purple prose and parallels abounded between the material and ethical realms: "virtue rests in adding to your treasury; vice in spending from it."[74] Everyone must learn to see his true self-interest [*avantage*], as God has intended. The kingdom's morals were its greatest asset.[75] Mirabeau could therefore conclude in his comments to Quesnay: "When we address behaviour [*moeurs*] in this chapter, as it pertains to our principles, the reader will be able to conclude quite easily that it is the most significant external manifestation [of our system] that speaks the most directly to our interior selves and that we treat, one might say, like mathematicians [*calculateurs*] in offering only first principles, relegating to moralists the laudable great task of backing them with the necessary sanction of the law."[76]

[71] Mirabeau and Quesnay, *Traité de la monarchie*, pp. 10–11.
[72] Ibid., p. 29.
[73] [Mirabeau and Quesnay], *La théorie de l'impôt* (Paris, 1760), p. 23.
[74] Ibid., p. 27.
[75] Ibid., pp. 3 and 10.
[76] AN M784 41.

Their next and final joint text, the *Philosophie rurale* (1763) followed the same pattern: Moral principles preceded the description of the natural order. This suited them both since Quesnay meant to entrench property rights within natural rights. Virtue and awareness of Nature's commands were gifts from God, ensuring that each generation would realize that its material well-being depended on the right moral choices.[77] The work closed with Mirabeau's call for "good bread and good conscience," tying economic prosperity explicitly to moral regeneration.[78] His *Leçons économiques* of 1769 offered similar moral and economic instruction. He explained to his target audience of "young readers" that God had created nature, and nature in turn had instituted a 'natural order' geared toward the nourishment and improvement of mankind.[79] "Man's main concern being his preservation, everyone's interest was the same as everyone else's, the interest of one is the interest of all"[80] Human beings shared a common purpose and, although brute instincts were powerful, "nature had bestowed intelligence and reason to our species" to enable us to overcome those baser impulses.[81]

Mirabeau had found his niche within the physiocratic project. Unable to do more than parrot its mathematical argumentation, he devoted himself to building physiocracy's moral edifice. The results were unfortunate for the doctrine. Since he could not challenge or fully explicate the *Tableau*, Mirabeau inflated the place of intuition and morality in physiocracy. In "Evidence," Quesnay had concluded that truly rational, enlightened human beings would sense God's higher purpose and know with utter certainty the right path to follow. Social conventions, religion, and laws existed merely to fortify this inner inkling of a "higher justice." Whereas Quesnay trusted in the power of self-evidence, Mirabeau, on the contrary, insisted that physiocratic ideas were extremely complicated. "We have come to this great truth [of the common interest of all classes] by following a long chain of principles and by looking very closely at their consequences. This is not within everyone's reach. This type of analysis is difficult and demanding because it challenges all our dearly held beliefs ... those we acquire from the cradle, through example and education. Still, the human understanding is clearly capable of grasping the true order."[82]

---

[77] [Mirabeau and Quesnay], *Philosophie rurale*, p. iii.
[78] Ibid., p. 412.
[79] Mirabeau, *Leçons économiques* (Amsterdam, 1769), pp. 156–7.
[80] Ibid., p. 188.
[81] Ibid., p. 190.
[82] Ibid., p. 202.

Quesnay and Mirabeau agreed that all individuals sought their self-preservation and safety and could be persuaded to follow their "deepest" self-interest. For the Doctor, however, human weakness endangered the natural order, and only reason could restrain disordered inclinations. Mirabeau, however, was interested in human motivations and granted people aspirations beyond their material well-being, including self-fulfillment which could be inspired by transcendental goals.[83] In his calls for (aristocratic) action, Mirabeau emphasized the double gratification of living up to one's personal and social potential.[84] Quesnay rarely addressed self-interest (of any sort), preferring to base his system on reason's highest capacities, but *Homo economicus* lurked in the shadows. Their views overlapped insofar as Mirabeau admired Quesnay's stoic principles and wished he could live up to them, and he too called on men to improve themselves by controlling their impulses. But he could not deny the strength of his own enthusiasms and the conflict between his impulses pervades his writings. Such wavering was most obvious in correspondence: "Believe me, my worthy friend, that I do not wish to make men's opinions any more indistinguishable than I would their features; but they must nonetheless share common traits," he told Longo.[85] Statements of this sort suggest that if physiocracy held out the possibility for an open exchange of ideas, as Jürgen Habermas argues it did,[86] it lay principally with the Marquis.

Yet by temperament, and as the self-appointed guardian and chief disseminator of the system, Mirabeau opted for a lofty mode of address, dispensing wisdom to his less-enlightened brethren. He meant to convey the grandeur of the project and the literary sublime, with its high-flown rhetoric, was the most obvious candidate. The *Tableau* "in its very simplicity" was itself a manifestation of the sublime, according to Mirabeau.[87]

---

[83] Philippe Steiner in his introduction to a special issue on physiocrats of *Revue française d'histoire des idées politiques*, 20:2 (2004), 228, states the physiocrats' political theory was based on an utilitarian anthropology resting principally on material self-interest.

[84] Michael Sonenscher argues that contemporaries viewed the physiocrats above all as moralists, which would have pleased Mirabeau but not Quesnay. *Before the Deluge*, p. 190. See also Marisa Linton, *The Politics of Virtue in Enlightenment France* (New York, 2001), pp. 8–16.

[85] Letter to Longo, 31 March 1778, in Lucas de Montigny, *Mémoires biographiques*, III, p. 406.

[86] Jürgen Habermas, *The Structural Transformation of the Public Sphere* (Cambridge, Mass., 1991), p. 99.

[87] Mirabeau, *Lettres sur la législation ou l'ordre dépravé, rétabli et perpétué, par l'Ami des hommes* (Bern, 1775), p. xliii.

Yet its rendition in language, despite Mirabeau's desire to let the "science" speak,[88] tended to the grandiloquent, tripping Mirabeau up. As he himself recognized, his vocabulary grew more archaic.[89] The ease that he had displayed in marrying morality and political economy in L'Ami des hommes vanished. Once again, he explained himself to Longo:

Despite my disordered style, strewn with symbolism and metaphors, my taste for proverbs and archaisms [*marotismes*], my penchant for neologisms, and all of my rustic jargon, one can glean some useful truths here and there, indeed the kind of truth we get from God and that is a sign of distinction. What is more, I have never claimed nor do I pretend to be a universal spokesman or to compete with the trumpets of judgment. Let everyone follow my example and speak to and address his fellows as best he can and enlightenment is sure to follow.[90]

Perhaps for these reasons, the Doctor had always insisted on the inclusion of the *Tableau* and of detailed explanations of its fiscal consequences in their "joint" texts such as *La théorie de l'impôt* of 1760 (although only Mirabeau would pay the price of brief imprisonment).[91] Even if most readers would merely glance at the figures and "think themselves awfully clever," educated policymakers would be able to reflect at length on their data.

Those who examine matters seriously and like to dig deeper will not stop there; they will take apart, check, and recombine the findings of our complex science. It is for them that we labour because they are the true guardians and true apostles of the sciences; the true custodians of learning; other readers, who only seek amusement and fodder for their meaningless babble, are not my concern since they have no power in society.... Scientific texts that contain mathematical proofs have the longest life and are reread the most if they properly fulfill their purpose,

---

[88] See his aforementioned letter to Quesnay of 13 June 1761. "Morality will not redress these destructive mistakes; only calculation, the endless renewal of riches and needs."

[89] He acknowledged the convoluted nature of is writing on more than one occasion. See for example the letter to Marquis Longo of 28 August 1777, cited in Lucas de Montigny, *Mémoires biographiques*, III, pp. 135–7.

[90] Letter to Longo, Paris, 28 August 1778, in Lucas de Montigny *Mémoires biographiques*, III, Appendix 2, pp. 446–7.

[91] On the composition of the text see Quesnay's letter to Mirabeau, n.d. [end 1760], Quesnay, *Oeuvres économiques complètes et autres textes*, pp. 1206–9. On Mirabeau's imprisonment see BN, manuscrits occidentaux, nouvelles acquisitions françaises, No. 3348, folios 218–46. The dossier includes letters from the duc de Nivernais to Malesherbes (15 and 17 December 1760). In the first he explains that he told Mirabeau to go to Versailles to plead his case with the duc de Choiseul and Mme de Pompadour; and in the second that he had done his duty as a friend and arranged for a temporary exile. There are also letters from the lieutenant of police Sartine to Malesherbes, 27 December 1760 and 2 February 1761.

because one has to dip into them to refresh one's memory, given that it is difficult to remember all the calculations involved in sciences where computation is always key and its most precious educational legacy.

How could one demonstrate to landowners that they would not lose by becoming the kingdom's sole taxpayers without such calculations? Quesnay had to remind Mirabeau – yet again – that no science worthy of the name dismisses mathematics. "Without it, we would be mired in confusion, opinions, errors, and baneful practices. Reconcile yourself to calculations," he urged his collaborator, "they are your guardian angels. They are the ultimate judges of men's monetary interests, and they must find pride of place in your volume, although they can be relegated to the end of chapters.... On the other hand, do not place them at the end of the volume. The reader would not be able to make sense of the different parts of the tableau [that we are describing]." He also reminds Mirabeau of his special task: "I have worked as hard as I could on the calculations because they are the essence [*l'extrait décisif*] and the *compendium* of this science, they show the logic [*le raisonnement*] behind the mysteries; you are far better suited to do this than I who only care about the results."[92] But *La théorie de l'impôt* bore Mirabeau's distinct *imprimatur*, and one has the sneaking suspicion that Quesnay knew that if he let him invoke honor, emulation, and duty, as was his wont, there would be no doubts that Mirabeau was the author.

### Beyond the Tableau

Let each man explain the *Tableau économique* to his class; for by doing so he will have participated in the holiest and most important endeavour here below.[93]

By the late 1760s, focus on the *Tableau* was not winning as many converts to the doctrine as physiocrats had hoped. They therefore shifted to the promotion of agrarian reform and to touting principles that would facilitate the adoption of their "natural order" at some future juncture. The *Tableau* still appeared in the collection of the movement's foundational texts, *Physiocratie* (1768), although Quesnay had by then altered the zigzag to a more complex *formule* that depicted more facets of economic

---

[92] Letter to Mirabeau, n.d. [end 1760], Quesnay, *Oeuvres économiques complètes et autres textes*, II, p. 1209.
[93] Ibid., p. xxiii.

exchange, without clarifying its calculations.[94] In his introduction, Du Pont de Nemours reduced the enterprise to simple precepts: (1) man's natural rights, (2) the natural order of society, and (3) the natural laws "most beneficial to men organized in societies." The three variables were intimately linked, he added, and could not be understood independently.[95] They constituted *the natural laws of the social order*. Man had a fundamental right to self-preservation and instituted laws to that end, "secured by reflection, judgment, moral and physical arithmetic, and by the proper calculation [*calcul évident*] of where his real interests lay." Preservation of our lives and that of the species must follow "the pattern mapped out by Nature herself to ensure the welfare of mankind on this earth. The Creator fashioned the useful workings of our minds to this end." As Du Pont went on to explain, properly run human societies upheld property rights and secured the reproduction of foodstuffs – in other words adhering to those very laws that physiocrats had "rediscovered" – and the reader who had followed him thus far might well wonder why he was preaching at so primitive a level. Du Pont reduced physiocracy to a natural law, "those truths perceived by Quesnay, the author of the texts I have assembled in this volume, and that everyone should rediscover. This law is so basic that we find traces of it lodged in our minds. Physiocracy would spread once the sovereign laws that it expresses have been properly understood and men have yielded to its evidence."[96] This version still required readers to look inward to tap into their cognitive processes in order to perceive evident truths, but they need not contemplate the *Tableau*.

Du Pont claimed to be addressing legislators and citizens.[97] It was they who must understand the importance of physiocratic doctrine but, even more, its necessity. But, should the nation's leaders fail to rid themselves of ingrained prejudices, the public at least would be enlightened. For it now appeared that the human mind experienced blockages like the body (or society), so that physiocracy had to be distilled more simply and the population's minds habituated to its discourse. The order of argumentation was reversed: Once one understood the natural order, the *Tableau* itself would become self-evident. The visual and mathematical "proofs"

---

[94] As of 1766. See "Présentation du Tableau économique," p. 395, in Quesnay, *Oeuvres économiques complètes et autres textes*, I, p. 395.
[95] Du Pont, *La Physiocratie ou constitution essentielle du gouvernement le plus avantageux au genre humain* (Leiden and Paris, 1767), pp. ii–xx.
[96] Ibid., pp. lxxv–lxxvi.
[97] Ibid., pp. xcii–xciii.

were there for those who wished to examine them, but self-interest and natural law would now be invoked more frequently to persuade readers to endorse the natural order.

Rather than using Mirabeau, the most obviously politically engaged of his followers, Quesnay called on a new advocate, the Paris magistrate and former *intendant* of Martinique (from 1759 to 1764), a physiocratic convert and short-lived advisor to Catherine II, Pierre-Paul Le Mercier de la Rivière, to devise the movement's political theory.[98] In 1767, La Rivière published the key text of Physiocracy's "second period."[99] *L'Ordre naturel et essentiel des sociétés politiques* expanded the economic dynamics discovered by Quesnay to social and political institutions suited to the "natural order."[100] When Quesnay published *Le Despotisme de la Chine* in the *Ephémérides* in 1769, he adopted a similar approach in the same parlance, changing the tone and emphases of his earlier collaborations with Mirabeau.[101]

Le Mercier began with an unsentimental ascription of self-interest to all men, explaining that they were driven solely by the search for pleasure and avoidance of pain. The former *intendant* made clear from the outset that he was addressing rulers, although he would demonstrate in the process to all members of society how they would benefit from a "restoration of" the natural order. "It is not because men are gathered in society that they have mutual rights and duties; but it is because they naturally and *necessarily* have mutual rights and duties that they naturally and *necessarily* live in society. Moreover, those rights and duties which are absolutely necessary to the physical order constitute justice."[102] The right to property, especially landed property, arises from this, and a tutelary

---

[98] On Le Mercier's career, see Florence Gauthier, "Le Mercier de la Rivière et les colonies d'Amérique," pp. 261–83, and Eric Gojosso, "Le Mercier de la Rivière et l'établissement d'une hiérarchie normative. Entre droit nature et droit positif," *Revue Française d'histoire des idées politiques*, 20:2 (2004), 285–305. See also Georges Weulersse, *Le mouvement physiocratique en France*, I, p. 137. Like Rousseau and Mably, Le Mercier presented Poland with his plan for a new constitution in 1772 where he confirmed his physiocratic beliefs.

[99] Le Mercier de La Rivière, *L'Ordre naturel et essentiel des sociétés politiques* (London, 1767).

[100] Melchior Grimm was no more sympathetic to this work than to any other Physiocratic text, *Correspondance littéraire*, vol. VII (Paris, 1879), October 1767, pp. 445–7.

[101] *Ephémérides du citoyen*, March 1767, III, Part I, pp. 5–88; April 1767, IV, Part I, pp. 5–77; May 1767, V, Part I, pp. 5–61; June 1767, VI, Part I, pp. 5–75. The original draft of the essay with a different chapter organization can be found at the Hagley, W2-5678 which is included in Quesnay, *Oeuvres économiques complètes et autres textes*, II, pp. 1009–114.

[102] Le Mercier de la Rivière, *L'Ordre naturel et essentiel*, p. 24.

authority (*autorité tutélaire*) is necessary to guard property against theft or seizure. Physical needs reveal and dictate the *essential order* and "there is no better proof that the Author of Nature meant us to be happy than men's capacity to understand this natural order, nothing easier to grasp than the essential order of society or the immutable principles on which it is founded."[103] They are embodied in three types of property: personal, movable, and landed. All the features of the social order devolve *necessarily* and *obviously* from these fundamental principles; this evidence, in turn, must guide legislation.

Since society will be rebuilt around the natural order, legislation would consist of the simple, evident laws that such an order entails. Legislators, per se, would not be necessary. The sovereign would oversee the system and guarantee its perpetuation, while magistrates made certain that laws are obeyed and always accord with the natural order. The sovereign or "titular authority" had an even greater stake in this natural order than his subjects because his rights of "eminent domain" made him coowner of all land and thus entitled him to collect taxes from its produce. The system would be known as "legal despotism" since the ultimate authority would rest with the hereditary monarch, who was himself but the servant of nature. Different political arrangements would be inconceivable once everyone understood that this new order embodied nature's plan. La Rivière presumed that only an absolute monarch would agree to be bound by the laws of nature, proving that "legal despotism" was the only appropriate form of government. Under royal supervision, the natural order would perpetuate itself "through the mechanism whereby the same causes always produce the same results, and those results become causes in turn."[104]

Knowledge of these fundamental truths had to be conveyed to the common man who must be given access to physiocracy's "fundamental texts" (*textes doctrinaux*). He would be swayed by the evidence because the mind cannot refuse what it "sees so clearly," even if this might take a little time, and might even involve debate (*choc des opinions*). La Rivière was sure that evidence, meaning the ability to form clear and distinct ideas, would eventually dispel all errors.[105] Cognitive processes ensured this outcome, but he didn't devote much time to explaining them except

---

[103] Ibid., p. 40.
[104] Ibid., p. 55.
[105] Ibid., p. 72. Evidence is "a truth that thorough examination has rendered so certain, so manifest, that it is not possible for the human mind to have cause to doubt it, once it has grasped the reasons that led it to adopt it."

for repeating commonplaces about sensation. Yet dispersed here and there are reminders that the mind may not reign supreme. Thus, we *feel* within us a disposition to acquire and hold on to our goods.[106] By paying attention to our sensations, we are informed of our duties. Once we have accepted that evidence is true, we *feel* uplifted and shaken (*transports et secousses*) out of ourselves. We have reached, as he puts it, a "sublime understanding of justice and injustice," which conforms to the immutable, essential order or, put more simply, to universal reason. To sin against this law is to sin against God.[107] This does not correspond to a sublime flash of insight, but rather to the mind saying hurrah to itself, and then bowing to a higher authority.

The rest of the volume reaffirmed the physiocratic version of the creation of renewable wealth ("the entire social order is encapsulated in property, security, liberty"[108]) and called on physiocrats to begin the restoration of the natural order by disseminating their "evident truths." The work's organization is significant, moving from self-evidence to political structures and closing with physiocratic economics. The basic principles are presented as incontestable: Necessity and self-evidence are invoked right and left, with nothing to back them up besides an unflinching "logic." The argument is blunt, impossible to miss, and it is this version that affixed itself in the public's mind as the ultimate word on physiocracy.[109]

Mirabeau continued to disseminate his own simplified versions of the doctrine, as did Du Pont, now editor of the *Ephémérides du citoyen*.[110] But he was troubled by the new reductivism and reminded fellow-physiocrats, in 1774, just as Quesnay had reminded *him*, of the importance of the *Tableau*.[111]

The *Tableau économique* ... is a gift from heaven that we owe to the venerable Prometheus of the land, it is the necessary core of the science that several of our

---

[106] Ibid., p. 441.
[107] Ibid., p. 444. Both Saint Paul and Aristotle are cited as authorities here.
[108] Ibid., p. 448.
[109] See Weulersse, *Le mouvement physiocratique*, I, pp. 141–2 describes Diderot's (temporary) enthusiasm, when he deems Le Mercier "superior to Montesquieu," although he would soon change his tune and support Galiani's campaign against the physiocrats.
[110] See his letter of 12 May 1770 to Carl Ludwig of Baden describing *Leçons économiques* as a primer. Knies, *Carl Friedrichs von Baden*, I, p. 39. Knies divided the correspondence into three parts: Volume I contains Mirabeau's correspondence with Carl Friedrich; Volume II contains Part II, Du Pont's correspondence with Carl Friedrich, and Part III, paginated anew, with Carl Ludwig in the 1770s and Part IV, his correspondence with Carl Ludwig in the 1780s.
[111] Letter from Du Pont to Carl Ludwig of Baden, no date [1774] that includes Mirabeau's address to the Tuesday Economic Assembly, Knies, II, p. 324.

acolytes and perhaps some of our students consider as a useless hurdle, as long as they have accepted its principles and understood its consequences, but no one who has not grasped it or learned how to use it can be considered a true economist or even statesman. Without it our nephews would soon lose sight of this science and would regard us, to their loss, as just an edifying sect of modern-day Platonists.

He asserted this again a few months later, challenging anyone to understand the pivotal seventh chapter of *Philosophie rurale* without recourse to the visual model.[112] He was moreover troubled by his discovery that Charles de Butré, the trusted mathematician, was reexamining the relationship between Man and Nature in a distinctly non-physiocratic way.[113] The *Tableau* was clearly necessary to keep devotees in line.[114]

As Mirabeau watched the doctrine dissolve into separate strands in the 1770s, despite his physiocratic salon, a new awareness dawned that the realms of the imagination and reason had to be more clearly demarcated. In *Les Devoirs* (1780), he argued that to grasp the significance of "magnanimity" in human relations, and to absorb the notion fully, one had to turn to reason because "any feeling that is solely indebted to the imagination misleads us by its capacity to inflame us, ends up consuming itself, and is, for that very reason, evanescent, leaving us, or at least most of us, without guidance or resources." Therefore,

He would first explain the difference between feelings that arise from thought and those that arise from the imagination. I know that men of feeling [*hommes sensibles*] will tell me that true sentiments come from the heart, but, if no other organ is involved, I will call this an emotion. Feelings cannot last unless they engage the mind.

"Reason, above all reason," he insisted, "which is nothing but logical calculation, just like calculating is nothing but mathematical logic."[115] Yet he does not mean "esprit géométrique" but rather a mathematical turn of mind that is applied in all circumstances.[116] One might contrast this to his earlier contention, in *La théorie de l'impôt*, despite its touting of rationality, that "moral virtue should be treated as a thoughtful calculation that

---

[112] Mirabeau, *Lettres sur la législation*, p. xliii.
[113] Letter to Butré, Paris, 8 April 1779, in Knies, *Carl Friedrichs von Baden*, I, p. 112.
[114] Letter to Carl Ludwig of Baden, no date [1773], in Knies, *Carl Friedrichs von Baden*, II, p. 54. Du Pont turned Quesnay's article "Observations sur le droit naturel des hommes réunis en société," into the centerpiece of *Physiocratie* (Leiden and Paris, 1767–1768).
[115] Mirabeau, *Les Devoirs* (Milan, 1780), pp. 12–14. Religion, however, comes from the heart, p. 275.
[116] Ibid., p. 104.

prefers the enthusiasm that comes from doing good to the mechanical profit that shrewdness and aloofness hold out."[117] Quesnay would have been pleased with his progress.

## The Critics

In 1763 and 1764, resolved to encourage agricultural production, the French government passed edicts allowing the free circulation of grain inside the kingdom and even permitting exports in years of plenty. The improvements that Quesnay advocated converged with administrative plans to transform the economic landscape. Agriculture now featured prominently in political discourses and, with concrete measures to support it, physiocracy found its public but also resolute opponents.

The more tracts the *économistes* published, the more their peculiar use of language generated irritated barbs.[118] Mirabeau riposted that their terminology was necessary to habituate the mind to think clearly.[119] The financial expert Forbonnais attacked their theory *and* their vocabulary, but Quesnay refused to engage in real intellectual debate, merely responding with a defense of physiocratic terminology.[120]

The royal censor, Moreau, urged them to be more flexible: "you wish to address the public so do not scare them away with words.... Your science deserves to be widely known, so simplify your vocabulary and no one will attack your doctrine; some mock your expressions: render yourselves appealing to the multitude, and remind yourselves that if truth does not always rule the human race, it is always the fault of its ministers."[121]

---

[117] Mirabeau, *Théorie de l'impôt*, p. 10.
[118] Melchior Grimm was among their fiercest critics: "I wish their ideas were not so confused, that instead of ideas, they did not often present us with words that do not mean anything, and that they bothered or were able to think before they wrote and tried to indoctrinate us." Were this the case he would be ready to read their work, despite their "barbaric and apocalyptic style," but all he finds "at the end of a long and painful perusal is nothing but commonplaces which I have long known, delineated emphatically and often exaggerated beyond all bounds, or else vapid words without any meaning." *Correspondance littéraire*, volume VII, October 1767, p. 432. Not all reviews were critical, however. The *Journal Encyclopédique* of June 1770 endorsed Mirabeau's *Les Économiques* (Amsterdam, 1770) as a science "on which some have striven to throw disrepute because they did not know it; the enthusiasm of some others did perhaps greater harm." Vol. XXIX (Geneva, 1967), p. 442.
[119] Mirabeau, *Leçons économiques*, p. xiii.
[120] "Lettre de M. Alpha, maître-ès-arts, à l'auteur des *Ephémérides* sur le langage de la science économique" in *Ephémérides du citoyen*, October 1767. Quesnay, *Oeuvres économiques complètes et autres textes*, II, pp. 1116–32.
[121] Moreau, "Opinion d'un magistrat" Paris, 12 February 1770, in Mirabeau, *Leçons économiques* (Amsterdam, 1769), pp. lvi–lvii.

Voltaire poked fun at them in *L'homme aux quarante écus*, while the abbé Galiani famously lambasted them in entertaining dialogues on the grain trade, which took Paris by storm in 1770.[122] His *Bagarre*, circulated privately, parodied whole segments of Le Mercier de La Rivière's defense of freedom of the grain trade.[123] As we saw, Le Mercier was an easy target because each of his claims came accompanied with assurances of its "necessity" and "evidence," practically begging to be lampooned. Mirabeau remained unrepentant:

We have created the vocabulary for a language that is meant to be understood from one end of the planet to the other. We did this without changing any existing expressions, but only by defining and extending then to natural, universal, and necessary phenomena. This is the only service that we have rendered.[124]

He told his readers, moreover:

In the early days we focused our efforts on establishing truths that went against the grain, refuting widely accepted, harmful prejudices, which were not only believed but were even consecrated. We entered this combat armed at first with what seemed paradoxes; our ideas, despite the fact that they were simple and drawn from the unchanging, eternal order of nature, seemed to others so strange that we were even accused of creating a special language, whereas there isn't a single new word or meaning in our entire vocabulary.[125]

Of course, the more serious attacks extended to their economic and political ideas.[126] The abbé de Mably questioned the logic of the "natural and

---

[122] Voltaire, *L'Homme aux quarante écus* (Geneva, 1768); abbé Galiani, *Dialogues sur le commerce des blés* (London, 1770). The *Mercure de France* published an ecstatic review of the *Dialogues* in April 1770, Vol. XCIII (Geneva, 1971), p. 241.

[123] Le Mercier de la Rivière, *L'Intérêt général de l'Etat, ou la liberté du commerce des blés* (Amsterdam, 1770). Galiani's *L'Intérêt général de l'Etat ou la liberté des Bagarres* was circulated in manuscript soon after and has been published by Steven L. Kaplan as *La Bagarre, Galiani's "Lost" Parody* (The Hague, 1979). Dena Goodman sees the quarrel between the *économistes* and Galiani and his supporters as a turning point. The incident challenged their notions of friendship and of civil debates. The nastiness of the quarrel, she contends, rent the façade of unity and the belief in the dominance of polite discourse. Goodman, *The Republic of Letters*, Chapter 5.

[124] "Discours prononcé par Mirabeau à la rentrée des assemblées économiques, 4 décembre 1775" in M 780/6. Weulersse, *Les manuscrits économiques*, p. 128

[125] Mirabeau, *Leçons économiques*, p. xxxix.

[126] In a letter of November 1767 to Le Mercier de la Rivière who was then in Russia, Du Pont stated that Grimm, the abbé de Gua and a few others, unfortunately including the abbé Raynal remained opposed to the system, whereas Diderot, the baron d'Holbach, the abbé de Condillac and baron Gleischen continued to support it. Winterthur Mss, Group 2, Series A, W2-11. See on this also Yves Citton, *Portrait de l'économiste*, pp. 141-8, and Emma Rothshchild, *Economic Sentiments*, pp. 34-7.

## A Delicate Balance 143

essential order of society."[127] "What I find obscure may also not be sufficiently clear to other readers." The physiocratic order, he continued, was anything but natural. He saw instead a human construct resting on unjust discriminations that actually reversed the natural order.[128] In naturalizing agriculture, the Economists contended that Nature mandated laws and magistrates to protect harvests, whereas what they truly meant was that nature should display their own biases.[129] The lawyer and essayist Linguet, like Mably, accused the *économistes* of justifying inequality.

A ruthless heart dictates your doctrine, whatever its pretense to nobility and highmindedness. You mock human tragedy, telling the human race that it is a pity that it is experiencing hard times, but that, based on evidence, this is their lot; it claims that God has essentially decided that the few will have everything, and the remainder nothing; … all the while, you claim to love their fellow men, despite such strictures. [You] embrace the loved one simply to cut his throat.[130]

Jean-Jacques Rousseau was equally dismayed by La Rivière's book and expressed his reservations to Mirabeau who had thrust a volume of *L'Ordre naturel et essentiel des sociétés politiques* on this reluctant reader. After admitting that he had lacked the stamina to read it to the end, he addressed a number of physiocratic presuppositions.

I have never been able to understand the nature of the evidence which serves as the basis for legal despotism, and nothing seemed less evident to me than the chapter that dealt with all this evidence.… This evidence necessarily disappears once one considers particular governments which are composed of so many different elements. For the science of government is nothing more than the science of combinations, implementations, and exceptions, which vary according to time, place, and circumstances. The public can never see with evidence all the connections and the interplay of forces.… Even were we to concede that this theory of natural laws is perfectly obvious, including its implementation, and so clear that it is plain for all to see, how can philosophers who know the human heart grant this evidence so much power over men's actions, given their awareness that individuals very rarely heed reason and much more often follow their passions.[131]

---

[127] Gabriel Bonnot de Mably, *Doutes proposés aux philosophes économistes sur l'ordre naturel et essentiel des société politiques* in *Collection Complète des Oeuvres de l'Abbé de Mably*, 15 vols. (Paris, 1795), XI, p. 4.
[128] Ibid., pp. 10–11.
[129] Ibid., p. 26.
[130] Simon-Nicolas-Henri Linguet, *Réponse aux Docteurs modernes ou Apologie pour l'auteur de la théorie des loix et des lettres sur cette théorie, avec la réfutation du système des philosophes économistes*, 3 vols. (Paris, 1771), I, pp. 118–19.
[131] Rousseau to Mirabeau, 26 July 1767 in *Correspondance complète*, XXXIII, pp. 238–9.

He argued for the force of contingency and the great variety of human arrangements, berating the physiocrats for their delusions concerning human nature: "Gentlemen, permit me to inform you that you give too much weight to your calculations and not enough to the inclinations of the human heart and to the play of the passions. Your system is excellent for the residents of Utopia, but will not do for the sons of Adam."[132] Mirabeau denied Rousseau's allegation that the physiocrats had given in to the "esprit de système." Since all those accused in the eighteenth century of concocting rigid, deductive systems automatically denied it, this comes as no surprise. Mirabeau merely repeated that Nature was the source of physiocratic laws and that their purpose was to steer governments back to the rightful path and men to their best interests.

> Knowledge of the natural order could not emerge as the science that shows all other sciences to have been false ... until the discovery of the simplest truth in the world, that everything here on earth depends on the creation of a surplus product, which our master has called the *net product*.... All the physical and moral advantages of human society are contained in this one statement: *increasing the net product*; all the harm done to society comes down to this fact: a *decrease in the net product*. This means that we can set all laws, mores, customs, vices and virtues on a scale and weigh them; the *Tableau* calculates it all: everything that lowers the one hundred percent that must be produced as net product is harmful to society, all that increases it, adds to its prosperity.[133]

Mirabeau could have invoked self-interest against the passions, or pointed out that a few incorrigible souls did not threaten their overall system, or even that physiocrats did not meddle in private decisions as long as they caused no serious harm. Instead he, Le Mercier, and others touted physiocracy as the only viable system for mankind so that it would be foolish, if not suicidal, to reject it. The annual creation of the net product depended on *every single* human being performing his or her assigned task (even if these were gauged in aggregate). Ironically, the more their arguments on behalf of free trade, their opposition to corporative regulations, and their single-tax proposals found an echo within the higher administration, the more such reforms came to be associated in the public mind with the physiocratic movement, the less receptive the public became to their overall project to "institute the natural order."

The abbé Galiani had raised serious objections to the doctrine in the *Dialogues sur le commerce des blés*, through his mouthpiece, the

---

[132] Ibid., p. 240.
[133] Mirabeau to Rousseau in *Correspondance complète*, XXXIII, p. 258.

Chevalier. He sensed the danger in physiocrats' unwillingness to acknowledge differences or to lend any weight to circumstances and put to them the contrary proposition that no system could be applied universally: Countries, climates, and conditions varied too greatly, as Rousseau had similarly remarked. Of course, they had no satisfactory answer since their goal was to overcome such contingencies. Galiani insisted, moreover, that *equity* must enter into considerations of free trade. While mankind might (perhaps) benefit in the long run (as physiocrats argued) from a free market, it was unethical to subject present populations to the harsh effects of dearth. Rising grain prices in the wake of free trade in cereals had led to rioting in the streets by the late 1760s, and Galiani, like Linguet and Mably, blamed the penury on physiocratic ideas. They were not far wrong: Quesnay had warned Mirabeau against tender-heartedness toward merchants who found no outlets for their goods, and hence, by extension, toward the suffering masses. "Discuss the good of the nation, and do not decide where it lies by commiserating with French merchants.... Your reason has now been enlightened to the point where it is its judgment you must fear." Individuals did not matter; a soft heart was "counter-productive."

Although Galiani's attacks undermined the physiocrats' moral claims while amusing his readers, the greatest intellectual challenge to the doctrine came from the royal administrator and historian of French finances, Véron de Forbonnais, who had briefly collaborated with Quesnay.[134]

The normal run of readers is not always able to understand the physiocrats ... because the authors, overly preoccupied with what they have perceived most vividly, make little effort to organize and tie their ideas together.

The *Tableau*, Forbonnais conceded, demonstrates (in millions of livres) how agriculture multiplies capital investments and industry does not. Physiocrats would have been more persuasive had they shown how 600 million livres advanced to agriculture produced 1,200 million while the 300 million to industry produced no more than 300 million, rather than demonstrating how the so-called sterile class, just like the farmers, reproduced 100 percent, but were obliged to turn it over to the agrarian sector. The *Tableau*'s demonstrations supposed that all commodities were exchanged in the same manner, neglecting the variety of transactions and sales. The flows depicted in the model distorted commercial exchanges and these errors were then treated as dogma.[135]

---

[134] François Véron de Forbonnais, *Principes et observations oeconomiques* (Amsterdam, 1767), pp. 162–3.
[135] Ibid., pp. 177–9.

The *Tableau* was premised on "preposterous, untenable notions."[136] Forbonnais recommended a more critical methodology: "In order to avoid exaggeration and inaccurate calculations (which the imagination concocts from incomplete understanding), we should not shirk, when engaging in such speculations, from the examination of all the possibilities that bring us nearer to the truth."[137] The *Tableau* was an "obscure metaphysical construct and so is the doctrine that supports it."[138] He wondered: "Do they believe that they will only be understood if they exaggerate, or that an *obscure and scientific format* which is attached to some commonly accepted truths will suffice to entrench such figments of the imagination?"

Forbonnais remained a mercantilist and was not afraid to say so.[139] He opposed the *économistes* and touched a raw nerve: He treated their doctrine as a product of the imagination – the very response Quesnay had meant to prevent. For his very fears that ideas might be treated as chimera had been realized. Rather than convincing Forbonnais that he had created a scientific system, the system has been refuted and consigned to the realm of fantasy. The inexpressible *je ne sais quoi* behind the *Tableau* that physiocrats believed would make people think (and that did intrigue some, like Turgot) proved rebarbative to most. Quesnay responded to these criticisms in the *Ephémérides* stating that their positions were simply incommensurable.[140]

If the physiocrats' ponderous style incited ridicule, it wasn't for lack of thinking about writing. While reciting their mantras about the natural order, physiocrats struggled for the right formulations that would persuade readers of the truth of their doctrine. Melchior Grimm, who consistently challenged their ideas, berated them for making the obvious overly obvious, while shedding no light on what remained obscure:

I recall reading an entire work by these gentlemen, which was certainly no picnic, from which I gathered little beyond the necessity for capital investments for large-scale farming so that it yield big profits whereas small farms require only small

---

[136] Ibid., pp. 193–4. "qu'on a prétendu faire sortir du Tableau, en le fondant sur des notions affligeables quoique incroïables."

[137] Ibid., pp. 279–80.

[138] Ibid., p. 285.

[139] Ibid., p. 245.

[140] Quesnay, "Lettre de M. Alpha ... sur le langage de la science économique" in *Ephémérides du citoyen*, October 1767. Quesnay, *Oeuvres économiques complètes et autres textes*, II, pp. 1116–32. "Forbonnais confuses commerce and traffic and this leads him then to confuse and muddle his discussion of the effects of both commerce and traffic."

investments and return only small profits. Begging your pardon, I do believe that, although I do not have the honour of being affiliated with the Economists, I could have come up with this great truth all by myself, had anyone asked.[141]

He concluded sarcastically after perusing a pamphlet by the abbé Baudeau: "I have already stated that the net profit for the reader is zero and that the glory achieved by the author is also zero."[142]

Physiocracy thus advanced with the dual purpose of demonstrating the value of agriculture and of converting readers to the natural order. The two endeavors had been present from the start but melded together once transforming men's minds became an obsession, since it was the precondition to their seeing the light. Jean-Claude Perrot treats the physiocrats' diverse writings as a sign of the movement's struggle to find an appropriate voice. Steeped initially in humanist rhetoric, they inched their way toward a new scientific language.[143] Perrot adopts the position, therefore, that innovators fumble their way by trial and error before they eventually succeed, and he believes that physiocrats succeeded in turning economics into a science. The merit of this approach lies in its very close reading of physiocratic texts and the attention paid to nuances without which it is impossible to follow the movement's development. Yet rhetoric was not a tool in its kit, bending to its strong scientific content. The theory was prisoner to its rhetoric because persuading readers to accept this new "outlook" was the precondition for understanding it.

We get a very different perspective from Loïc Charles and Christine Théré's joint endeavor to depict physiocratic writing "workshops."[144] While the authors usefully cull information scattered in secondary texts and correspondence to offer lists of physiocratic collaborators, they less happily contrive to distinguish between a Versailles-based Quesnay model and a later, Paris-based, Mirabeau model. In this typology (and the tables that accompany it) the first group, clustered around the Doctor, were closely supervised, whereas the second rested primarily on the "papers" read at Mirabeau's Tuesdays. Although they purposely leave out analysis of the "content" in order to focus on the "structure" of these encounters, the ultimate goal is to demonstrate the existence of

---

[141] Grimm et al., *Correspondance littéraire*, VII, p. 432.
[142] Review of abbé Baudeau, *Exposition de la loi naturelle*, in the second October 1767 issue, p. 451.
[143] Perrot, "Economie politique," *Une histoire intellectuelle*, pp. 63–95.
[144] The latest chapter in this endeavor is Christine Théré and Loïc Charles, "From Versailles to Paris: The Creative Communities of the Physiocratic Movement," *History of Political Economy*, 43:1 (2011), 25–58.

a close-knit physiocratic movement. Unfortunately, the typology recalls twentieth-century higher education with, on the one hand, the French research institute "laboratory" model and, on the other, the University-style "seminar," more than eighteenth-century practices. It also blurs the boundaries between convinced physiocrats and those who contributed the odd text to the *Ephémérides* or who attended Mirabeau's Tuesday salon when they happened to be in Paris (for any number of reasons). Their *parti pris* is especially problematic in explaining physiocracy's ultimate failure. As Mirabeau himself put it to Count Carl Friedrik Scheffer, Swedish royal councilor and tutor to Gustav III, in a letter of 8 November 1772:

> Economic science was strongly contested at first and now merely finds itself thwarted [*contrariée*]. The number of true Economists is infinitely small, although without them the rest would be lost, and those who grasp the principles of this science in their entirety is very small indeed compared to the other blatherers [*babillards*].[145]

Physiocrats failed to focus exclusively on economic questions not because economics had not yet matured into a separate discipline, but because their system was predicated on self-evident axioms that could only be verified in the soul. Redoubled efforts to persuade the public that ultimate happiness rested on acceptance of the natural order reached its low-point with the elaboration of its political vision.

---

[145] Oswald Sirven, "Ur Markis de Mirabeau's Brev Till Greve Carl Fridrik Scheffer," *Lychnos*, 9 (1948), 51–84, 55.

# 5

# Representative Assemblies

The Marquis brought to his collaboration with Quesnay political goals and ambitions yet did not become the movement's political theorist. Instead it was Le Mercier de La Rivière and Quesnay himself who developed the theory of legal despotism as the appropriate expression of the natural order. The Doctor had striven for years to dissuade Mirabeau from attaching their new economic program to his personal political beliefs, and enthusiastically endorsed the muscular version of "legal despotism" put forward by his new favorite, La Rivière. Since the small body of core physiocrats were divided on the notion of representation, it is worth revisiting this question, which demonstrates, once more, the gulf between Quesnay and Mirabeau.

Mirabeau defended representative institutions, building on a well-established aristocratic critique of absolutism. Proponents of decentralization wished to restore the authority of the nobility and of the old system of estates and weaken the intrusions of the royal government which was spreading its tentacles through its envoys, the *intendants* who administered the provinces in its name. These criticisms had been at the heart of the reforms touted by the circle of advisors of the duc de Bourgogne, Louis XIV's heir presumptive, but all went to their grave in the hecatomb that befell the Court from 1711 to 1715.[1] A more radical position had been voiced by the marquis d'Argenson in his *Considérations sur le gouvernement ancien et présent de la France* of 1737 which circulated in manuscript

---

[1] The arguments for reform of the kingdom were summarized in the *Tables de Chaulnes* written by Fénelon and the duc de Chevreuse, 1711. The duc de Chevreuse died in 1711, Bourgogne in 1712, and Fénelon in 1715, followed later that year by Louis XIV.

and would be published in 1764 (posthumously). He proposed creating local assemblies to oversee local affairs while maintaining the oversight of the central government in the hopes of bolstering the flailing monarchy and counteracting aristocratic pretensions.[2] Mirabeau's criticisms were in line with the older tradition that sought to strengthen rather than weaken the second order. As historians have noted, Mirabeau's support of provincial assemblies, coming in the middle of a national crisis over taxation, stressed the fiscal advantages that the treasury would reap by reestablishing local governance.[3] Given the centrality of financial crises and of the rising national debt to the fate of the eighteenth-century monarchy, Mirabeau's ideas on fiscal responsibility and consent to taxation have attracted recent scholarly interest. But his solicitude for provincial estates was principally intended to increase the political clout of the nobility, even if it was presented as serving the fiscal interests of the monarchy. It is here that the ambiguities of Quesnay's project become most apparent. When choosing Mirabeau as ally and spokesman, Quesnay was fully aware of his determination to enhance the power of the second order, and yet he presumed that he could bring him to see the light on this as on other questions. But the fact that the one envisaged a kingdom led by a revitalized landed aristocracy whereas the other wanted an enlightened monarchy that privileged agriculture without a special role for nobles, impeded a cogent enunciation of the doctrine. Quesnay gradually eroded the Marquis's trust in representation, although in this, as on his other strongly held beliefs, he continually wavered, and this set him apart from Quesnay's other collaborators.[4]

Thus, scholars have found it difficult to reconcile the support for representative assemblies associated with Mirabeau, Le Trosne, and Du Pont (as of the mid-1770s) with the movement's equally strong rejection of representative bodies in the theory of legal despotism put forward by Quesnay and Le Mercier de la Rivière. They have therefore opted for one version over the other as physiocracy's official line, although more attention has been paid recently to the twists and turns in Mirabeau's positions.[5] Georges Weulersse had minimized Mirabeau's commitment to representation by reducing it to an expedient for efficient tax

---

[2] See Pierre Renouvin, *Les Assemblées provinciales de 1787. Origines, développement, résutats* (Paris, 1921), pp. 7–10.
[3] Ibid., pp. 11–15.
[4] Georges Weulersse, *Le mouvement physiocratique*, I, pp. 57–8.
[5] Renouvin offers once again a good example of this by focusing on Mirabeau's letters to the *Ephémérides* of 1767–8.

collection.⁶ For Antonella Alimento, the reversal in Mirabeau's thought occurred while he was composing the *Théorie de l'impôt* (1760) when he began to treat representative assemblies as the means to transform the existing system.⁷ Keith Baker has argued that physiocrats altered French political discourse by recasting sovereignty as the representation of "society" ("understood as an association of individuals engaged in the common production and enjoyment of economic and social values") thereby legitimating the representation of landowners over that of the traditional orders.⁸ To bolster this argument, Baker had to include Turgot and Condorcet among the physiocrats.⁹ Whatever position they have taken on this, scholars have had to brush aside internal divisions on representation itself to extract a single physiocratic political vision. Most recently, Manuela Albertone attempted this reconciliation by arguing that all shared similar assumptions about property as a natural right.¹⁰ I will stress, instead, how Quesnay marginalized Mirabeau's position and how a second generation of physiocrats revived it after the doctor's death.

In 1767 Quesnay endorsed Le Mercier de la Rivière's contempt toward representative assemblies as inherently disruptive. The year of the publication of *L'Ordre naturel et essentiel des sociétés politiques* he offered a similar description of legal despotism in *Le Despotisme de la Chine*, while Du Pont disseminated this version in the *Ephémérides* as the doctrine's political catechism. Sovereignty lay in an hereditary monarchy but the King, like everyone else in the state, had to obey the laws of the natural order to ensure human welfare. Political authority existed in order to secure the reproduction of basic resources and to protect property, yet by moments it sounded as if the very survival of humanity were at stake. Be that as it may, the ruler had legislative and executive duties to perform, while his subjects fulfilled their productive functions. All social organization rested – or ought to rest – around the continuing production of foodstuffs and raw materials and the profits that they engendered. This barebones understanding of economic productivity translated into

---

⁶ Weulersse, *Le mouvement physiocratique*, I, p. 43.
⁷ Antonella Alimento, "Tra fronda e fisiocrazia: il pensiero di Mirabeau sulle municipalità (1750-1757)," *Annali della Fondazione Luigi Enaudi*, XXII (1986), 97–141, 124–5.
⁸ Keith Michael Baker, "Representation," in Keith Baker, ed., *The French Revolution and the Creation of Modern Political Culture*, I, *The Political Culture of the Old Regime* (Oxford and New York, 1987), pp. 469–92, 482.
⁹ Ibid., pp. 481–3.
¹⁰ Manuela Albertone, "Fondements économiques de la réflexion du XVIIIe siècle, Autour de l'homme porteur de droits," *Clio@Themis*, 3 (2010), 25 pages.

a barebones political system whose sole purpose was to guarantee the annual reconstitution of the net product.

Whereas Montesquieu's *Spirit of the Laws* (1748) or Rousseau's *Social Contract* (1762) – despite their support, respectively, for mixed monarchy and republicanism – were cast as general speculations, there could be no doubt that Le Mercier's theory of legal despotism grew directly out of physiocracy. Whether "Nature" necessitated such a political order might be open to debate; whether physiocrats thought that this was the system appropriate to Nature's dictates did not appear to be in doubt. Mirabeau, however, could never bring himself to endorse it completely.

It is not my intention to revisit mid-century struggles between the monarchy, the sovereign courts, and provincial estates on which there is a distinguished scholarship, although I will allude to those conflicts that engaged physiocrats directly.[11] Mirabeau was wont in later years to complain of the ridicule heaped on him because of his collaboration with Quesnay,[12] and to take special pride in the continued popularity of his prephysiocratic texts *L'Ami des hommes* and essays on provincial estates. He had endorsed Quesnay's discoveries believing in their scientific soundness, trusting that they would add *gravitas* to his own projects. He had not expected to reject so many of his own ideas, that is beyond conceding that a nation's wealth rested on agricultural productivity not in its population, yet he sacrificed them time and again to Quesnay's higher logic. The place of the nobility in particular caused him much grief since Quesnay treated them merely as landowners (as Baker rightly maintains), whereas they remained charged for him with a special destiny. It was only in *Les Devoirs* (1780) that he finally acknowledged that the nobility was not a natural institution after all, and that merit should be rewarded instead, yet he also still insisted in letters to Marquis Longo that feudalism had had its uses.[13] By then, however, he confined himself to disseminating physiocracy in increasingly simpler form, referring to himself as the doctrine's chief "educator."[14] But as his son – the "famous

[11] A good place to start would be David Bell's *Lawyers and Citizens: The Making of a Political Elite in Old Regime France* (Oxford, 1994).
[12] See his letter to Carl Friedrich, 11 August 1776, in Knies, *Carl Friedrichs von Baden*, I, p. 96.
[13] Mirabeau, *Les Devoirs* (Milan, 1780), pp. 128, 132; Letter to Longo, 31 March 1778, in Lucas de Montigny, *Mémoires biographiques*, p. 406; in his letter of 3 November 1778 he offers his criticisms of "modern" nobility, III, p. 474.
[14] He explains this role, for example, in a letter to Carl Friedrich of Baden, 31 March 1770, in Knies, *Carl Friedrichs von Baden*, I, p. 22. See also his correspondence with Count Scheffer edited by Osvald Sirven (e.g., letter of 8 November 1772, pp. 57–60).

orator" – understood, the Marquis was first and foremost a political theorist, and hence a highly frustrated one.[15]

## Provincial Estates

In 1750, Mirabeau had crafted an anonymous pamphlet supporting provincial estates.[16] As he later explained in *L'Ami des hommes*, the publication of Montesquieu's *Esprit des lois* had galvanized him.[17] But there were also immediate reasons for his support of provincial estates: He was taking a stand on behalf of his friends and of his own order.[18] The widespread opposition to a new universal levy on revenue, the *vingtième* (5 percent), decreed in May 1749, had led the Controller general Machault d'Arnouville to abolish the fractious Languedoc estates later that year.[19] Few of France's provinces still possessed their old representative assemblies and Machault was determined to overcome the opposition of surviving privileged bodies (such as these provincial estates) and make everyone contribute his share to the treasury.[20] Under Louis XIV, a universal *capitation* (head tax) had been added to direct taxes (*tailles*) paid by the nonprivileged, and had become permanent in the eighteenth.[21] In 1710, moreover, a supplementary 10 percent tax on revenue had been collected to meet an especially grave economic crisis. It was abolished in 1717, reestablished in 1733 for four years, and again in 1741 during the war of Austrian Succession. In May 1749, it was abolished for good, the intention being to substitute a permanent peacetime 5 percent tax, the *vingtième*. Technically, the percentage reduction would have lowered taxation were it not for the systematic investigations of personal income

---

[15] Loménie offers a quotation from the comte de Mirabeau's letter to a friend in 1788: "I wanted to do justice to my father as a political philosopher," Loménie, *Les Mirabeau*, I, p. 345.

[16] *Mémoire concernant l'utilité des Etats provinciaux* (1750) followed by an expanded *Précis sur l'organisation ou mémoire sur les états provinciaux*, published seemingly in 1755, and reproduced with a long introduction in *L'Ami des hommes*, IV (Paris, 1757).

[17] Mirabeau, *L'Ami des hommes*, III, p. 408.

[18] Mirabeau, *Mémoire sur les états provinciaux* in *L'Ami des hommes*, IV, pp. 131–2.

[19] The Burgundy Estates did not meet until 1751 and the tax was levied there without opposition. See Julian Swann, *Provincial Power and Absolute Monarchy: The Estates General of Burgundy, 1666–1790* (Cambridge, 2003), p. 306.

[20] Joël Félix makes a very persuasive case that the vingtième ended up increasing inequalities. *Finances et politiques au siècle des Lumières* (Paris, 1999), pp. 64, 281. See also Riley, *The Seven Years War*, who argues that the effect was to increase tax evasion (p. 59).

[21] On revenues from the *capitation*, see Michael Kwass, *Privilege and the Politics of Taxation*, p. 72.

Machault insisted on.[22] Unlike previous versions, no *abonnements* (or fixed sums negotiated with the treasury by those provinces that still retained estates) would be allowed, nor would the privileged orders, such as the clergy, be entitled to contribute, as they had in the past, through a gracious donation (*don gratuit*). Revenues would be assessed by specially named government agents who answered to the royal provincial *intendants*, ensuring that everyone paid his rightful share and that the few provinces with estates would be brought into line with the rest of the kingdom. And indeed, as of 1715, so Michael Kwass demonstrates, universal taxes (*capitation*, *dixième* or *vingtième*) provided over half of direct state revenues, displacing the *taille*, which fell from 64.3 percent (in 1695) to 41.8 percent of overall intake (by 1789).[23]

The groups with the most to lose – the nobility, the clergy, and the provincial estates – remonstrated against these invasive measures.[24] Some prominent writers, like Voltaire, lent their pen in support of the embattled minister, eager to see the Church finally contribute its share. The Assembly of the Clergy, meeting that year, outraged at the attack on its special privilege to grant monies to the crown as it saw fit, denounced the tax.[25] The strongest opposition to the *vingtième* arose in Languedoc, a province where the diocese functioned as both civil and religious districts and where prelates controlled the provincial estates.[26]

Mirabeau's friend Jean-Jacques Le Franc de Pompignan, magistrate at the Montauban *cour des aides*, and his brother the prelate Jean-Georges Le Franc de Pompignan, were actively involved in combating the new tax. The *cour des aides* oversaw the land registers on which taxation in the province rested, and as its deputy, Pompignan voiced his objections to the new levy, which granted the royal *intendants* even greater

---

[22] Marcel Marion, *Machault d'Arnouville*, pp. 78, 196. The *vingtième* was doubled during the Seven Years War, and a third was added between 1760 and 1763. Jean-Jacques Le Franc de Pompignan, *Dissertation sur les biens nobles avec des observations sur le vingtième* (Paris, 1758), p. 87, remonstrates against the "evil consequences" of "uncovering family secrets, the necessary mysteries of wealth, and the financial situation of merchants." Riley, *The Seven Years War*, p. 70, on the French belief that they had the right to privacy.

[23] Kwass, *Privilege and the Politics of Taxation*, p. 68.

[24] Marion, *Machault d'Arnouville*, pp. 261–6 on the pamphlet war that erupted in spring 1749.

[25] See James Collins, *The State in Early Modern France* (Cambridge, 1995), p. 202. Kwass, *Privilege and the Politics of Taxation*, p. 85, and Marion, *Machault d'Arnouville*.

[26] Marion, *Machault d'Arnouville*, p. 90. Antonella Alimento, *Réformes fiscales et crises politiques dans la France de Louis XV, de la taille tarifiée au cadastre général* (Brussels, 2008), pp. 18, 63–5.

powers over tax inspection than before.[27] In a second brief he endorsed the special exemptions from taxation of "noble lands" drawing on history to support their longstanding rights.[28] Noble property, he argued, dated from the Salic laws and its privileges were therefore "sacred" and could never be abrogated. It was the sovereign's duty to uphold liberties sealed by binding treaties.[29] Like illustrious predecessors in the duc de Bourgogne's reforming circle (such as Fénelon), Pompignan blamed reduced taxation on the deluge of exemptions caused by inappropriate ennoblements.[30] "This is not abuse, it is prostitution of this privilege." Besides, nobles already contributed by their services and through the onerous upkeep of their properties so that taxing them additionally was unfair.[31] His brother, meanwhile, fought for the retention of the clergy's traditional privileges. Mirabeau positioned himself within this alliance of privileged bodies that challenged the Crown's claims to override the "fundamental laws of the kingdom."

In December 1749, exasperated by the Languedoc estates' refusal to endorse the *vingtième*, Machault granted all their tax-collecting authority to the *intendant* and abolished them.[32] Fearing that this abolition would extend to the remaining handful of provincial estates, Mirabeau decided to demonstrate their *utility* to the realm and their loyalty to the monarch. In a pamphlet on provincial estates, he therefore championed Languedoc's ancient "liberties," and assured the public that by their consent to levies provincial estates facilitated the collection of taxes. Provinces with estates did not pay less than regions under direct government fiscal control.[33] To the contrary, the trust that existed between taxpayers and the deputies who negotiated their tax rate encouraged them to pay. Using their

---

[27] On land registers, see Gilbert Larguier, "Normes, production et évolution des compoix terriens en Languedoc XVIe–XVIIIe siècles" in Mireille Touzery, ed., *De l'estime au cadastre en Europe, L'époque moderne* (Paris, 2007), pp. 339–72, 348, 352–5, 358–9. On the fury of the *cours des aides*, see Kwass, *Privilege and the Politics of Taxation*, pp. 53–4.

[28] Pompignan, *Dissertation sur les biens nobles*. The work was revised in 1758 and the remonstrances on the *vingtième* appended to the volume dated from 7 July 1756 (on the occasion of an additional levy).

[29] Ibid., pp. 31–2.

[30] In the 1711 *Tables de Chaulnes*, for one. See Nagle, *La Civilisation du coeur*, p. 227.

[31] Ibid., pp. 42, 53, 61–3.

[32] Marion, *Machault d'Arnouville*, p. 132. Once he had broken their resistance, Machault reinstated them on 10 October 1752.

[33] Marion, *Machault d'Arnouville*, pp. 114–15 contests this as do other historians, but Marie-Laure Legay agrees. See *Les états provinciaux dans la construction de l'état moderne* (Geneva, 2001), p. 234.

"deep knowledge" of local customs and of the region's peculiar features, less visible to an outsider, the deputies enlightened the monarch about the real economic state of their province. Quite unlike those arrogant grandees who used to rebel against the king, responsible elites drew up remonstrances after a temperate deliberation of the three orders.[34] A system that involved "nobles and landowners" in its administration was much preferable to one "in which decisions were taken arbitrarily, local practices disregarded, people had no say and felt that decisions had been foisted upon them."[35] Provincial assemblies, moreover, called and dismissed at the will of the monarch, inculcated civic spirit and quelled "Republican" agitation. Provincial estates were the pillars of the monarchy.[36]

In the expanded version written some years later, Mirabeau called more boldly for the reinstatement of provincial assemblies throughout the realm.[37] After examining the form and efficacy of the Brittany, Burgundy, Languedoc, and Provence estates (leaving aside those in smaller border provinces), he settled on Languedoc as the most advantageous, as had Fénelon before him.[38] In rejecting the other versions, he

[34] *Mémoire sur l'utilité des états provinciaux* (Rome, 1750), 44 pages, described in Henri Ripert, *Le marquis de Mirabeau (L'Ami des hommes), ses théories politiques et économiques* (Paris, 1901), pp. 92–7. The 1750 text was reprinted in 1787 as part of a series of proposals for the restoration of provincial estates. *Objets proposés à l'assemblée des notables par de zélés citoyens. Premier Objet: administrations provinciales* (Paris, 1787), pp. 3–23. This is the version I used.

[35] Mirabeau, *Mémoire sur l'utilité*, pp. 12–13.

[36] Mirabeau, *Mémoire sur l'utilité*, p. 9. Legay views Mirabeau's efforts to reinvigorate the estates as crucial to a changing perception of these bodies, turning them from "opponents" of the monarchy to guarantors of public order (pp. 322–4).

[37] As a great prince had hoped would happen, Mirabeau adds, referring to the Duke of Burgundy, who died in 1712 (*Mémoire sur les états provinciaux*, p. 218). The second version is only available in its 1759 version but is presumed to have been written or even published earlier. Pierre Renouvin dates the new version to 1751 (op. cit., p. 12); Henri Ripert supposed that the expanded edition came out in 1757 and is the source quoted in the Bibliothèque nationale catalogue (where it appears as *Mémoire concernant l'utilité des Etats provinciaux* (no place of publication, 1757). As Loïc Charles notes, this date must be wrong since Grimm reviewed the book in 1755. Quesnay, *Oeuvres économiques complètes et autres textes*, II, p. 1234. See Grimm et al., *Correspondance littéraire*, III, July 1755, p. 100. The longer version with a new introduction, included in Volume IV, part I of *L'Ami des hommes* (Paris, 1759) is the one commonly used.

[38] Mirabeau, *Mémoire sur les états provinciaux*, p. 244, drawing as he says his analysis from Boulainvilliers (p. 242). On Fénelon, see Renouvin, *Les Assemblées provinciales de 1787*, p. 8. See Anne Blanchard, Henri Michel, and Elie Pélaquier, eds., *Les assemblées d'Etats dans la France méridionale à l'époque moderne* (Montpellier, 1995). The archbishop of Narbonne headed the Estates, twenty-three prelates sat for the clergy, and the king named twenty-three barons. The third estate had sixty-eight representatives but only forty-six were allowed to vote. Alimento, *Réformes fiscales*, p. 64. Marion

explained that Brittany allowed too many representatives from the nobility, Provence not enough. The more people participated in administration (not "decision making") the stronger the body politic and the feeling of solidarity. A state that relied on force, ruled men's bodies; one that governed equitably, won over their hearts. It was better, in other words, to be loved than to be feared. Representative assemblies gave a voice to the nation's diverse interests and allowed for harmonious resolutions.

Mirabeau went on to explain that society actually consisted of four different orders. Each had a different function and as a consequence had developed a different ethos. The clergy, of course, oversaw morality in general. The military nobility embodied generosity, disinterestedness, and true honor (not atavistic brutality as some regrettably insisted). The magistracy – or civil order, as Mirabeau calls it – personified wisdom and ensured that legislation conformed to the kingdom's "fundamental laws." A final group of worthies were part of the "municipal order," in charge of urban administration. This last "order of citizens," drawn from among the commercial classes, was essentially driven by self-interest.[39] Representative assemblies at the regional or provincial level brought together the three traditional orders, whereas local councils or municipalities were overseen by the "fourth order," whose particular skills lent themselves to administering local affairs.[40] Of course, since property was the "foundation and principal bond" of society, all deputies to provincial assemblies would own land, but Mirabeau did not consider that they represented landed *interests*, since each remained bound to the

---

summarized the situation in Languedoc as follows: "The real nobility hardly bothered to assert its rights to participate in the assembly and showed little interest in discussing business in which the ultimate decisions rested with the bishops. This predominance of the clergy represented the real danger in the struggles over the vingtième because the privileges of the clergy were even more at stake than the privileges of the province." Marion, *Machault d'Arnouville*, p. 90. Mirabeau declared that he did not feel the bishops had too much power. Mirabeau, *Mémoire sur les états provinciaux*, p. 246. If he began the new version in 1751 (as drafts in the Archives nationales suggest), it was at a time when the Languedoc estates had not yet been reestablished.

[39] Mirabeau, *Mémoire sur les états provinciaux*, pp. 58–61. This group of citizens concern themselves with the productivity of agriculture, trade, etc.
[40] Cupidity and sociability might be the pivots of *L'Ami des hommes*, but they weren't enunciated so openly earlier. On Mirabeau's moral philosophy, see Sonenscher, *Before the Deluge*, pp. 191–200, defining physiocratic morality as "The first was the conception of human nature underlying the idea of the natural and essential order of political societies. The second was the place of property in human society. The third was the broader system that was designed to force what the Physiocrats called the unnatural and retrograde order in which actually existing political societies were based to revert to one that was natural and progressive" (pp. 191–2).

outlook and ethos of his order.⁴¹ Peasants, guided by benevolent landowners, of course, needed no voice. Taxes, freed from the clutches of financiers, should be collected by public receivers.⁴² The king could count on the loyalty of his people: His authority coursed through the land like "electricity," but he must uphold natural social distinctions and preserve the historical rights of provinces.⁴³ Furthermore, by recognizing the special virtue attached to each social group and rewarding merit in *each separate sphere*, he would rekindle civic virtue. Did not "the source of good laws lie in men's hearts"?⁴⁴

In 1759, while preparing a revised edition under the "guidance of a wise man [Quesnay]," Mirabeau offered a long rejoinder to his critics. It began with a praise of the "great genius and political philosopher" [Montesquieu] who made intermediary bodies the bulwark of the monarch.⁴⁵ Mirabeau repeated that the old feudal nobility was especially suited for service.⁴⁶ Quesnay however urged him to emphasize the utilitarian aspects: "only enlightened men, who reside in their provinces, are capable of overseeing, examining, and observing, on the spot, in detail and with precision, the impediments to agricultural production and to the trade in foodstuffs and come up with the proper remedies."⁴⁷ Thus, a possible conflict was looming between the economist-doctor who attached representative bodies to agricultural productivity, and the nobleman-moralist who sought to reinvigorate a flagging political institution, and to reform tax collection.⁴⁸ To further complicate matters, historians working on provincial estates have demonstrated that by the middle of the eighteenth century these ancient institutions worked quite closely with the royal administration, even while keeping alive the notion of a "right of consent to taxation" and the protection of ancient freedoms.⁴⁹ They

---

⁴¹ Mirabeau, *Mémoire sur les états provinciaux*, pp. 45, 62.
⁴² Ibid., pp. 100, 166–7.
⁴³ Ibid., pp. 173–4.
⁴⁴ Ibid., p. 73. "There is only one solution: rekindle the bond between the best and most august of masters and his most faithful subjects. Reinstating power to local bodies would strengthen the state and make it more vigorous than ever before" (p. 243).
⁴⁵ Ibid., Book IV, part II, p. 15.
⁴⁶ AN, M784/36/1, draft of a new introduction to the *Mémoire sur les états provinciaux*.
⁴⁷ Ibid.
⁴⁸ As Alimento also notes, since Mirabeau altered his positions, one has to monitor the changes very carefully. Mirabeau, as Joël Félix points out, also argued that provincial estates allowed borrowing at lower rates. *Finances et politiques*, p. 254.
⁴⁹ See for example Legay, *Les états provinciaux*, pp. 239, 245, 32–4, 350. Michel Peronnet, "Réflexions sur les Etats de Languedoc: une histoire intermédiaire à l'époque moderne" in Anne Blanchard et al., *Les Assemblées d'Etats dans la France méridionale*, pp. 107–28,

were therefore already viewed in a positive light, although not necessarily for the reasons Mirabeau put forward, because they served the absolutist state.

His engagement on behalf of provincial freedoms went beyond public advocacy. He revealed a decade later that he had been secretly instructed in December 1749 by representatives of the three orders of Provence (where a weak system of representation still prevailed) to lobby for an *abonnement* of their *vingtième* but that the Comte de Saint-Florentin, minister of the King's Household, had explained to him in April 1750 why such a course was inadvisable.[50] Mirabeau had nonetheless counseled a number of communities to add the *vingtième* to their regular assessments (without going through the complicated procedures demanded by the state) on the understanding that the government would turn a blind eye.[51] He had not broadcast these negotiations although "they were known to his friends." He "lifted this veil of secrecy" when he offered his services to his native province once again in 1758.

## A Call for Change

The success of *L'Ami des hommes* satisfied Mirabeau that he had made the right decision in linking his destiny to writing.[52] He was now broadly regarded as an authority on national welfare. "They no longer dare say in my presence that it is the peasant's lot to be miserable," he told his brother, and reported on his newfound fame: "I am received graciously everywhere at Versailles, and my friends tell me to seize the day, because the moment you leave here, you cease to exist." "Aside from the favour [*bontés*] displayed by the royal family and other notables, I can tell from

---

115, and Marion, *Machault d'Arnouville*, p. 284. The vingtième survived all these attacks, as long as Machault remained minister, but the beginning of a new war and urgent need for money, meant the return of expedients such as the *abonnements*. See also James Collins, *The State in Early Modern France*, p. 202, and Legay, *Les états provinciaux*, p. 245. Antonella Alimento, "Tra fronda e fisiocrazia" pp. 97–141, and *Riforme fiscali*; Baker, "Representation" pp. 469–92; and Claude Michaud, "L'assemblée provinciale du Berry, 1778–1789)," in Anne Blanchard et al., *Les assemblées d'Etat dans la France méridionale*, pp. 215–38, 218–19.

[50] AN, K1219/9, n.d. in "Recueil et mémoires aux Etats de Provence" [Mirabeau 1758–60]. Mirabeau refers to "une assemblée particulière des procureurs des gens des trois états nés et joints tenue le 6 décembre 1749."

[51] Ibid.

[52] Letter to his brother, the Chevalier de Mirabeau [later *bailli* of the Order of Malta], 27 July 1758, in Ch. Laurent, ed., *Les voyages en Bretagne du Chevalier de Mirabeau 1758–1760* (Mayenne, 1983), p. 110.

their faces, and friends like Brun confirm this, that I am well-liked and that subordinates [*peuple de sous-ordres*] speak well of me. Providence only knows whether any of this will bear fruit."⁵³

That summer and throughout the following year, Mirabeau believed he would come to play a leading role in French affairs (and to promote his brother's career in the navy). The Chevalier warned him not to be overly sanguine, judging Quesnay too timid to promote their ambitions, the court too rife with intrigue, and, as the brothers endlessly lamented, the nation too depraved. The Marquis summed up their position: "It all comes down to my habitual refrain: do you wish to reform things? Reform men. Do you want to abolish things? Get rid of the *chosiers* [racketeers]." Four days after this sally, Mirabeau reported that his friends were urging him to strike while the iron was hot but that the powers-that-be "seemed unwilling to hear him preach." Yet his popularity remained at its peak, as he boasted to his brother, referring to himself in the third person.⁵⁴

As for consideration, *Victor* is treated as a rarity, an excellent citizen, and the country's last hope, but, until now, there has been insurmountable opposition to putting him to work [*le mettre en oeuvre*]. So he exhausts himself in swimming between two streams and does not even know before God and his conscience whether he should persist or give up altogether. Were he ambitious or a courtier, his choice would be simple, because he has heard from others what [he] is reporting to you here. Since he threatened to leave [claiming he had run out of money] he has been offered over 100,000 *écus* to support himself.

In his response, on 24 August, the Chevalier put his finger on one of the problems:

I am glad that you are giving it a go [*tentes fortune*] and it has occurred to me that I might harm rather than serve you in this. People have noticed that I have never paid a visit to the mighty one; could Mme de Pompadour resent you for that reason? Secondly, they are afraid that, should you succeed [*si tu allais en avant*], you would seek to ram me in there [*m'y fourrer*]. I have scared them enough on my own; imagine what they would make of the two of us, since they also fear you? Think it over and consider whether my absence is more useful to you than my presence. Then let me know what you think and I will act accordingly.⁵⁵

---

⁵³ Letters to the Chevalier of 29 July and 4 August 1758 in Laurent, *Les voyages en Bretagne du Chevalier de Mirabeau*, pp. 111 and 114.
⁵⁴ Ibid., Letters of 8 and 16 August 1758.
⁵⁵ Ibid., p. 135, letter from Chevalier to Marquis, from Brest, 24 August 1758.

The Marquis reassured him that he was the worthier of the two, and in September was hoping to see his brother named Minister of the Marine.[56] "The order of primogeniture will hopefully be reversed. The second knows something they need." Despite their machinations, neither the Marquis nor the Chevalier obtained government positions, although a year later, at the fall of Silhouette's ministry, Mirabeau hoped once again that he might be called to the helm. As he explained to his brother on 29 October 1759, he would only accept the ministry of finance if his brother got the navy.[57] His program, as expressed to the Chevalier, included the dismantlement of the current provincial administration (getting rid of royal *intendants*), the restoration of provincial estates, the abolition of tax farming and indirect taxation (even if this meant declaring bankruptcy), the abolition of the *corvées* (forced labor on the roads), and other fiscal reforms. This was a standard conservative program, voiced by other critics of the absolutist state.

Local estates continued to feature in the brothers' correspondence as the Chevalier travelled in Brittany commenting on local institutions. Mirabeau "having plumbed to the depths of economic processes" [*cavé* is the term he uses], realized he should have placed less emphasis on the legal rights and authority of the nation's "arcane assemblies," offering the first hint that he was questioning his commitment to provincial estates. He despaired of ever getting his "message" across, despite the success of the fifth volume of *L'Ami des hommes* – the first to address Quesnay's system directly.[58] The Chevalier doubted whether the fifth volume would be as popular as his brother imagined but the seed has been sown and future generations would reap the benefits. The brothers remained of one mind about the value of feudalism and, on 15 July, the Marquis expressed his conviction that Providence meant him to examine the "origins of all governments."[59] Since republics were only suited to city-states, and the historical record showed that "pure absolute monarchies never lasted ... more than four reigns" without fomenting revolution, a solid monarchy "requires intermediary bodies. An English style assembly... is unsuited to a vast country like ours that is surrounded by neighbours. ...France once had such general assemblies, which were,

---

[56] Loménie, *Les Mirabeau*, I, p. 227.
[57] Ibid., II, pp. 398–9.
[58] Laurent, *Le voyages en Bretagne du Chevalier de Mirabeau*, p. 203, letter of 30 June 1760.
[59] Ibid., pp. 210–11, letter of 15 July 1760.

in their original and truest form, just assemblies of oligarchs (if I might put it this way)." There was nothing for it, he concluded, but to restore the authority of the old provincial estates. Yet he doubted at times of their success in a century "obsessed with self-interest" and feared he was becoming a "moral Don Quixote." Without Quesnay's tenacity, in that summer when they were working on *La théorie de l'impôt*, he admitted, he would have given up long ago. He admired the doctor's "studious, even apostolic zeal" and his ability to "see the power and ill-effects of moral turpitude so clearly and yet continue working tirelessly, putting him [Mirabeau] to shame."[60] The Chevalier however, found the doctor a cold fish, altogether too self-serving in benefitting from a system he supposedly decried – or actually had *others* criticize, since he did not write those things himself.[61]

Mirabeau was simultaneously engaged in a dispute regarding the *vingtième* in his home province, maneuvering as *Realpolitician* rather than prophet of a new world order. Provence had not possessed formal estates since 1639 but was governed by an assembly composed of 37 representatives of its 700 "communities," a body dominated by urban elites, although the archbishop of Aix, the first two consuls and assessor of that city, and two royal representatives had the right to attend. The three traditional orders, however, were represented on the executive committee.[62] Fief-owning nobles had been permitted to hold a separate assembly as of 1548. Should they also possess judicial authority as part of their feudal attributes, their lands were exempt from regular taxation. Since Provence was a region of *taille réelle* (where the status of the *land* and not of the *landowner* determined who paid taxes) this created a loophole that fief-owners were keen to preserve. As Rafe Blaufarb has demonstrated, the erosion of their feudal privileges in the eighteenth century made the old nobility particularly touchy about their status.[63]

---

[60] Ibid., p. 212, letter of 21 July 1760.

[61] Ibid., p. 224, letter from the Chevalier of 18 August 1760.

[62] François-Xavier Emmanuelli, "Les assemblées provinciales en Provence et en comtat venaissin aux XVIIe et XVIIIe siècles" in Anne Blanchard et al., *Les assemblées d'Etat dans la France méridionale*, pp. 91–105 and "Réflexion sur les Etats Provinciaux au XVIIIe siècle: Provence, Comtat Venaissin, Corse," *Parliaments, Estates and Representation* 16 (1996), 131–9. All the communities represented were urban; there were no representatives of the countryside. *Fiefs* were exempt from the bulk of direct taxation but nobles were still responsible for an annual lump sum, which they divided among themselves (pp. 134–5).

[63] Rafe Blaufarb, "Noble Tax Exemption and the Long-Term Origins of the French Revolution: The Example of Provence, 1530s to 1789" in Jay M. Smith, ed., *The French Nobility in the Eighteenth Century* (University Park, 2006), pp. 141–65.

When Mirabeau intervened in the dispute between representatives of the communities and those of the nobility over the allocation of the 1757 *vingtième*s, he was therefore stepping into a highly charged situation, but one with which he knew intimately as a Provençal landed magnate. On 8 August 1760, the representatives of both bodies thanked Mirabeau for his services in helping them resolve their differences.[64] Each side had argued that it could not meet the new tax. Mirabeau, in his inimitable style, had called on them to show public spirit, "to take on the mantle and spirit of the patriot," forget their discord and help each other handle these new fiscal demands.[65] At the last minute, the syndic for the communities Pazéry[66] alerted Mirabeau about a sub-clause dealing with communal justice, which allowed communities to purchase the right to meet without seigneurial consent. Mirabeau responded by berating the procurators of Provence on 26 August for debasing local authority and by courting the favors of the royal treasury in so ignoble a manner. Ancient rights were being bartered away. The foreseeable result would be a string of lawsuits before the Royal Council that would undermine "equity, justice, and confraternity." They should rally instead to "defend traditional Provençal law and its ancient Constitutions which would allow them to re-establish [their] authority [*nous nous rétablirons*] in more favourable times."

Mirabeau's support of the nobility's traditional prerogatives is clear in his response to Pazéry. He hoped that the "communities" would choose to delete the offensive article. He would have no "scruples in serving the nobility on this score, because it would mean upholding the public law of our land." While calling for a revamped national tax system and new economic order, Mirabeau was deploying equal energy to maintaining the status quo. His fame as provincial advocate led to requests for help with their briefs by the estates of Artois and Maritime Flanders in the late 1750s.[67]

---

[64] AN K1219/9 two letters dated Aix, 8 August 1760. Additional materials concern the negotiations, including letters from Pazéry on behalf of the *procureurs du pays*, 26 August 1760, from Mirabeau to Pazéry of 20 August 1760, and to the syndics of the nobility on 20 and 26 August 1760.

[65] AN, M784/25 "Plan d'arrangement pour l'affaire de la représentation du 20e pour les différents corps qui composent la province."

[66] The assemblies' legal representatives, or syndics grew more powerful during the eighteenth century. Emmanuelli, "Les assemblées provinciales en Provence," p. 99, and Blaufarb, "Noble Tax Exemption," p. 146. Cubells, *La Provence des Lumières*, p. 282; The Pézary, father and son, like Mirabeau's friend the Président d'Eguilles, supported the Jesuit Order against the attacks that culminated in the dissolution of the Order.

[67] See AN783/14 and M784/15. Also Alimento, "Tra fronda e fisiocrazia," p. 123 referring to AN K1161/37 (Artois).

## The Problem of the Nobility

This commitment to his order had been a major stumbling block in the composition of the *Traité de la monarchie,* which Mirabeau had envisaged as a pendant to his *Mémoire sur les états provinciaux,* and whose sorry fate we have already encountered.[68] He meant to demonstrate that monarchy was the earliest form of government and that monarchic states were necessarily composite in nature.[69] Despite Quesnay's skepticism, he clung to the nobility's antiquity "lost in the mist of time" and its innate qualities. A good monarch, he argued, not only respected social distinctions, he acknowledged the special worth of his nobility. True enough, Montesquieu had been wrong in associating honor with the order, since they had often acted dishonorably, but by tying honor to the performance of duty, they would recover their pride and manifest the highest degree of virtue, not least because they performed the most onerous services.[70] A monarchy depended on intermediary bodies for its stability, and the nobles' natural function was to assist their king: "a republic elected its administrators but a monarchy received them from nature."[71]

Mirabeau still had much to learn since he insisted that "a monarchy is guided by a military ethos [*esprit militaire*]. By ethos, I do not mean the government itself, whose competence is civil and economic, but rather a military outlook. A monarch must have an army; military service should be rewarded with the highest ranks and honours to ensure that this ethos is passed down the generations [*dans les races*] and become a national characteristic [*préjugé de nation*]."[72]

Quesnay objected on several grounds. The French nobility owed its privileges to feudal usurpations and the power attached to fiefs. It could not be defined ahistorically. Ancient titles disguised the more prosaic origins of a noble family but could not vouch for its merit. The nobility had distinguished itself through military service but had no monopoly on bravery, in fact Mirabeau should stress its "patriotic zeal" in order to demonstrate its multiple virtues.[73] There were other kinds of merit besides nobility. It might be treated as "an order [*corps*] in the monarchy,

---

[68] Mirabeau and Quesnay, *Traité de la monarchie,* p. 33.
[69] Ibid., pp. 36, 48.
[70] Ibid., pp. 67–72, 91–3.
[71] Ibid., pp. 95–6.
[72] Ibid., p. 83.
[73] Ibid., pp. 131–2.

with special functions and rank," but one had to acknowledge that merit and virtue were distributed evenly among the population.[74] Given its recent history, Quesnay added, the French mistrusted the high nobility, so Mirabeau should be careful about praising them too highly or he would risk alienating his readers. In a final sally Quesnay thought it would be appropriate to denounce "the tyranny and evils of the sword which turned noblemen into beasts." Educate, civilize and inspire the nobility, Quesnay urged his friend.

As for the monarch, Quesnay took a different tack altogether. He should be guided by natural law and positive laws should align themselves so closely on the former that the two became indistinguishable.[75] Quesnay explained that he privileged natural law above religion because it was immutable. The multiplicity of faiths (where only Catholicism, of course, could claim to be true) meant they could not reflect natural law. Besides, there was always a risk that the clergy would gain undue authority.[76] Should one find religion necessary, there were advantages to a natural religion that upheld belief in a Creator, Providence, rewards and punishments in this life and next, and the existence of a necessary law (*obligatoire*).[77] Subsistence was the primary goal of every society. The population remained ignorant of the sources of wealth, and not even those ministers or kings who had established special councils to oversee trade and agriculture had bothered to enlighten their subjects. It was no coincidence that in his famous novel Fénelon had his hero Telemachus instructed by Mentor [the goddess Athena] on this important matter for who else could have done it?[78]

In the body of the text, Mirabeau elaborated on the administration of local affairs by his "municipal order," charged with overseeing "production, manufacture, commerce, finance, and the maintenance of order [*police*]." Quesnay added functions that Mirabeau had left out: looking for the best ways to promote agricultural productivity and the prosperity of the state, overall order, and the most equitable system of taxation.[79] Physiocratic priorities were not yet ingrained in Mirabeau's consciousness. Quesnay's response to Mirabeau's continued call for intermediary

[74] Ibid., pp. 85–6.
[75] Ibid., p. 120.
[76] Ibid., pp. 29, 42, 58.
[77] Ibid., p. 59.
[78] Ibid., pp. 53, 142.
[79] Ibid., p. 139.

bodies was that "monarchic despotism" was an oxymoron because no man could rule arbitrarily over millions of subjects. He did it through laws.[80] This was legal despotism in a nutshell. The Doctor and his pupil failed to find sufficient common ground but Mirabeau blithely disregarded their fundamental divergences when he called for provincial assemblies and praised the nobility once more in *La théorie de l'impôt*.[81] In condemning indirect taxation and tax farming, he repeated his longstanding criticisms of the *intendants*.[82] Taxation should be handled by the "people's natural magistrates," be they village or town councilors, whom they were more likely to trust and who would oversee tax collection more cheaply and efficiently than the current collectors.[83] It seemed reasonable to insist on some form of inspection so Mirabeau proposed the creation of a tier of assemblies, starting at the village level, answerable to the nearest town, then county, and culminating in provincial bodies that would report to the central government.[84] This could be implemented very easily if the king invited representatives of the three orders to meet in each provincial capital to undertake whatever tasks the king mandated.[85] Trust was necessary for the success of such endeavours and this entailed the kingdom's moral reformation.[86] Quesnay and Mirabeau's positions were still far apart. They overlapped in seeking fiscal reform, the promotion of agricultural productivity, and moral education. In insisting on representative assemblies and the distinction among classes, the *Théorie de l'impôt* reflected Mirabeau's political vision. Insofar as it touted a radically new fiscal system based on agricultural productivity, the volume was Quesnay's.[87]

---

[80] Ibid., p. 111. Finally, Quesnay finding Mirabeau too unsystematic offered twelve points on the origins and development of different types of political regimes from their earliest origins to patriarchal societies all the way to variants of absolutism and despotism which Mirabeau might develop chapter by chapter (pp. 181–2).

[81] On Mirabeau's tenacity on the role of nobility, see Jay Smith, *Nobility Reimagined*, pp. 99–100.

[82] Mirabeau, *La Théorie de l'impôt*, p. 307.

[83] Ibid., p. 45.

[84] Ibid., pp. 346–7.

[85] Ibid., pp. 364–5. This was the suggestion that Du Pont made to Turgot upon hearing he had been made Controller general. See Chapter 8.

[86] Ibid., p. 455.

[87] For a fine analysis of Mirabeau's notion of the moral bond between monarch and subjects, see Kwass, *Privilege and the Politics of Taxation*, pp. 235–8. Marion, *Histoire financière*, I, p. 202. Alimento, *Réformes fiscales*, pp. 123–5. Félix reminds us that the popularity of such writings spurred the Controller general L'Averdy to create the *Journal d'agriculture, du commerce, et des finances* in 1765, *Finances et politique*, pp. 208–9 to encourage public debate on economic matters.

Unfortunately the work provoked the tax farmers' ire and Louis XV fumed at the criticism of Louis XIVs reign.[88] Mirabeau was arrested and taken to Vincennes, and the volume was withdrawn from circulation.[89] The Marquis spent ten days in captivity before the duc de Nivernais persuaded the king that the author was a well-intentioned but misguided fool and had him exiled to Le Bignon.[90] He stayed there but a few months, invoking his mother's poor health to return to Paris. This incident did not end Mirabeau and Quesnay's collaboration but they proceeded more cautiously. The principles of the natural order got pride of place in the *Philosophie rurale*, published in 1763.

Mirabeau continued to disseminate the doctrine's main points in *Éléments de la philosophie rurale* in 1766 and, as of 1767, contributed regularly to the *Éphémérides du citoyen*, the journal edited by the abbé Baudeau who had been converted to physiocracy, and which Du Pont would take over in 1768. The *Lettres sur la législation* began to appear in the journal in February 1767 and reveal Mirabeau's thoughts on politics at the very time when Quesnay was promoting legal despotism.

Mirabeau began in Rousseaunian fashion by asserting that one could not judge mankind or social institutions based on their current "degenerate and corrupt" state.[91] He called on his readers to "look inside" themselves to see if legal sanctions had been necessary at the dawn of time for men to co-operate, or if man had not been born with such inclinations.[92] Still, one could not simply rely on man's feelings – for his senses inform but do not enlighten him – and his "lack of certainty" opens the door to all sorts of enthusiasms. Reason grants him the means to move beyond instinct and to realize that man has a place in the great order of creation.[93] The physical and moral domains must be united once more.

"We have deluded ourselves that there are differences between civilized and barbarian nations when all are barbaric in different ways since none has adhered to the natural order or learned how to perpetuate our

---

[88] B.N. manuscrits occidentaux, nouvelles acquisitions françaises, No. 3348, folios 218–46. The dossier includes letters from the duc de Nivernais to Malesherbes (15 and 17 December 1760).

[89] Ibid., folio 227. Order from the Chancellor to his son Malesherbes, 21 December 1760. This raised the issue of the tacit permission granted to Mirabeau's other books (and others that criticized the government) in folios 232v and 233.

[90] Loménie, *Les Mirabeau*, II, pp. 233–5. The Marquis was annoyed and then angry when he heard that Nivernais had advised his brother to stay away from Versailles.

[91] Mirabeau, *Lettres sur la législation*, pp. 7, 17.

[92] Ibid., p. 3.

[93] Ibid., pp. 13–15.

species safely."[94] Mirabeau waffles on how we are to gain such insights. An interior voice tells us that our personal (enlightenened) self-interest lies in serving the general interest.[95] This does not make us equal or abolish distinctions, since they are rewards for services rendered.[96]

There is a significant shift, however, as Mirabeau concedes that the internal divisions within each of the three orders render them unworthy of acting as "counterweights" to royal authority.[97] What is more, the initial usefulness of specialization that answered men's multiple needs, had been transformed beyond recognition to claims of exclusive rights and privileges. Surely this was not how societies were meant to be organized.[98] Given this, representative assemblies were unsustainable because they could only represent corrupt selfish interests. The prince, whose only interest was the general good, would find himself continually at war with his subjects and they with each other.[99]

This did not stop Mirabeau from condemning centralization and inflated court spending, and suggesting that local assemblies might prove useful in daily administration.[100] There, landowners could assess and allocate local taxation, without risk that they might defraud the state.[101] The king and the landowners would therefore share the common goal of improving the land and its cultivation, without anyone seeking to challenge royal authority.[102] Although he insists in one of his *Lettres sur la législation* that the king must abandon military pursuits, he argues elsewhere that strong nations need armies, and that only nobles perform selfless acts of valor.[103] Mirabeau was not yet ready to abandon his longstanding support of his caste.

[94] Ibid., pp. 390–3. It is here that Mirabeau becomes "Malthusian," arguing that man without the natural order soon reaches the physical limits of his independence. Mirabeau also expressed such sentiments in a letter to Charles de Butré where he explains that left to their own devices, without physiocracy, population would explode, properties would be endlessly subdivided, men would work themselves to death unable to afford animals or tools, 8 April 1779, in Knies, *Carl Friedrichs von Baden*, I, p. 109.
[95] Mirabeau, *Lettres sur la législation*, p. 129.
[96] Ibid., pp. 189–90, Letter 4 (n.d.).
[97] Ibid., pp. 199–202.
[98] Ibid., pp. 126–8, letter 3 (18 August 1767).
[99] Ibid., pp. 100–2, letter 2 (18 March 1767). This was the problems with republics and the moment when bad institutions, created to answer momentary needs, grew entrenched.
[100] He makes no mention of controller general L'Averdy's municipal reforms of 1764–5. See Félix, pp. 246–8 on the reform, and p. 237 on the presumption that it was inspired by Mirabeau and d'Argenson.
[101] Ibid., pp. 676–9.
[102] Ibid., p. 683.
[103] Mirabeau, *Lettres sur la législation*, pp. 242, 246–7.

In the post-*Economie rurale* years, therefore, Mirabeau was still mulling over the role and format of consultative assemblies, the best way of enshrining the natural order, and attempting to sort out, unsuccessfully as yet, general from particular virtues which he had previously attributed to specific groups in society. Despite his suspicions of special interests, he invoked men's capacity for selflessness, with the nobility still the most selfless of all, although, given their "honesty," landowners come pretty close.

In the meantime Quesnay and his newly consecrated political theorist, Pierre-Paul Le Mercier de La Rivière, had posited outright that nature needed no intermediaries. *L'ordre naturel et essentiel* condemned every form of representation as mere platform for distorted, selfish interests. In other words, Le Mercier did not distinguish between degenerate and regenerated representation, which Mirabeau was in the process of articulating. Thus, *L'ordre naturel* stated:

The sharing of authority among several administrators undermines the essential order of society in three ways: 1. It divides an authority that cannot, by its very essence, be divided. 2. It exposes public interest to the furies of private interest and creates a disparity between our duty and motivations. 3. It ties an all-powerful authority to popular suffrage whereas it must, and can only, be beholden to evidence.[104]

Elections "would not place evidence at the forefront, pandering instead to opinion or, if you prefer, to the wishes of men controlled by opinions." We should understand by this that the only option was to obey the natural order. All other positions were dismissed as "opinions," that is to say as products of imagination (dangerous), not of rational thought (trustworthy). There were no grey areas: To believe that authority lay in a plurality of votes was to deny the evidence of the natural order, for once men understood it, they would automatically endorse it.

Moreover, temporary assemblies (like provincial estates that only met for a few weeks) with conflicting interests could never reach binding decisions nor claim to speak on behalf of the "nation." Majority rule simply meant the temporary triumph of one faction over another, since dissidents might disregard the law or change it at the next session. Assemblies composed of big landowners (or worse, just aristocrats) would do no better, since they would exclude the people, and should they include deputies from both groups, they would spend all their time quarrelling and get

---

[104] Le Mercier de la Riviére, *L'Ordre naturel et essentiel des sociétés politiques*, p. 147.

nowhere.¹⁰⁵ Despite statements to the contrary, it would appear that men remained wedded to their "opinions," so that Le Mercier and Quesnay felt the natural order would fare best without representative bodies. In their physiocratic state, the system would be its own guarantee, since the nation would know that it embodied the order of nature. Magistrates would review legislation to ensure it remained faithful to nature's dictates. A monarch has to be as absolute as the law. "Knowledge of the natural and essential order being public and evident, this government will benefit everyone by instituting a true legal despotism; it will also benefit rulers by granting them personal despotism; arbitrary despotism is not true despotism because it is not *personal*, it is not *legal*, it fails to represent the interests of the person who exercises it…. legal despotism, on the other hand, is natural, perpetual, and absolute."¹⁰⁶ This is a universal imperative: "each nation is but a province of the great kingdom of nature; so all should be governed by the same laws, laws, which would all resemble each other because they have a common essence, dependent on the same absolute justice and injustice."¹⁰⁷

Quesnay adopted the same tone in his defense of the legal despotism that he believed existed in China.¹⁰⁸ The shilly-shallying was over and done with.

Legislative authority and the power to levy taxes seem to give rise to endless claims, disorders, and strain relations between the monarch and the nation. This has been the bane of every government imagined by men, but man can no more create and constitute the natural order than he can create himself. The constitutive order of societies is contained within the general logic [*l'ordre général de la formation*] of the universe where everything has already been foreseen and arranged by the supreme Wisdom.¹⁰⁹

Heeding the natural order would satisfy, by definition, everyone in the kingdom.¹¹⁰ This is physiocracy at its starkest, embracing all features of the economy and polity, securing what supposedly mattered most to everyone: their survival. Like Rousseau's "general will," to which it is

---

¹⁰⁵ Ibid., pp. 149–50, 168–70.
¹⁰⁶ Ibid., p. 78.
¹⁰⁷ Ibid., p. 325.
¹⁰⁸ *Despotisme de la Chine*, (1767) in Quesnay, *Oeuvres économiques complètes et autres texts*, II, p. 1012.
¹⁰⁹ Ibid., pp. 1014–15.
¹¹⁰ Le Mercier de la Rivière, *L'Ordre naturel et essentiel des sociétés politiques*, p. 97. This is the physiocratic dogma Steven Kaplan takes to task in *Bread, Politics and Political Economy*, I, pp. 114–17, 152.

often compared, debate would be pointless both within the imagined polity and about the proposed system.[111] One either agreed or disagreed with its propositions. But, unlike Rousseau, legal despotism came tied to specific economic goals and could not be separated from them. Once one had understood the law of reproduction of the net product, one no longer needed to consult Nature herself (or what it inscribed in men's soul). Nor was one expected to infer the general will, since it was already clearly defined.

Quesnay, Du Pont and Le Mercier's political vision began with the necessity of a legal despot. Theirs was a top-down vision of the exercise of power. Mirabeau, however, without relinquishing his loyalty to the monarchy, had been deeply engaged in struggles to balance royal authority through consultation of the three orders, rather than of the Parlements who claimed to represent the nation. Once he adopted physiocracy's analysis that the king was "co-owner and overseer" of the nation's landed revenues, and that, at best, the nation's landowners might be engaged in the assessment and allocation of the tax burden, Mirabeau had far less need of a monarch than his fellow physiocrats. All societies need chiefs, he concludes, but the monarch of the new order will, of course, rule but need not govern, that is, not engage in the details of administration.[112] No matter how hard he tried, Mirabeau couldn't conceive of government that did not entail civic participation, even if these local administrators possessed no legislative attributes. To this extent, Mirabeau does indeed correspond to Tocqueville's famous description of his ideas as "the invasion of democratic ideas within a feudal outlook."

## Provence Again

Mirabeau's attention was distracted by a new government undertaking to carry out cadastral surveys throughout the realm, and the demand that Provence proceed to a new *affouagement* (the local term for the evaluation of taxable properties).[113] He addressed the representatives of his province with physiocratic arguments but not before he had reminded

---

[111] See for example Sonenscher, *Before the Deluge*, chapter 3.
[112] Mirabeau, *Les Devoirs*, pp. 209–11, 192.
[113] The last dated from 1731 and a full affouagement would follow in 1773. See on this Alimento, *Réformes fiscales*, p. 73, Marie-Laure Legay, "L'état, les pouvoirs intermédiaires et la réforme cadastrale dans la France du XVIIIe siècle," pp. 373–89 in Mireille Touzery, *De l'estime au cadastre en Europe: l'époque moderne* (Paris, 2007), pp. 383–4; Félix, *Finances et politique*, pp. 289–304.

the "assembly of the province" that he was not only a native son but also a major landowner who had supported representative institutions in the past, earning plaudits from several provincial estates.[114] He now appeared before them in the guise of a citizen whose only purpose was to enlighten them about their true interests and to explain, by means of the new "geometrically demonstrated economic science," why they should refuse a new land survey. Only leases offered an accurate measure of taxable income because they deducted the costs of running a farm from the estimate of its value.[115]

The dilemma facing Provence, he presumed, was that requests from communities and individuals had poured in after a run of poor harvests pleading to be taken off the tax rolls. While they were certainly owed relief, a new *affouagement* was not the answer. Constant revisions discouraged landowners from improving their properties, and neither Languedoc nor Brittany, nor any of the *pays d'élections* for that matter revised their land registers. With his "physiocratic perspective" he wished to stimulate true and lasting prosperity by means of agricultural improvements and capital advances to farmers.

New cadastres involved of course intrusive investigations into landed income, which, as James Riley has ruefully remarked, the French particularly detested.[116] Whether from his new physiocratic insights or from an atavistic dislike of government meddling, Mirabeau repeatedly intervened to block governmental initiatives to improve tax collection, siding with local (or particular) interests against the state. On the whole, however, physiocrats supported piecemeal initiatives, such as the freeing of the grain trade, while waiting for a dramatic shift in economic priorities. Quesnay informed the Intendant of Soissons how to proceed with revenue assessments, just like Mirabeau would suggest to the Margrave of Baden.[117] It was easier to challenge government policy when one disliked the Controller general. Therefore, when in 1768 Mirabeau was asked to mediate yet another Provençal fiscal dispute (whose resolution once again affected him directly), he was ready to tackle L'Averdy, although he was the minister who had enacted free trade in cereals in 1764. The city

---

[114] AN, M784/53 [n.d.].
[115] See on this Alimento, *Réformes fiscales*, p. 346.
[116] Riley, *The Seven Years War*, p. 70.
[117] Letter from Quesnay to the Intendant of Soissons, January or February 1761, in Quesnay, *Oeuvres économiques complètes et autres textes*, II, p. 1209; see Mirabeau's letters to Carl Friedrich of 4 October 1769 (p. 79) and of 9 June 1774 (pp. 80–2) in Carl Knies, *Carl Friedrichs von Baden*, I.

of Marseilles had voted to charge absentee landlords in its jurisdiction an extra tax (10 percent on revenue and the 2 *sols pour livre*) although they had already paid their share in their province's general *abonnements*. The frustrated nonresidents asked the Marquis to remonstrate on their behalf (since he counted among their number).[118] The various briefs and correspondence reveal Mirabeau's delight in his role as "intermediary." First, however, he paid obeisance to the single tax and expressed his disapproval of all indirect taxes.

It would be unseemly for me more than anyone to speak against a territorial levy. I demonstrated publicly long ago that it was the only equitable tax, the only one that conforms to the law [of nature], the only one that would prevent the ruin of the nation and of the monarchy. My ideas have not changed on this score because the principles are invariable and mathematical. But such a tax can only be envisaged in places where there are no levies on consumption.

Marseilles had a particular status (as royal town and trading center) whose revenues were raised through a combination of customs duties and sales taxes. Mirabeau contested the town's right to tax its nonresident property owners since the latter already contributed in Provence. To add them to the urban tax rolls was double-dipping. Since the new levy was no doubt intended to reduce the city's debt to the treasury, the Marseillais should beg the king's mercy rather than tax nonresidents.[119] As an additional affront, Mirabeau charged, absentee landlords had not been invited to send representatives to the municipal hearings and thus had not "consented" to this tax. Joël Félix presumes that Mirabeau would have been pleased to see his "suggested reforms" adopted in cities like Marseilles, whereas Mirabeau, who detested L'Averdy, directly opposed him on this.

The deputies for each side, however, presented only technical arguments to the royal council. Could the city legitimately claim the special levy of 1716 as a precedent, and were nonresidents protected under an *arrêt* (decision) of 1666? To help him sort out the legal issues and to advise him on strategy, Mirabeau called on the services of Pazéry, who was now the province's deputy at Versailles. Mirabeau wondered whether to approach L'Averdy directly or to deal with the *premier commis des finances*, Ménard de Conichard instead, and whether to argue the case

---

[118] AN M806/2 an 187-page notebook includes the correspondence between Mirabeau and various Provençal notables from March to August 1768.
[119] See Félix, *Finances et politique*, pp. 252, 256.

at the royal council or have it transferred to the *cour des aides* or Aix *parlement*? The discovery that the Marseilles city council had cooked the books caused another flurry of correspondence.

Mirabeau initially sought a negotiated settlement, as he explained to "his dear cousin," the Marquis de Castellane, back in Aix. He had met with L'Averdy, who just wanted a quick resolution, given Marseilles' 12 million-livre debt to the treasury. A fleet had gathered at Toulon ready to invade Corsica that summer, and the nation must be prepared to "make sacrifices." Mirabeau had retorted that these must be "general and the same for everyone." When L'Averdy advised the nonresidents to raise a separate *abonnement*, Mirabeau understood that the Controller general had no interest in the particulars and that the nonresidents had no choice but to seek some accommodation with the Marseillais. The government would not back down from fear of embarrassment even if, as Mirabeau believed, the nonresidents had right on their side. Nonetheless, it was in "everyone's interest to uphold the government's dignity." Mirabeau swore to be tactful, even if he was ready to face "exile, prison, and disgrace," as he had once already. Although "known for his courage, he would hold back for the good of his compatriots." Such testimonials to his own character are strewn throughout this correspondence: "I only know how to speak the unvarnished truth [*la raison toute crue*], although it sometimes gives [me] indigestion." He told an Aix friend, "It goes against social proprieties to speak unpleasant truths without cause and by a sort of ill-humor, but when it comes to truths that matter to us, then they must be expressed as forcefully as possible."

On 18 June L'Averdy had informed the Marquis that the 1666 regulation did not apply to Marseilles so that the city was justified in demanding the *vingtième* from nonresidents. As Mirabeau had requested he was applying the law uniformly. For Mirabeau, "the snake's" (as he referred to L'Averdy) reply demonstrated the government's bias and its inability to rise above the fray, as it was meant to. The time had come, therefore, to plead their cause before the "true organs of the people." By August 1768, the case moved to the *cour des aides* in Aix.

This allowed Mirabeau to castigate the Marseilles city council once more for its high-handed treatment of its nonresident notables. "What would become of citizens if one arbitrarily presumed to represent them and allowed their adversaries to make decisions for them?" True, delegates were sometimes able to represent general interests regardless of their rank, and priests or townsmen had at times represented the whole province at meetings of the Estates General. But, should a member of the first estate decide that only the third estate was liable to taxation or vice versa, each would become a spokesman for his own special interests and cease to act as a universal deputy. This was the dilemma of representation in the degenerated order that Mirabeau was applying himself to correct.

Mirabeau expressed this to Butré who had briefly succumbed to spiritualist influences and thought that there were ways, beyond physiocracy, to pierce the mysteries of nature.[120] Mirabeau brought him back to the principles of political economy.[121] His role at the Margrave's court, he reminded him, was to help calculate the net product and to spread physiocratic ideas, as slowly and gently as need be. It might prove useful to involve landowners in the calculation of the net product and tax collection.[122] The Margrave might be induced to create village councils in which landowners would be granted minor administrative tasks and Mirabeau suggests that those with a revenue of 500 livres should have one vote, those with 1,000 livres two votes, those with 250 livres half a vote, and so on. A similar system could be adopted at the district level where communities would send representatives. "This will familiarize landowners with the practices and jargon of correspondence and accustom them to co-operate with each other to improve their conditions. You will then be able to negotiate with them about the repurchase of indirect taxes and their replacement levy. Thus will the great family [of man] be instructed and brought to collaborate ... This is how I would have operated in France."[123] He had thought of adding this to the *Théorie de l'impôt* but the details had been too hazy for the purposes of the book.

By the mid-1770s, Mirabeau appeared to be recapitulating his own difficult journey: from sudden illumination – a step enshrined in the *Tableau* itself – to doubts, confusions, resistance, and finally acceptance. The process entailed a deep intellectual surrender and Mirabeau understood that most physiocrats, never mind fellow-travelers, did not invest enough effort to achieve such insight. He had initially understood the process to mean grasping the *Tableau*'s message by reenacting a particular cognitive process; later, he saw it as training the mind slowly to rid

---

[120] Rodolphe Reuss, *Charles de Butré 1724–1805, Un physiocrate Tourangeau en Aslace et dans le Margraviat de Bade* (Paris, 1887), p. 22 believes he was attracted by hermeticism in its current German Rosicrucian incarnation.
[121] Letter to Carl Friedrich of Baden, 17 August 1776, Knies, *Carl Friedrichs von Baden*, I, p. 96.
[122] One might note in this respect that the Margrave only abolished serfdom in September 1783, see Knies, *Carl Friedrichs von Baden*, I, pp. 117–21.
[123] Letter to Butré 8 May 1777, in Knies, I, pp. 106–7.

itself of its ingrained prejudices and patterns of thought. Mirabeau's duty became to aid his readers. Enlightenment no longer came as a species of Grace, as Quesnay sometimes suggested, but through profound reflection on the nature of things, which he was no better at explaining.

## Les devoirs

*Les Devoirs* (1780) a little known work published in Italy under the care of Marquis Longo (and, incidentally, not yet available online) finally restored Mirabeau's confidence about human psychology and motivations. In the volume Mirabeau returned to his argument in *L'Ami des hommes* that men were torn between cupidity and sociability (rephrased here as "magnanimity"). Disinterestedness was the product of *reason*, a logical calculation that superseded narrow self-love.[124] Imagination led us astray through its very power to rouse us but it could only create fleeting impressions. "A long chain leads from the physical to the moral ... but the progression must be properly understood."[125] One must spot the links between morality and the social order, and the relation between our individual physical needs and the creation and conservation of the universe. In sum, "our morality must be entirely economic."[126]

In isolation, man is a fearsome brute; in society, he becomes a companion and ally to his fellows as soon as he acknowledges that he depends on them to meet his daily needs (serving, in other words, his self-interest), and that all his rights come accompanied by duties. "Obedience, love, and resignation turn him into God's friend."[127] Here's the rub: Mirabeau now presumes a limited set of impulses, restricting humans to material necessities and the urge to "live, grow, multiply, fulfill [their] physical duties, and know [their] moral duties."[128] By abiding to the system intended for mankind, men will obey God's dictates (and feel his benevolence). The "benefits" they will reap have been calculated and demonstrated by the new *economic science*. Physiocracy, Mirabeau, had come to accept, required a reductive approach to human psychology.

Although good qualities are unevenly parceled, man can improve himself through education since he is naturally given to emulation. Magnanimity and nobility of soul are less likely to prevail in degenerate societies so it will

---

[124] Mirabeau, *Les Devoirs*, pp. 10–12.
[125] Ibid., p. 15.
[126] Ibid., p. 40.
[127] Ibid., p. 16.
[128] Ibid., pp. 32–3.

take time for education to "seep in ... and trickle down the generations. We must keep this constantly in mind and not get discouraged if changes occur too slowly."[129] In common physiocratic fashion, humanity is quickly abstracted from its current environment and transferred to a physiocratic realm where needs are simple and people contented since they are defined by their physical requirements. After looping this loop, Mirabeau ascribes similar drives to a complex society, presuming that the same interactions would obtain. Thus, he cast "this science of life" (as he called it from 1769 onward),[130] onto a "modern," post-feudal world where caste distinctions had disappeared and landowners "served the sovereign and society."[131] This, as the reader might recall, was when Mirabeau admitted that virtue was *not* inherited, so that the passing down of titles made no sense. Public service required honesty and ability, not titles, and the nobility, which had emerged from feudal anarchy (he now conceded) as a form of public power, was bound to disappear once true sovereignty was restored, for such sovereignty could not be divided. Nobility had ceased serving a useful purpose, but it had taken decades for Mirabeau to reach this point.[132] "In a properly ordered agricultural society, the sovereign need only consult landowners who are his co-adjutants."[133] Assemblies of landowners at the county level might help assess annual productivity and revenues. As for national consultation, it might be required once a century if something in the constitution needed to be altered.[134]

The sovereign had to make sure that all his subjects knew their duties and the ways to create agricultural surpluses.[135] Transformations, he repeated, would take *time*. Institutions changed as slowly as mentalities. "Different customs, rules, languages, weights and measures, habits, and practices will not fuse readily into a single, uniform system."[136] As Michael Sonenscher reminds us, Mirabeau worried that societies only changed through bloody revolutions.[137]

He had finally made sense of the great physiocratic order to his own satisfaction. The apprenticeship had been long and Mirabeau warned others

---

[129] Ibid., pp. 23–4.
[130] See for example his letter of 4 October 1769 to the Margrave of Baden, in Knies, *Carl Friedrichs von Baden*, I, p. 79.
[131] Mirabeau, *Les Devoirs*, p. 128.
[132] Ibid., p. 133.
[133] Ibid., p. 173.
[134] Ibid., p. 224.
[135] Ibid., p. 166.
[136] Ibid., p. 221.
[137] Sonenscher, *Before the Deluge*, pp. 29, 192–3.

of this. His initial adhesion had been his Road to Damascus but moving beyond this enthusiastic endorsement had required patient reflection and the recognition of his "true" interests. Mirabeau, therefore, understood only too well how difficult it was to accept physiocracy and the social, political, and psychological sacrifices it entailed. One could begin by accepting the *Tableau* even if one never understood it fully, because this was the first step to a greater renunciation. For Mirabeau this became a story of Christian redemption with an economic twist: from sinfulness to grace, from pride to humility, and from food in the fields to food on the table. The psyche as a whole had to yield, renouncing worldly ambitions and that aspect of "self-fulfillment" to accept, as Quesnay had argued, that the only thing at stake was survival.

### Le Trosne

Despite the development of the doctrine of legal despotism and the relegation of Mirabeau to a "minority position" on representation, others had begun to see their worth, especially for practical ends. This might frustrate the reader who is looking for a clear line, a single physiocratic position, but divergences matter a great deal here and should not be brushed away. They get at the heart of the contradictions that drove physiocracy into the ground, no pun intended. Quesnay's frustrations with Mirabeau's *need* and *inability* to "feel" physiocracy's finer points from *within*, his impatience with overwrought moralizing, made him prefer a pared down version of human motivation and to construct a political system around it, bolstered by a punitive system of laws and strict policing. To pursue my metaphor, with this, physiocrats dug their own graves.

The authoritarianism that Yves Citton noted in physiocracy is most evident in Le Mercier's work.[138] Stridency compounded it. Guillaume-François Le Trosne, the Orléans magistrate who adhered to physiocracy in 1765, expressed similar views with far greater finesse.[139] As his biographer remarked – and is quickly apparent to anyone who peruses his work – his style is far more accessible than "Quesnay's drier or Mirabeau's apocalyptic tones."[140] In two treatises (one published posthumously), Le Trosne examined the fiscal consequences of the new system and imagined

---

[138] Citton, *Portrait de l'économiste*, p. 163.
[139] Jérôme Mille, *G.-F. Le Trosne (1728–1780) Etude économique, fiscale et politique* (Paris, 1905), p. 8.
[140] Ibid., p. 29.

its future administrative structure. Fantasy played its part here. Le Trosne however departed from "strict" legal despotism in detailing a tier of representative assemblies of landowners that would, to be sure, be merely advisory.[141] Landowners, he presumed, would happily participate in the administration of their provinces.[142]

Privileging harmony above all other social values, he too rejected republicanism or counterweights to the monarchy that, despite their apparent prudence, actually granted "dangerous authority" to the public.[143] There is, he argues, a higher authority that unites all interests, including those of the ruler, that of the natural order, as will become apparent once the system is established.[144] Men's passions do not pose much of a threat because there are laws to contain them. One must beware, however of the administrators' passions, because "nothing can stop them in a benighted age when prejudice and error hold as much sway as the arguments one can muster against them, and where intermediary bodies do as much good as evil, where the sovereign can be deluded, where counterweights are just platforms for blind, oppressive, and arbitrary passions which keep society in a state of war, all the more readily and inevitably because they are a part of the governing structure."[145] The passions will never disappear but it is possible to limit the damage through education, a proper constitution, and the recognition of the value of collaboration. Le Trosne does not presume that the "order" will ever prevail "absolutely and perfectly," but rather that one must strive toward that goal.[146]

Government based on this order necessarily entails that the nation be a polity, a real civic entity endowed with real life, movement, and activity, a common will which has a chance to express itself and which can formulate its wishes, needs, and demands. It supposes national bodies [*formes constitutives et nationales*] erected to perform their proper administrative functions, enact new laws, oversee justice, with a proper hierarchy, and appropriate competence of its law courts, for taxation, its allocation and collection, for the assessment of public expenditures and accounting thereof.[147]

---

[141] *De l'ordre social* (Paris, 1777) followed by *De l'administration provinciale et de la réforme de l'impôt* (Basel, 1779, 1788), *De l'ordre social*, p. 234, calls for the creation of a provincial administration.
[142] Ibid., p. 340.
[143] Ibid., pp. 247–8.
[144] Ibid., p. 258. Educating the public would, of course, help.
[145] Ibid., p. 264.
[146] Ibid., pp. 265–6.
[147] Ibid., p. 278.

He asserts, as a good physiocrat, the importance of proper cognition to achieve certainties, but from his pen it reads like common sense. Moreover, he approaches the *Tableau* in the same matter-of-fact way as an *illustration* of the doctrine. Although this comes close to heresy in the version I've been detailing, one should note that Le Trosne does not explain how the *Tableau* works and therefore sidesteps the difficult issues.

> The science of economics deals in measurable quantities and can therefore be treated as an exact science, open to calculation. It requires the use of a specific formula which also serves to bolster [*serve d'appui*] the proofs reached through reasoning. This formulation is called the *Tableau économique*, an invention that is as important as it is ingenious, painting to the eye the distribution of what the three classes produce annually, their mutual payments, and the salutary or harmful actions of the government with regard to agriculture.[148]

When he counseled the adoption of provincial assemblies in a later work,[149] Le Trosne deemed them essential for fiscal reforms, and for inculcating a patriotic spirit that would replace *esprit de corps*. "One needs to offer citizens an alternative attachment, ... and this can be done by involving them in local administration, showing them that they have a common interest, and raising this national interest above their private interests."[150] How different from Le Mercier's version.

Antonella Alimento argues that Mirabeau changed his views on representation by order to assemblies of landowners once he combined his own ideas with Quesnay's, building on his own "fourth category," the "municipal order" that oversaw urban affairs.[151] The distinction he created between an order of magistrates and a civil administration allowed him to tie representation to utility and, once he adopted Quesnay's

---

[148] Ibid., p. 319, note 1.
[149] Le Trosne, *De l'administration provinciale*. If the work was initially composed for a Toulouse essay competition in 1775, it was clearly revised since it contains references to Moheau's 1778 work on population (p. 465), and only published posthumously. Le Trosne died in 1780. On the competition, Michel Taillefer, *Une Académie interprète des Lumières, L'Académie des sciences, inscriptions, et belles-lettres de Toulouse au XVIIIe siècle* (Paris, 1984), p. 138. The particular competition was sponsored by the Toulouse Chamber of Commerce in honor of Louis XVI's coronation on a "topic of political economy": "Agriculture and trade being recognized as the true sources of national wealth, what and how much protection and encouragement should the government allot them in order to promote the greatest benefit to the state?" The prize went to Le Trosne on 1 September 1776 at a special public meeting of the Academy of Sciences which had been charged with reviewing the entries.
[150] Le Trosne, *De l'administration provinciale*, p. 209.
[151] Alimento, "Tra fronda et fisiocrazia," pp. 97–141.

definition that property created government, to switch from the protection of the "fundamental laws of the kingdom" to the protection of the "fundamental rights of property." Representative assemblies would serve as the natural allies of the monarchy, and local knowledge would continue to matter. Likewise, Michael Sonenscher sees Quesnay's economic vision answering Mirabeau's dilemma about how to reconcile the interests of the provinces with those of the king.[152] Keith Baker traced the physiocrats' switch from feudal assemblies to social representation back to Mirabeau. Yet Mirabeau's journey from representation by order, and especially of his own order, to administration through landowners was painful and tortuous and he only endorsed it once he had developed the right moral framework within which he could place his own physiocratic convictions. Quesnay rejected representative institutions as unnecessary (unstable and unreliable) no matter what their composition. In allowing Le Mercier de la Rivière to enunciate the new political order, he revealed the degree to which his physiocracy was authoritarian, unyielding, and harsh. Physiocracy's political legacy was salvaged by Du Pont de Nemours who abandoned Quesnay's position and, in summer 1775, revived Mirabeau's project and submitted it to Turgot as the blueprint for a new participatory form of government.

---

[152] Sonenscher, *Before the Deluge*, pp. 215–16.

# 6

# The Journalist

The time has come to introduce the third major player in this story, Pierre Samuel Du Pont, who fathered the Delaware Du Pont dynasty and became physiocracy's prime proselytizer both as author of physiocratic texts and as editor of the *Éphémérides du citoyen*. For Quesnay and Mirabeau, he embodied the future. "We must take good care of this young man for he will speak for us when we are dead," the doctor had remarked.[1] Du Pont fulfilled his mission, continuing to believe until his dying day that Quesnay had changed economics forever. He survived both the Revolution and Empire to offer his services to the returning Bourbons, a dynasty he had served so faithfully in younger days.

More attuned to the sensibilities of the age, Du Pont left behind autobiographical writings that organized his being around two poles: the cultivated and sensitive influence of his mother, and the practical, materialistic drive of his father. Du Pont would frequently comment on the contrary pulls of the poetic and of the scientific, which he associated with these early influences, and Quesnay and Turgot would offer alternative father figures.

He was born in Paris in 1739, the son of a Protestant clockmaker, Samuel Du Pont, who had moved from Rouen to Paris to pursue his craft, and of Alexandrine de Montchanin, a noble coreligionist whose family had fallen on hard times.[2] Du Pont Senior, ineligible as a Protestant

---

[1] "Il faut soigner ce jeune homme, car il parlera de nous quand nous seront morts." Hagley, Wintherthur Manuscripts, W2-4796, *Mémoires de Pierre Samuel Du Pont adressé à ses Enfants, 4 septembre 1793*, chapter XIV, p. 5 (each chapter in the manuscript is paginated separately).

[2] Details regarding Du Pont's life are drawn from Du Pont's manuscript memoirs, translated with notes by Elizabeth Fox-Genovese as *The Autobiography of Du Pont de Nemours*

FIGURE 6.1. *Portrait and Coat of Arms of Pierre Samuel Du Pont de Nemours* (1789), Hagley Museum and Archives.

for guild membership, had purchased his mastership as clockmaker to the King from the *Prévôté de l'hôtel*. This office entitled him to carry

(Wilmington, 1984); his 1814 letter on his "accomplishments" (W2-5098); Ambrose Saricks, *Pierre Samuel Du Pont de Nemours* (Lawrence, KS, 1965), and Schelle, *Du Pont de Nemours* (Paris, 1888). See also Liana Vardi, "Du Pont's Autobiographical Writings" in 2009 *Selected Papers from the Consortium on the Revolutionary Era* (2012).

a sword to the endless delight of his son. His mother had accompanied the Jaucourt family to Paris as companion for their daughter. They seem to have quarreled, and Du Pont does not mention knowing the famous contributor to the Encyclopedia. Alexandrine met her future husband through her brother, a clockmaker's engraver. With characteristic Rousseaunian sensibility and lack of gallantry, Du Pont confided to his sons that he had worshipped his mother and had looked for her in every woman he met. "Alas, I am obliged to admit, to my shame, that most of those who induced this illusion subsequently applied themselves to destroying it, so that I learned by painful experience that women like my mother were extremely rare."[3] His mother imbued him with chivalric dreams and the striving for finer things; as for his boorish father, all he wished was for his son to follow in his footsteps. "He feared that with my taste for reading and my already distinct bent for Poetry, I should not wish to follow his art."[4] Alexandrine nonetheless persuaded her husband to send their son to school and invented subterfuges to train him for a liberal career, including some higher mathematics, which at least met his father's approval.[5] Unfortunately Alexandrine died from complications from childbirth at age 36 in 1756, when Du Pont was still in his teens. Du Pont's one surviving sibling, a younger sister, was living in Geneva where she had been sent from fear of renewed persecution of Protestant girls.[6]

Relations between father and son soured and Pierre ran away from home on 17 April 1757 (following a particularly ferocious argument) leaving behind a letter he later retrieved and took with him to America, explaining that he was giving up watchmaking.

> I have reflected on the conduct I ought to follow, as you wished me to do, after the sad circumstances in which we found ourselves. It seems to me that the miseries I have suffered come less from the craft itself than from the misfortune of displeasing you, and my inability, as of yet, to fulfill your wishes.[7]

In the end, Du Pont applied himself to learning the trade and was received as master clockmaker on 1 January 1763.[8] When his roommate

---

[3] Fox-Genovese, trans., *The Autobiography of Pierre Samuel Du Pont de Nemours*, p. 104.
[4] Ibid., p. 123.
[5] Ibid., p. 132. She took him to see d'Alembert, so that he might recommend a tutor.
[6] Ibid., p. 157. Fleeting references show that Du Pont kept in touch with various family members throughout his life.
[7] Hagley, W2-5097, around 1810 he would list fifty-four occupations that he had engaged in.
[8] As Du Pont made plain to his sons, they were part of an extensive Protestant network that stretched across France, England, the Netherlands, and Germany, but appeared to play no visible role in his subsequent life.

contracted smallpox, Du Pont watched with fascination the treatments he received from a local surgeon and started attending lectures at the Saint-Côme Academy of Surgery.

> I was not rich enough to be admitted to the [Medical] Faculty of Paris: but I was counting on being received as a Doctor in one of the provincial faculties as soon as I could practice without danger to my patients; then I hoped to find someone who could lend me enough to buy a small office as a doctor at the court, the property and wages of which would remain with him and which would give me the right to practice medicine in Paris.[9]

This scheme fizzled out once he realized that he only came up with diagnoses after he had left the patients' bedside but, as he added in 1792, his association with Quesnay and the lack of doctors in the countryside, prodded him to hone his medical skills and to offer his services to the peasants near his country retreat.[10]

Like many a young man, he composed verses and even tried his hand at tragedy and enjoyed the pleasures of the capital. He also began composing essays on public affairs and sent one to the war minister, the duc de Choiseul, prefaced by an ode in his honor, but failed to obtain a post.[11] He first addressed agriculture in a pamphlet published anonymously in July 1763, *Réflexions sur l'écrit intitulé Richesses de l'État*, arguing that taxes were too high and should be paid only by landowners. He had had this epiphany, he would recall in his autobiography, while strolling through the countryside. A second pamphlet, published a month later, advocated free trade. He dedicated the first text to the poet Voisenon who introduced him to one of his relatives, Charles-Blaise Méliand, intendant of Soissons. Méliand hired the young man to make surveys of farm production in his generality and sponsored his membership to the Agricultural Society of Soissons. The Controller general had been promoting such associations in the hopes of stimulating agricultural productivity. Du Pont would also be named to the Agricultural Society of Orléans and as corresponding member of the London Society for the Encouragement of Arts, Manufactures, and Commerce.[12] He was

---

[9] Fox-Genovese, *Autobiography of Du Pont*, p. 193.
[10] Ibid., p. 194.
[11] Hagley, W2-4571, "Stances irrégulières au sujet de l'Ordonnance qui établit trente-deux régiments de recrues pour tenir lieu de milice" [1763]. The Duke thanked him but offered no preferment.
[12] Du Pont kept the notifications of memberships. See W2-5036 for Soissons (4 September 1763); W2-5037 for Orléans (16 November 1754), and W2-5038 for London (18 November 1766).

extremely proud of these achievements as he would of any mark of favor (French and foreign) throughout his life.[13]

Voisenon counseled Du Pont to send his pamphlets to celebrities, including Voltaire and Mirabeau (whose works he now read). Voltaire praised the young author's combination of "finance and poetry."[14] Mirabeau urged him to acquaint himself with Quesnay's articles in the Encyclopedia. The doctor himself had found much to approve of in Du Pont's conclusions: "Quesnay, who perused every morning those [tracts] that had been published the previous night, only to consign them to his watercloset, accepted mine, and jotted 'good' on the front page and held on to them."[15]

Quesnay advised his new protégé to accompany Méliand on a tour of his generality, and packed him off with a list of questions. He also urged him to write a treatise supporting free trade in grain. Ensconced in Méliand's library, Du Pont spent his days reading rather than producing the expected agricultural surveys. He did, however, work on the treatise and handed a draft to Quesnay that pleased him so much that he suggested that Du Pont dedicate the work to Mme de Pompadour. She died in April 1764 after a brief illness, but Du Pont retained the dedication, although he knew he would incur the wrath of Choiseul who had quarreled with the favorite and detested Quesnay.[16] The doctor's loss of influence at Court after Mme de Pompadour's death had deleterious effects on Du Pont's love life as his fiancée's parents broke off their engagement. They evoked his Protestantism as an excuse, so had to relent once he converted and allow the couple to wed on 26 January 1766. The groom's witnesses included the Controller general L'Averdy, Trudaine de Montigny, Méliand and the farmer general Mézières, a mix of physiocratic allies as well as nonphysiocratic sponsors.[17]

Du Pont's pamphlet on the grain trade had caught the attention of Jacques Turgot, Intendant of Limousin who introduced him in turn to Daniel Trudaine and his son Charles-Louis Trudaine de Montigny of the

---

[13] The passport that permitted Du Pont to travel to Poland on 3 July 1774 described him as "conseiller aulique de notre très cher et très aimé cousin le margrave de Baden." Hagley, W2-5045. H. Arnold Barton, "Gustav III of Sweden and the Enlightenment," *Eighteenth-Century Studies* 6:1 (1972), pp. 1–34, reminds us that Mirabeau was among the first recipients of the Order (p. 17).

[14] Hagley, W2-1516, Letter from Voltaire to Du Pont, 16 August 1763.

[15] Du Pont, *Mémoires*, chapter XII, p. 10, my translation.

[16] The work appeared as *Sur l'exportation et l'importation des grains* (Paris, 1764). See Du Pont, *Mémoires*, chapter XIV.

[17] Saricks, *Du Pont*, p. 45.

Bureau of Commerce and Inspection of Manufactures.[18] In 1764, Turgot and the Trudaines were working on the details of an edict that would free the grain trade and Du Pont was invited to assist them. At Turgot's insistence, moreover, the Controller general L'Averdy hired him to compile agricultural statistics in the Soissonnais and Limousin.[19] Soon after L'Averdy offered him the editorship of the new *Journal de l'agriculture, du commerce et des finances* he was subsidizing, but Du Pont's editorial meddling with submissions, in open support of Quesnay's system, led to his dismissal in October 1766.[20] Unemployed, Du Pont returned to toting up leases, claiming to Voltaire that he had visited over 3,000 farms.[21]

In October 1767, Mme Du Pont gave birth to a son who was called Victor in honor of his godfather, the marquis de Mirabeau. A second son, Pierre-François, died aged a few months in 1769, and Turgot acted as godfather to a third, born in June 1771.

> Here is my proxy, my dear Du Pont, for the baptism of the child that Mme Du Pont is carrying. If it is a boy, why don't you call him Eleuthère-Irénée in honour of liberty and peace. Both names would also suit a girl. If you wish to give less meaningful names, you know that I am called Anne-Robert-Jacques and this should give you plenty of choice.[22]

Du Pont produced the first compendium of physiocratic essays, giving pride of place to Quesnay's article on "natural law."[23] At this point he was also asked to take over the editorship of a monthly review founded by the abbé Baudeau in 1765 that focused on public affairs in the manner of Addison's *Spectator*. Baudeau had been seduced by Quesnay's theory and the journal began to feature articles on the Economists' program. Under Du Pont's stewardship the *Éphémérides du citoyen* flourished, circulation reaching five hundred subscribers.[24] Unfortunately collaborators were few and Du Pont ended up penning most of the articles, contributing 110 articles and 40 brief commentaries to the 48 volumes under his

---

[18] On this body, see Minard, *La fortune du Colbertisme*.
[19] Schelle, *Du Pont de Nemours*, p. 43.
[20] Du Pont reported this opposition to Le Trosne on 24 July 1766 [Hagley, W2-5] and was still complaining to Trudaine de Montigny on 20 October 1766 [Hagley, W2-6].
[21] Letter to Voltaire of 10 September 1769 [Hagley, W2-18] and letter to Méliand of spring 1767 [Hagley, W2-10].
[22] Letter from Turgot to Du Pont, Limoges, 24 May 1771 in Gustave Schelle, ed., *Oeuvres de Turgot et documents le concernant*, III, p. 487.
[23] *Physiocratie* (Paris, November 1767) and *De l'origine et des progès d'une science nouvelle* (London, 1768).
[24] Schelle, *Du Pont de Nemours*, p. 102.

direction.²⁵ Repeated delays in publication and a regime less favorable to economic reform led to the suppression of the journal at the end of 1772.

Du Pont was once more adrift. Through the marquis de Mirabeau he had met the Margrave of Baden, Carl Friedrich and his wife, Carolina Luisa, a noted art collector.²⁶ Du Pont kept the Margrave and Margravine abreast of the latest Parisian publications and art salons, and began tutoring their son Carl Ludwig from afar, hoping in vain to transform these tasks into an actual post at the court in Karlsruhe. In desperation, with no steady source of income, he accepted an offer from the Polish magnate Adam Czatoryski to tutor his children and become an honorary councilor of the Republic of Poland with the added duties of Secretary of the Polish National Education Council and directorship of its Academy.²⁷ A very despondent Du Pont set off for Warsaw with his wife and sons. He reported unhappily to Quesnay:

It has been a torment for me to live in a Republic without a Republic, a den of plunderers, where only a small, infinitely small number of worthy citizens are enlightened, where few show perseverance, and even fewer have the means to. The legislators are paid by the usurpers [Russians] at the expense of the public or of individuals who displease them, and they only care about two things: augmenting their already scandalous wealth and smothering all Enlightenment, undermining institutions that might restore order to the state, morality to the nation, and freedom to it people.²⁸

In August 1774, the new monarch, Louis XVI, named Turgot Controller general and Du Pont was summoned back to France with the title (and remuneration) of Inspector General of Commerce and as Turgot's personal assistant.²⁹ In a long letter, expressing his hopes for the new era

---

²⁵ Saricks, *Du Pont*, p. 53.
²⁶ Patrick Michel, "Caroline Louise de Bade 'La Minerve de Hesse', collectionneur exemplaire" in Pierre Rosenberg, ed., *Peintures françaises dans les collections allemandes XVIIe–XVIIIe siècles* (Paris, 2005), pp. 65–74.
²⁷ Saricks, *Du Pont*, pp. 58–60.
²⁸ Hagley, W2-38, letter written from Saxony on 18 December 1774, as Du Pont was on his way back to France. He went on to complain that all funding for education had been cut and as for his tutoring duties: "You can imagine what a boring task it is for a man, and for my breed of statesman, to have to raise a four-year old tot [*marmot*]." There was no place on earth equal to France, he concluded. It was "the least corrupt, the least debased, the most amiable" of nations.
²⁹ Hagley, W2-5050, letter recalling Du Pont sent from Versailles on 19 September 1774, signed by the King. Hagley, W2-1672, letter from Turgot to Du Pont from Versailles, 21 September 1774; Hagley, W2-37 Du Pont's response to Turgot, dated 29 October 1774. Prince Czatoryski would be reimbursed, Du Pont would be able to recover the property he had sold when he left France. Hagley, W2-4589, Du Pont's project for

that was about to dawn, Du Pont explained to Turgot what reforms he ought to undertake, warning him, however, that it would probably take four to five years to convince the public of their worth.[30] The minister was determined to act quickly, but his reforms garnered such opposition from the Court and various vested interests that he was ousted from office in May 1776.[31] After Turgot's fall, Du Pont was once more unemployed and penniless. Disconsolate and self-pitying, he composed his own epitaph in 1778:

Here lies Pierre Samuel Du Pont, knight of the Royal Order of Vasa, intimate councilor of the Legations of Baden, honorary councilor to the Supreme Council on Education in Poland, General Inspector of Commerce of France, after having been graced with the benevolence of Carl Friedrich, Gustav III, Stanislas Augustus, enjoying the full confidence and close friendship of Anne Robert Jacques Turgot, deprived by that minister's disgrace from the hope of being useful to his country and to Europe, retired to this rustic haven, wonderfully assisted by Nicole Charlotte Marie Louise Le Dée, his amiable, active, prudent, benevolent and beloved wife, where he has built a country retreat, planted trees, introduced the cultivation of new plants, provided work and lessened poverty, and cured the inhabitants of their illnesses. May his agricultural activities be happier than his political occupations, and prove so successful that this inscription never see the light of day.[32]

Despite the great rivalry between Turgot and the neo-mercantilist finance minister Jacques Necker, the latter offered Du Pont some work gathering trade statistics.[33] In his spare time, Du Pont translated the opening cantos of Ariosto's *Orlando Furioso*, publishing the work anonymously while sending copies to the crowned heads of Europe, making plain he was the author.

His great patron Turgot died in 1781. "The age of illusions is past! I no longer flatter myself that I might be useful to mankind," he wrote to Carl Friedrich of Baden, in winter 1782.[34] Despondently, he added: "I lost Mr. Quesnay, my first teacher. I witnessed all the improvements that

---

Polish education: "Projet d'une académie et des universités en Pologne par Du Pont de Nemours" [1774].
[30] Hagley, W2-36, "Fragment d'une lettre à M. Turgot en date de Varsovie, le 12 octobre 1774."
[31] For an excellent analysis of Turgot's ministry, see Edgar Faure, *La Disgrâce de Turgot* (Paris, 1961).
[32] Hagley, W2-5095. Epitaph 1778.
[33] Hagley, W2-60, letter from Du Pont to Necker of 25 December 1778, thanking him for employing him on reports of the balance of trade.
[34] Letter of 4 February 1782 in Knies, *Carl Friedrichs von Baden*, I, pp. 202-3.

Mr. Turgot brought to France undone.... I watched this virtuous citizen, this most learned, amiable, and best of men, whose love I had the honour to enjoy, die in my arms, in the prime of life." He felt alone, rudderless, and unloved. Despite his goodwill and kindness, Mirabeau "lacked tolerance and could not stand opinions that differed from his own." Moreover, Mirabeau did not love him the way Turgot had or "the way I once had the unbelievable joy to believe that Your Highness condescended to love me."

Salvation would arrive in the guise of the comte de Vergennes, Louis XVI's foreign minister, who befriended Du Pont and in 1783 found him work in the ministries of the navy, foreign affairs, and finance.[35] Although not as instrumental as he liked to claim in the drafting of the Treaty of Paris that ended the American War, it did win him the friendship of Thomas Jefferson. In December 1783, again through the good offices of Vergennes, Du Pont was granted letters of nobility.[36] Just when his professional prospects seem to be stabilizing, his wife died in September 1784. Du Pont found lodgings for himself and his sons in Paris. He worked on the commissions that established free trade between France and England and France and the United States. In November 1786 Vergennes helped him acquire the title of *conseiller d'état*, ensconcing him within the French administrative hierarchy.

France was entering a period of financial crisis so dire that it could not negotiate new loans. In desperation, the Controller general, Calonne, called an Assembly of Notables with representatives from the old nobility and high clergy hoping it would agree to major changes in the tax base. Du Pont was named second secretary and therefore witnessed firsthand the prerevolutionary upheavals that failed to achieve any reforms. He had clearly acquired enough *gravitas* to be included in the so-called Committee of Thirty that brought together like-minded men to work out strategies for the upcoming Estates General. The group met at the house of Adrien Duport and included Lafayette, La Rochefoucauld-Liancourt, Condorcet, Talleyrand, and Siéyès.[37] Du Pont was elected deputy for Nemours on 17 March 1789, despite a few protests that a "noble" should not be allowed to represent the Commons.[38] During the Revolution, Du Pont sided with the more moderate reformers, supporting the retention of the King's veto

---

[35] Saricks, *Du Pont de Nemours*, p. 76.
[36] Ibid., p. 84. This incited Du Pont to concoct domestic ceremonies for each of his sons when they turned twelve when he formally handed them their first sword. These are detailed in Hagley, W2-5075 and W2-5076.
[37] Saricks, *Du Pont de Nemours*, pp. 135-7.
[38] Letter from Irénée Du Pont to his brother Victor, from Nemours, dated 18 March 1789. Hagley, Wintherthur Ms., Series E, "Smith transcripts" vol. 13, pp. 26-31. "Father's

and pushing for physiocratically inspired legislation. Since there were several deputies by that name, he became known as "de Nemours" to distinguish him from the other Du Ponts. His activities and writings during the Revolution will be discussed in the last chapter. It is now time, therefore, to return to the Du Pont of the late 1760s and 1770s.

While still in his twenties, Du Pont had become physiocracy's most assiduous propagandist. Unlike Quesnay or Mirabeau he owed all his successes to the doctrine. Without it, he might have eked a living as clockmaker or joined the many literary aspirants who roamed the capital.[39] His adherence to the physiocratic creed opened doors for him in the royal administration and secured him livings (as long as his patrons were in power). Other early supporters of Quesnay, like Louis Paul Abeille, inspector of manufactures and later secretary of the bureau of commerce, distanced themselves from the movement once they encountered its rigidity.[40] Few stuck with it through thick and thin, and Du Pont was one of the rare devotees whose commitment survived momentary expediency. Physiocracy had not only been kind to him as he told Sophie de Monnier, the comte de Mirabeau's mistress:

Various circumstances attached me to the Economists. They did me both good and harm; they taught me a real and profound science and made me look ridiculous.

> [Papa] speech was intended to bring them to accept union; but as you will see, this did not happen. As soon as the Third had been assembled, Mr. Fouquet, a Nemours lawyer who hoped to be elected deputy opposed Father for this reason. He reproved him most sharply for wishing to unite the Third with people it should regard with suspicion. Father retorted squarely and stood by his opinion for a long time with only Mr. de la Comble on his side. The barking [*clabaudages*] and cabal of the people of Nemours won in the end, and the Third voted to keep the three orders separate." Several days later, he reported: "They had planned a bread riot at the time when Father had persuaded the Duke of Orléans to abolish his banal flour-mills [*moulins banaux*]. They are attempting by means of calumny to gather signatures in the countryside for a protest against Father's election and his *cahier*. He took precautions, however, to ward off the effects of such a manoeuvre."

[39] See for example, Robert Darnton's "The High Enlightenment and the Low-Life of Literature in Pre-Revolutionary France," *Past and Present* No. 51 (May 1971), 81–115; *The Great Cat Massacre and Other Episodes in French Cultural History* (New York, 1985); and "An Early Information Society: News and the Media in Eighteenth-Century France," *The American Historical Review* 105:1 (2000), 1–35; Daniel Roche, *Les Républicains des lettres*; Dena Goodman, *The Republic of Letters*; Paul Bénichou, *Le sacre de l'écrivain 1750–1830* (Paris, 1973), [*The Consecration of the Writer, 1750–1830*], translated by Mark K. Jensen (Lincoln and London, 1999).

[40] When Abeille complained that Du Pont had included his work in his list of Economic texts in the *Ephémérides*, Du Pont wrote him a letter that revisited their longstanding conflicts, including Abeille's "theft" of notes that Quesnay had intended for Du Pont. n.d. [1768] Hagley, W2-17.

Had I done half as much for another organization as I did for theirs, I would be twice as famous. I am barely known in France, although Turgot's ministry showed that I was a good and disinterested man, even somewhat talented.... Ask around Paris, ask men of letters: some will tell you that I am mad, others that I am a fool, and others still will say they have never heard of me.[41]

Du Pont acquired firsthand experience of agricultural statistics in the mid-1760s, and parlayed it into positions in the high administration and a seat on fiscal committees during the Revolution.[42] He continued to write on financial questions but never produced the full-fledged treatise on the French economy that one might have expected from a self-styled *économiste*. Instead, he expanded the cultural side of the doctrine reserving, it would seem, his more sober reflections for actual government work. As his personal papers and publications demonstrate, he never abandoned his interest in poetry, belles-lettres, and the arts – which spoke to the "feminine" side he associated with his mother and that he sometimes had trouble reconciling with his more "manly" aspirations. Most of his literary offerings took the form of poems and fables for his family and friends, or of translations of the classics,[43] but in the early 1770s he also began to consider seriously how the arts might be brought into line with the natural order. Since Du Pont's more standard dissemination of Quesnay's doctrine is well known, I will spend the next several chapters dealing with his less familiar efforts to render physiocracy in other modes.

## Physiocratic Aesthetics

One might be tempted to treat the reviews of plays and poems or the speculations on the nature of the arts that Du Pont began to offer in the *Éphémérides* as mere fillers and relatively benign ones at that. This would be to forget the role that culture played in the Enlightenment and the seriousness with which Du Pont and his fellow physiocrats viewed the "decay of morals" and the "frivolity" of contemporary arts. One of his intentions, therefore, was to monitor the portrayal of the countryside for the benefit of his readers, and to praise all those who contributed to the moral elevation of their fellow men. In the process, Du Pont added "physiocratic aesthetics" to the doctrine's ever-extending

---

[41] Hagley, W2-74. Letter to the marquise de Monnier, from Bois des Fossés, 27 October 1779.
[42] See for example his pamphlets on the *aides* (taxes on alcoholic beverages) of the 1790s. *Douze pamphlets sur les droits des aides* (reproduced on Gallica).
[43] In prison, he also began a translation of Samuel Richardson's *Sir Charles Grandison*.

tentacles and began to envisage what cultural life might be like in a "regenerated kingdom."

Du Pont's association with Jacques Turgot reassured him that there was no shame in appreciating the arts. Over the years, they exchanged hundreds of letters and Du Pont brought about one thousand with him to Delaware. As his edition of Turgot's works demonstrates, Du Pont was both aware of and sympathetic to Turgot's writings on language, poetry, and translation.[44] In the 1750s, while learning German, Turgot had helped Michel Huber translate Salomon Gessner's lyric poems and, fluent in English, had been the first French translator of Ossian, fueling in both instances the French "pre-romantic" craze for these writers.[45] In the 1770s, Turgot undertook a translation of Virgil's *Aeneid* in measured verse (*vers métriques*), the only poetic form he now deemed acceptable.[46] Plunging into cultural debates was therefore commensurate with a life devoted to the "new science of economics." As a matter of fact, Turgot had suggested that Du Pont vary the offerings in the *Éphémérides*:

It is true that one gets tired of always repeating the same things; but then why do you always wish to say the same things? Why do you confine yourself to a single theme and insist on being nothing but an *économiste* when you could easily treat all sorts of subjects relevant to politics, the happiness of mankind, morals, or legislation? You all want for Quesnay and his first disciples to have said everything. You forbid any discussion of all the things he didn't talk about, and when you do address such topics, you always bring them back to what these masters said about them. This then lends all your writings the same monotonous ring.[47]

Du Pont and Turgot disagreed, however, about the transformative capacity of the arts. Although he did not deny that they might encourage virtuous behavior, Turgot focused principally on their internal merits,

---

[44] See my "Writing the Lives of Eighteenth-Century Economists," *The American Historical Review*, 114:3 (2009), 652–61; Pierre Samuel Du Pont de Nemours, ed., *Oeuvres de Mr. Turgot, ministre d'état*, IX (Paris, 1811); Daniel Droixhe, *La linguistique et l'appel de l'histoire (1600–1800), Rationalisme et révolutions positivistes* (Geneva and Paris, 1978); Nathalie Vincent-Munnia, *Les premiers poèmes en prose: généalogie d'un genre dans la première moitié du dix-neuvième siècle français* (Paris, 1996); Christian Leroy, *La poésie en prose française du XVIIe siècle à nos jours* (Paris, 2001); and Paul Van Thiegen, *Ossian en France* (1920) and *Le Préromantisme*, 3 vols. (Paris, 1929–1947).
[45] See Du Pont, *Oeuvres de M. Turgot*, IX; Salomon Gessner, *La mort d'Abel* (Paris, 1760); Turgot, "Lettre de M. Turgot aux Auteurs du *Journal étranger* sur les poésies Erses," *Journal étranger* (September 1760), 3–16.
[46] It replicated the "natural cadence of speech" according to Turgot.
[47] Gustave Schelle, ed., *Oeuvres de Turgot et documents le concernant*, III, p. 484, letter from Turgot to Du Pont, Limoges, 7 May 1771.

the revitalization of literary expression, and cultural exchanges among nations. He did not extend his theoretical explorations beyond poetry and translation, even if he appreciated music and painting as a man of sensibility and taste.[48]

He could therefore wonder on the one hand at Du Pont's dislike of Greuze: "Would this be because of his [paintings] of the *Fils ingrat* and *Fils puni*? These two sublime pieces, set alongside, depict a heart-rending situation. They are more eloquent and useful than a sermon."[49] The arts might arouse emotional responses, but this did not mean that poetry or drama should be used to change people's positions on economic matters. The public would be persuaded by rational demonstrations, not by fairytales, and in this Turgot went farther than Quesnay, who allowed Mirabeau to digress into anecdotes.[50] A lover of both poetry and economics, Turgot saw them as complementary realms, speaking to different sides of the human experience.

For Du Pont not only were the two realms intertwined but knowledge arose from a single powerful source. The "dismal science" was far from that, he reassured Carl Ludwig, the Margrave's son: "There is no reason to think of philosophy as something dour, and least of all economic philosophy. All that is beautiful, honest, tender, touching, sunny, and pleasant falls under the dominion [*est du ressort*] of the science whose object is human felicity."[51] Consequently, Du Pont presumed that moral uplift would accompany Turgot's ministry: a "rebirth of morals, which is always preferable to a rebirth of letters," as he put it to the Margrave, although he lamented that "in the midst of our successes we have so many enemies, so many cabals to defeat, such corrupt mores to redress or combat."[52]

When Du Pont began addressing art and literature in the *Éphémérides*, literary and art criticism were developing into distinct realms, each with

---

[48] Charlotte Guichard, *Les Amateurs d'art à Paris au XVIIIe siècle* (Paris, 2008), p. 35, describes the enthusiasm of the Academy of Painting when Turgot was named Controller general.

[49] Schelle, *Oeuvres de Turgot et documents le concernant*, III, p. 497, letter from Turgot to Du Pont, Limoges, 15 October 1771. The works were purchased by the marquis de Véri, brother of Turgot's friend, the abbé Véri. Colin C. Bailey, *Patriotic Taste, Collecting Modern Art in Pre-Revolutionary Paris* (New Haven, 2002), p. 117.

[50] Schelle, *Oeuvres de Turgot et documents le concernant*, III, pp. 481–2, letter from Turgot to Du Pont, Limoges, 12 April 1771 (and see Chapter 7).

[51] Hagley, W2-4582, Du Pont to Carl Ludwig of Baden, Paris, 22 January 1772.

[52] Knies, *Carl Friedrichs von Baden*, I, pp. 182–3. Letter from Du Pont to Carl Ludwig, Paris, 4 September 1775.

its rules and particular expectations. Such a split challenged the traditional search for "the attributes common to all the arts" and the old association between poetry and painting based on the Horatian dictum *ut pictura poesis* (poetry comes from painting), which had been commonly invoked in the seventeenth century. Yet the public still responded to poetry, drama, and the fine arts based on the hierarchy of genres dating back to Aristotle and Horace, and demanded that they offer moral lessons, pleasurable responses, emotional release, as well as probing investigations of the human condition.[53] Two additional concepts had joined the aesthetic arsenal: *belle nature* and the *je ne sais quoi*. In the first case, the arts were called on to represent ideal nature (*belle nature*) rather than "imitating" the debased version that met the eye. It was the artist's task to capture this inner essence, emphasizing the creative and transformative power of art. The source of his inspiration and the extent to which it arose from actual contact with nature remained vigorously debated.

In attempting to capture *belle nature*, a great artist tapped into a *je ne sais quoi* ("I know not what"): an indescribable dimension that lay beyond the reach of reason. The term had originated in Spain but found a home in seventeenth-century France where it fit the new understanding that great art transcend the very rules it was meant to embody.[54]

[53] There is a vast literature on the subject. Enlightening overviews can be found in H. B. Nisbet and Claude Rawson, *The Cambridge History of Literary Criticism*, vol. IV: *The Eighteenth Century* (Cambridge, 1997); Annie Becq, *Genèse de l'esthétique*; Paul Bénichou, *Le sacre de l'écrivain, 1750–1830* (Paris, 1973); Thomas E. Crow, *Painters and Public Life in Eighteenth-Century Paris* (New Haven and London, 1985); André Fontaine, *Les doctrines d'art en France, peintres, amateurs, critiques de Poussin à Diderot* (Geneva, 1989); Marian Hobson, *The Object of Art*; Jean Starobinsky, *L'Oeil Vivant II: La relation critique* (Paris, 1970); John Brewer, *The Pleasures of the Imagination: English Culture in the Eighteenth Century* (Chicago, 2000); Lionello Venturi, *Histoire de la critique d'art* (Paris, 1969); Serge Trotthein, ed., *L'Esthétique naît-elle au XVIIIe siècle?* (Paris, 2000); Edouard Pommier, *Winckelmann, inventeur de l'histoire de l'art* (Paris, 2003); John C. O'Neal, *The Authority of Experience, Sensationist Theory in the French Enlightenment* (University Park, Pa., 1996).

[54] See Hobson, *The Object of Art*, p. 37, Becq, *Genèse de l'esthétique*, pp. 67–72; Richard Scholar, *The Je-Ne-Sais-Quoi in Early Modern Culture: Encounters with a Certain Something* (Oxford, 2005); Lawrence Kerslake, *Essays on the Sublime: Analyses of French Writings on the Sublime from Boileau to La Harpe* (Bern and New York, 2000); Jean-Paul Sermain, "Le code du bon goût (1725–1750)" and Peter France, "Lumières, politesse et énergie" in Marc Fumaroli, ed., *Histoire de la rhétorique*. Orla Smyth, "La sympathie des belles âmes: réflexion sur la théorie des Belles-Lettres au début du XVIIIe siècle," pp. 131–48; and Daniel Dumouchel, "Le problème de Du Bos et l'affect compatissant: l'esthétique du XVIIIe siècle à l'épreuve du paradoxe tragique," pp. 473–95, in Thierry Belleguic et al., *Les Discours de la sympathie, Enquête sur une notion de l'âge classique à la modernité* (Quebec, 2007).

Artists had always been expected to display "inventiveness" (*ingenium*). Now inspiration would enable them to capture an elusive dimension that turned representation into art.[55] Great poets and painters were thus born and not made, and works of everlasting value were expressions of individual genius. Such originality was prized despite the Royal Academy of Painting and the Académie française's insistence on a rigid separation of genres, and continued to equate beauty with the classical principles of reason, order, symmetry, and hierarchy.[56]

The new sensationalist philosophies brought new perspectives on how to stimulate audiences and elicit sympathetic responses from them, as classical rhetoric itself demanded.[57] Speculations arose on the effects of pain and pleasure on audiences and whether the responses engendered by the arts were automatic – and hence universal reflexes – or whether they could be acquired and taught. Yet not all responses were meant to be pleasurable as the translation in 1674 by Boileau of the *Treatise on the Sublime* (dating from Late Antiquity) reminded readers. The arts could employ strong, disturbing imagery to induce feelings of awe and unease.[58] This sublime went beyond lofty and elevated expression and spiritual trances, to induce jolts that reminded viewers that human beings were subject to forces that they could not always control and spoke to the "disquiet" that John Locke attributed to the human condition.

[55] As John Barrell points out, the "originality" demanded of eighteenth-century artists entailed the contradictory demands of novelty and remaining true to nature. *The Political Theory of Painting from Reynolds to Hazlitt* (New Haven, 1986), p. 125.
[56] Different criteria therefore governed the arts and the sciences. In the first, it was the particular manifestations of general rules that mattered; in the second, the particular example only made sense within general laws. This question was debated in the Republic of Letters as an offshoot of the "quarrel of the Ancients and the Moderns." In his *Preliminary Discourse to the Encyclopedia of Diderot* (1751), d'Alembert argued for the bond between the arts and sciences (p. 5). The eighteenth-century's considerations on their relationship are investigated in articles edited by François Azouvi, Michel Baridon, and Christine Rolland, "Mouvement des sciences et esthétique(s)," in a special issue of *Dix-huitième siècle* 31 (1999). See also Marc Fumaroli, *La Querelle des Anciens et des Modernes* (Paris, 2001); Douglas Lane Patey, "Ancients and Moderns" in H. B. Nisbet and Claude Rawson, eds., *The Cambridge History of Literary Criticism*, vol. IV: *The Eighteenth Century* (Cambridge, 1997), pp. 32–71; Stuart Gillespie "Translation and Canon-Formation," pp. 9–20, and Stuart Gillespie and Robin Sowerby, "Translation and Literary Innovation," pp. 21–37, in Stuart Gillespie and David Hopkins, eds., *The Oxford History of Literary Translation in English*, vol. 3: *1660–1790* (Oxford, 2005).
[57] See Becq, *Genèse de l'esthétique*, pp. 340–4.
[58] Nicolas Boileau-Despréaux, *Traité du sublime ou du merveilleux dans le discours traduit du grec de Longin* in *Oeuvres diverses du Sieur D\*\*\** (Paris, 1674). The original work is no longer ascribed to "Longinus." Edmund Burke's *A Philosophical Enquiry into the Origins of our Ideas of the Sublime and Beautiful* (London, 1757) provided the standard English formulation in the second half of the eighteenth century.

But such jolts also focused the attention of an otherwise jaded public. Influential eighteenth-century French art theorists like the abbés Du Bos and Batteux argued that the strength of the arts lay in their capacity to move and interest audiences.[59] Du Bos spoke of an aesthetic sensation which recalls contemporary British speculations about a spontaneous enthusiastic response in the human psyche which Lord Shaftsbury turned into a sign of natural sociability. Francis Hutcheson built on Shaftesbury's idea of an independent moral sense to propose that men also possessed an inner sense of beauty (or sixth sense) that made them respond instinctively to its manifestations.[60] That human beings possessed distinct aesthetic sensibilities was becoming increasingly accepted. If such responses were universal, they were not confined to elites, and one was duty-bound to introduce the public to such "pleasures of the imagination."[61] In Germany, Alexander Baumgarten proposed the imagination as a separate form of cognition, aroused by aesthetic responses, which differed from but were as valid as intellectual cognition. At the end of the eighteenth century, Immanuel Kant would bring together these various theories, asserting that aesthetic experience and moral goodness were one and the same thing.[62] The arts did not merely entertain or use their wiles to manipulate audiences, they spoke to an internal sense that stimulated the public to unselfish and generous actions. A lesson one might learn, if one

---

[59] Ernst Cassirer, *The Philosophy of the Englightenment* (Princeton, 1951), chapter VII; Du Bos, *Rélexions critiques sur la poësie et sur la peinture*; and Batteux, *Les beaux-arts réduits à un même principe*. In England, more emphasis was placed on the duty of the arts to instruct and not just please or move audiences. Barrell, *The Political Theory of Painting*, p. 43.

[60] See Alexander Broadie, "Art and Aesthetic Theory" in Alexander Broadie, ed., *The Cambridge Companion to the Scottish Enlightenment* (Cambridge, 2003) pp. 280–97; Paul Guyer, "The Origins of Modern Aesthetics: 1711–35" in Peter Kivy, ed., *Blackwell Guide to Aesthetics* (Oxford, 2004), pp. 15–44; and Cassirer, *The Philosophy of the Enlightenment*, pp. 312–31 and 338–60. Anthony Ashley Cooper, third earl of Shaftsbury published in 1711, *Characteristics of Men, Manners, Opinions, Times*, the following year Addison would publish his series on the "Pleasures of the Imagination" in his magazine, *The Spectator*. Francis Hutcheson's *Inquiry into the Original of Our Ideas of Beauty and Virtue* appeared in 1725.

[61] Joseph Addison in *The Spectator* (1712), numbers 411–421. See, among others, John Brewer's *The Pleasures of the Imagination*. Richard Steele's *Tatler* (1709–11) and Joseph Addison and Richard Steele's *The Spectator* (1711–12) were copied throughout Europe.

[62] For example, Montesquieu's *Essai sur le goût* (Paris, 1993), p. 11, in rebuttal to Du Bos, ascribed separate pleasures to the soul, independent of the senses. Baumgarten first published his views in *Philosophische Bertachtungen über einige Bedingungen des Gedichts* in 1735 and *Aesthetica* in 1750. Kant, *Critique of the Aesthetic Power of Judgment* (1790). See Guyer, "The Origins of Modern Aesthetics: 1711–45," p. 41.

was so inclined, was that the arts might be harnessed to educate, elevate, and reform social behavior.

It was within such contemporary developments that Du Pont began to reflect on the nature and especially the usefulness of the arts. In articles in the *Éphémérides* he called on belles-lettres and the fine arts to teach the public virtue, and, like physiocracy, to do so by delving deep into the foundations of the physical and moral order.[63]

> However enjoyable it is to study Belles-Lettres, these must never be treated just as entertainment. They are a form of instruction whose purpose is to encourage honest and virtuous behaviour and discourage vice, disorder, and crime. Poets, Orators, and Philosophers (whose mission is to guide the other two), can only fulfill these worthy goals by painting nature faithfully, embodying its principles and awe-inspiring laws and, if possible, attaining its level of energy.

Inner sensibility drew us irresistibly to the beauty that virtue exuded but Du Pont offered no psychological explanation for this, taking it for granted.[64] Since the arts stimulated instinctive responses, they must use this power for good.

> Let the Poet and Orator urge us ever forward, let them reinforce and confirm our hearts' first impulses and illumine them with vivid and warm images and they will be sure to move and affect us, and to make a powerful and lasting impression.[65]

Du Pont repeated that the arts inspire us to virtue "because man has a natural propensity to prudence and justice."[66] "The role of Art is to show men, prove to their reason, and open their hearts to the great truth, which they have disregarded for so long, that it is in their best interest on this earth, to follow a stern yet benevolent justice." In relying on the arts to teach men to "see properly, think properly, speak appropriately," he turned them into physiocracy's natural allies. They would convince the public to adopt the natural order.[67]

In Antiquity Du Pont informs his readers, "all philosophers were poets and all poets philosophers."[68] Poetry can once again aspire to that goal

---

[63] He begins with a multipart review of Saint-Lambert's third version of *Les Saisons* in *Éphémérides* (1769), volume III, pp. 133–58, volume IV, pp. 120–34, and volume V, pp. 169–89.
[64] Ibid.
[65] "Du principe commun aux beaux-arts," p. 46.
[66] "Traité des droits du genie," *Éphémérides* (1769), vol. XI, p. 132.
[67] Du Pont, "Du principe commun," p. 55.
[68] Du Pont, "Idées sur la Poésie en général et la poésie dramatique en particulier," *Éphémérides* (1771), XII, p. 131.

and demonstrate that philosophical ideas could be rendered in verse.[69] Du Pont ranks very highly "the new poetry and plays coming out of Germany that glorify goodness and Diderot's and Saurin's plays that render virtue appealing and show the dangers of misbehaving." Another example was *The Druids*, a drama that "showed that reason had to be respected, the laws obeyed, the Supreme Being venerated, and fraternity extended to all men."[70] On the other hand, he condemned Turpin's play *Cyrus* for suggesting that the greatest Roman authors, Horace and Virgil, owed their genius to the turmoil of the age.[71] As far as Du Pont was concerned, Turpin could say such things because the Parisian public had become so jaded that it needed strong emotions to arouse it, indifferent to the harm they might cause or the falsehoods they peddled. Horace and Virgil should be vilified for flattering tyrants. They had led princes to believe that no matter how corrupt, cruel, or unjust, all would be forgiven if they supported the arts. Talent must be used wisely. Du Pont's aesthetic philosophy thus rejected art's entertainment value, its pleasurable qualities (even with occasional jolts) unless manipulated for virtuous ends, indeed because he acknowledged art's lasting effects.

A rustic poem, which by its very nature and that of its subject matter must sow a thousand useful seeds in the hearts of young men who read more poems than moral or political treatises, seems to us so important that we would fail in our duty if we did not analyse them thoroughly: we are not interested in literature *per se*. Purely literary beauties do not move us as much as those that can contribute to the main goal we have set ourselves, and that the Author shares as well. We gaze with pleasure at the brilliant flowers that promise great harvests, but we prefer the harvests themselves. The great merit of the Poem of the *Seasons* is that the charm of its beautiful verses is almost always deployed to ornament the precepts, advice, or images directed toward general utility and people's happiness. The author always links these crucial aspects.[72]

The Physiocrat and the Poet both endeavored to reveal man's true nature and nature's true plans. Since peasants and farmers were already aware of these realities, art had to educate city folk and the landed elite. It could not do so if poets resorted to age-old clichés. Saint-Lambert, for example, had confused support for agriculture with operetta peasants when he

---

[69] Du Pont, "Idées sur la Poésie," p. 137.
[70] Du Pont further approved Le Blanc de Guillet's depiction of the "imperfections of savage life." Review of *Les Druides* in *Ephémérides* (1771) vol. 12, p. 146.
[71] Discussion of *Cyrus, A Tragedy in Five Acts* for the benefit of Carl Ludwig of Baden, Knies, *Carl Friedrichs von Baden*, II, pp. 33–9 (1 February 1773).
[72] Du Pont, review of Saint-Lambert's *Seasons*, *Éphémérides*, (1769), IV, pp. 125–6.

lauded their small houses and tiny plots of land. *The Seasons* should have celebrated *big* farms, *big* barns, and *big* profits. Once artists grasped the importance of the "natural order," art, like politics and economics, would be rejuvinated.[73]

Like other physiocrats, Du Pont relied on the enlightened despot to oversee society and morals, but this monarch had to be persuaded to institute the natural order in the first place. "Belles-Lettres can convince Sovereigns.... that the greatest happiness they can feel, that their greatest power, authority, and wealth will result from the increased well-being of their subjects and from the care they devote to protecting their subjects' rights, their natural freedoms, and facilitating their mutual exchanges."[74] Turgot disagreed, detaching art from physiocratic didacticism.

> I did not have to wait for my attack of gout to reflect on the nature and principles of taste. Hence it is not grief that made me find fault with your principles of literature. Besides which, the issue here is neither disgust nor sentiment but logic and logic is not the Economists' strong point. Their weakness [*leur maladie en général*] is always rushing ahead and not stopping to analyse the meaning of words scrupulously enough.[75]

Turgot was put off by the physiocrats' relentless preaching and urged Du Pont to abandon it, for it merely created enemies.[76] What is more, Du Pont's argument that "only *honnêtes gens* understand poetry" had made him smile. "There are plenty of people who write very good verses and who are far from decent – although there is something in what you say."

None of these arguments dissuaded Du Pont from writing sixteen-year-old Carl Ludwig of Baden, his princely pupil: "In our course on Belles Letters, Your Highness has learned that the charms of eloquence and poetry lie in their ability to paint true pictures that foster in us a preference for worthy deeds, a horror of vice, and enthusiasm for virtue."[77] Properly pursued the arts would permit a monarch to present his program to his people in an appealing way. The heir to the throne was lucky to be living in the eighteenth century.[78] For Du Pont, the Moderns surpassed

---

[73] Du Pont, "Du principe commun," p. 53.
[74] Ibid., p. 54.
[75] Hagley, W2-1639, Letter from Turgot to Du Pont, Limoges, 29 October 1771.
[76] Schelle, *Oeuvres de Turgot et documents le concernant*, III, p. 497. Letter from Turgot to Du Pont, Limoges, 15 October 1771.
[77] Hagley, W2-4582, letter from Du Pont to Carl Ludwig of Baden, Paris, 22 January 1772. Carl Ludwig was born on 14 February 1755 and died 16 December 1801.
[78] Knies, *Carl Friedrichs von Baden*, II, p. 64, Du Pont's reflections on Chapters III and IV of François Jean de Chastellux's *De la félicité publique ou considérations sur le sort des hommes dans les différentes époques de l'histoire*, 2 vols. (Amsterdam, 1772).

the Ancients because they had added a moral dimension to the arts.⁷⁹ Despite his call for moral uplift, Du Pont realized that this demand might prove too programmatic:

But, they will object, must drama be turned into a sermon? Yes and no. What harm would there be if its lessons were as worthy as a sermon? Still, it must be a drama, have a plot, a theme, dialogues, charm, eloquence, power and especially be interesting. It should sweeten the lesson for those who would otherwise reject it. For if, despite a worthy message, this drama were poorly done, it would be bad, because it would fall into the boring genre [Voltaire's *bon mot*].⁸⁰

For all his arguments about the fusion of virtue and beauty, Du Pont did not trust in their automatic combination. Like physiocratic economics, the arts had to be guided and monitored. And so he wrote Caroline Luisa about the 1773 salon:

What is true of our artists is just as true of our men of letters, our merchants, and even our big landowners. There are plenty of individual talents, plenty of isolated lights, but there is too little mutual help, and almost no public spirit. Everyone runs in a different direction, without a plan or trustworthy guide, doing as he pleases, without a rallying point, might I say without enough education about what is truly beautiful and accords with good taste? It is nonetheless true that all the arts can speak to the soul and that nothing surpasses in beauty the art which rouses it to honest feelings and useful ideas.⁸¹

Human responses had been perverted and art had lost the guidance and energy it had once drawn from nature. Like the tableaux "in disequilibrium," therefore, Du Pont could point to the problems with the arts. He could even imagine an ideal state of the arts, in the way that the *Tableau économique* displayed an ideal economic circulation. But, as with the *Tableau*, there was an irreducible mystery to art, a *je ne sais quoi* that went beyond words.

In his physiocratic utopia written during the Revolution, *L'Heureuse nation ou gouvernement des Féliciens*, Le Mercier de La Rivière envisaged a future role for the arts: "The theatres show only plays that have been approved by a Censorship Board and they must all express a moral

---

⁷⁹ Du Pont, "Idées sur la poésie," p. 146.
⁸⁰ Ibid., p. 158. In fact, Du Pont had written to Voltaire, praising him for his combination of beautiful *and* useful verses. Hagley, W2-18, Letter from Du Pont to Voltaire, 10 September 1762. Also in Besterman, ed., *Correspondance de Voltaire*, vol. 63 (Geneva, 1962), pp. 3–8.
⁸¹ Hagley in manuscript, W2-4585, published in *Archives de l'art français*, nouvelle période, Tome II (1908) "Lettres sur les salons de 1773, 1777 et 1779 adressées par Du Pont de Nemours à la Margrave Caroline-Louise de Bade," pp. 1–123.

message; they must aim to improve the population both as human beings and as citizens."[82] A few pages sufficed to cover this topic. Du Pont, on the other hand, would return time and again to the arts, hoping that "beauty might become the reward for virtue." Sadly, beauty proved more elusive than the net product.

### Paris Art Salons

Du Pont ventured beyond the realm of the written word to comment on the visual arts, searching for their moral utility. He reported on three salons to the Margravine of Baden, appealing to her as a celebrated patron of the arts, having learned that she was looking for reports on the 1773 salon. He was still hoping to be granted a post at the Court at Karlsruhe, and establishing an affinity of taste and outlook might ingratiate him with Carolina Luisa.

Public exhibitions of the latest artworks submitted to the Academy of Painting and Sculpture began to be held regularly in 1737. Held every two years, the salon opened in late August for several weeks.[83] There were printed catalogues of the paintings and sculptures on display and the exhibition produced flurries of reviews. The most famous no doubt remain those of Denis Diderot composed for Melchior Grimm's *Correspondance littéraire*, starting with the 1759 salon.[84] By sheer coincidence, he did not cover the years 1773, 1777, or 1779 on which Du Pont reported.[85]

In all three salons, Du Pont fully approves those who use color well. Color, he argues, is central to the painterly effect, and this accords with his sensualist approach.[86] Jean-Baptiste Greuze (1725–1805)

---

[82] Le Mercier de la Rivière, *L'Heureuse nation ou gouvernement des Féliciens*, 2 vols. (Paris, 1792), II, p. 61.

[83] See Thomas E. Crow, *Painters and Public Life in Eighteenth-Century Paris* (New Haven and London, 1985). For an overview, see also Mark Ledbury, "Imagining the *Salon*: Mapping Art Criticism in the Eighteenth Century," in Jonathan Mallison, ed., *The Eighteenth Century Now: Boundaries and Perspectives*, in *Studies on Voltaire and the Eighteenth Century* (2005), 10, pp. 205–19.

[84] See the complete salons in Laurent Versini, ed., Diderot, *Oeuvres*, vol. IV, *Esthétique-Théâtre* (Paris, 1996).

[85] Hagley, "Sallons," Salon of 1779, pp. 145–6.

[86] In the late seventeenth century, a controversy had raged about the primacy of drawing (over color) as the Academy of Painting maintained (stressing the importance of form), opposed by those, most notably Roger de Piles, who asserted that color gave texture and life to images and represented nature as seen by the eye more faithfully. See on this Becq, *Genèse de l'esthétique*, pp. 88–9, and Romira M. Worvill, *"Seeing" Speech: Illusion and Transformation of Dramatic Writing in Diderot and Lessing* (Oxford, 2005), pp. 29–35.

and Jean-Honoré Fragonard (1732–1806) were Diderot favorites, and Du Pont rarely deviates from Diderot's judgments. Du Pont's principal demands were that painters follow "nature" and display "talent." He would therefore have to face the fact that the two did not necessarily coincide.

His overall impression of the 1773 salon was that the artists might have surpassed themselves had they communicated with each other better and been guided by "a superior genius" – like the Margravine – who could have steered their particular talent to better ends and with surer taste. Louis Lagrenée (1725–1805) lacked genius and his paintings were mediocre because he was but a "servile imitator of what he sees and cannot rise to the level of ideal beauty because he cannot see it." Joseph-Marie Vien (1716–1809), on the other hand, was one of Du Pont's favorite painters, and his painting of a sleeping nude mesmerizes him.[87]

One wanders off, goes this way and that, and is always drawn back to the beautiful Greek woman he [Vien] has captured in so voluptuous a dream that the image lingers and makes one appreciate the gift of Heaven we call Beauty. So, when one is a philosopher, one dreams of the means by which societies might treat Beauty as a reward for virtue, moving men to be good to others in ways that satisfy the Soul and the Senses, so that all faculties which the Supreme Being has granted our species work together to make us love his just and benevolent laws.

Sensationalist philosophy had its drawbacks, forcing Du Pont to confront his instinctive stimulation, and he rationalized his responses as best he could. He praised Claude-Joseph Vernet and regretted the absence of Greuze and Philippe de Loutherbourg who were no longer showing at the Salon. "Greuze has painted moral tales that inspire virtue," [he now agreed with Turgot] while "Loutherbourg throws onto the canvas poems filled with warmth, honesty, feeling, and strength" (hence inverting *ut pictura poesis* by favoring a scenic, narrative approach to painting).

Du Pont directs his highest praise to sculptors, since he deems that French painting is getting progressively worse whereas French sculpture continues to improve. Perhaps, he reflects, this is because sculptors have to observe nature closely, from all angles, and are clearer about their objectives, or "is it because they work more slowly, in greater isolation, unlike painters who seek out sparkling company, become vain and lazy, greedy and hasty? Is it because there is no room left on our walls for paintings, but plenty of gardens, stairwells and porticos for statuary?"

[87] The painting is now in a private collection and there exists, to my knowledge, only a single reproduction in an exhibition catalog.

This is not to say that Du Pont admires sculptors unreservedly. He is especially frustrated by the unfaithful depiction of famous men. Thus, the prince de Condé (or Grand Condé) who was very short, the maréchal de Luxembourg who was short and hunchbacked, and Turenne who was of medium height were all rendered as six feet high, whereas the maréchal de Saxe who was taller than all of three, and of Herculean build, was reduced to average height and bearing. "Such negligence cannot convey the proper idea of the heroes they mean to celebrate." This is a theme that Du Pont will return to with increasing virulence. But all is not lost as Du Pont admires the great beauty of Augustin Pajou's bust of Mme du Barry (perhaps because, he claims, "it bears little resemblance to the original"), and others of Buffon, Catherine the Great, Helvétius, and Diderot. Above all, the statue of a boy weeping over his dead bird moves him so much that he wishes he might console him.

Moral judgment predominates in his approach to the 1773 salon: "It is invariably true that all the arts speak to the soul and that beauty awakens honest feelings and useful ideas. It is equally true that a man of taste must be a man of feeling, who knows what pleases and suits other men, guided by that species of fraternal love that renders valuable everything than can please or serve them."[88] It was not unusual to argue in the 1770s that the improvements of mankind went hand in hand with the progress of the arts. Du Pont's oddity, of course, was to associate such progress with physiocracy.

He penned his second Salon four years later in a despondent state since he was still recovering from Turgot's and his loss of favor, and his current unemployment. "My sight has dimmed, my enthusiasm has vanished. My ardent heart has lost its bearings, it can make no plans, and is consumed with grief. I have nothing to reproach myself, but I have so many regrets!"[89] This is the shortest of his three Salons, and its most important feature is Du Pont's renewed insistence that great men must be rendered accurately. He applauds the Crown's initiative, under the sponsorship of the Superintendant of Royal Monuments, the Comte d'Angiviller, to commission statues of celebrated Frenchmen and paintings of major events in French History. He is perturbed, however, by some depictions. For example, showing Bishop Fénelon in pontifical robes, holding his masterpiece *Télémaque*, was inappropriate because it suggested he had written the work as part of his sacerdotal duties rather than in his capacity as tutor

---

[88] Du Pont, *Lettres*, Salon of 1773, p. 40.
[89] Du Pont, *Lettres*, Salon of 1777, p. 62.

to the Dauphin. He is truly horrified by Jean-Antoine Houdon's bust of Turgot which, "with its rounded forms, could have been a portrait of his sister, except that she does not resemble him." The features of great men must be rendered precisely (insofar as one knew them) because physiognomy offers a window to the soul. Faithful portraits, especially once compared to the feats these men had performed, would reveal how such traits became imprinted. Armed with such information rulers would be able to assess candidates for posts more perspicaciously. Although the "science" was as yet in its infancy, Du Pont vouched for its potential. Portraits would offer the raw materials and history the testing ground. To this end, he hoped that keeping family portraits would turn into a "filial duty."

Being of short stature himself, he seemed particularly sensitive to the oversized depiction of national heroes that implied that great men had to be tall. It was important to show "the man as he had been" and this went beyond facial features: "the build, the thickness of the neck, the curve of the loins, the position of the hips reveal a great deal about the nature of a man's soul." "He who studies nature, especially nature as manifested in great men, must observe it from head to toe and above all refrain from placing different heads on a single mannequin."

He also had suggestion for painters who wished to depict the countryside. Rather than Noël Hallé's "ridiculous scene of a toadying fool who knocks down the walls of his garden to hand out pears to little rascals, why not paint instead a paterfamilias enclosing his plots?" Since Du Pont does not explain how one might go about this, this was yet another chance to score rhetorical points. He waxes ecstatic about Vernet – *comme de rigueur* – having spent "half his time at the Salon" gazing at his seascapes.

Greuze's pupils, despite their best intentions, do not match his skills. "He is peerless in painting morality, charity, beautiful souls, but more importantly, nature and truth." Du Pont was once more confronted with the evidence that good intentions did not necessarily produce great art. He knew this from his visceral (rather than intellectual) responses to the artworks. Perhaps once artists "truly" heeded nature they would produce both moral and aesthetic masterpieces but Du Pont has no recipe for ensuring this.

He returned to the Salon in 1779, in far better spirits, impressed by all he saw, and yet still "able to feel and judge" amid such riches.

Enough of the fields; enough of being a man of nature. Has the art lover vanished? The rye, the oats, the corn, and the last of the hay have been stored.... Let us fly to Paris.... Let us see if the heroes painted by Vien, Doyen, Brenet, Beaufort or Lépicié match the manliness of our hardy labourers, if they capture the nobility of those who have returned to their native land, having shed blood for their country, foreheads covered with praiseworthy scars and arms toughened for farming by their stay in the army. Let us gauge whether the women and children of the two La Grenées display the freshness, bright eyes, sprightliness [*ressort dans les nerfs*], and life force [*la vie dans les chairs*] of our country urchins who frolic in the grass, or of our farmers' daughters dancing under the elms, holding the hand of their strong rather than "charming" lovers. Let us see if the elderly and the mothers painted by Greuze, Wille or Aubry, have the respectable bearing of our rustic patriarchs; ... Oh, you magicians, favoured by the Muses, who animate marble and canvas, my teachers, my friends, fear me! I have lost the logical thread of your lessons. I am no longer swept up by your style. I will no longer compare you to your teachers or rivals. I have swept aside all schools. I arrive newly minted from the school of nature, I have just seen all that you must imitate.

The rustic idylls that Du Pont presumed he would fail to encounter at the Salon were of course the stock-in-trade of rural depictions on which he based his own imaginary vision. Perhaps all he meant was that he had become a better judge of artistry knowing what truly mattered. "It is not enough to paint and to represent. One should only paint and express what ought to be transmitted to posterity. To paint atrocities for no reason and immortalize them is to belie the intentions of art and the moral ends of history painting."

He feels let down however by the Younger Wille[90] (although he describes him as Greuze's ablest disciple): "Your Highness would be most disappointed with the *Seigneur and the Poacher*. The catalogue describes an indulgent seigneur when, to the contrary, he seems curt and haughty, his physiognomy lacks nobility, his temples are too close together, his chin is pointy, his constricted gait [*taille génée*] suggests narrow-mindedness and callousness; his wife, on the other hand, who is seated beside him with her head on his shoulder, seems to be urging him with charming grace to show more leniency." That Wille's women outshone his men marked him as a "man of sensibility" in Du Pont's estimation: it brought to mind the "sublime Richardson" who displayed much more sympathy toward women than his own sex.

Lagrenée offers Du Pont another occasion to ruminate on the female form. "There is nothing more natural than painting a beautiful woman totally naked, without a hint of the clothing that disfigured her. It can

---

[90] Pierre-Alexandre Wille, known as Wille le fils, was the son of the famous engraver Johann Georg Wille.

be respectable, even pious. She is Eve in Eden, the mother of humanity, a goddess, a symbol of fertility and life, or even wisdom. She is Virtue, Truth. But, should I notice on her body the traces of an unflattering garment and how it pressed on her body, then I just see a woman without her clothes, who took them off for money, in order to display herself at the Salon, or at least to the painter who shows her to us; she is no longer a model: she is indecent and vile." Realism proves merely sordid: *belle nature* is what is wanted. And he ends with the revealing observation: "Ah! Sensuality, sensuality, you ensnare with rings of flowers the very philosophers who denounce you!" But he can always turn to depictions of maternal love to warm the cockles of his heart, and he is "moved to tears" by the sacrifice of a Vestal priestess[91]:

The grief of the victim and her parents pierce the soul of the spectator. She stands on the fatal ladder, one foot already in the grave, close to the stone that will smother her. She looks up at the sky. Her rounded form hints at the accident for which she is being so cruelly punished and deepens our sympathy. The executioners themselves are filled with compassion, although to different degrees; if the executioners themselves weep, why should we be ashamed to have tears in our eyes?

This Salon, like the two previous ones, returns him to his hobbyhorse, the misleading depiction of great men.

I preferred his [Brenet's] *Cincinnatus*. I am naturally partial to ... men who work the land. The composition of this painting is rich and ingenious, but Cincinnatus was a tall [*grand*] man and the one I see here is barely 5 foot two inches. He is short and fat. What, haven't there been diminutive heroes? For sure and, when we know this for a fact, we must depict this, but if there is no reliable evidence about their size, then we should give them handsome proportions in order, as Montaigne put it: "to lend extra support to the objects of mankind's veneration."

The portraits of Benjamin Franklin and of Linnaeus pleased him because they encapsulated the essence of the men, as did the busts of Voltaire and Rousseau. The latter's sensibility and susceptibility were rendered as clearly as his narrow-mindedness, emotional equivocation, and deceit. In other words, the artist had captured the flesh-and-blood Rousseau.[92]

---

[91] Du Pont, *Lettres*, Salon of 1779, p. 92.
[92] Rousseau's opposition to the doctrine was well known to the physiocrats. On Quesnay and Rousseau, see Loïc Charles and Philippe Steiner, "Entre Montesquieu et Rousseau. La Physiocratie parmi les origines intellectuelles de la Révolution française," *Études Jean-Jacques Rousseau*, 11 (1999), 83–159.

The "warts and all" approach served a purpose, therefore, which was to reveal the inner man, but was reprehensible if it broke the illusion that the model was a goddess. Yet Du Pont did not seem fond of allegory: "Above all, be clear: a painting should not be an enigma." And he continues to endorse physiognomy:

Your Highness knows how much I approve of the science of physiognomy and how far I am from believing it is just conjecture, as those who have not studied it imagine. The best library to extend and perfect such a useful science, which would be especially useful to princes and philosophers, would be an immense gallery of portraits of all the men whose character is well-known, executed by Largillière, de La Tour, Roslin, or Duplessis."[93]

In favoring observation of *actual* characteristics, Du Pont was rejecting the reductive prototypes devised by Charles Le Brun in his *Physiognomic Studies* of the late 1660s, which associated specific facial expressions with different emotional states.[94] Where was *belle nature* now?

Physiognomy was discredited for most of the eighteenth century, and both Jaucourt in his article *Physiognomy* in the Encyclopedia and the naturalist Buffon had criticized the very notion that outer appearance was a guide to the inner person.[95] Du Pont's approach, which included the entire body, reflected the late eighteenth-century revival of physiognomy that would evolve into osteology and craniometry to characterize human differences. But he also read the "visible" body with the help of new medical theories that gauged its fitness through its degrees of vigor and torpor.[96] The joining of the "physical" and "moral" fastened on nerves, fibers, toning, and increasing the body's natural resistance.[97] Hygiene, sanitation, fresh air would not only keep the population healthy, it would stop it from degenerating. Thus regeneration of morals was linked to the regeneration of the body, just like that of the state required the regeneration of agriculture. But Du Pont also accepted the longstanding association of physiognomy with "civility." Since courtiers and the socially ambitious alike had learned to put on masks or develop impassivity, finer

---

[93] Du Pont, *Lettres*, Salon of 1779, p. 106
[94] See Norman Bryson, *Word and Image French Painting of the Ancien Régime* (Cambridge, 1981), pp. 43–52.
[95] Jean-Jacques Courtine and Claudine Haroche, *Histoire du visage* (Paris, 1988), pp. 91, 97–8.
[96] Courtine and Haroche, *Histoire du visage*, pp. 98, 118, and Daniel Arasse in Georges Vigarello, ed., *Histoire du corps*, vol. 1: *De la Renaissance aux Lumières* (Paris, 2005), p. 465.
[97] See, for example, Barroux, *Philosophie, maladie et médecine*, chapters 6 and 7.

tools were now required for the analysis of character.[98] Du Pont seemed content to rely on moral exemplars to inspire the public – as long as their features were not grossly misrepresented.[99] The Revolution that taught him so much else, would lead him to abandon the hope that personality, like art, could yield its secrets. He criticized phrenology for its reductive approach to criminality, arguing the importance of education, social institutions, and accidental circumstances.[100]

Although he probably welcomed Diderot and Sébastien Mercier's efforts to catalogue Parisian types and "conditions" in their physiognomies of the city with their various characters, he was never fully satisfied by "social realism."[101] Despite his remarks on physiognomy, Du Pont had difficulty reducing human beings to simple primal needs as Quesnay seemed to be doing, and Mirabeau conceding after a protracted battle. The doctrine's theory of selfhood went no farther than the contention that a properly trained mind would resist the lure of the passions, and that men would be content with food, shelter, security, and doing the right thing. Du Pont, like his physiocratic confreres ultimately sought refuge in aggregate identities and broad distinctions based on gender and the stages of life (as we will see in the next chapter). So in the end he retreated to the safe conclusions that insofar as physiocracy's realization required preparatory work, the arts could serve such ends, since they touched the heart (the source of fellow-feeling) as well as the mind (where useful ideas came together), already a departure from Quesnay's condemnation and Mirabeau's waffling over the role of emotion. A cleansing of the Augean Stables of the soul might perhaps be in order, but in the guise of a reorientation rather than outright repression. In a prosperous physiocratic nation culture would incite to virtue by making it irresistibly beautiful. Yet Du Pont conceded that the arts involved *creation* and not simply *imitation*, in line with the new aesthetics. *Je ne sais quoi* turned pedestrian subjects into works of art. In effect, the flash of insight which led Quesnay to compose the *Tableau* was at work when artists produced *their* tableaux.

---

[98] Courtine and Haroche, *Histoire du visage*, pp. 128–30.
[99] See on this Peter J. Schneerman, "Lire et parler. La réception de l'*exemplum virtutis*," in Thomas W. Gaehtens et al., eds., *L'art et les normes sociales au XVIIIe siècle* (Paris, 2001), pp. 44–57, and Jean-Claude Bonnet, *Naissance du Panthéon, Essai sur le culte des grands hommes* (Paris, 1998), pp. 115–32.
[100] Du Pont, "Sur les assertions du Docteur Gall," from *Publiciste,* 8 pages (1805) in Collection of Pamphlets by Du Pont, Hagley, N* B2019. D815.02.
[101] See Courtine and Haroche, *Histoire du visage*, pp. 125–6. The extent to which he would have accepted Nicolas-Edme Restif de la Bretonne's variants is more questionable, since they included "unsavory" characters.

Physiocrats had attempted to reconstitute Quesnay's stroke of genius through a series of cognitive steps, but artistic creation belonged to the realm of imagination that Quesnay had condemned. Art drew its potency directly from the forces of creation at work in the universe. Du Pont was therefore stepping on dangerous ground in acknowledging his impotence to govern the arts. This domain would thrive without the intercession of doctrine. Trust that nature would do its work directly raised the possibility that individuals might be released from physiocratic oversight altogether, free to listen to the voice of nature rather than learning how to think through the doctrine's "sacred texts," as Le Mercier de la Rivière called them. Could man be trusted? Taming artistic creation was as daunting as taming man himself.

# 7

# The Education of Princes

Neither Quesnay nor Mirabeau had sought to translate physiocracy into the cultural idioms of art and literature even if their writings called for a reformation of morals and Mirabeau encouraged like-minded authors. Quite the contrary, Quesnay had distinguished the steps in the constitution of true ideas, insisting on the dangers of letting the imagination roam freely since it would inevitably interfere with rational analysis. He was equally wary of analogy, so often misused by the medical profession. Mirabeau had finally conceded that appeals to imagination induced ephemeral enthusiasms and should be avoided.[1] Emotions were suspicious, aroused, as he put it, "as easily as the sound of trumpets sets horses galloping." He had taken it upon himself "as Quesnay's first disciple," to disseminate the physiocratic message to the unwashed masses by means of digests and educational treatises. But as he warned Du Pont in September 1773: "You find yourself, my dear Du Pont, in a situation where you cannot help being known as the first and principal student and disseminator of the science and, in this guise, the words you utter to the world are taken as dogma so you must be very careful not to let emotional enthusiasm [*du coeur*] smother the spirit of calculated reason."[2]

Quesnay was furious with Du Pont for writing poetry. "My Master scolded me so sharply, so frequently, for having written these verses that he

---

[1] Quesnay was not alone in his suspicions: see Lorraine Daston, "Fear and Loathing of the Imagination in Science" in Peter Galison, Stephen R. Graubard, and Everett Mendelsohn, eds., *Science in Culture* (New Brunswick, 2001), pp. 73–95, and Fleury, *Métaphysique de l'imagination*.

[2] Hagley, W2-1655, letter from Mirabeau to Du Pont, rue Saint-Jacques, Paris, 21 September 1773.

almost stifled my tendency to indulge in versifying," Du Pont would recall. "I spent four years without daring to read Poets, never mind following in their step, and it was only after I spent time with M. *Turgot* at Limoges and applauded his energetic verses, so rich and so harmonious, that I allowed myself to return occasionally to my natural inclination."[3] Quesnay's mistrust of poetry was longstanding as Mme Du Hausset reported, although he had briefly yielded to the muse in his youth. A friend of hers wondered why he didn't seem to appreciate an ode by Marmontel, "Did he not admire great poets?" "'Like great *Bilboquet* [cup-and-ball game] players' he responded in that way he had of making everything sound amusing."[4] Poetry was a just a pastime, and a waste of time at that. Du Pont was well aware that, albeit for different reasons, Quesnay, Mirabeau, and Turgot would strongly disapprove of his efforts to render physiocracy in artistic form, yet he was determined to employ new genres to move the public in the right direction. "The nation's mores are such nowadays that one must turn Morality and Justice into song and can only preach effectively at the Opera house," he caustically remarked.[5] Melchior Grimm had once accused the physiocrats of dreaming of a society with no room for the fine arts.[6] Du Pont retorted to his readers: "those who do not know me accuse me of not liking poetry; those who know me well, accuse me of liking it too much."[7]

## A Physiocratic Play

In 1771 Du Pont began to neglect his editorial duties in order to write a play that would transpose into the literary realm the economic program to which he was devoting his life. Du Pont called his work, a *comédie héroïque,* a genre he adopted from Corneille who had used it to describe his play *Don Sanche d'Aragon* (1650), a comedy that did not confine itself to the low-born as the genre required, but used princely characters in situations "that did not put their kingdoms or themselves at risk" (and hence did not infringe on tragedy's domain).[8]

---

[3] Du Pont, *The Autobiography of Du Pont de Nemours*, p. 272.
[4] Du Hausset, *Mémoires*, p. 52.
[5] Du Pont's review of the operetta *Sylvain,* by Marmontel and Grétry, in *Éphémérides* (1770), I, pp. 174–97, 176–7.
[6] Grimm et al., *Correspondance littéraire*, VIII, p. 436.
[7] Du Pont, review of new edition of Saint-Lambert's *Seasons*, *Éphémérides* (1771), VI, p. 163.
[8] Pierre Corneille, dedication of the play to M. de Zuylichem, councillor to the Prince of Orange, "This is a new type of poem, without parallel among the ancients." See "Épître dédicatoire" of *Don Sanche d'Aragon* in Maurice Rat, ed., *Théâtre complet de Corneille* (Paris, 1960), II, pp. 607–10.

Du Pont's play, *L'Empereur Joseph Second*, recast in verse a familiar anecdote that he had already described at length in the *Éphémérides*.⁹ It involved an "act of charity" performed by Joseph II in granting a pension to the widow of an Austrian army officer who was living in abject poverty with her daughter. Du Pont expanded the incident into a full-blown melodrama with a spunky heroine, an impoverished suitor, an evil aristocrat, an inconsolable widow, and a savior in the form of a prince in disguise. The plot was an excuse for Du Pont to demonstrate how a monarch with a strong will and powerful moral sense might transform his nation's economy. Quotations will therefore be inevitable.

In the opening scene we hear Joseph's thoughts as he wanders the streets of Vienna incognito:

| | |
|---|---|
| Je goûte le bonheur de posséder l'empire | *I relish the happiness of ruling the empire* |
| Au bien de mes enfants consacrant mon pouvoir, | *devoting my power to my children's welfare* |
| Dans leur foule inconnu, je vais apprendre à voir. | *hidden in their midst, I will learn to see.* |
| Autour de moi les Grands apprêtent leur figure | *Around me, the Nobles disguise themselves* |
| Mais ici j'entendrai le cri de la nature. | *But here, I will hear the cry of Nature.* |
| Je saurai si ces grands qui composent ma cour, | *I will learn if the Nobles at my court* |
| De mon Peuple en effet ont mérité l'amour; | *Deserve the love of my People;* |
| Et je saurai surtout ce qu'on dit de moi-même | *Foremost I will learn what is said of me* |
| De la voix du Public l'importance est extreme, | *For the Public's voice is extremely important,* |
| Et jamais ses leçons ne sont à dédaigner. | *And its lessons should never be disdained.* |
| Qui les mépriserait ne saurait pas régner. (Act I, Scene IV). | *He who scorns them would be a poor ruler.* |

---

⁹ *Les Ephémérides du citoyen*, 1770, volume VIII, part III, pp. 176–85. A copy of the play exists at the Hagley Museum and Archives, W2-235. This particular anecdote, the Du Pont informs us, was well known, having already been published in Viennese newspapers (*papiers publics*). "No other Prince would furnish so many worthy anecdotes" (p. 179). It was indeed one of the stock stories circulating about Joseph. The *Mercure de France*, for instance, had reported it (as was mentioned in March 1775 in their review of Le Blanc de Guillet's play *Albert Premier ou Adeline* (1775) (Geneva, 1970), p. 253.

He sees a young woman carrying a bundle of clothes. She is young; she is pretty; she looks distraught, and obviously in need of help. She tells him her sad tale. She is off to sell her last belongings because she and her mother are pursued by a relentless creditor. Her father was a famous officer, who served his king bravely and nobly, but who died penniless leaving his widow without any support. He did leave a son, of equal valor, eager to serve his country, but who needed first to claim a small inheritance. When he arrived on his estate, he learned that he was ruined. Arbitrary taxation had hampered trade and his farmers had fled, abandoning their fields. The young man tried to find ways to remedy his losses, encouraging his peasants to return to the land, when an unlucky yet worthy friend pleaded for his help in salvaging some foreign cloth which had been seized from him.

| | |
|---|---|
| Mon frère ne croyant qu'obliger un ami | *My brother believing he was merely helping a friend,* |
| Prenant pour des brigands leur troupe mercenaire | *Taking their mercenary troop for brigands,* |
| Aux employés du fisc, imprudent, téméraire | *Boldly, recklessly, resisted the agents of the* |
| Il osa résister, et périt sous leurs coups. | *Fisc, and perished under their fire.* |

### The Emperor

| | |
|---|---|
| Ah! Grands Dieux! | *Oh! Heavens!* (Act 1, Scene VII) |

The injustice of the creditor pursuing the mother is paralleled by the cruel demands of the treasury. In both cases innocents are harmed and havoc ensues. Du Pont was asking his audience (or imaginary audience) to feel and empathize with the sufferings of landowners and farmers in the way they would with a helpless maiden and widow. Thus, Joseph's exclamation of horror, followed by "I shudder at your sad tale!" For if there is a villain in the personal melodrama, as we are about to discover, the state is also a villain. Whatever personal disappointments they suffered, the family might have found some solace on their land and enjoyed a modest but honorable income. The system denied them this possibility with the same ruthlessness that allowed a courtier to deceive them for his own cruel ends, in the hope that poverty will force the young woman to become his mistress.[10] Have you appealed to the

---

[10] Should a denunciation of indirect taxation seem incongruous, Louis Sébastien Mercier suggests similar topics, *Du Théâtre ou Nouvel Essai sur l'Art dramatique*, (Amsterdam, 1773), pp. 159–60.

Emperor, Joseph asks? A courtier has done so (the evil Count Krait), she replies, but to no avail.

Perhaps he can be of some help. Sophie doubts this, because "Ministers, Grandees, and Kings have been unable to, or if they could have helped, they chose not to."[11] The evil that Joseph feared has been revealed in all its horror. His kingdom is filled with supplicants who are misled and betrayed in his name. Come to the palace tomorrow and I will make sure that the Emperor hears your case. I know him personally. Alone, Joseph reflects:

| | |
|---|---|
| Tarissons cette Source d'abus et de crimes, | *Let is extinguish this source of crime and* |
| Simplifions l'impôt; hâtons tous nos projets. | *Abuses. Let us simplify taxation* |
| Qu'on ne puisse en mon nom opprimer mes Sujets | *hasten all my projects. Let no one oppress my Subjects in my name.* |
| Leur bonheur, leur amour, leurs travaux, leur aisance, | *Only their happiness, their love, their labor, their well-being* |
| Peuvent seuls m'enrichir et fonder ma puissance, | *Can enrich me and steady my power* |
| Par de plus sages lois, il faut les protéger | *Wiser laws must protect them,* |
| C'est le premier travail auquel je dois songer. | *This is the first task I must set myself.* |

Indignation and concern share the spotlight. Though the initial appeal is to the king's heart, the more important recourse is to his mind, that which connects the particular misfortune to a greater evil, a larger social pattern. It is not enough to remedy particular wrongs when a decisive act might fix similar problems, avert potential misfortunes. The ruler's sensibility allows him to feel his subjects' pain. His more important capacity is to use his pity to prevent further disasters.

Hence before the happy conclusion when the heroine is able to marry her impoverished suitor (who gets a commission in the Emperor's Personal Guard) and the evil minister who hopes to seduce Sophie is unmasked, Joseph makes long physiocratic speeches to his cabinet, outlining his plans for the future.

As Act III opens, the Emperor is instructing his Minister of Finance and other ministers in the tenets of physiocracy. We are in the presence

---

[11] "Les Ministres, les Grands, les Rois ne l'ont pas pu: ou bien, s'ils le pouvaient, ils ne l'ont pas voulu."

of a scientific monarch, an enlightened, educated ruler.[12] You must understand, he tells them, that taxation comes from the land, that it originates in the soil. Taxation should not throttle its source, but find a way to encourage its growth.

| | |
|---|---|
| Craignons surtout, craignons d'arrêter dans sa course, | Let us beware, above all, of slowing the |
| Du bonheur des Etats, cette abondante source. | course of this abundant source which |
| C'est elle qui fournit, par ses biens renaissans, | ensures the happiness of States. Its constant renewal gives |
| Le pain à tout le Peuple et l'opulence aux Grands. | the people bread and grandees wealth. |
| Vous verriez ce pays tomber en décadence | The country would decay were I |
| Si j'allais dans vos champs exiler l'abondance | to exile abundance from your fields by |
| En gênant le débit de leurs productions | Interfering with their sale or with the freedom |
| Et le droit que chacun a sur ses actions. | Of choice. |
| Je ne le ferai pas | I shall not do it. |

Yet, the Minister argues, this is the way of all states. Abuses, rather, Joseph answers, abuses that must be removed *(qu'il nous faut extirper du Sein de la Patrie)*. Indeed, agrees the Minister, and that is why he thought he would lighten the load of the countryside by taxing other productive activities. No, retorts the monarch, for this would make artisans flee to the city. Nature will yield its fruits.

| | |
|---|---|
| ... on n'a rien des mains de la nature | Nature yields nothing freely and only |
| Qu'à force d'avancer des frais qu'avec usure | repeated investments make her surrender |
| Elle rend à la fin. | at last. |

The play tells us that, if women must be taught to protect their virtue (against evil seducers like the one featured in Act II), nature, to the contrary,

---

[12] Interestingly, Du Pont does not indicate whether Joseph is still wearing his republican cloth coat. The real Joseph, in fact, usually donned a uniform like his hero Frederick II. Derek Beales, *Joseph II*, vol. I: *In the Shadow of Maria Theresa, 1741–1780* (Cambridge, 1987), p. 173.

must be seduced or forced to yield hers. Higher taxes would reduce consumption and sales, making farming a pointless, unprofitable occupation. The land would be abandoned and the citizens would starve.

| | |
|---|---|
| Ils tomberaient en friche, et tous les Citoyens, | The fields would lie fallow, and the Citizens |
| Qu'alimentent leurs fruits, dénués de moyens, | whose production they sustain, shorn of |
| Périraient par la faim, sans qu'il ne fut possible | their revenue, would die of hunger, without |
| D'apporter des secours à leur misère horrible. | any way to assist them in their terrible misery. |

Du Pont has Joseph continue in this vein, detailing the horrors that would befall the nation, including an empty treasury, should indirect taxation be instituted. And so, the Minister queries, how does he foresee levying taxes?

| | |
|---|---|
| Quoi! Vous me demandez, vous, ce que j'imagine? | What? You ask what I imagine? |
| Je n'imagine point; mais une Loi divine, | I imagine nothing; a divine law |
| Fixe mon intérêt ainsi que mon devoir. | Dictates my interest and my duty. |
| Aisément cette Loi se peut appercevoir | A law that is easy to perceive |
| … | …. |
| Telle est la grande Loi de la Société. | This is the great Law of Society. |
| Je veux m'y conformer; que mon autorité | I mean to obey it; to make my authority |
| Soit toujours tutélaire et toujours protectrice. | Always titulary and always protective. |
| Régner par la terreur me serait un supplice. | To reign through terror would be torture. |
| Je veux être estimé, chéri de mes Sujets; | I want to be esteemed, loved by my Subjects |
| Je veux fixer chez eux l'abondance et la paix. | I want to bring them abundance and peace. |

Joseph has turned from practical physiocratic concerns about wealth and taxation to the doctrine's first principles: benevolent design, natural law, and property rights. The Minister repeats his question: Where would the money come from? From that part which nature meant to be taxed, the Emperor finally reveals: agriculture. For the monarch has, as it were, rights of eminent domain on the land that property rights cannot extinguish. Under the reign of liberty that he means to institute, more land would come under the plough, increasing production and thus the monarch's natural share in the fruits of the soil. "I will do my best, Sire, to be worthy of you." replies the Minister obediently. "I count on it," says the Emperor. Joseph continues to build his dream of a nation of farmers and soldiers with its classic conflation of prowess, physical fitness, and labor. Toward the play's end, meaning to resolve everyone's problems to their satisfaction, Joseph savors the pleasures of giving:

| | |
|---|---|
| Quel plaisir je m'apprête! | *What pleasures await me!* |
| Combien douce est la joie où je livre mon coeur! | *How sweet is the joy I feel!* |
| Qu'à remplir un devoir on trouve de bonheur! | *What happiness to fulfill one's duty!* |
| Dieu des coeurs bienfaisans! ô Dieu, qui vois mon âme, | *Lord of kind hearts! You who see inside me, fill me with these gifts for* |
| Verse sur moi les dons que mon zêle réclame! | *which I yearn! Let me be Surrounded by* |
| Que de mortels heureux je puisse m'entourer | *happy mortals and have no more* |
| Et n'avoir plus mes torts à plaindre, à réparer! | *faults to reproach myself for or fix!* |

Although Du Pont was expressing an eighteenth-century commonplace about the joys of doing good and how kings ought to view this as their special domain, he captured something specifically Josephine: the Emperor's obvious need to appear as a benefactor. The playwright elevated it, of course, to a function of statecraft.[13]

This dramatic rendering of physiocracy was no mere diversion. Du Pont spent months on his play and revised it for an additional two years. What had brought him to this pass? We might take it in part as a response to the movement's recent humiliation at the hands of the abbé Galiani

---

[13] Fénélon's *Télémaque* inspired these associations throughout the eighteenth century. Thomas Kaiser, "The Abbé de Saint-Pierre, Public Opinion, and the Reconsitution of the French Monarchy," *Journal of Modern History*, 55 (1983), 618–43, and "Louis *le Bien-Aimé* and the Rhetoric of the Royal Body," in Sara E. Melzer and Kathryn Norberg eds, *From the Royal to the Republican Body* (Berkeley, Los Angeles, London, 1998), pp. 131–61.

whose *Dialogues sur le commerce des blés*, an incisive attack on physiocratic ideas, had been greeted with wild acclaim in 1770, the naysayers being none other than the physiocrats.[14] The Italian's witty dialogues mocked their ideas and their angry responses merely worsened their case. Turgot, for example, counseled silence on the matter, since pompous refutations could not compete with Galiani's lightness of touch. Du Pont's play was an attempt to beat Galiani at his own game by providing a literary counterpart to his bestseller. Unlike Galiani who relied on "cheap irony" to deride the physiocratic project, as Du Pont put it, he would provide a high-minded lesson in civics and economics.

Du Pont's choice to write his play in verse rather than prose reveals his literary aspirations and his desire to be taken seriously by a traditional audience. Despite his careful staging and attention to facial expressions and bodily gestures – which place him in a cohort of theatrical innovators – he only rarely introduced Diderot's halting style meant to reproduce actual speech.[15] His characters use the nobler artifice of rhyme to communicate their thoughts and feelings. For monarchs did not habitually chat on stage. When they did speak, it was indeed in the *alexandrin* favored by classical dramatists. Actually, monarchs, living monarchs that is (at least French ones), did not appear on stage at all, and Du Pont was courting lèse-majesté.[16] His countrymen had been turning to historical subjects recently, with kings as heroes – but they were dead kings, preferably of another dynasty.[17]

Fearing rebuke, Du Pont was secretive about his enterprise. We first learn about it in Turgot's letter of 12 February 1771. Du Pont had

---

[14] Ferdinando Galiani, *Dialogues sur le commerce des bleds* (London, 1770). Weulersse also saw the publication as a turning point for the Physiocrats, *Le mouvement physiocratique*, I, pp. 227ff, but paid no attention to Du Pont's play. For Du Pont's response to Galiani, see *Ephémerides* (1770), I, pp. 27–34.

[15] Denis Diderot, *De la poésie dramatique* and *Paradoxe sur le comédien*, which Du Pont would have been familiar with. On Diderot's theatre, see for example Michael Fried, *Absorption and Theatricality, Painting and Beholder in the Age of Diderot* (Chicago, 1980) and Pierre Frantz, *L'esthétique du tableau dans le théâtre du XVIIIe siècle* (Paris, 1999).

[16] Louis XV was notoriously sensitive about depictions of the monarchy on stage. After his death plays featured acts of charity by Frederick II and Marie Antoinette: *Auguste et Théodore, ou les Deux Pages*, comédie, 2 actes, by Faur (Paris, 1789) *Le Billet de Mariage* by Desfontaines, Octobre 1772 reworked as *La Dot*, performed in 1785 and *La Chasse* by Desfontaines (Paris, 1778) all performed at the Théâtre des Italiens

[17] Even this did not save Collé whose *La partie de chasse de Henri IV* could not be performed in Paris until after the death of Louis XV who had taken umbrage at the suggestion that Henry IV's populism was France's salvation. In Jacques Truchet, ed., *Théâtre du XVIIIe Siècle*, 2 vols. (Paris, 1974), II, pp. 599–655.

been neglecting the *Ephémérides*, it turned out, only to pen a comedy. Distractions of this sort were dangerous, Turgot warned, because they took up valuable time. He knew this from personal experience (*J'en dis tous les jours mon mêa culpa*).[18] A month later, Turgot shared his impressions of the actual manuscript.[19] There were charming bits but overall the play lacked polish. The scene with the minister of finance was totally out of place. It interrupted the flow and distracted attention from the main plot. Joseph pontificates and his speeches to his advisors were the most poorly written in the play. For the first time, Du Pont is confronted with the political implications of his work. "It is shockingly anachronistic given its contemporary subject matter. Everyone knows that the Emperor has no lands to govern and therefore cannot have a minister of finance. What is more, can you really believe that one can put words into a living monarch's mouth that may not correspond to his beliefs and might even completely go against them"?

Turgot's final letter on the subject of 12 April 1771 went into more detail but also tried to smooth the author's ruffled feathers.[20] He apologized for his roughness and for his delayed response. He realized that their friendship was being sorely tried for, like any author who had invested as much as Du Pont did in *Joseph*, he bristled at criticism. But, as a lover of truth, Du Pont deserved the truth. He must give up this project. "Well, my friend, I must tell you that my advice is to give up doing anything, absolutely anything with *Joseph the Second*. I have read and reread it several times and my opinion has never wavered." Then, Turgot really let loose. The ideas were not only poorly presented; they were pedestrian. Didactic verse was an abomination. It is sometimes possible to cloak commonplaces in regalia or to launch into lengthy philosophical debates, but, as far as he was concerned, there was no way to write the long scene in Act III that Du Pont has in mind.

Turgot demolished Du Pont's efforts without grasping his fundamental point: the metonymic relationship between private and public. Eighteenth-century audiences, as far as we can tell, would have responded to his play by treating it as a touching tribute to royal benevolence. They would have been puzzled by the physiocratic segments and like Turgot would have considered them out of place. Such sermons belonged rather

---

[18] Hagley, W2-1621. Letter from Turgot to Du Pont, Limoges, 12 February 1771. The letters can also be found in Schelle, *Oeuvres de Turgot et documents le concernant*, III.
[19] Hagley, W2-1624. Letter from Turgot to Du Pont, Limoges, 13 March 1771.
[20] Hagley, W2-1626. Letter from Turgot to Du Pont, Limoges, 12 April 1771.

in Virgil's *Georgics* or James Thomson's descriptive poems. Despite his ambitions to create a new genre, Du Pont would have been defeated by the aesthetics of recognition: the eighteenth-century propensity to confine art to established genres. But Du Pont believed, very much like Diderot, that theatre would prove a powerful vehicle for moral reformation, especially if it depicted "realistic" scenes, drawn from daily life, with which the audience could empathize.[21] Such belief in the contagion of emotions was completely contrary to Quesnay's teachings.

Turgot ended his critique by raising a more serious objection that went right to the heart of Du Pont's project. He tried to disabuse Du Pont of his illusions about educating monarchs.

I see no value in presenting useful ideas to the Emperor in an accommodating way. Trying to instruct Princes who are no longer children is a pure waste of time. It is the public one must instruct. If these princes are men they will understand books written for men and won't require fairytales like children. If they are only princes, they will listen to the tale without understanding it and only truly believe what everyone else around them believes, meaning what is popular rather than a publicly acknowledged truth. A few pages of honey-tongued praise and veiled truths will have no effect on those kings who have sided against the economists or against works like the abbé Galiani's. You can be sure that a prince who remains unmoved by that book will appreciate the simple truth without having to be praised. As a general rule, my friend, we must instruct and persuade the public and we will do this, in the long run, by proper demonstrations that sensible men will find convincing, since the public which controls men in power is in turn led by the enlightened. And enlightened men are not persuaded by good or bad verse, however much they like the good ones. They look for reasons and they want them stated simply. As you know, they recoil when they are lectured or at displays of sectarianism. Forgive me once more, dear friend, but don't make a spectacle of yourself and let the public make fun at your expense. Have the courage to sacrifice a work that you wrote in a moment of distraction and that you haven't perhaps had time to consider more coolly.

Turgot's enlightened public who preferred cogently argued works was apparently not Du Pont's target. He took up Turgot's challenge instead, deciding to reach the frivolous with frivolities. For why should one restrict oneself to singing the praises of dead heroes when there existed more compelling examples whose actions affected the present generation?[22] This

---

[21] See on this Diderot, *Oeuvres* (Paros, 1996), IV, pp. 1071–73.
[22] He states in the preface to his manuscript: "I deemed that it was this Prince's fate to serve Europe by publicizing his exemplary actions, as by the wisdom of his behaviour." On French theatre audiences, see Jeffrey S. Ravel, *The Contested Parterre: Public Theater and French Political Culture, 1680–1791* (Ithaca, 1999); Gregory Brown, *A Field of Honor:*

was an "avant-garde" declaration despite its traditional versification.[23] He had intended "to remain faithful to the original dialogue reported in the *Ephémérides*. Of course, he had invented the cabinet discussions since these gatherings were not public. Admittedly, he ought to have had Maria Theresa preside the council, but he did not feel up to putting both the noble mother and her worthy son on stage.... He had hoped rather that the great man whose name it bore would find it to his taste and that the drama might be published. For this prince's destiny was to serve Europe by his example." Yet Du Pont's intended audience for this play remains murky. Was he addressing the Emperor and by extension Louis XV, as Turgot concluded, or had he a larger public in mind? Much has been written about the physiocrats and public opinion yet no one has come up with a satisfactory definition of their ideal public – because they failed to come up with one themselves.[24] It cannot be denied, however, that time and again physiocrats declared that they were addressing monarchs first and foremost. Turgot's exhortations certainly gave Du Pont pause, but he was not dissuaded, and, in fact, continued to revise the work.

Turgot did not share Du Pont's adulation of Joseph. "Your dear Emperor," he wrote Du Pont in that third missive, "is about to ignite all of Europe once again; so, for heaven's sake, please forget these ferocious and incorrigible types, and speak to men instead." As an afterthought, he added: "I see that you are planning to send your play to the Emperor. I beg you not to do it. Should M. de Saint-Mégrin be made ambassador to Vienna, as is rumored, I fear that he might encourage you to do so; were he really your friend, he would not." Austria was then allied to France, a tie reinforced by the recent marriage of Marie Antoinette to the Dauphin. The alliance, however, was becoming more precarious with the forthcoming partition of Poland, France's traditional client, so Du Pont's endeavor might have produced unintended diplomatic consequences.[25]

---

*Writers, Court Culture, and Public Theater in French Literary Life from Racine to the Revolution* (New York, 2005); and Maurice Lever, *Théâtre et Lumières: Les Spectacles de Paris au XVIIIe siècle* (Paris, 2001).

[23] On this point, see Worvill, *"Seeing" Speech*.

[24] On this, see for example the introduction by Bernard Delmas, Thierry Delmas and Philippe Steiner, eds. to *La Diffusion internationale de la physiocratie (XVIIIe–XIXe)*, (Grenoble, 1995).

[25] In fact there was no response from Vienna or from Mercy-Argenteau the Austrian ambassador, at least none to be found in the diplomatic papers at the Ministère des Affaires étrangères. Mme de Pompadour had been instrumental in the reversal of alliances but we have no notion whether Quesnay approved or disapproved. He did not get along with the Duc de Choiseul who continued to enforce this policy.

Turgot need not have worried: Du Pont never published the play and it was never performed.

As far as I have been able to establish, Joseph never saw a copy, although Marie Antoinette did (so Du Pont reported to the Margrave of Baden).[26] The Margravine Carolina Luisa acknowledged receiving a copy of the play with a friendly note, on 22 September 1772, praising Du Pont's worthy intentions.[27] After a great deal of prodding, Du Pont had garnered some appreciation, but no help toward publication nor any hint that she would approach the Emperor. Carl Friedrich was equally circumspect. He finally responded in late December 1772 apologizing for the delay and thanking Du Pont for sending him the play, without further comment.[28] This is all we know about the play and its fate.[29]

Yet it had a strange afterlife. In the fall of 1772 the Théâtre français included in its repertoire *Albert Premier ou Adeline* slated to open on 26 October.[30] The play had received official sanction, but the performance was canceled at the last minute by a direct order from the Court.[31] Its author was revealed to be Le Blanc de Guillet. Voltaire to whom it was first attributed, reported a rumor that Du Pont had written it.[32] Le Blanc's play finally had a ten-day run in February 1775 (when Turgot was Controller general). Reviews were mixed. It was then whispered that the *économistes* had helped revise the play after its lackluster first performance.

---

[26] Hagley, Winterthur Mss, 10/E, Eleutheria Du Pont Smith transcripts of Du Pont correspondance with the Margrave of Baden, Volume 3, pp. 134–5. In Knies, *Carl Friedrichs von Baden*, I, p. 142.
[27] Hagley, Du Pont Smith transcripts, vol. 3, p. 119. This letter is not in Knies.
[28] Ibid., p. 118. Letter from Carl Friedrich, Margrave of Baden to Du Pont de Nemours, Karlsruhe, 25 December 1772.
[29] Hagley, W2-1928. In the late 1780s, reflecting on this youthful exercise, he admitted to Mirabeau that the play had been a failure but that he had hoped it would serve a didactic purpose.
[30] Le Blanc de Guillet, *Albert Premier ou Adeline, comédie héroique en trois actes, en vers de dix syllabes* (Paris, 1775).
[31] Georges Weulersse, *La Physiocratie à la fin du règne de Louis XV*, p. 11. This is also the explanation that Grimm provides in the *Correspondance littéraire* in November 1772, X, p. 91, but, in January 1773 he tells a different story: "M. Le Blanc, ... who preached a sermon in the *Druids* against human sacrifice on the stage of the Comédie française ... has chosen to preach at that same arena, the sermon Adeline ... but the Archbishop of Paris found some inappropriate mentions in this sermon and forbade Father Le Blanc from preaching on the stage" which is why Le Blanc is reduced to composing verses for Mirabeau's Tuesdays (vol. X, p. 173).
[32] Voltaire's letter of 11 November 1772 to Henri Lambert d'Herbigny, Marquis de Thibouville in Voltaire, *Correspondance* (Paris, 1987), XI, p. 127.

Despite its title and its medieval setting, the play was clearly based on the same anecdote that had inspired Du Pont (although Le Blanc focused much more on the melodrama). As Grimm pointed out, the incident was so thinly disguised that Le Blanc had sought the Austrian ambassador's blessing before submitting his play to the censors.[33] Sartine, the chief censor, had approved the script but the government decided that its physiocratic speeches mocked the ministry – Terray's provisioning policies had infuriated the *économistes* – and its performance was stopped by a writ issued from Fontainebleau.[34] In another version by a nineteenth-century compiler, the play's focus on a disloyal courtier had displeased the Austrian ambassador.[35] The abbé Baudeau explained what he knew of the affair.[36]

M. Le Blanc, author of *The Druids* and *Manco* showed the queen this morning his drama called *Albert I*. It had been announced for last year, and was about to be performed when an order came to hold it back. For its subject is one of the Emperor's traits. The duc d'Aiguillon informed about the play, said curtly: "Apparently someone wishes to give the King a lesson." "It is too strident" some said. They might have added, "and the pupil too old." Du Barry feared that it might mortify the Dauphine and *Albert* was banned. Madame de Villeroy was curious to read the play and found it very good. She was so diligent that a few days before the King's last illness, she had the Dauphin and Dauphine hear it read by a M. Tessier from Lyons who has the knack of doing the voices of the men and women in an entire comedy. The listeners were won over. The Dauphin stated: "This is the sort of play I like." He remembered this once he became King and said: "This play *Albert I* is very good and I will have it." As a result permission was requested to dedicate it to the Queen; it has just been granted.

## Gendering the Economy

Du Pont spent so much time on the play because he believed that he might move the Emperor to reform [his future] state along physiocratic lines. At that time Joseph seemed particularly apt to fill that role. The fact that Du Pont and Joseph were nearly the same age (Du Pont was born on 14 December 1739 and Joseph 13 March 1741) might have encouraged this

---

[33] Grimm et al., *Correspondance littéraire*, X, pp. 90–1 and 118–19, November and December 1772.
[34] Weulersse, *La Physiocratie sous les ministères de Turgot et de Necker*, p. 19.
[35] Bibliothèque de l'Arsenal, Fonds Rondel, "Notice biographique sur Antoine Le Blanc de Guillet 1730–1799" par M. Claude Perroud, in *Annales de la Société d'Agriculture, Sciences, Arts et Commerce du Puy*, XXV (Le Puy, 1864), p. 283.
[36] June 14 1774, Nicolas Baudeau, "Chronique secrète de Paris sous le règne de Louis XVI (1774)," in *Revue rétrospective ou Bibliothèque historique* (Paris, 1834), III, pp. 85–6.

identification. At thirty, they were both ready to tackle the world's problems, both perhaps equally chafing at the bit.[37] Du Pont's liberties with the political situation in Austria were not accidental. He felt no qualms at denying Maria Theresa's actual power – she was the ruler and Joseph the co-regent, both were not co-regents, as Derek Beales reminds us[38] – for gendering was central to physiocracy and hence featured prominently in the play. The natural order involved distinctions between Nature/Woman and Society/Man. Mirabeau had expressed this quite plainly to one of his economic assemblies, in 1774:

Let us return to the bosom of our mother, she will guide us toward happiness, success, and prosperity ... our prosperity rests in following nature's wishes for she is always maternal, always benevolent.... Let us take man at his origins, surrounded by the bountiful fruits of the earth, spread every which way, which were mother's milk to him. He was then handed the responsibility of looking after them so that he might enjoy his right to life and to the perpetuation of his species.[39]

Du Pont's version of the story is not completely distorted but slants the hagiographic treatment of Joseph to his own ends. The Chevalier du Coudray's *Anecdotes intéressantes et historiques de l'illustre voyageur pendant son séjour à Paris* comes closest to Du Pont's version.[40] Grimm's retelling in the *Correspondence littéraire* is basically the same although the young woman's destitution is linked to economic crisis. She tells Joseph that the Emperor is reputed to be stingy – which accounts for her nervousness when she discovers his true identity.[41] The propaganda piece *Le Monarque accompli*, however, spins this differently: A saintly Joseph alerts his saintly mother, *"la plus auguste et la plus religieuse des reines."*[42]

She learns with a shudder the horrible and desperate straits of the family of a soldier who had so often shed his blood in the service of the state, and how barbaric

---

[37] Beales, *Joseph II*, p. 194. Between 1771 and 1773 Joseph tried to wrest power from his mother.
[38] Ibid., p. 135.
[39] Letter from Du Pont to Carl Ludwig [nd 1774] citing this text. Knies, *Carl Friedrichs von Baden*, II, pp. 319–22.
[40] Alexandre-Jacques Coudray, *Anecdotes intéressantes et historiques de l'illustre voyageur pendant son séjour à Paris*, 2nd edition (Paris, 1777), pp. 136–8, and Joseph Lanjuinais, *Le Monarque accompli ou prodiges de Bonté, de Savoir et de Sagesse qui font l'éloge de Sa Majesté impériale Joseph II et qui rendent cet Auguste monarque si précieux à l'humanité*, 3 vols. (Lausanne, 1774).
[41] Grimm et al., *Correspondance littéraire*, X, pp. 89–90. "They say he is a miser."
[42] Lanjuinais, *Le Monarque accompli*, I, p. 48.

ministers devoid of humanity had refused to hear his widow, denied her access to the throne, despite her repeated attempts. But starting now, admittance to the most humane and best of Emperors is as easy for the poor, indigent, and downtrodden as it is for the rich and mighty. What better spectacle than that of a Prince who avenges humanity in so striking a manner in front of the entire court!

The Emperor might have been granted the dominant role but Maria Theresa is integral to the story. Joseph II was Holy Roman Emperor and co-regent of Austria, until his mother's death in 1780: a man with absolute power in one sphere but strictly limited in another. He traveled incognito as the Count of Falkenstein (as rulers were wont to do when they wished to avoid ceremonial). In his version, Du Pont insinuates that despite her apparent supreme authority, Maria Theresa could not stop Joseph from exuding sovereignty and being recognized for who he truly was. By abandoning his regalia in the first scene, he was misrepresenting himself. But in Maria Theresa's realm, to wear the crown was a parody of power, a denial of where the true power lay. It is no accident that Joseph repudiated so strongly the court ritual in which he played second fiddle. He was reclaiming his true majesty by letting it surface naturally. Thus could the unnatural situation of a man without power be resolved for Du Pont. His Joseph was ruler and man, Emperor and Joseph – a king with multiple bodies.[43]

Du Pont's gendered fantasies permeated the ideal society he fantasized about in letters to Carl Ludwig.[44]

The house is their [women's] republic. It is there that they exercise the most affectionate and most powerful rule. It is through their perpetual care and constant prudence that they make themselves worthy of the respect they must always inspire. The more they keep to this private realm the more virtuous they become. It is therefore most seemly that they should only appear in public at designated times, when they reach the age of marriage, to take part, under their mothers' gaze, in the dances at major and minor national festivals.

In Rousseaunian fashion, he asserted that, since their role was domestic, they had no need of the same education as men. They should rule over their own sphere as wives, mothers, citizens worthy of worship, give up useless fripperies, and agree to dress simply. But, Du Pont sighed, "we are still far from this; and perhaps it will be a protracted battle. If anyone

---

[43] Beales, *Joseph II*, I, pp. 33 and 155 citing Joseph himself: "It would be a sad situation if the status of Man were incompatible with that of Emperor."
[44] Knies, *Carl Friedrichs von Baden*, II, pp. 300–4, undated letter from Du Pont to Carl Lusdwig [1774].

escapes royal control, it is women, for they belong to the family far more than the state."⁴⁵ In Sophie, however, Du Pont shows us that his ideal woman is competent and self-possessed. She expresses her disapproval of the cold-hearted Joseph (before she discovers he stands before her); she takes care of her mother and has strength for both of them, since protecting the family was treated as a typical female responsibility in the Old Regime. She has no vanity (or for that matter, excess clothing) and is naturally upright. Du Pont's gendering does not require mousy spinelessness. It just demands that women know their place.⁴⁶ And should one imagine that these were mere literary conventions, he explained quite clearly what he expected from his son Victor: "You do not lack kindness and I myself possess sensibility and tenderness. But we are *virile*."⁴⁷

## An Education Fit for a Prince

In the midst of all this, at the end of 1771 Du Pont began tutoring Carl Ludwig the Margrave of Baden's son and heir, through periodic long letters on history, economics, and the arts.⁴⁸ Carl Ludwig was born in February 1755 and would marry in 1774. This happy event did not end these epistolary lessons. They were interrupted by Du Pont's departure for Poland.⁴⁹

The Du Pont of the early 1770s was juggling the editorship of the *Éphémérides*, whose issues were coming out with increasing delays, along with the composition of a physiocratic play. He also had a young family

---

⁴⁵ Knies, *Carl Friedrichs von Baden*, II, p. 304. Letter from Du Pont to Carl Ludwig of Baden, on Peter the Great, festivals, and military dress [n.d., 1774].

⁴⁶ Review of Mirabeau's *Economiques* in *Éphémérides* (1769) XII, pp. 163–4. As Du Pont gleefully points out, Mirabeau shares his assessment of the fairer sex: "The farmer needs a prudent and faithful wife, a confidante and a sweet companion, a woman who, while he oversees the labours on the fields, will keep the interior of the house in order, a woman who is prudently thrifty, highly charitable, always gentle, always even-mooded, mother and mistress of everything under her care, in other words, the loving star that lights up the domestic sphere, never agitated, illuminating everything around her, and whose very presence brings order, life and activity. Such a mixture and perfect embodiment of all the useful virtues belong to this sex only." This strict gendering of roles in the running of a farm was as old as Hesiod. As for what it says about Mirabeau's psychological yearnings, I leave this to the reader to decide.

⁴⁷ He was objecting to Victor addressing him as "mon cher petit papa." Hagley, W2-386. Letter from Du Pont, 22 May 1790.

⁴⁸ Carl Knies, *Carl Friedrichs von Baden*, II, Part III (Du Pont's correspondence with Carl Ludwig of the 1780s).

⁴⁹ News from Paris would henceforth be conveyed by the abbé Baudeau. Knies, *Carl Friedrichs von Baden*, II, Part III, p. 203, n.d. (mid-1774).

to support and the state of France to consider, since the new Controller general, the abbé Terray, was opposed to free trade. In December 1772, permission to publish the journal was withdrawn and Du Pont grew deeply anxious about his prospects. The advent of a physiocratic state seemed to be receding in France itself, although Du Pont took comfort from the reforms undertaken in Italy by the Duke of Tuscany, in Sweden by Gustav III, and in Germany by the likes of the Margrave of Baden, by Maria Theresa's creation of a chair of political economy in Milan, and the grand reforms he expected from her son, Joseph II. Still, he had to reflect on the failures of reform in his own country. Were the "prejudices" plaguing the science of the natural order insurmountable or could they be confounded? Would the nation unite to fulfill Nature's commands?

The letters to Carl Ludwig, despite their obsequious tone, relay with unselfconscious candor Du Pont's continuing search for means to inculcate his economic program. Mirabeau and Du Pont supported the research and speculations of Antoine Court de Gébelin (1725–1784) – and vice versa – because of their own interest in ancient cultures, although Mirabeau was not taken in unlike his younger colleague. As students of the occult are likely to know, Gébelin gained lasting fame for his interpretation of the Tarot. In his lifetime he was famous for his multivolume investigation of ancient languages and rituals, the *Monde primitif*, that revealed their common origins and began appearing in 1773. He died by electrocution in a Mesmerist bathtub before bringing the endeavor to a close. He had anticipated volumes on ancient history, agrarian laws and festivals but died before they were written, although he left outlines of their arguments which centered on Man's agrarian avocation. At the dawn of civilization, agriculture had flourished and been venerated.

Du Pont and Mirabeau were listed among the first subscribers to his opus.[50] Gébelin read extracts from his work at Mirabeau's physiocratic Tuesdays and, in his last published volume, thanked the Marquis for the use of a country retreat.[51] Although it appears never to have materialized, a project had been mooted that Gébelin offer a course on physiocracy

---

[50] Court de Gébelin, *Plan général et raisonné du Monde Primitif analysé et comparé avec le monde moderne* (Paris, 1773), p. 98.
[51] Court de Gébelin, *Monde Primitif analysé et comparé avec le monde moderne* (Paris, 1781), VIII, p. ix. Knies, *Friedrichs von Baden*, II, letter from Du Pont, 21 June 1773, "Discours pour la clôture des assemblées économiques tenues cette année chez M. le marquis de Mirabeau," p. 113, and "Discours pour la clôture de la huitième année des assemblées économiques tenues chez M. le marquis de Mirabeau le 13 mai 1774," p. 201.

starting 15 September 1767, in which he would explain the *Tableau* in all its various incarnations, and "describe the different classes in civil society, their rights and duties; the source of riches, their distribution and reproduction, and what a man, citizen and head of household might usefully and rightfully contribute to ensuring his own prosperity, that of the nation, and the happiness of humanity."[52] Du Pont was not merely sympathetic to Gébelin's anthropological project, it inspired him to propose agrarian festivals in the antique mode for the state of Baden, while commenting on the marquis de Chastellux's recently published examination of human happiness.[53]

Like Gébelin and the Economists, Chastellux took man's physiological needs as his starting point. He then proceeded to consider whether reliance on different resources affected the type of society they founded. Ultimately, he decided that such speculations on the "state of nature" were pointless, since no traces remained of these primitive arrangements.

> Let me conclude this long digression by stating that one cannot assess the happiness of peoples in earliest antiquity either from their frugality or their opulence; a simpler lifestyle is no more an indication of their virtue than their magnificence would be of their happiness: everywhere ignorance, despotism, war and superstition have taken from men the benefits that nature bestowed on them.[54]

Du Pont gleefully noted that Chastellux looked forward to the establishment of a "physiocracy," which he defined as "a government resting on the powers of nature, its energy and activity." This could only occur once the laws of nature were properly understood and thoroughly analyzed, although he did not explain how this might be achieved.[55] Du Pont however took issue with Chastellux's contention that "there was nothing left of the state of nature."[56] He informed Carl Ludwig that the family, for example, dated from the earliest days, since agriculture and organized societies developed simultaneously with all the conventions that went with them. These early states had withered from a neglect of education, and an unfettered and selfish pursuit of wealth that transformed

---

[52] A.N. M784/1.
[53] Hagley, W2-1642, Turgot to Du Pont, Limoges, 14 July 1772. François-Jean Chastellux, *De la félicité publique ou Considérations sur le sort des hommes dans les différentes époques historiques*, 2 vols. (Amsterdam, 1772). See Darrin M. McMahon, *Happiness, A History* (New York, 2006), pp. 214–16.
[54] Chastellux, *De la félicité publique*, I, p. 74.
[55] Ibid., p. 135. He called for a physical and moral medicine. Voltaire, who annotated the edition, remarked: "La médecine qui fait naître la politique! Ah!"
[56] Knies, *Friedrichs von Baden*, II, part III, p. 46 [n.d. 1773].

their "ministers" into oppressors and governments into despotisms. "An uneven distribution of abundance and riches led to a loosening of morals, the communication of ideas was hampered; religion steeped in allegories and image-based writing-systems restricted learning to priests whose ambition, avarice, and vanity stopped them from spreading it to the people. They seduced rulers and abased their subjects." True education ceased (and hence the only brake to injustice and arbitrary government vanished), frivolous arts filled the void to distract people from their misery; philosophical speculation, meanwhile, became increasingly abstruse and detached from reality.

Willy-nilly Du Pont found himself constructing a plausible alternative narrative that explained why the "natural order" had not been "perpetuated" from the outset. Unlike Mirabeau who sought to root modern institutions, such as nobility, in ancient practices – although he would concede the more conventional "usurpation" by feudal barons in his later writings – Du Pont's intellectual horizons were defined by physiocracy. The contradiction between the "necessity of the natural order" and its sporadic realization was bound to preoccupy him more.[57]

Yet for all this, Du Pont was a Modern, whereas Quesnay and certainly Mirabeau were on the Ancient side of the Querelle. Du Pont praised his era for reviving the "science of public felicity" from the doldrums into which it had sunk since the dawn of civilization. Whereas Chastellux reproved the Greek military outlook, Du Pont again begged to differ.[58] Martial arts could easily be transformed into public games that improved the moral and physical conditions of the nation's youth. Military training should not be restricted to professional soldiers. A free nation must be protected by its citizenry. Chastellux proves no better with the Romans, apparently, since he is clueless about the true sources of good government.[59] Chastellux made the additional mistake of "denying that traces of man's original language still existed, revealing yet again our indebtedness to the primitive world."

---

[57] Le Trosne was doing this as well in his texts of the mid 1770s, displaying a similar awareness of the contradiction and no better able to account for it.

[58] Knies, *Friedrichs von Baden*, II, part III, pp. 65–7 [n.d. 1773].

[59] Ibid., p. 55. Court de Gébelin, *Plan général du Monde primitif* (p. 7). He is a true physiocrat according to Anne-Marie Mercier-Faivre, *Un supplément à "L'Encyclopédie": Le "Monde primitif" d'Antoine Court de Gébelin, suivi d'une édition du "Génie allégorique et symbolique de l'Antiquité" extrait du "Monde primitif"* (Paris, 1999), pp. 54–5, on the Eloge delivered by Quesnay's son, Quesnay de Saint-Germain at the Musée de Paris [the Mesmerist headquarters] in June 1784.

## The Education of Princes

[You] will observe that agrarian nations enacted the best codes, which survive among the most ancient peoples of Asia. We [Du Pont and his pupil] will examine the degree of respect accorded to those who devoted their lives to agriculture and how their status accorded with the natural order necessary to societies, to which the peoples of Europe will have to return once they seek to perfect their laws and ideas.

Du Pont agreed with Gébelin that early rituals were allegorical celebrations of humans' fulfillment of the divine plan. They therefore reached their acme in the "exuberant celebrations of the golden age that saw the birth of agriculture and of judicial institutions, ... with thanksgivings ... and prayers imploring divine blessings on ... ploughing, sowing, first fruits, harvest, vintage, and the dead season."[60] Early civilizations had understood the need to celebrate agriculture. The "self-esteem" of the rural workforce had been stimulated through "feasts, spectacles, and amusements." Poetry disseminated important messages through its power to influence people who had no leisure to read or study, "less by an appeal to reason than the power to move, stimulate, surprise, and ... educate the people while they thought they were simply being entertained.... One can learn twenty songs in less time than it takes to grasp ten arguments, and one will remember the first while the second leaves no traces."[61]

Du Pont's response to Gébelin was not unique and, besides its naiveté, appears to reflect the sensibilities of his generation and its responsiveness to emotions in ways that seemed perverse to the older, more analytical group that comprised Turgot, Mirabeau, and of course Quesnay imbued with seventeenth-century rationalism. Thus, Jacques Turgot and the (much older) Bern physiologist Albrecht von Haller expressed skepticism about Gébelin's speculations to their respective correspondents Du Pont and Charles Bonnet.[62] Turgot agreed to subscribe to the *Monde primitif* in November 1772 but added, "I must admit that his ideas seem to be a tissue of fantasies [*rêveries*] and that he lacks the finesse of a critic or the necessary metaphysics to deal with such a subject. But, as you say, despite this, one might glean a few good insights and some useful facts."[63]

[60] Court de Gébelin, *Du génie allégorique et symbolique de l'antiquité* (Paris, 1776), p. 147.
[61] Gébelin, *Du génie allégorique*, p. 149, and *Monde Primitif*, part VIII, vol. 1 *Dissertations mêlées* (Paris, 1781), p. xix.
[62] Albrecht von Haller, *The correspondence between Albrecht von Haller and Charles Bonnet*, ed. Otto Sonntag (Bern, Stuttgart, Vienna, 1983), pp. 1145–7, letter from Charles Bonnet of 12 November 1774, praising Gébelin and Haller's reply of 17 November, "fearing to express his views on *Le monde primitif*."
[63] Letter from Turgot to Du Pont, Limoges, 27 November 1772, in Schelle, *Oeuvres de Turgot et documents le concernant*, III, p. 570.

Mirabeau was equally indulgent, telling Charles de Butré not to criticize Gébelin overly much, since he would immediately cave in, and that celebrating agriculture was worthy in itself.[64]

Turgot was a serious student of history and etymology, contributing a lengthy article to the *Encyclopédie* on the subject, and Haller was a celebrated lyric poet, author of *Die Alpen* (1729–1732) and recently of a 400-page oriental fable *Usong* (1771). He was also an innovative researcher who had added the concepts of the sensibility of nerves and irritability of muscles to eighteenth-century medicine. To the Genevan physiologist Charles Bonnet's often sentimental responses to poetry, Haller opposed a more hard-headed interest in rhythm and cadence (very much, in fact, like Turgot's). Bonnet had moved from anatomy to metaphysics, developing a theory of the perfectibility of living things as their potential regenerative capacities unfolded over time (in readiness for the Second Coming) based on his study of the polyp and butterfly.[65] His starting point remained anatomy, however, whereas Du Pont was poised between political economy and culture wondering how he might bring the two together. He was therefore much taken with Gébelin's "demonstration" that all spheres of life had cohered at the dawn of society. Taking his cue from him, Du Pont would present agrarian festivals as moments of unalloyed joy, which united all members of society and "inculcated them with the same principles, the same tastes, promoting the love of order, virtue, and useful work."[66] This was not the only available interpretation of such rituals. In his widely read *L'Antiquité dévoilée par ses usages* Nicolas-Antoine Boulanger argued instead that the Flood had been a turning point for humanity, leaving its traumatized survivors fearful, melancholic, and superstitious.[67] The dominant mood of their rituals, in commemoration of the great disaster, was funereal. This explained why they burst into tears in the midst of joyous occasions such as the Bacchanalea or tributes to the deities of agriculture such as Ceres, Cybele and Atys, Venus and Adonis, or Osiris and Isis. Pagan rituals thus lamented the fate of gods and mortals.[68] He used sources from as far afield as ancient Palestine and Persia, Japan and China, Brazil and Canada, finding in each reminders of the bitterness of the human condition.

[64] As Mirabeau reported to Carl Friedrich after he had introduced Butré to the Margrave.
[65] Charles Bonnet, *La Palingénésie philsophique* (Geneva, 1769).
[66] Knies, *Carl Friedrichs von* Baden, II, Part III, p. 16. Letter from Du Pont, 31 December 1772.
[67] Nicolas-Antoine Boulanger, *L'Antiquité dévoilée par ses usages*, 3 vols. (Amsterdam, 1766).
[68] Ibid., I, pp. 270–9.

# The Education of Princes

Du Pont, having failed to arouse interest in his physiocratic play, now turned his attention to another medium, imagining the festivals of a future physiocratic state in excruciating detail. Easily carried away and a lover of ritual (as witnessed by the "first sword" ceremonies he wrote for his sons) he elaborated on his project unlike other eighteenth-century authors who merely hinted at their content in one or two paragraphs. Montesquieu's contented Troglodytes honored the gods in festivities where young women, crowned with flowers, danced with their sweethearts to rustic music. In the feast that followed they sang of nature, virtue, and love, opening their "hearts to give and to receive."[69] A page sufficed to get this across. Rousseau harked back to the Lacedaemonians of ancient Greece as his example of the festivals that befit a true Republic.[70] Poland, he suggested elsewhere, might regain its civic spirit if hearts were moved by public ceremonies, modeled on the ancients.[71] Mirabeau himself had briefly alluded to civic rituals (and his son would openly encourage them during the Revolution). Enlightenment invocations of bygone festivities were often laden with teary-eyed accounts of contemporary village festivities.[72] Du Pont offered no such comparisons.[73]

His vision belongs to the utopian genre described by Mona Ozouf and Jean Ehrard where rituals are conceived as encouraging public spirit by involving the entire population and emphasizing communal harmony (as envisioned by elites). Their aim was fundamentally didactic. While some versions might commemorate local heroes, others celebrated a new order

---

[69] Montesquieu, *Lettres persanes* (Paris, 1989), Letter XII, pp. 43–4.
[70] Jean-Jacques Rousseau, *Lettre à M. D'Alembert*, in *Du contrat social* (Paris, 1962), pp. 232–4.
[71] Jean-Jacques Rousseau, *Considérations sur le gouvernement de Pologne et sur sa réformation projetée en avril 1772* in *Du contrat social* (Paris, 1962), pp. 343–5. His *Essai sur l'origine des langues* was equally prescriptive, see Jean Starobinsky's introduction to the reprint of the 1763 manuscript (Paris, 1990), p. 53. See also Michael Culoma, *La Religion civile de Rousseau à Robespierre* (Paris, 2010), pp. 31–4.
[72] Mona Ozouf, *La Fête révolutionnaire, 1789–1799* (Paris, 1976), pp. 16–17, and Jean Ehrard, "Les Lumières et la fête," pp. 27–44, in Jean Ehrard and Paul Viallaneix, eds., *Les Fêtes de la Révolution, Colloque de Clermont-Ferrand (juin 1974)* (Paris, 1977). See also Alain Corbin, "Préface," pp. 7–11, in Noelle Gérôme, "La tradition politique des fêtes: interprétation et appropriation," pp. 15–23, in Alain Corbin, Noelle Gérôme, and Danielle Tartakowsky, eds., *Les Usages politiques des fêtes aux XIXe–XXe siècles* (Paris, 1994).
[73] Béatrice Didier, "La fête champêtre dans quelques romans de la fin du XVIIIe siècle de Rousseau à Senancour," pp. 63–72, and Roland Mortoer, "Prélude à la fête révolutionnaire: la 'fête bocagère' dans la poésie descriptive de la fin du XVIIIe siècle," pp. 73–84, in Jean Ehrard and Paul Viallaneix, *Les Fêtes de la Révolution. Colloque de Clermont-Ferrand (juin 1974)* (Paris, 1977). See also my "Imagining the Harvest in Early Modern Europe."

or existing hierarchy by calling on different social groups to partake in the solemnities, in the ways of traditional urban corporate pageantry. Others yet, eager to transcend social distinctions focused their festivals on cycle of the seasons or stages of life, masking potential conflicts and stimulating "heartfelt" declarations of mutual love and friendship. Two additional features typified the eighteenth-century festive imaginary: an obsession with both dancing and martial exercises.[74]

The festivals that Du Pont envisioned conformed to the social harmony model, although quite clearly associated with physiocratic ideals. They were important to his physiocratic project and he appeared to have given them much thought. It is in this light that we might treat his wholehearted endorsement of Court de Gébelin's depiction of ancient festivities and the spirit that imbued them, for this fitted his purpose admirably.[75]

## Agrarian Festivals

In December 1772 Du Pont presented the Margrave with a scheme for seasonal festivals that he thought might be overseen by the heir to the throne.[76] "In a state which had rekindled awareness of the natural order, where people had been led back to nature, celebrations of this kind could not only be revived but become the prime means of teaching virtue."[77] These festivities need not be costly or extravagant and could easily be planned to coincide with existing feast-days. Additional pomp would encourage emulation as each participant became infused with the

---

[74] Abel Poitrineau, "La Fête traditionnelle," in Jean Ehrard and Paul Viallaneix, *Les Fêtes de la Révolution. Colloque de Clermont-Ferrand (juin 1974)* (Paris, 1977), pp. 11–26, 16–17.

[75] Knies, *Carl Friedrichs von Baden,* II, letter from Du Pont to Carl Friedrich of Baden, 5 January 1773, pp. 149–50, in which he vaunts Gébelin's enterprise and sends him some preliminary chapters. He also returns the loan of the Margravine's three volumes of d'Anquetil, a writer he deems far beneath Gébelin. He had needed the volumes for "his work," although what that mysterious enterprise might be is left for the modern reader to guess. Presumably the work by D'Anquetil was his two-part translation of the Zoroastrian *Zend-Avesta*, published in three volumes in 1771. Du Pont was less flattering about Gébelin's second volume which he forwarded to the Margrave on 30 July 1774, pp. 171–2. Du Pont describes his projected fêtes in a letter to Carl Friedrich of 3 December 1772. Knies, *Carl Friedrichs von Baden,* pp. 145–6.

[76] Knies, *Carl Friedrichs von Baden*, II, p. 146.

[77] The notion of the convergence of heart and mind is central to the later eighteenth century according to Robert Mauzi, *L'idée du bonheur dans la littérature et la pensée française au XVIIIe siècle* (Paris, 1994), p. 544. It is not certain that Du Pont was convinced of this so much as tried to convince himself of this.

ambient fraternal spirit, and thus "receptive to the legislator's plans."[78] Du Pont had a full program in mind and never doubted that these gatherings would delight one and all and spread good cheer.[79]

The spring festival was devoted to adolescence. "The best pupils would receive prizes and winners would move up in rank as in the old Roman *juvinalia* and what the Germans, Franks, and Gauls called the *champ de mars* and *champ de mai*." The summer festival would outshine all other festivities since it came right after the harvest, and Du Pont explained that it was modeled in part on the Chinese ploughing ceremonies and Samnite nuptial rituals. An autumn feast would follow the grape harvest and honor adults during a day of reconciliation and harmony, inspired by the feast the Romans called *charisties*. New wine would stimulate good cheer. The winter festival, based on the Chinese feast of the Ancestors, would extol the merits of old age and fatherly love. Homage would be paid to elders seated by the fireplace. The winter festivities would not supplant but rather supplement Christmas, New Year, and the Epiphany. Given the harsh northern European climate, only two of these seasonal festivals would be held outdoors. The fall and winter celebrations would have a more intimate setting and hence feel more domestic. In spring and summer, on the other hand, people would gather outdoors.[80]

The summer festival, described in painstaking detail, opened to the sound of trumpets and the chiming of bells. People would gather on the green (*la plaine*), the men dressed in plain uniform. The Prince or his envoy would arrive. The farmers would raise their weapons in greeting, and then fetch the sheaves that had lain behind the women and pile them in a mound big enough to support a platform on which the monarch and his family would sit, reminding everyone that the prince's authority rested on the products of the earth. This demonstrates Du Pont's determination to make symbols transparent to facilitate the didactic thrust of the festival. The troops then paraded as the men fired salvoes, and it was time for the women to appear, ushered in by the local elders. "I am

---

[78] Knies, *Carl Friedrichs von Baden*, Letter of 31 December 1772 to Carl Ludwig, II, part III, p. 23. "le législateur, qui les trouve émus, les porte où il veut."

[79] Du Pont, of course, shared the sensationalist assumption that positive feelings were "contagious." See Ozouf, *La Fete révolutionnaire*, pp. 201, 252, 327 for how this affected festivals. See also Nicolas Mariot, "Qu'est-ce qu'un 'enthousiasme civique'? Sur l'historiographie des fêtes politiques en France après 1789," *Annales Histoire, Sciences Sociales* 63:1 (2008), 113–39 who regrets that Ozouf's insights into the delusional quality of the festival organizers has been forgotten.

[80] This idea had been revived by Morelly in 1755 in his *Code de la nature*, Jean Ehrard, "Les Lumières et la fête," p. 40.

sending a battalion of old men to do this," Du Pont explains, "in order to stress that families remain under the authority and care of their elders and that unions are contracted under their aegis." The brides led the cortege, decked in white linen and pink ribbons. They were so overwhelmed with excitement that they could barely walk, and had to lean on their mothers (and some elders), embodying literally their "weaker sex." Fanfares would greet their arrival and the brides would line up on the right side of the field to face the grooms, escorted in by their fathers. As the music died down, the young men would step forward, remove their hats, and fall to one knee, while still holding their muskets, to ask their fathers for their blessing and permission to marry. The fathers would come forward and murmur a blessing with one hand on their sons' head, embrace them and remove to their allotted place. The young men would rise and move toward the battalion [this is again Du Pont's term] of women, in a light, brisk step, while maintaining a respectful demeanor. They would fall to their knees before the mothers and beg them to bestow on them their hearts' desire. The brides' mothers would assent and exhort them to love and respect their daughters. With a kiss on the forehead, mothers would remind their daughters of their duties, take their hand and place it in that of their intended. The couples thus joined would line up before the Prince and pay homage to his stewardship of their nation. The Prince would respond with a simple, moving (*pathétique*) and noble speech about the sanctity of the vows they had just exchanged. He would explain how important they were to society and bid them to be honest, active, virtuous, and hardworking. At this, the grooms, still holding their musket in their right hand, would place their left arm around their brides and kiss them on the cheek, as the Prince looked on. This kiss sealed both their love for each other and for the nation.

The grooms, however, still needed to prove their fitness to found new households by their readiness to defend the realm. Martial sounds would suddenly erupt as a squadron, saber in hand, galloped toward the bridegrooms. The brides would be quickly borne to safety, while their men-folk, resolutely affixing their bayonets, would form three lines and prepare to meet the onslaught. As the cavalry veered to the left, the bridegrooms would set off in hot pursuit reaching the women before the squadron could harm them. The chase would continue around an expanse whose size, Du Pont specifies, would be proportional to the number of women. The cavalry, rebuffed by a volley of fire, would retreat at last. Hoops of joy and victory songs would erupt, and the Prince would congratulate the winners but remind them that the ruler retained his monopoly on warfare and would protect them and their property.

Canon and ploughs had, meanwhile, been dragged in front of the dais. The Prince, or his eldest son, stepping down from the platform, would be greeted on all sides by tearful admirers cheering, clapping, and shouting their thanks. He would start to plough, replaced in turn by the most important landowners, most prosperous farmers, and lastly by winegrowers, as the women and old men looked on (replicating the Chinese ritual that Pierre Poivre had described, as Du Pont had earlier pointed out).[81] A trench would be dug and an encampment set up, after which all would retire for the night. The following day a priest blessed the proceedings. Festivities and martial exercises would resume (described in loving detail), with banquets at the camp, and lastly dancing. On the third day, the prince would ask the grooms to break their weapons and to devote themselves to useful work. He would then bid them farewell after participating in the sowing of the following year's crop, and the festivities would come to a close.

Even this abbreviated summary reveals the importance that Du Pont attached to these rituals and the delight with which he described every phase, apparently convinced that the Margrave would implement these festivities forthwith and that they would inspire other rulers. Civic spirit and social harmony would emerge from the fusion of participants in this theatrical performance. Du Pont's festivals were fully participatory although women were often relegated to the role of tearful "observers." By *enacting* their place in society, each was reminded of his or her duties and appreciated in consequence. There was no "role-playing" nor special regalia (or at least kept to a minimum) since the rituals were intended to reinforce the status quo. A year later, Du Pont had not given up, writing Carl Ludwig about the King of Sweden's plan to create a national uniform.[82]

There are several ways of achieving this. The simplest, Your Highness, seems to me to return us to that other important institution that we have already discussed, that of a national militia, or of the military discipline one might teach an entire nation through festivals, exercises, entertainments, and public games.

---

[81] Pierre Poivre (1719–1786) was intendant of the French Pacific islands Iles de France and Bourbon (Réunion), a botanist and physiocratic fellow-traveler. Du Pont married his widow after the death of his first wife. Mably, for one, could not bear the Chinese civic rituals so vaunted by Physiocrats. Mably, *Doutes proposés aux philosophes économistes*, pp. 109–110.

[82] Knies, *Carl Friedrichs von Baden*, II, part III, p. 302, n.d. [1774].

Persuasion would be all the easier, he explained to his teen-age pupil, since the human soul retained within it traces of the "natural order." Du Pont did not neglect this side of Carl Ludwig's education and he explained the gist of sensationalist cognition. All knowledge came from our senses and their responses to pain and pleasure (another way in which he simplified Quesnay's more complex version).[83] After going through the steps whereby our nerves processed sensory data and the mind then stored, recalled, combined and contemplated this information, Du Pont moved on to the proof of the existence of God. "[Humans] cannot hide from themselves that they have sensations; that they do not give these to themselves, because, were this the case, they would only have pleasant ones; they cannot determine the intensity of these sensations, which are sometimes stronger and sometimes weaker than they would like; there must therefore be something outside of them, a cause, a being, a *je ne sais quoi*, which limits their faculty to feel and which acts upon that faculty." Sensations of hunger, smell, or pain point us to what is useful and protect us from harm. "Hence our one duty on earth is to study the laws of the natural order so that we might govern our behaviour and our efforts, provide for our necessities, pleasure and enjoyment." Knowing this, we realize that others feel the same things, and that kindness or services rendered will move them to respond in kind. We must therefore always display our gratitude for the bounties we receive from nature.

"Let us not hold back our tears," he tells Carl Ludwig, "but instead praise, yes praise the great Being, the sublime benefactor to whom we owe our existence, our subsistence, our sensibility, our intelligence, our reason, and our love." Since human prosperity rests on agricultural surpluses, when he tends his fields the farmer does God's work.[84] "Only he finds a noble and worthy use for Providence's gift of intelligence. Only he behaves like a true human being, a creature favoured by the Creator, understanding Nature's assets and turning them to his own advantage."[85] This leads to the standard recapitulation of the physiocratic laws of profit, investment, and politics. "The more one studies the order that

---

[83] "Extrait et réfutation du livre intitulé *Le Bon Sens* et de toutes les folies des athées," n.d. [1773] in Knies, *Carl Friedrichs von Baden*, II, pp. 87-99. The work was by Baron d'Holbach and, given its atheism, one that Du Pont felt the need to contradict.

[84] Du Pont, *Éléments de philosophie économique*, p. 16. The unpublished full draft is at the Hagley library, W2-4579 (A fragment was published in the *Éphémérides* in 1771). The manuscript is 120 pages long and was begun in 1771 and finished apparently in 1774. Du Pont mentions on pp. 94-5, the simultaneous composition of an essay which the Hagley dates to 1774: "Essai sur les prix" W2-4590.

[85] Du Pont, *Éléments de philosophie économique*, pp. 16-17.

the Supreme Wisdom has granted the universe, the more one comes to admire the reciprocal ties that bind together the diverse parts of this mighty assemblage. Nothing is isolated, everything supports the rest, all causes are effects and all effects are causes."[86] One must moreover be prepared to meet any contingency (including, of course, foreign attack), and not fall prey to Troglodyte idealism, so Du Pont indulges his love of manly pursuits to propagate a "muscular physiocracy."[87]

These speculations came to an abrupt end as Du Pont left Paris for Poland, having failed to secure a post in Kalrsruhe.[88] He had been offered a position to tutor the children of Prince Czaroryski, and simultaneously invited to serve as secretary to a commission establishing a new educational system for Poland.[89] The commission achieved nothing lasting, much to Du Pont's chagrin, and he reported to Quesnay how he and his colleagues had been sidelined by "an illegal ad hoc commission" that claimed it would be legitimated by a future decree. Sixty professors had been left without revenue and schools had closed as a result of the rapine and corruption that prevailed in Poland.[90] He had yet to be paid himself but he abandoned his unrewarding tasks to hurry back to France where he had been recalled by order of the King, at Turgot's request. His Polish adventure had lasted only a few months but educational reform remained very much on his mind as he traveled back to his homeland.

Du Pont, like Mirabeau, conceived of education as teaching the public to rid itself of prejudices and imbibe the true dictates of Nature. Yet his version differed drastically from his elder's. Whereas Mirabeau devoted increasing energies to physiocratic primers aimed at the young, often in the form of dialogues, Du Pont sought to appeal to princes and adults.

---

[86] Ibid., p. 55.
[87] Du Pont's letters to Carl Ludwig engage in a critique of Rousseau that permeates physiocratic writing as a whole. Not only did they dispute his version of inequality and of man's bondage, they also saw agriculture as the greatest benefit to mankind, not its downfall. For a slightly different take on the physiocrats' relationship to Rousseau, see Michael Sonenscher, *Sans-Culottes, An Eighteenth-Century Emblem in the French Revolution* (Princeton, 2008), pp. 248–60, especially p. 259. Jean-Jacques Rousseau, *Discours sur l'origine de l'inégalité parmi les hommes*, p. 73. Rousseau's judgment on physiocracy is summed up in his letter to Mirabeau of 26 July 1767 discussed at the end of chapter IV.
[88] He was granted permission to travel to Poland by the King on 8 July 1774, Hagley, W2-5046.
[89] See on this Manuela Albertone, "Du Pont de Nemours et l'instruction publique pendant la révolution, de la science économique à la formation du citoyen," *Revue francaise d'histoire des idées politiques*, 20:2 (2004), 353–371.
[90] Letter from Du Pont to Quesnay, from Battelstedt in Saxony, between Hamburg and Erfurt, 10 December 1774. Hagley, W2-38.

Future generations could not be weaned away from error without the collusion of families, hence the idea of festivals that would include everyone. Alternately, they might follow the guidance of their enlightened rulers, hence his play. Thus, despite Turgot's remonstrations, Du Pont believed that both princes and their subjects could learn through entertainments and that emotions were contagious. His inspirational civic rituals were predicated on this. Despite their common root in sensationalism, his understanding of the way human beings responded was a far cry from Quesnay's and the version that Quesnay had worked so hard to instill in Mirabeau. For Du Pont's generation appealing to the heart was as legitimate as appealing to the mind, for this was no longer a matter of imagination versus reason, or the infusion of spirituality, but of a new physiology centered on sensibility. Du Pont turned himself into orchestrator of emotions, hoping that exaltation in the right arena would strengthen individual commitment to serve the commonwealth. Selfhood resolved itself through emotional bonds. We cannot understand Du Pont's version of physiocracy without his literary outpourings, which supported the mathematico-rationalist arguments of the original doctrine by appeals to social action and mutual harmony.

# 8

# Changing the World

Du Pont hurried back from Poland to take up a post in Turgot's administration and to act as his private secretary, but arrived too late to attend Quesnay's funeral. Turgot had been named Controller general in August 1774. He embarked on a program of liberal reforms, some of which had been attempted before such as freeing the grain trade and cutting state expenditures. A spike in grain prices in spring 1775, blamed on deregulation, unleashed riots in various cities and cost him the popular goodwill he had initially garnered. He opposed all trade monopolies, including the guild system, yet believed the state should intervene in some instances and he took energetic measures to prevent the spread of a cattle epidemic. In other words, he threatened vested interests while seeming to embody "ministerial despotism," not least to those grandees whose pensions he was trimming. The abolition of the guilds and of the *corvée* in February 1776 mobilized the Parlements against him, and Louis XVI finally gave in to pressures, including from his family, and dismissed him from office in May 1776.[1]

Turgot's mix of *dirigisme* and laissez-faire suggested a "vision" that he was eager to enact and in short order at that, having explained to his friends that he had no time to lose because men in his family died young. During his twenty-month ministry, Turgot was indeed incapacitated by congenital gout, which tied him to his bed for months on end. Yet we only know second-hand, from Du Pont and Condorcet, that he entertained more radical measures, such as instituting a universal tax on

---

[1] For an analysis of what was at stake see Steven L. Kaplan, *La fin des corporations* (Paris, 2001) and Faure, *La disgrâce de Turgot*.

land or representative assemblies.[2] In summer 1775 Turgot thus asked Du Pont to draft a memorandum on the establishment of local assemblies, looked it over (and perhaps annotated it), and then set it aside. This *Memoir on Municipalities* is so often regarded as Turgot's plan that it is important to set the record straight.

Calls for a mixed form of monarchy were getting louder in the eighteenth century, and the reader has already encountered such proposals in a previous chapter. Criticisms of centralization evoked strong ripostes from the royal government. The Parlements and associated lawcourts, like the *cours des aides* (that dealt with fiscal litigation) were at the forefront of the agitation and Chancelier Maupeou abolished them in 1771. Guillaume-Chrétien de Lamoignon de Malesherbes, the *Président* of the Paris *cour des aides* penned remonstrances on behalf of his court in 1771 and again in May 1775, after it had been reinstated. Among other complaints, he called for the reestablishment of provincial assemblies and for transparency in state finances. The response was not altogether negative, although all concrete suggestions were shelved.[3] Malesherbes was persuaded to reenter state service as Minister of the King's Household in July 1775, although neither he nor Louis XVI was enthusiastic about the prospect. Perhaps it was his presence that encouraged Turgot to contemplate the creation of local assemblies. Despite this, Malesherbes proved a lukewarm ally in the struggles of spring 1776, although he did resign in solidarity when Turgot was removed from office.

Although they have attracted less attention than the calls for representative bodies from opponents of absolutism, similar, more pragmatic proposals were mooted within the royal administration. In August 1764, for example, Controller general L'Averdy abolished municipal offices and reestablished elections for city councilors. The choice of mayor, however, remained a royal prerogative. The reform encountered some setbacks and L'Averdy conceded that it could not be applied universally. Nonetheless, as Joël Félix rightly argues, historians have unfairly dismissed this major effort to involve the public in local affairs. The prime purpose of this

---

[2] D'Ormesson had drafted a proposal for a land tax, *subvention territoriale*, for Turgot, see John Hardman, *Overture to Revolution, The 1787 Assembly of Notables and the Crisis of France's Old Regime* (Oxford, 2010), p. 10.

[3] Elisabeth Badinter, *Les "Remontrances" de Malesherbes* (Paris, 1978), "Remontrances Relatives aux impôts, 6 mai 1775," pp. 169–276, 232. He had served as Director of the Librairies from 1750 to 1763, and as President of the Paris *Cour des aides* from 1763 to 1771 and again in 1774-5. He would volunteer to act as Louis XVI's lawyer at his trial in December 1792–January 1793 and would himself be guillotined in April 1794.

municipal reform was to facilitate tax collection, but Félix believes that L'Averdy saw it as a step toward decentralization, reducing the *intendants'* control over municipal administration and giving notables a say in their own affairs.[4] Officeholders were no happier than the *intendants* at their loss of privilege and the challenge to their authority.

L'Averdy's system, it should be said, was somewhat cumbersome: Every guild and corporate body sent a deputy to a local Assembly of Notables, which elected the councilmen (based on strict criteria of eligibility) and drew up a list of mayoral candidates. The councilmen would be answerable to the said Assembly, presumed to meet at least twice annually. It was therefore quite possible to involve local elites in tax assessment and collection without envisaging a system of representation culminating in a national body. It was also in 1764 that the Marquis d'Argenson's political reform plan, initially composed in 1737 and privately circulated, was finally published. It too argued for representative assemblies at the local level where they would be least threatening to royal authority.[5] As mentioned in Chapter 5, eschewing the old representation by order, d'Argenson believed landowners should be put in charge of local fiscal affairs.[6] Unlike a host of other reformers, he suggested retaining the *intendants* but reducing the size of their generalities. Otherwise, we find the rhetoric common to other moral reformers (including Mirabeau): Public participation would develop civic spirit, the nobility would return to the countryside, greater attention would be paid to agriculture, and laissez-faire would hopefully be enacted.[7]

One can see why Du Pont was retroactively impressed and would claim in his 1792 autobiography that d'Argenson had taken a shine to him when he came to wind his clocks (as his father's apprentice) and gave him a copy of his manuscript.[8] He mused appreciatively on d'Argenson's conclusion that "democracy is as much of a friend of monarchy as aristocracy is its enemy."[9] By 1814, he would go even further, claiming that

---

[4] Félix, *Finances et politique*, p. 246.
[5] René Louis de Voyer d'Argenson, *Considérations sur le gouvernement ancien et présent de la France* (Amsterdam, 1764), p. 31.
[6] Ibid., p. 222.
[7] Ibid., pp. 272, 293.
[8] Du Pont, *The Autobiography of Du Pont de Nemours*, p. 160. Fox-Genovese presumed that at the time of writing, Du Pont was referring to the "physiocratic" 1784 edition, which scholars now attribute to d'Argenson's son, although he most likely meant the 1764 edition. It too appeared posthumously, right after the marquis's death. Perhaps d'Argenson lent him a copy of the manuscript version.
[9] D'Argenson, *Considérations*, p. 148.

"since age fourteen [he had been] the pupil of the Marquis d'Argenson, to whom we owe such a great book on the government of France; and since then of all the writers and all the administrators who offered great insights into political economy."[10]

Although Controller general abbé Terray had swept away L'Averdy's municipal system in 1771, just as Chancellor Maupeou was dismantling the Parlements, some physiocrats, as we saw, were beginning to take more kindly to representative bodies, most notably Le Trosne.[11] We can't say for certain when Du Pont abandoned Quesnay's and La Rivière's theory of legal despotism.[12] The physiocratic ruler, he long continued to argue, should have tutelary authority over the kingdom and its resources and, of course, encourage the teaching of physiocratic principles. "In order for the Nation to be sufficiently enlightened on the natural laws [of the reproduction of wealth], a public and general system of education must be established and the publication of doctrinal texts encouraged, so that its tincture might rub off on the least of its citizens."[13] Those who contested the natural order should be pitied, but if they persisted they would understandably face public indignation.[14] In 1774 Du Pont had not yet abandoned such views, eliciting the following response from Turgot: "I still insist that you purge the term 'tutelary' from your vocabulary. Besides the question of its appropriateness, the word bears the Economist stamp, and indeed displays the most shameful aspect of the Economists' system. Nonetheless, I would like the word authority to be accompanied by an epithet, and I would say *public authority* which doesn't prejudge in favour of one system over another."[15] Turgot was referring to Du Pont's contribution to an essay competition on peasant landownership from the Saint-Peterbsurg Academy where he spelled out his views

---

[10] Listing his accomplishments, n.d. [1814] W2-5098.

[11] His texts in favor of such representation within a physiocratic state, composed in the early 1770s, would be published in 1777 as *De l'ordre social*. Le Trosne not only stands apart from other major physiocrats for his restrained tone but also for not living in Paris or idolizing Quesnay. In July 1766 Du Pont responds to a reproach from Le Trosne explaining why he had praised Quesnay so extravagantly in the *Journal de l'agriculture*. He knew that no one would think that he was doing this in order to curry favor but only to praise the doctor's great merit. Letter of 24 July 1766, Hagley, W2-5.

[12] Physiocratic support of education often came down to spreading their catechism to the people rather than endowing them with the 3 Rs. Nonetheless they are taken as pioneers in this domain. See François Furet and Jacques Ozouf, *Lire et écrire: l'alphabétisation des Français de Calvin à Jules Ferry*, 2 vols. (Paris, 1977), I, p. 97.

[13] Du Pont, *De l'origine et des progrès d'une science nouvelle*, p. 38.

[14] Ibid., pp. 83–4.

[15] Letter from Turgot to Du Pont, Paris, 14 March 1774, Hagley, W2-1667.

on (physiocratic) government.[16] In the preamble, Du Pont explained that after feudal government "whose constitution was far from perfect" had disintegrated, no constitution had been put in its place. Landed magnates had lost much of their revenue and status, but so had sovereigns who failed to establish new constitutions leaving their kingdoms prey to men's passions and to the contingency of events.[17] This anarchy would end only once the reproduction of wealth (through the net product) had been properly grasped and used in the "constitution of a government based on reason and men's universal interests." Granting states a "proper constitution" was thus very much on Du Pont's mind. How to educate the public followed close behind. "If one wishes to get an idea of the degrees of perfection and happiness that humanity can attain, one should examine those empires that teach all their citizens the rules that govern public welfare and explain all their features. This promotes perfect concord among citizens, for who would dare disturb it? Evidence would immediately reveal the troublemaker as a traitor to the Fatherland [*Patrie*] and to the human race."[18] As ever, the "rule of evidence" was much harsher than the "rule of reason" touted by contemporaries such as Turgot, and the two should not be confused.

Louis XVI on ascending the throne rid himself of the triumvirate who had directed policy in the last years of his grandfather's reign, recalled the Parlements, and allowed his new Controller general Turgot to enact a number of "positive" changes to encourage economic growth. Turgot had already introduced reforms in tax assessments in his own *généralité* of Limoges (where he had served as *intendant* from 1761 to 1774) and promised the King, on being named to the ministry, that he would not declare bankruptcy, increase taxation, or take out new loans. He assured the monarch that he would willingly endure every calumny so long as he had the King's support, for he foresaw that his economic policies and

---

[16] "Mémoire sur la question proposée par la Société économique de Petersbourg: Est-il plus avantageux et plus utile au bien public que le paysan possède des terres": the term "tutelary authority" occurs on page 13 of this 18-page "Discours préliminaire," Hagley, W2-4581. Du Pont also reduced government to "tutelary authority" in *Elements de philosophie économique*, pp. 114–15. The draft began with the same citation from Plato: "Rather than calling governments monarchies, aristocracies, or democracies, all should have been called theocracies since God is men's true lord and master."
[17] The term "constitution" had various meanings in the eighteenth century, and Du Pont appears to use it in the sense of a rational organization. See on this Alain Guéry, "Principe monarchique ou roi très chrétien? Les funérailles des rois de France," *Revue de Synthèse*, CXII:3–4 (1991), 443–54.
[18] "St. Petersburg Memoir," p. 16.

especially his attempt to remedy fiscal abuses would cause anxiety and arouse opposition. But he believed that a healthy economy would ensure peace at home, recognition abroad, and the happiness of the Nation and the Monarch.[19]

Calling Du Pont back to France from Poland, Turgot explained that he had named him Inspector General of Commerce, a post that would keep him nearby. "It would be more pleasant for me to have you by my side" and hence preferable to the possibility, he had earlier mooted, of naming him *Intendant* of Ile de France "with the mission of giving a good constitution to a country that needs it most, to challenge [*faire nargue*] the English company, the Dutch, and even the colonies of North America."[20] Whatever Turgot intended by these cryptic remarks, Du Pont took them to heart, responding with three letters from Warsaw explaining to Turgot how he ought to proceed. He knew that Turgot had just freed the grain trade, and later found and kept the minister's four-page outline for the Declaration of 13 September 1774 that insisted that the public be told the rationale behind the edict. This entailed detailing the nefarious effects of protectionist and provisioning policies, reassuring Frenchmen that monopolies could not arise (to raise prices) in a situation of total freedom, and assuring them that the King desired the happiness of his people. The preamble would therefore "serve to educate [the public] on this question and present, so to speak, its core principles, in a precise yet strong and clear manner, so as to still all doubts and prevent alarms that might be raised later to undermine [*ébranler*] this legislation."[21] Turgot thus presumed that "reason" would prevail over fears and superstitions, as he no doubt deemed them.

Du Pont, ever wary of the abbé Baudeau, had heard that the latter had made his own suggestions to the minister and countered them with his "eminently practicable" plan of action, dismissing the other as chimerical. All provinces, he advised, should immediately calculate what they paid in indirect taxes, what it cost to collect them, and how much the royal treasury actually received. The major landowners in each province

---

[19] Du Pont possessed his own copy of the letter, dated from Compiègne, 24 August 1774. Gustave Schelle, *Œuvres de Turgot et documents le concernant*, IV, pp. 109–13.

[20] Letter from Turgot to Du Pont, Versailles, 21 September 1774, Hagley, W2-1672. Du Pont refers later to that mooted intendancy in a letter to the Marquis de Pezay that details all his conflicts with the abbé Baudeau. From Versailles, 12 March 1776, Hagley W2-50.

[21] Turgot, "Canevas pour la déclaration du 13 septembre 1774 sur le commerce des grains," Hagley, W2-5694.

should be called together and confronted with the evidence of sums they paid, assured that the king meant to lessen their burden, and "enjoined to sign an agreement [*en obtenir un contrat*] to pay the sum that the treasury actually received." "Estates, security, and a law [*règle*] would thus be established in one fell swoop."[22] This could be done immediately for it should never be said of Turgot that he had been minister without accomplishing anything. "If the law is properly written, if the facts are clearly and straightforwardly enunciated, with the greatest exactitude, it is impossible that the provincial estates should not consent, especially in the initial burst of enthusiasm that will greet you and the King." This constitutional innovation would seemingly be instituted by fiat. In a second letter, dated October 12, Du Pont urged the creation of a national education system to explain the need for fundamental reforms, although "it will perhaps take four to five years to persuade everyone."[23] Du Pont was eager, he explained, to show himself worthy of the King's and Turgot's trust and he thanked the Lord for sending this Prince, who would not only save France but set an example of "good order, justice, enlightened humanity, and good mores," to all of Europe.[24] Du Pont therefore had no doubts about the course Turgot should adopt, and believed that "landowners" would be swayed by evidence and endorse fiscal reform put forward by the central government. Turgot and Du Pont shared a similar ambition to educate the public in economic principles, Turgot piecemeal through legislation, and Du Pont more systematically through an educational system. Turgot appeared content to inform the French about deregulation edict by edict. Du Pont, on the other hand, wanted a system that created and perpetuated a physiocratic nation.

It would seem that the debacle of May 1775, when freedom of the grain trade provoked food riots that the minister harshly put down, led Turgot to consider that local assemblies might facilitate the adoption of his reforms and he asked Du Pont to draft the outline for such legislation. What we know of Turgot's plans for administrative reform is limited to a few comments.

I wanted a municipal administration based on small districts of twenty, thirty, or at most forty parishes. I rejected any distinction of rank or order. Landownership was furthermore made a precondition, and I dismissed corporative privileges or association of orders. [These assemblies] were to be restricted to the allocation

---

[22] "Fragment d'une lettre à Mr. Turgot du 7 octobre 1774," Hagley, W2-35.
[23] "Fragment d'une lettre à Mr. Turgot en date de Varsovie, le 12 octobre 1774." W2-36.
[24] Letter from Du Pont to Turgot, 29 October 1774. Hagley, W2-37.

of the tax burden, the settlement of disputes arising from local administration, and routine improvements of the district, including roads. I left those matters that concern the nation as a whole, peace, war, the rules and amount of public contributions, to the government. By creating so many of these assemblies and granting them so little power, I did not fear that royal authority would suffer any harmful effects.

Thus, in the summer of 1778, did Jacques Turgot express to his friend, the abbé Véri, the difference between his version of local assemblies and the one recently enacted by his successor at the Control general, Jacques Necker.[25] Having no stake in the realization of such a plan – unlike Du Pont de Nemours or Condorcet – Véri offers plausible evidence of what Turgot had in mind for the restructuring of French administration. Upon hearing of Necker's reform, Turgot had scoffed at the rumors that Necker had carried out his own plan, since their versions were so "dissimilar." Thus, Necker's new assemblies included representation of the three orders, whereas Turgot's would have been composed solely of landowners, and would not have extended to whole provinces.[26] For Turgot believed in a strong executive and did not like to see its power reduced or "balanced" by either a parliament as in England or "state rights" as in the new United States.[27] His representative assemblies served neither as participatory government nor as a form of constitutional monarchy, but were complementary, incommensurable forms of authority, where one was subordinate to the other. All we know, besides this, of Turgot's intentions comes from two brief notes, dated September 1775, that he sent Du Pont. "You can continue working on the municipalities at your leisure.... Like you, I think it is necessary to act, but one must bring measure and precision in the articulation, all the more so since there will be objections to contend with, so that the result on its own is not enough." Two weeks later, he remarked: "I am sorry, my dear Du Pont, that you have wasted all this time writing down your ideas with superfluous assiduity [*perfection superflue*]. I only needed an outline [*canevas*]. I have thought too deeply on this matter for the last fifteen years not to have my own opinions on this subject that you had no way of guessing, and only by pure chance could our ideas have corresponded exactly. This means that

---

[25] Joseph-Alphonse de Véri, *Journal de l'abbé de Véri*, 2 vols. (Mâcon, 1930), II, p. 148.
[26] Letter from Turgot to Du Pont, 28 July 1778, in Schelle, *Œuvres de Turgot et documents le concernant*, V, p. 563.
[27] Lettre au docteur Price, 1778, in Schelle, *Oeuvres de Turgot et documents le concernant*, V, pp. 534–6.

the final version will doubtless need to be rewritten: but, let's wait."[28] Turgot fell from grace before he could move the plan any further.

Du Pont, however, kept the project alive for years afterward. In 1778, he sent a copy of the draft to the Margrave of Baden, explaining that he had written it but that Turgot had intended to promulgate it.[29] When he published Turgot's works in 1809 he included a longer version, insisting more openly that it embodied Turgot's intentions, even if he had been the one who expressed them.[30] Gustave Schelle, who edited how own collection of Turgot's writings, dismissed this second version as untrustworthy, although he placed some faith in the first.[31]

The famous memorandum of 1775 called on the King to create municipal assemblies, premised on Du Pont's distillation of physiocracy. "The science that embraces them, although it is not very extensive, rests on principles of justice that everyone carries within [*dans son coeur*] and an intimate awareness of our own sensations that is endowed with a great degree of certainty."[32] The rights of men in society, Du Pont continues, do not arise from history, but rather from "their nature," meaning their physiological needs. As he explains the wisdom of involving the public in the details of administration – on which the *intendants* remain ill-informed – he urges the monarch to use his full legislative authority to establish municipal bodies to end the abuses in the assessment and collection of taxes. Then comes the oft-cited paragraph (which is taken to embody Turgot's credo):

The root of the evil, Sire, comes from your Kingdom's lack of a constitution.[33] It is a society composed of poorly united orders and of a population whose members are bound by very few social ties: where, as a result, almost no one cares about anything other than his own self-interest, where almost no one bothers to fulfill his duties, nor to know how he is connected to others. So that ... Your Majesty must make every decision Herself or through deputies [*mandataires*]. Everyone

---

[28] Schelle, *Oeuvres de Turgot et documents le concernant*, IV, pp. 675–6. Letters from Turgot to Du Pont of 11 and 23 September 1775.
[29] Du Pont, "Mémoire sur les municipalités" in Knies, *Carl Friedrichs von Baden*, I, pp. 244–83.
[30] *Oeuvres de Mr Turgot, Ministre d'Etat*, VII (1809), pp. 386–484.
[31] Schelle, *Oeuvres de Turgot et documents le concernant*, IV, p. 574: "It would seem that at this juncture [1809] Du Pont revised the original text quite significantly and that the version initially published by Mr. Knies gives a better sense of what Turgot's ideas might have been in 1775."
[32] Du Pont, "Mémoire sur les Municipalités" in Knies, *Carl Friedrichs von Baden*, II, p. 244.
[33] Thus, Guéry cites it, "Principe monarchique ou roi très chrétien?," p. 444.

awaits Your special orders to contribute to the public good, to respect the property of others, sometimes even in order to use those in one's possession. This compels You to legislate [*statuer*] on everything, and most often by special dictate [*volontés particulières*] whereas You might govern, like God, through general laws, if all the constitutive parts [*parties intégrantes*] of Your realm possessed a regular organization within a well-defined hierarchy [*rapports connus*].[34]

The kingdom was presently divided into provinces, districts, towns and villages and each was in turn composed of families and individuals called on to perform various duties. They were not clear about these duties, so that havoc and confusion reigned as people pursued their individual interests, and were so selfish and self-regarding that they hid their actual revenues "as if Your Majesty were at war with her people." There was no public spirit "because the kingdom lacked a clearly articulated and visible common goal."[35] The first step must therefore be to institute an educational system that would clearly explain the "highly evident common interest that binds [his subjects] together and let them discuss it and conform to it."[36] This would ensure that representative bodies shared the same vision and end the dissention still so prevalent in Provincial Estates. Moreover, thus would "virtuous and useful men, just souls, pure hearts, and zealous citizens be fashioned in all classes in society," and the arts and sciences stimulated to useful rather than frivolous ends. People would work harder, labor would acquire a more "virile" connotation and come to be valued in itself as people set themselves to achieving "honest ends." This, Du Pont assured the monarch, would be "the fruit of the uniform patriotic outlook that an Education Council would impart to the young."[37] This was the gospel that Du Pont had been preaching for years.

The assemblies that Du Pont foresaw would be responsible for local administration and the upkeep of roads, but their principal task would be to oversee taxation, and this would surely have met with Turgot's approval. Du Pont culled the organizational structure he proposed from similar reform projects by the likes of Mirabeau and d'Argenson. Thus, landowners would have a voice in such assemblies along a sliding scale based on the amount of land they owned or farmed. A landed income of 600 livres would grant them one vote; those with less land would have

---

[34] Du Pont, "Mémoire sur les Municipalités" in Knies, *Carl Friedrichs von Baden*, II, pp. 245–6.
[35] Ibid., p. 246.
[36] Ibid., p. 247.
[37] Ibid., p. 248.

partial votes; those who owned more, multiple votes.[38] "Municipality" was understood to mean a "township," but cities themselves were saddled with prohibitive property requirements (10,000 livres) to ensure that the countryside would be far better represented than the towns. Nonetheless Du Pont was confident that this system would breed harmony and cooperation since the rich would have no reason to oppress the poor or find any loophole to evade taxation.[39]

Such assemblies would be called at the district and provincial levels with deputies from the lower assemblies (going into great detail about their roles, the nature of their mandates and the registers that they must keep). Deputies from the provinces would then gather annually in the capital to hear the king's wishes for the following year and then disperse. The draft closed with Du Pont's characteristic soppiness: "Ah! Sire, if I weren't moved by the desire to witness such a happy day and if tears weren't welling in my eyes, I would not deserve the kindness which Your Majesty has bestowed on me."[40] This was toned down in the 1809 version, probably because the intended recipient had died under unfortunate circumstances. In the version Du Pont sent the Margrave the expectation was that the new assemblies would meet in October 1776, once the harvest had been assessed.[41]

Perhaps because Quesnay had died in December 1774 and he was serving a new master, Du Pont now found it possible to incorporate representative institutions with limited authority within his vision of government, as Le Trosne was doing at the same time, and as Mirabeau had advocated in *La théorie de l'impôt*.[42] His ultimate goal, like theirs, was to provide a political framework for a *physiocratic* order whereas Turgot was looking to create more efficient tax collection. The memorandum therefore reflected the program Du Pont wished Turgot to adopt rather than conveying Turgot's ideas faithfully. For example Turgot did

---

[38] In his own proposal for representative assemblies, the marquis de Condorcet would object to this very feature, supporting the "one man, one vote" alternative. Condorcet, *Essai sur la constitution et les fonctions des assemblées provinciales* in A. Condorcet-O'Connor and M. F. Arago, eds., *Oeuvres de Condorcet* (Paris, 1847), vol. 8, pp. 117–659. We do not know Turgot's own views on this.

[39] Ibid., p. 256. Keith Baker quite appropriately equates this to a "joint-stock company in land, in which the largest shareholders naturally held the largest share of votes, *Condorcet*, pp. 253–4. Mirabeau and Le Trosne made similar proposals.

[40] Du Pont, "Mémoire sur les Municipalités" in Knies, *Carl Friedrichs von Baden*, II, p. 283.

[41] Ibid., p. 279.

[42] Mirabeau, *Théorie de l'impôt*, pp. 222–6.

not mean to propose to Louis XVI a full tier of assemblies (at least at this stage) nor to establish a National Education Council, but, after Turgot's death, Du Pont felt increasingly free to make claims about the project that had grown in his mind as a precondition for the realization of physiocratic goals.

This was one of the wisest and most far-sighted plans envisioned by this excellent statesman, which, along with the other two I just discussed [including a territorial tax], were completely finished by September 1775; and, had not the pointless sedition occasioned by the grain trade eaten up six weeks, would have been ready at the end of July and could have been presented to the [Royal] Council for discussion, and enacted in October, for this was when they had to start functioning or else everything must be delayed a year. It would be a great service to the Nation (*Patrie*) to publish what has been retrieved [*ce qu'on a pu recueillir*] of the general plan that Mr. Turgot had conceived, and since only a full transcription can do it justice [*donner une juste idée en le transcrivant*], this duty will be fulfilled.[43]

Both in this biography of Turgot (reprinted in 1788) and the revised version of 1811, Du Pont showcased the plan on municipalities and increasingly presented it as Turgot's blueprint for a national constitution.[44] Turgot had desired "all levels of municipal administration from parishes to the entire kingdom."[45] In 1813, he even vaunted it as one of Turgot's greatest achievements.[46]

In a further projection, Du Pont insisted that Turgot had not only wished to promote public instruction, he had also envisaged "public festivals that would spread gaiety and concord while recalling man's duties to Society and that of the citizen to the Fatherland."[47] Despite this ridiculous claim, he continued to insist:

All the ideas in the following Memoir are M. Turgot's. They contain the *Constitutional Project* that he had wished to give France for the mutual advantage of the King and the Nation. It was composed by another hand. He had confided the task of a first draft to his most intimate friend, had approved it, even if

---

[43] Du Pont, *Mémoires*, I, pp. 202–3. Note that the date is given here as October 1775, whereas the date he told the Margrave had been October 1776.

[44] Ibid., (1782), II, pp. 49–54; I, pp. 199–204. Du Pont, *Oeuvres de M. Turgot, Ministre d'Etat* (Paris, 1811), I, p. 336. The overall "project" is summarized on pp. 194–7, followed by its pendant, the Board of Education, as in the previous versions.

[45] Du Pont, *Mémoires*, I, pp. 193–4.

[46] Du Pont, letter to the Editors of the *Mercure de France*, "[Turgot] left behind a project on provincial assemblies justifiably applauded by his successors." *Extrait du "Mercure de France" du 31 juillet 1813*," Hagley Library.

[47] Ibid., p. 251.

he meant to correct and rewrite it from scratch with the severe scrupulousness he brought to all of the writings in which he allowed his friends to cooperate.[48]

Despite the contradictions in the above statement regarding drafts, revisions and collaborations, history has accepted that the "Memoir" reflected Turgot's intentions (or that he had actually written it). In the years following his dismissal from office and his death in 1781, as successive Controllers general failed to resolve the nation's fiscal crisis, his reputation rose and his name was once more invoked with reverence.[49] Du Pont whose fortunes had been tied to the minister's was both hagiographic and opportunistic, eager to reinforce his own credentials among influential high administrators sympathetic to Turgot's projects (although, oddly enough, his new patron, the foreign minister Vergennes, had disliked the Controller general).

Du Pont was not the only keeper of the flame. In 1786 the marquis de Condorcet would publish his own biography of the minister and would write a 500-page plan for representative assemblies in 1788 alluding to "[Turgot's] similar projects" with which he did not fully agree.[50] Better-known to posterity than Du Pont, Condorcet was successful in transmitting his version of Turgot as "man of science," ever-engaged in scientific investigations (he lists them), a believer in progress, in reason, and in the extension of the scientific method to social phenomena, in other words, being in all ways, Condorcet's spiritual father. That Condorcet was concocting a Turgot of his own desiring has escaped some but certainly not all historians.[51] Condorcet spent half of his biography on "Turgot's long-term projects" based on his "conversations with the minister and his surviving papers."[52] They included the plan to create assemblies, "without distinctions of order."[53] "He wanted these institutions to be the product

---

[48] Du Pont, *Oeuvres de Mr Turgot*, (1809) VII, p. 386.
[49] Gilbert Faccarello, "Le legs de Turgot. Aspects de l'économie sensualiste de Condorcet à Roederer" in Faccarello and Ph. Steiner, eds., *La pensée économique pendant la Révolution française* (Grenoble, 1991), pp. 67–107.
[50] Letter from Du Pont to the marquis de Saint-Lambert, 8 August 1782, Hagley, W2-122, about Condorcet's demand that Du Pont turn over all of Turgot's writings in his possession. Du Pont offered copies of some. Condorcet, *Vie de M. Turgot* in A. Condorcet-O'Connor and M.F. Arago, eds., *Oeuvres de Condorcet* (Paris, 1847), vol. 5. p. 49.
[51] Not however Elizabeth and Robert Badinter, *Condorcet, un intellectuel en politique* (Paris, 1988), p. 214: "En vérité, ce que Condorcet attribue à Turgot est précisément son propre crédo en 1785."
[52] Condorcet, *Vie de M. Turgot*, a single tax (p. 85), other major reforms (p. 91), representative assemblies (pp. 114–24).
[53] Ibid., p. 147.

of reason, unlike those created by force of circumstances or by pure chance." Unlike Du Pont, Condorcet maintained that Turgot would have started with municipal assemblies and then followed with district assemblies [*assemblées d'élection*] but that he had "no desire to move beyond that" because these lower-level bodies were sufficient for his purposes and he wanted to accustom the public to this new institution. Yet Turgot also had a larger project in mind:

> M. Turgot was planning to obliterate, one by one, all of the disorders in the administration, to create an entirely new one based on the indubitable principles of political economy, and to offer the necessary instruments to those ministers who wished to engage in similar reforms in other branches of government, that would ensure the success of their enterprise and earn the trust of the nation.[54]

Such "recollections," coupled with Du Pont's contention that Turgot asked his "collaborators" to draft proposals for legislation "from which he would pick the best," fed myths about Turgot's work habits that reinforced Du Pont and Condorcet's claims to speak for him: For example, that he consulted a small group of friends and collaborators on every decision.[55] Yet in his more lucid moments, Du Pont scoffed at his supposed influence on Turgot. He berated the abbé Baudeau in March 1776 for his criticism of Turgot's Six Edicts, calling him an ungrateful wretch. He himself was working tirelessly on the minister's behalf, even if "he does not follow my advice more than four or five times a year, although he hears it every day; and I would spill every drop of my blood for him because I am certain that if he is given freedom to act (*si on le laisse faire*), he will save France."[56] The temptation to inflate his credentials was always greatest when Du Pont feared his career was at an end,[57] and the

---

[54] Ibid., pp. 149–50. Note that by political economy, Condorcet meant more than physiocracy.

[55] Charles Gillispie describes a "Turgot circle" that the minister consulted regularly and that functioned practically as a secret cabinet during his ministry, in *Science and Polity in France at the End of the Old Regime* (Princeton, 1980), pp. 37, 50. Eric Brian enthusiastically endorses this in *La mesure de l'Etat, administrateurs et géomètres au XVIIIe siècle* (Paris, 1994), pp. 30–1, 140, 143. See also Richard Whatmore *Republicanism and the French Revolution: An Intellectual History of Jean-Baptiste Say's Political Economy* (Oxford, 2000); Keith Baker in his biography of Condorcet does not describe a "real" Turgot circle, so much as treat Condorcet "as the most passionate and possessive member of an intimate, exclusive, and frequently intolerant circle that claimed the minister as its own" (pp. 40, 72). A different treatment of the relationship between Condorcet and Turgot can be found in Emma Rothschild, *Economic Sentiments*.

[56] Letter from Du Pont to Baudeau, from Versailles, 12 March 1776, Hagley, W2-49.

[57] In a letter to the marquise de Monnier (Gabriel de Mirabeau's mistress) while he was unemployed, Du Pont expressed his common delusion that he was undervalued in his

*Memoir on Municipalities* helped to bolster his own standing by claiming that he had had the minister's full confidence. As for the draft itself one might consider the story he told Malesherbes, who had been named trustee of Turgot's papers. Du Pont was seeking to retrieve a memoir he had partially authored on the policy to follow vis-à-vis England and the thirteen colonies; and a second, "totally by his own hand on municipalities, containing a plan for parish, county, provincial and general administrations." His personal copy had so many corrections that it was practically unreadable and he wanted the clean copy by Villard, (a clerk in his office) that Malesherbes now possessed. The memoir, he explained, "was in the form of an address to the King which, although based on Turgot's views and principles, was not truly his plan, but rather the way I thought it might be executed. He wanted me to change two things: one was to restrict the number of parishes within the first level to a circumference of two leagues, those of an *élection*, or next level up, to four or five leagues, provinces to twice that, with each county or *élection* containing four to five district and each province sixteen to twenty-five districts." Turgot had meant to ensure that landowners would be able to attend these meetings without any difficulty, so that the assemblies were to be held within half a day or at most a day's ride. From the district level upward, these assemblies would also judge civil cases. "He had very wise views on the nature of these courts, which he confided to me. But I was in a hurry [*pressé de jouir*], and found his grand plan too utopian [*tenaient trop à l'eutopie*] and urged him to change it so that it might be implemented quickly, by tampering as little as possible with existing structures.... It was with this in mind that I composed the said Memoir." Turgot had agreed that the plan would have to be modified before it could be implemented, "but that, meanwhile, every detail should be thoroughly worked out, as if it were intended for a new land, as a model of perfect government, so that it would be easy to judge what could be changed or omitted altogether, meaning that some things might stay as they were. He was planning to write it himself but I don't believe he got very far. Perhaps all that is left are the principles that he confided to me in

own land, although his reputation was high abroad, claiming he had been "the Margrave of Baden's minister, enjoyed the esteem of the Grand Duke of Tuscany, the Kings of Sweden and Poland (who showered him with favors), had turned down a pressing offer to got to Russia, and was known to the Emperor and King of England. He had rushed to join Turgot although he had countless offers to stay in Poland, and the King of Sweden was offering him a post at that same moment." Du Pont to the marquise de Monnier, 27 October 1779, Hagley, W2-74.

our conversations."⁵⁸ The omniscient scholar, unlike Malesherbes, knows the existence of Turgot's notes to Du Pont stating that he there was no call for a full-blown plan, and that he had ideas on the matter that Du Pont had no way of divining. The heavily "marked up" version does not survive among Du Pont's papers and one wonders whether it is the one he claims to have shown to Calonne containing "Turgot's annotations."

The memorandum indeed resurfaced in 1787 during the Assembly of Notables. By December 1786, Controller General Charles Alexandre de Calonne, despairing of a remedy for France's fiscal crisis, had called together an Assembly of Notables composed of hand-picked deputies, unlike the Estates General where they were elected by their constituencies. Pierre-Michel Hennin was made first secretary and Du Pont was named second secretary. Du Pont was beside himself. On January 30 he wrote the marquis de Mirabeau: "I do not answer for my health or my life, but I will try to spare them as much as possible, while dazzling the world with the quantity and strength of my public and private labors.... I am no longer the advisor of a minister, but the secretary of the Assembly, of one and of all."⁵⁹ He hoped that the plan for provincial assemblies that Calonne had presented to the Notables would survive and that "he [himself] wouldn't have to carry the weight of the world on his shoulders."

It was widely believed that Du Pont had urged the creation of assemblies on Calonne, presenting these as Turgot's greatest wish.⁶⁰ Yet he had competitors on this score. The comte de Mirabeau [Mirabeau's eldest son and future revolutionary leader] presented Turgot's text as his own to the Controller general some time that winter. Du Pont demolished this claim by showing the minister his hand-written version "with Turgot's annotations." Mirabeau was not put off and published the Memoir (which his associate Clavière had been instrumental in concocting) as emanating from Turgot's pen, leading Du Pont to a more public rejoinder. He

---

⁵⁸ Letter from Du Pont to Malesherbes, 7 April 1781, Hagely, W2-101.
⁵⁹ Letter from Du Pont to Mirabeau, Paris, 30 January 1787, Hagley, W2-272.
⁶⁰ Pierre Chevallier, *Journal de l'Assemblée des Notables de 1787* (Paris, 1960), p. 65. Loménie de Brienne referred to Le Trosne and Turgot (the latter as Condorcet presented him) on municipal assemblies, pp. 13–16. Renouvin, *Les Assemblées provinciales*, pp. 80, 352. Robert D. Harris, *Necker and the Revolution of 1789* (Lanham, Md., 1986), p. 83. John Hardman, *Overture to Revolution*, pp. 119–20. Hardman accepts Véri's explanation that Turgot, as he reported, had not wanted to push Louis XVI to reforms for which he was not yet ready. On Du Pont's participation in the Assembly of Notables, see also Egret, *The French Prerevolution*. Gruder, *The Notables and the Nation*, p. 184, describes the renewal of interest in Turgot's plans. The version that Calonne initially presented to Louis XVI in November 1786 differed from the version to the Notables the following spring. Renouvin, *Les Assemblées provinciales*, p. 82.

declared in the *Journal de Paris* on 3 July 1787 that he was the author of the Memoir and explained, moreover, to Turgot's irate brother, how Mirabeau had come to see this draft.

When your brother was still alive and the comte de Mirabeau was at Vincennes, dying of boredom, applying himself and developing a commendable interest in useful endeavors, I would visit him every Sunday to cheer him up. He always asked me to bring him materials, memoirs, or papers that would further his education, to enable him to do something useful when he was released. Among the countless personal writings that I loaned him, there was one which was not the worst among the ones I had composed. He returned it to me without saying he had copied it. And he has since presented it to M. Calonne as his own. I had to bring the original to the minister (which contained annotations by your brother) to show him how the Comte de Mirabeau sometimes operates.[61]

Interestingly, the marquis de Mirabeau's own Treatise of 1750 was making the rounds.[62]

Du Pont said that I would be gratified to learn that my books are spread on every desk in the minister's offices in Paris with each copy earmarked in thirty places. I told him that although this might tickle another's man academic vanity [*chatouillement académique*], I would rather a minister who had done his homework.[63]

Since 1778, when Necker had succeeded in establishing provincial assemblies in Berry and Haute-Guyenne, such initiatives were associated with the Control general, and raised fears that rival institutions would be weakened in consequence. Necker fell from power in 1781 after he proposed the creation of other such assemblies.[64] Similar conflicts arose during the Assembly of Notables. Du Pont complained in the course of that spring that Necker's supporters were attempting to undermine him.[65]

---

[61] Schelle, *Oeuvres de Turgot et documents le concernant*, IV, pp. 571–4.
[62] Sections of the marquis de Mirabeau's own work were reprinted in a compendium of proposals for provincial estates in *Objets proposés à l'assemblée des Notables par de zélés citoyens* (Paris, 1787), "Numéro Ier: Mémoire concernant l'utlité des états provinciaux, Par M. le Marquis de M." "*Note:* Ce Mémoire fut imprimé en l'année mil sept cent cinquante; les exemplaires en étaient en petit nombre & et il ne s'en trouve plus," pp. 3–23.
[63] Letter from Mirabeau to Longo, Paris, 8 July 1787, Montigny, *Mémoires biographiques*, IV, pp. 494–5.
[64] Renouvin, *Les Assemblées provinciales*, pp. 59–63, 68. As Renouvin notes, physiocrats were opposed to Necker's assemblies because they did not give the entire responsibility to landowners (p. 64).
[65] Letter from Du Pont to the comte d'Angiviller, Paris, 13 April 1787, Hagley, W2-288. Necker had warned Bouvard de Fourqueux not to associate with Du Pont whose ideas had displeased the Assembly of Notables.

"They make light of my projects saying that the Notables find them distasteful. I have no projects. I worked on those of M. Turgot which were adopted by M. de Calonne and I contributed precisely those proposals that the Notables deemed agreeable and good, for which they gave thanks and on which the hopes of the nation still rest."[66] The proposal for provincial assemblies that the Assembly of Notables discussed and finally rejected, was very much the version that Du Pont had urged on Turgot and that Calonne presumed to represent Turgot's wishes.[67] As John Hardman explains, Calonne retained the spirit of "Turgot's plan," with parish/municipal and district assemblies composed of landowners whose function was purely "administrative." Provincial assemblies might retain representation by order. Turgot's plan for a "national municipality" was deemed too risky, since it could develop into a species of Estates General once convened.[68] The Notables agreed to a tier of assemblies but opted for the "Necker model" of provincial assemblies where half the seats were reserved for the privileged orders, although with a vote by head.[69] Calonne failed to persuade the Notables to agree to his tax reforms, and was sacrificed in the hope that they would prove more amenable without him. This was not the case and the monarchy's failure of nerve irritated the old marquis de Mirabeau. The notables had turned down the government's proposed reforms because it was weak.

Rather than banking on support from its notables, [the government] should have established assemblies and instituted tax relief by fiat, through monarchic decree. I had hoped that such assemblies would move to abolish fiscal privileges and redistribute taxation equitably. But their role should be only advisory and have no veto power.[70]

On hearing of Calonne's disgrace, so he says, Du Pont rushed to call on Bouvard de Fourqueux to convince him to accept the post he had already refused due to ill-health. He had been one of Turgot's strongest supporters

---

[66] Ibid., partly cited by Hardman, *Overture to Revolution*, p. 10. Hardman furthermore notes that Du Pont wrote d'Ormesson in June 1787 to say that "he was responsible for the central measures but that Calonne had toned down his proposals. He had recommended the adoption of Turgot's provincial assemblies without modification; a land tax payable in money" (p. 28).

[67] This is plain from Hardman's description (*Overture to Revolution*, pp. 120–7).

[68] Ibid., p. 127.

[69] Ibid., p. 143. This was the edict promulgated in June 1787 in the districts as well as at the provincial level.

[70] Ibid., pp. 495–6. In that same letter, Mirabeau criticized the decision to talk of "deficits" and to suggest new taxes.

and a friend of the physiocrats. Fourqueux only lasted three weeks at the Control general. Loménie de Brienne (one of Turgot's Sorbonne friends) who had desperately wanted the post and resented Du Pont for thwarting him, was named chief minister and proved a total fiasco. Du Pont was out of favor, although Brienne agreed to keep him as secretary to the second Assembly of Notables (which also failed).[71] Du Pont reported his travails to Baron Edelsheim, the Margrave of Baden's minister, on 11 July 1787. On 1 May France had been a monarchy, he commented. "On May 9 [after a special session] it had become a *republic*, not through the establishment of provincial bodies, which could work hand-in-glove with the monarch to create a symbiotic *monarcho-republicanism*, but by fixing the amount of the following year's taxes rather than agreeing to a proportional tax on landed revenues, as initially suggested." Moreover, they had opted for the "English principle" whereby taxation was based on state expenditures rather than the other way round. This would perpetuate both France's deficit and shortfalls in revenue and require constant recourse to national assemblies – for all intents and purposes thereby establishing a "Republic."[72] Du Pont was reiterating the physiocratic principle that the people did not "consent" to taxation (except by endorsing the theory of the net product) but merely apportioned them. In these months Du Pont had managed the incredible feat of presenting his own draft legislation as Turgot's and using the respect in which Calonne and other "physiocratically inclined" reformers held the former minister to propel himself onto the national stage.

Building on their discussions during the Assemblies of Notables, a group of like-minded reformers known as the Committee of Thirty continued to meet to devise strategies for fiscal reform and to prepare for the upcoming meeting of the Estates General.[73] After a tumultuous meeting where he was denounced as an interloper in the meeting of the third estate, since he had been granted a noble title, Du Pont was elected deputy for Nemours by a vote of 182 out of 208 on 17 March 1789.[74]

---

[71] Schelle, *Du Pont de Nemours*, p. 269.
[72] Du Pont letter to Baron Edelsheim, 11 July 1787, pp. 273–4 in B. Ermannsdoerffer et al., eds., *Politische Correspondenz Karl Friedrichs von Baden, 1783–1806*, vol. 1 (Heidelberg, 1888). Hardman addresses Du Pont's letter on p. 266, but misconstrues Du Pont's objections. The "social constitution" he refers to is representation of landed interests which are those of everyone in the state.
[73] Saricks, *Du Pont*, pp. 135–7.
[74] Copy of letter from Irénée du Pont to his brother Victor, from Nemours, 18 March 1789. Hagley, Group 10, Series E, volume 13 (Smith transcripts), pp. 26–31. And several days later: "They had begun to riot over the price of bread just when Papa had obtained from the Duc d'Orléans the abolition of his banality on windmills."

He sat on eleven of the Constituent Assembly's committees and served as one of its rotating Presidents from 16 to 31 August 1790.[75] Given the self-denying ordinance that forbade deputies from running for the new legislature in fall 1791, Du Pont established printing works with twenty-five presses on the Ile Saint-Louis. On 10 August 1792, he claimed to have rushed to Louis XVI's side at the Tuileries Palace, although historians view this as improbable.[76] After the King's capture by the Parisians, he managed to flee to his country home near Nemours.[77]

## Revolutionary Festivals

The healthy contagion of the seasonal fêtes Du Pont had imagined in the 1770s turned into dangerous pestilence as he witnessed the radicalization of revolutionary festivals. Rather than celebrating the physiocratic consensus he had hoped for earlier, or displaying national unity as they had initially, by April 1792 festivals were, he feared, being manipulated for partisan ends. Du Pont had been a prominent member of the Constituent Assembly, a moderate reformer disturbed by the radicalization of politics after the King's attempted flight from France in June 1791, who joined the conservative Feuillant faction, after it broke away from the Jacobins. In that guise, in April 1792, he denounced Pétion, the mayor of Paris, for planning a mammoth civic ceremony to honor members of the Swiss Guard of Châteauvieux who had been mutinied against their officers in Eastern France two years earlier. The National Assembly had deemed them

---

[75] Saricks, *Du Pont*, p. 176. On page 157 he lists: Agriculture and Commerce, National Treasury, Examination of Accounts, Public Assistance, Public taxation, Examination of the Caisse d'escompte, Imposts, Ecclesiastical affairs, Finances, Alienation of the national domain, Tithes, and as adjunct member of the Committee on the Constitution.

[76] Marc Bouloiseau, *Bourgeoisie et Révolution, Les Du Pont de Nemours (1788–1799)* (Paris, 1972), pp. 73–6.

[77] Hagley, Series E (Smith transcripts), vol. 13, p. 109. Du Pont's grand-daughter repeats the myth: "On 10 August 1792, Mr. P. S. Du Pont was adamant about going to the Tuileries to defend the threatened monarch. I heard from my father, Eleuthère Irénée Du Pont, that he was there as well but only to watch over his father. They found themselves in a downstairs hall with about 500 gentlemen when the King crossed it on his way to the Assembly with the royal family. Upon noticing Mr P.S. du Pont, the King stopped and said 'Ah M. Du Pont! You are always there when you are needed!' They all followed the King and his family, surrounding him on the walk. The populace, however, broke in from the other side of the palace, seized the Tuileries canons and fired on the troop and killed a great many. Only a hundred were left when they reached the Assembly.... Mr Irénée du Pont was lucky to have pulled his father away from this terrible scene, safe and sound. They climbed over the garden gate, and ran off through a warren of small streets to find refuge at a friend's where they changed their clothes for plainer ones, and went back home."

guilty of rebellion, and La Fayette had insisted on making an example of them, and urged his cousin, the marquis de Bouillé, to use all means to extinguish the rebellion. Three dozen of the rebels had been captured and executed at the time; the remainder being sent to the galleys. Yet a sense of excess and injustice lingered because the regiments had voiced legitimate grievances against their officers.[78] Further public sympathy had been nurtured by claims that the Chateauvieux regiment had sided with the people in July 1789. In the end, the radicals prevailed (despite the protests from the Swiss government) and the soldiers were granted amnesty on 31 December 1791 and, as they made their way from Brest to Paris, were hailed as heroes. At the Jacobin club, Collot d'Herbois and Robespierre (and Marat in *L'Ami du people*) treated the affair as a battle between the valiant "opponents of tyranny" and those who preached "obedience to unjust laws."[79]

After several deferrals, the city of Paris finally announced that a Festival of Liberty (as the event in honor of the Châteauvieux regiment had been renamed) would be held on April 15 to celebrate these "heroes of the Revolution" and their "martyred" brethren. Collot d'Herbois and Robsespierre lashed out against La Fayette and other "aristocrats," demanding that the celebration make plain to the public who "truly" represented law and liberty.[80] On April 9, the forty surviving soldiers arrived in the capital and were welcomed at the National Assembly where they received the official "thanks of the nation," much to the consternation of some deputies, since the rebellious regiment had killed men from other regiments before finally surrendering, and one of their victims, Désilles, had been officially mourned only eighteen months earlier. History was being rewritten with yesterday's heroes becoming today's suspects.

The festivity itself, masterminded by Jean-Louis Prieur and Jacques-Louis David, included a large statue of Liberty and the Tables of the Law, thus formally celebrating both, and such conflations have led Mona Ozouf to reject the standard view that these were primarily "political" ceremonies.[81] However lavish and well-organized, the festival remained

---

[78] The best description is in Alain-Jacques Tornare, *Vaudois et Confédérés au service de France (1789–1798)* (Yens, 1998). The sentence had been handed out by the officers of two other Swiss regiments organized by Bouillé into a martial court, because the regiment was not under direct French control.

[79] See P. J. B. Buchez and P.-C. Roux, *Histoire parlementaire de la Révolution française* (Paris, 1835), XIV, pp. 62–125; F.-A. Aulard, *La Société des Jacobins, Recueil de documents* (Paris, 1892), III, pp. 409–512.

[80] Aulard, *Société des Jacobins*, III, 6 April 1792, p. 464.

[81] Marie-Louise Biver, *Fêtes révolutionnaires à Paris* (Paris, 1979), pp. 47–52.

under the aegis of the Paris Municipality (similar events being organized in other towns), rather than by the National Assembly so that the bearing of arms was forbidden.[82] In this highly charged atmosphere, Du Pont responded to what he saw as a provocation, and wrote a pamphlet attacking the mayor, thereby engaging in one of the great symbolic battles of the Revolution.[83]

How dare Pétion organize a festival of liberty around insurgents "who had attacked the national guard in the Eastern departments of Meurthe and Moselle as well as threatened the Parisians?" he thundered.[84] The Paris Municipality had no right to speak in the name of France nor, as it claimed, of the "People," since the nation was now one and could only speak through its elected representatives. Pétion was trying to recreate the particularisms and divisions that had prevailed in the Old Regime. His festival was not a celebration of liberty but of a skewed and divisive vision of France. What is more, how dare the municipality advertise in its leaflet that representatives of the National Assembly would be present without ever asking for their consent? Pétion seemed confident that he could "give orders to [the National Assembly] and inform them either the night before or on the day itself: *Legislative body, obey your masters and ours, the instigators and organizers of the festivities on behalf of the men of Châteauvieux, send them your deputation, their seats are ready....* Some members might indeed abandon their duties to attend this ceremony and sit next to rebels and assassins: but there won't be many."

---

[82] The bearing of arms proved contentious: it was intended to reassure the public of the festival's peaceful intentions but others, like Du Pont, feared that it was intended to disarm the participants so that the "Federates" who were converging on Paris for the event might stage a coup.

[83] Buchez and Roux, *Histoire parlementaire*, p. 81, deemed him the most ferocious among outspoken opponents who included André Chénier. Warren Roberts, *Jacques-Louis David and Jean-Louis Prieur, Revolutionary Artists, The Public, the Populace, and Images of the French Revolution* (Albany, 2000), pp. 139–43, 168–70, 251–3, 281–4. Ozouf, *La fête révolutionnaire*, pp. 115–29, deems the celebrations in question a turning point in the elaboration of revolutionary rituals; Michel Vovelle, on the other hand, treats them as a "rehearsal" at best, with the turning point occurring on 10 August 1793. *La Révolution contre l'Église: de la Raison à l'Être suprême* (Lausanne, 1988), p. 28. See also James H. Rubin, "The Politics of Quatremère de Quincy's Romantic Classicism" in George Levitine, ed., *Culture and Revolution, Cultural Ramification of the French Revolution* (College Park, Md., 1989), pp. 230–44.

[84] Du Pont, *Lettre de M. Du Pont à M. Pétion, 13 avril 1792* (reprinted in 1796), *Réponse de M. Pétion à M. Dupont*, followed by *Seconde lettre de M. Du Pont à M. Pétion, 27 avril 1792*. In French Revolutionary Pamphlets, Kroch Rare Book Room, Cornell University. Ozouf, *la fête révolutionnaire*, p. 98.

Who was legitimately entitled to speak in the name of the nation and to organize festivals in its name? For Du Pont this responsibility rested solely with the Assembly. The people demonstrated their sovereignty through the electoral process. It was for the Assembly therefore to organize national festivities. Moreover, since the nation stood for the rule of law, it could not celebrate criminals. Ceremonies organized by local authorities had to be deemed private, in which case they had no right to halt traffic in the capital (Pétion had forbidden carriages to enter the day of the festival) or to be held on the *champ de la fédération*, the ground reserved for national festivals. What is more, Pétion's usage of the term "People" was shameful: He meant the radical neighborhoods of eastern Paris who were demanding the blood of their "enemies."

> The sovereignty of the French people is at stake here. The question is whether it will retain the freedoms it has won; whether it will support its constitution and the authority of those it chose freely to fulfil public duties, or whether it will allow itself to be controlled, to see its power usurped by men it has not chosen, who are a small minority of self-recruited trouble-makers [*factieux*] and who subjugate from one corner of the nation to the other its delegates and representative, by resorting, depending on the circumstances, to calumny, pillage, arson, and assassination.

Pétion offered a nineteen-page rebuttal. The festival had not meant to offend anyone. The organizers had been told to keep things simple and decent.

> Whom will you ever persuade that citizens who arrived singing and dancing committed all the atrocities that you ascribe to them; that they put a gun to onlookers' throats to force them to join them, or to swell the cortege, or to shout: "Long live Châteauvieux!" ... Oh you who show nothing but mistrust of the people, who believe that it is capable of every excess and disorder, this is how you deprave it and make it vicious. Few men have the courage not to be despicable when they are always despised.

People would look back on festivals that celebrated liberty and equality such as this one as of the "most remarkable signs of the progress of public spirit, inspiring the people whose moral instruction and edification is so important." His account of events is elegiac:

> At last the long awaited day dawned. What beautiful weather! What serenity! So was the festival. What an amazing sight watching three to four hundred thousand people freely displaying deep sentiments of joy and elation, maintaining the most perfect order and displaying the most touching harmony, without the need for police.... One cannot have a soul, one cannot love liberty if one does not feel

delight at how we are rising to our destiny.... Just look at the emblems and ornaments of the festival, which echo ... the civic festivities of ancient free peoples.

Du Pont rejected this rosy description (which was so painfully reminiscent of his own words to Carl Ludwig) and accused Pétion, in a pamphlet dated 27 April, of lying about the number of participants, and of continuing to describe the 15,000 who might support his views as the "People." "The People are no longer free. Elections in primary and electoral assemblies are now controlled, and those who are known, outside the clubs, to be men of merit and probity, are the butt of threats." This is contrary to the spirit of 1789. "There no longer exist two nations in France, equality has been irrevocably established; no matter how hard they try, and even at the cost of their little army, France will remain one nation and one public." Du Pont had warned Pétion in a personal missive that he was publishing a pamphlet criticizing him.[85] Its contents were similar to the published version, insisting on the dangerous course on which the mayor had embarked. Du Pont ended with the hope that reason would prevail.

These competing visions of legitimacy went beyond a war of words. Du Pont and a group of fellow moderates organized a counter-demonstration on 3 June, enlarging the celebrations planned since 6 March by the Legislative Assembly to honor Jacques-Guillaume Simonneau, mayor of Étampes, killed during a grain riot. The felled mayor's official insignia and sash would be placed in the Pantheon, and the event would be turned into a Festival of the Law, reminding citizens of importance of obedience at a time when grain riots were spreading and discontent against the government increasing.[86] The architect and member of the Committee of Public Instruction Quatremère de Quincy organized the pageant and David contributed a frieze for one of the parade's platforms, although this is disputed by some art historians.[87]

---

[85] Hagley, W2-399, draft of letter to Pétion de Villeneuve, 13 April 1792.
[86] The rival celebrations are summarized most fully in David Lloyd Dowd, *Pageant-Master of the Republic, Jacques-Louis David and the French Revolution* (Lincoln, Neb., 1948), pp. 55–77.
[87] Marie-Noelle Polino, "Quatremère de Quincy et la fête de la loi en l'honneur de Simoneau, maire d'Etampes (juin 1792)" in R. Chevallier, ed., *La Révolution française et l'antiquité* (Tours, 1991), pp. 285–309; Richard I. Kertzer, *Ritual, Politics, and Power* (New Haven, 1988), pp. 155–6; Jean-Claude Bonnet, "La mort de Simonneau" in Jean Nicolas, ed., *Mouvements populaires et conscience sociale* (Paris, 1985), pp. 671–6; Sukla Sanyal, "The 1792 Food Riot at Étampes and the French Revolution," *Studies in History*, 18:1 (2002), 23–50.

Robespierre who described Simonneau "a greedy speculator in public foodstuffs," denounced the event as a sign of "contempt and hatred for the people."[88] Ministers, deputies, magistrates, and national guards marched behind models of the Bastille and of a pyramid memorial to be erected at Étampes itself, a bust of the fallen mayor, a tribute to the Law on a golden throne crowned by a statue of Minerva, followed by another mammoth seated figure of the Law of "both stern and gentle expression, with one arm leaning on the tablets of the law and the other holding a golden scepter," held by sixteen men in antique garb, demonstrating that the "law governed the unruly."[89] The *Révolutions de Paris*, on the more radical side of the spectrum, derided the ornate representations of an "austere principle," and the banners that insisted not merely on the rule of law but that proclaimed that "truly free men are slaves to the law."[90] The editor, Prudhomme, was moreover mystified by a huge papier-maché shark aloft a pole bearing the label "respect the law," and he mused that the intent was no doubt to portray the people as the shark poised on top of the law, but could as easily be read as the law skewering the people. The more frequently reproduced image of the event by Jean-Louis Prieur, engraved by P.-G. Berthault, shows the shark on the left of the parade but is hard to make out. The entire parade, in fact, is dwarfed by the backdrop of a huge, partially demolished Bastille, although it no longer existed. The *Révolutions de Paris* provided its own illustration of the procession with the fish on the stick also appearing on the left-hand side, somewhat more prominently.[91]

The Festival of the Law, deemed to represent Quatremère's more learned and complicated antique leanings than those of his counterpart David, is part of ongoing debates regarding the nature and legibility of revolutionary festivals.[92] One should remember that the festival of 3 June was also

---

[88] Buchez and Roux, *Histoire parlementaire*, pp. 265, 268.
[89] Pitra, "Lettre à Meister sur la fête civique de 1792 en l'honneur de Simonneau, juin 1792" in "Corpus historique étampois," available online. Also In Grimm, Meister, et al., *Correspondance littéraire, philosophique et critique*, ed. Maurice Tourneux (Paris, 1882), XVI, pp. 139–45.
[90] Louis-Marie Prudhomme, *Révolutions de Paris*, Douzième Trimestre, Numéro 152, 2–9 June 1792, "Procession en mémoire du maire d'Etampes," pp. 450–5.
[91] Jean-Louis Prieur, *Tableaux historiques de la Révolution française*, Number 61, 3 June 1792, Musée Carnavalet, Paris.
[92] See Roberts, *David and Prieur, Revolutionary Artists*, pp. 282–3; Ozouf, *La fête révolutionnaire*, pp. 120–1, 124, arguing that David and Quatremère had opposite styles: David favoring realism, whereas Quatremère favored abstraction. Marie-Noelle Polino, "Quatremère de Quincy," p. 286, disagrees with Ozouf's conclusions, arguing the similarities, not least because both men contributed to both.

FIGURE 8.1. "Hommage funèbre au maire d'Etampes," *Révolutions de Paris*, June 1792, General Research Division, The New York Public Library, Astor, Lenox and Tilden Foundations.

a physiocratic event, insofar as it celebrated a man who had sacrificed his life for free trade in cereals.[93] To make matters clearer, the physiocratic triad "liberty, security, and property," was plastered throughout the procession.[94] But this message carried its own ambiguities in linking wheat and bloodshed, as Jean-Claude Bonnet notes, for could liberty embodied in "the laws" (not least those of the "economy") fill empty bellies?[95] Who was the real victim, here? For a committed physiocrat like Du Pont the difficulty lay elsewhere. Those who had fêted the Châteauvieux rebels and now mocked the memorial to Simonneau invoked the law of humanity to trump the decrees of the Constitution. In calling for obedience to the law, Du Pont denied that individuals possessed an inner sense of their

---

[93] It seems stubbornly and provokingly so. [Association Etampes-Histoire], *Étampes en Révolution, 1789–1799* (Le-Mée-sur-Seine, 1989), pp. 109–11.
[94] Ozouf, *La fête révolutionnaire*, p. 119.
[95] Bonnet, "La mort de Simonneau," p. 676. Sophie Wahnich finds a similar ambiguity in the petition for leniency for rioters from the local priest who nonetheless supports freedom of trade, "Un avocat sensible dans l'émotion de l'évènement: le curé Dolivier face au meurtre du maire d'Étampes, printemps 1792," *Journée d'histoire des sensibilités*, EHESS, Paris, 6 March 2006, in *Mundos Novos*, online publication, 16 March 2006.

"natural rights," although that is precisely what physiocracy had once claimed. Now that "rights" had been embodied in legislation, nature had been heeded, and demanding their expansion smacked of perversity and threatened the stability of the new order.

Although Prudhomme attributed the celebration to Du Pont and his friends among the Feuillants, Du Pont left no record of it.[96] We might conclude for him that the harmonious festivals that he had once scripted for Carl Ludwig had been subverted through partisanship and the invocation of the "wrong" inner sentiments. Rather than concord, the radicals' rigid notions of virtue produced division and violence, and unleashed the passions. In the pamphlet on "National Education" published a few years later, Du Pont would include the village festivities he had always favored: teaching children to write by copying maxims such "Equality, Liberty"; "Work, Property, Justice"; "Economy, Wisdom" after which they should partake in martial exercises while the women looked on "from their own sphere."[97] He had not abandoned the idea of civic participation but put his faith more strongly than ever in the family.

The Revolution had been a rude awakening. His prediction of the havoc wrought by the Paris municipality and the radicals in the Assembly came to pass, as we know. Du Pont fled to the countryside after the *journée* of 10 August 1792. There, reports of the September massacres and growing revolutionary violence prompted him to reflect on the question of evil and the possibility of human progress.

## Philosophie de L'univers

The poem and volume he produced, published jointly as the *Philosophie de l'univers*, have puzzled scholars, for Du Pont appears to have gone off the rails with a Creation myth that strove to account for evil and a theory of progress predicated on the transmigration of souls.[98] This was not Turgot's or Condorcet's notion of material improvements that

---

[96] See my forthcoming work on the organization of this event.
[97] Du Pont, "Vues sur l'éducation nationale par un cultivateur" (Paris, 1794), which Du Pont printed on his own press, 48 pages, pp. 18, 30, 33, 35, 41.
[98] Robert Darnton is a good example, *Mesmerism and the End of Enlightenment in France* (New York, 1970), pp. 136–8. There may have been mesmerist influences, since quite a few of Du Pont's Feuillants colleagues were seduced by the theory of animal magnetism. See Georges Michon, *Histoire du parti feuillant, Adrien Duport (1789–1792)* (Paris, 1924), pp. 4–5. On metempsychosis as literary theme, see Jean-François Perrin, "Métempsychose: soi-même comme multitude: Le cas du récit à métempsychose au 18e siècle," *Dix-huitième siècle*, 41 (2009), 169–86.

would bring enlightenment in their wake.[99] Du Pont detached himself from the material world and leapt into the unknown. He must find a way of accounting for individual pain and suffering – and not just the survival of the species – in the grand design envisaged by Quesnay.

Michael Sonenscher has argued that "physiocracy was a kind of theodicy" because, as he explains, it assumes "a God-given human ability to put a ruined world right."[100] Steven Nadler makes the important point for the uninitiated, that theodicy, as Leibniz understood it, sought to answer why a benevolent deity created a world in which evil existed at all rather than seeking to account for evil itself.[101] The "easiest" solution, he adds, and one frequently adopted, was to gauge the overall amount of good compared to the overall amount of evil in the world, and to treat evil as stimulus to the good to strive harder. Physiocrats, under Quesnay's tutelage, had privileged such aggregation without lingering on individual fates. As in Leibniz's theodicy, it was humanity's welfare as a whole that mattered.[102] Du Pont now addressed evil squarely as a pervasive and incomprehensible misery. Finding no other solution, he moved beyond man's material and moral constitution to offer the hope that the "soul" would transcend this pain when it became pure spirit, although it could never overcome its restlessness and disquiet totally. There was no final resting place, because even at its most purified, the soul would continue to yearn for the unattainable perfection of God. There was a limit on how high his creations could rise, even within God's benevolent plan.[103]

A long poem "Oromasis" acts as prelude, depicting the battle between good and evil. The Creator's plans for a perfect world are thwarted by an evil spirit Arimane, who insists on human mortality and pain, but the good Creator Oromasis remains sanguine as he addresses Arimane: "I know

---

[99] Anne-Robert-Jacques Turgot, "Tableau philosophique des progrès successifs de l'esprit humain" in Joel-Thomas Ravix and Paul-Marie Romani, *Turgot, Formation et distribution des richesses* (Paris, 1997), pp. 70–94: Condorcet, *Esquisse d'un tableau historique des progrès de l'esprit humain* (Paris, 1988).
[100] Michael Sonenscher, "Physiocracy as Theodicy," p. 335.
[101] Steven Nadler, *The Best of All Possible Worlds: A Story of Philosophers, God, and Evil* (New York, 2009), pp. 89–96. Also Jérôme Porée, *Le Mal, homme coupable, homme souffrant* (Paris, 2000), pp. 115–21; Rober Mauzi, *L'Idée du bonheur*, pp. 549–57.
[102] Hagley, W2-425, letter from Du Pont to the marquis de Saint-Lambert, addressed here as "citoyen," of 17 December 1794, shows that the Revolution changed his mind: "Alas! I have lost almost every single friend and, for a long time now, I have been unable to ask for news of any man without getting the answer *He is dead*. Some assassinated, others from the grief of having seen their loved-ones assassinated. I came close to the first calamity, and I suffer still from the second, which is far more cruel."
[103] Knies, *Carl Friedrichs von Baden*, II, Part III, p. 94. Letter to Carl Ludwig, n.d. [1773].

the limits of your power. In the nature of things, I cannot prevent living beings from suffering, but neither will you be able to prevent their being happy and finding life itself a joy." In the long text that follows the poem, Du Pont argues that physical and moral phenomena are at bottom the same. The laws of morality that must guide man's conduct are therefore as demonstrable and indubitable "as those of geometry or chemistry." Nature consists of destiny (which governs everything), a creative intelligence (God), and matter – in effect replacing that "other" Trinity.

Pain and suffering exist to spur us to action, for, just like life itself is animated by oxygen which keeps it in motion, so must men keep active.[104] Nonetheless, except for a few outstanding individuals, humans can only soar so high. To console them for their mortality, they have been given the gift of love. With this love comes the wish to help and support others. "This is how, at its beginning, the earth was peopled with couples that grew into families, and families into nations [*peuples*] where all loved, helped, and enlightened each other, gaining dominion over all living forms."[105] People understood that they had to cooperate in order to survive. But God had also endowed human beings with imagination. Envisaging the future filled them with hope and the capacity to plan. This had not happened by chance; it was all part of benevolent design.[106]

Unlike self-interest and the search for material profits, love is never exhausted and yields continued dividends. So, although man's self-interest will help him survive, friendship and love give his life meaning. Additionally, man possesses a conscience by which to gauge his own behavior. "[The Creator] has placed deep inside men's hearts a Minister: a soul within the soul to judge the soul. We have a self that desires and acts, and another self that weighs whether such desires are worthy or such actions appropriate. We become aware of this conscience each time we blush or feel remorse at our actions." Once intuition had been invoked and abused by his revolutionary opponents, Du Pont could no longer tell men to rely on instinctive responses. He had to posit an additional sense, separate from either reason or sentiment, which, like the teachings of the Scottish Enlightenment and those French proponents "of a sixth sense," entailed an "inner observer" that patrolled the soul.[107] Du Pont deems human responses to be universal, bound by material exigencies. Primitive men, for example, felt affection the way we do for they too needed food,

---

[104] Du Pont, *Philosophie de l'univers* (Paris, 1796), p. 57.
[105] Ibid., pp. 62–3.
[106] Ibid., pp. 67 and 122.
[107] See, for example, Adam Smith, *Theory of Moral Sentiments* and *Wealth of Nations*.

shelter, and companionship. In a footnote, therefore, Du Pont calls on conscience to dawn on "Laclos, even Danton, even Robespierre, even Marat, and even Philippe Égalité [the duc d'Orléans] and realize that these are terrible times".[108] Man can conquer evil (in himself), which is why God favors the virtuous.[109] For the goal is universal harmony, not just personal redemption.

Like the oyster that cannot understand how it is lifted out of the sea, humans lack sophisticated organs and senses to see beneath the surface of things. Nonetheless they can infer a higher reality by means of *analogy* (Quesnay's bête noire).[110] For beyond the chain of living things we are able to observe, lies another that leads us ever upward towards God (without ever merging with him). Du Pont had probed "Greek, Platonist, Chinese, Persian, Zoroastrian, and Christian" texts for explanations but had fallen back on his own conclusions that higher intelligent forms had to exist, based on the increasing cognitive complexity of animals in the chain of creation.[111] He had used his mind and listened to his heart to reach these conclusions. "Alone, surrounded by memories of my friends" he had felt the pull of "ethereal forces and heard the choirs of Seraphs seated by God's throne," and as his reason, conscience, and sensibility drifted away from his being, he "had contemplated ideal beauty and perceived a grander, nobler order." Imagination had served as his conduit:

Imagination helps us [see ideal beauty], she is the handmaiden of reason that enables us to perceive higher things that our senses, which we share with the lower animal forms, do not enable us to see. The imagination is an intermediary sense, thrown like a bridge between the animal realm and more exalted realms. This is why it was given to the most advanced species.

For the imagination, like "Noah's dove, flies off to discover new things." Reason judges on whatever it reports, compares the information, and then accepts as true (*certain*) what accords with existing phenomena, even if only by analogy. As we reflect, we realize that we are not mere bodies, mere intelligence, or mere machines, but all three, and that our intelligence survives our physical destruction to return in different form. What Quesnay would have dismissed as phantasms now served to bolster Du Pont's message of hope.

---

[108] Du Pont, *Philosophie de l'univers*, p. 103.
[109] Ibid., p. 119.
[110] Ibid., p. 128.
[111] Ibid., pp. 134–6. Du Pont once again calls upon analogy, which enables us to grasp the laws of the universe. This was also Charles Bonnet's argument in his *Palingenesis*.

Du Pont referred to wandering souls as *monads*, citing Leibniz and Pythagoras as sources but diverging from both. Pythagoras's universal harmonies and theory of reincarnation were clearly appealing.[112] The Pythagoras admired in the eighteenth century was the sage who imparted secrets to a healthy physical and moral life to his followers, which he deduced from the "same geometric laws" that governed the universe. Leibniz's idea of a preestablished harmony that made body and soul act in conjunction, and of simple substances, or monads, powered by an inner force were similarly attractive. Each of Leibniz's monads reflects the universe from its own vantage point – while always reacting to other monads – and this might have satisfied Du Pont's need to reconcile his newly minted individual path to salvation with the rest of Creation. The theological considerations behind Leibniz's theodicy play no role here. Du Pont is not questioning the distribution of God's grace, since we can all save ourselves through our own efforts. Nor is he interested in the questions of transubstantiation, miracles, or whether this is the "best of all possible worlds" God might have created (meaning with the most good and least evil congruent with the simplest natural laws) that Leibniz's contemporaries had been debating.[113]

Instead Du Pont posits his new "insights" as the reward for man's travails, the ultimate recognition of their efforts and merit. It is an otherworldly reward, however, although neither the Christian paradise nor the Hindu Nirvana. We fear death because we associate life with motion and growth, and therefore dread immobility.[114] There is nothing to fear. Intelligence survives the disintegration of the body and begins a series of spiritual incarnations, reaching ever higher toward the ultimate knowledge that belongs to God only. Man has been made *perfectible* to attain these higher planes.[115] Once rid of its mortal coil, the soul (or intelligence) enters a purgatory where the quality of its previous life is assessed: It then rises or falls along a ladder or chain of being, based on its merits, although remorseful souls sometimes choose voluntarily to move down a few rungs. Totally unrepentant souls will self-destruct and merge with the ooze from which they once emerged. "The evidence for all this springs

---

[112] See the recent overview by Kitty Ferguson, *The Music of Pythagoras* (New York, 2008) and for Pythagorean ideas during the French Revolution, James H. Billington, *Fire in the Minds of Men* (New Brunswick, N.J., 1999), pp. 100–6.

[113] See the comparison of Bayle, Leibniz, Malebranche and Arnauld in Nadler, *The Best of All Possible Worlds*.

[114] Du Pont, *Philosophie de l'univers*, p. 168.

[115] Yet only when it has shed all its earthbound and limited human perceptions will this essence remember its previous incarnations.

from the heart.... In medicine, listen to nature, in philosophy, listen to instinct."[116] In conclusion:

> There is a great presumption in favour of an hypothesis once we concede that it agrees perfectly with other known, proven laws, with all the facts of Natural History, and especially with the mercy, justice, and infinite goodness of God.[117]

Economics play virtually no role in this work. For Quesnay, morality was using one's reason to make the right choices. Now, for Du Pont, it has become: "our need for love, for esteem, which is much stronger, better developed and more expressive in man than other animals, because of that greater intelligence which elevates our *morality* far above theirs."[118]

Physiocrats had contended that man had the ability to learn and heed Nature's message as long as he let his thought progress step-by-step to the point of utter certainty. But what if nature's message was not heard or understood? After all, physiocrats also argued that perceiving self-evidence required huge levels of concentration. Very few were capable of such strenuous exercise, they repeated. How then might the remainder of humanity be brought to understand nature's message? As we saw, Du Pont moved increasingly away from Quesnay's and Mirabeau's epistemology to suggest that emotions could open hearts to the insights that only physiocrats truly possessed. Quesnay had posited that inklings of higher truths could come in sudden flashes, which was one of the accepted versions of the sublime. Physiocrats remained divided on the "efficacy" of emotions per se, and Mirabeau finally endorsed Quesnay's mistrust of imagination. Du Pont was the product of a younger generation that thought in terms of nervous stimulation resulting in "healthy contagion," until, that is, he witnessed its lethal effects during the Revolution. Metempsychosis took the realization of Nature's ultimate plan beyond men's power to destroy it. Du Pont abandoned "aggregates" to focus on individual destinies. Although one might reasonably conclude that eternal salvation (or "self-improvement") did not require an earthly commitment to the net product, Du Pont nonetheless tied spiritual rewards to the fulfillment of duties on earth. The physiocratic gospel represented the "best of all possible worlds."

Du Pont wrote the initial draft after he fled the capital in summer 1792, dedicating the poem to the Lavoisiers. He published it himself in

---

[116] Du Pont, *Philosophie de l'univers*, pp. 205–6.
[117] Ibid., pp. 235–6.
[118] Ibid., p. 91. He also refers to it on the same page as a "moralité profondément sentimentale."

1796 (two editions), with an expanded version in 1800.[119] It was Du Pont's most successful text and one that he clearly cherished.[120] He wrote his son, Victor, on 19 Nivose II (8 January 1794)[121]:

> I am sending you, as you asked, *La Philosophie de l'univers* or at least the important part of this book which is titled *Principes et Recherches sur la Philosophie de l'univers* with its epigram.... You can attach before it, *Le Serpent* and then *Oronasis*, and at the end the literary discussion of the *Religions antiques de l'Asie*. But its truly essential, new, rich, and precise depictions and sentiments [*les choses et les sentiments*] are contained in the little notebook that I am entrusting to you. Don't lose it, don't lend it: You know how much it means to me. Etch it in your mind and in your heart. If it is imprinted there, I will have fulfilled one of the principal goals that led me to write it.

## Theophilanthropy

The Committee of General Security finally tracked down Du Pont and arrested him on 13 July 1794 for "counter-revolutionary activities" and conveyed him to La Force prison in Paris.[122] The fall of Robespierre a few days later saved his life, and he was released at the end of August.[123] He proposed to Lavoisier's widow and, when she declined his offer, successfully courted the widow of the physiocratic fellow-traveler and Intendant in the South Seas Pierre Poivre. They married on 26 September 1795.[124]

Du Pont served both on the Directory's two chambers, the upper Council of Elders and the lower Council of Five Hundred between 1795 and 1797 and was elected to the newly founded Institut de France. He edited the journal *L'Historien* and contributed to others, such as his friend Pierre-Louis Roederer's *Journal d'économie publique, de morale et*

---

[119] His second son, Irénée had trained with Lavoisier.
[120] Schelle, *Du Pont de Nemours*, pp. 331–2. The title page of the first edition states a publication date of 1792, although the work itself was not completed until June 1793.
[121] Hagley, W2-409 letter from Du Pont to his son Victor, 8 January 1794.
[122] From prison, on 7 Thermidor he tries to reassure Victor and his wife Josephine: "Do not worry yourselves over me. I am allowed to give you news. I feel quite well. I am treated, like my comrades, most humanely. There is enough food and one might even call it abundant and healthy. It is based on good principles of hygiene and medicine, with a mix of animal and vegetable substances in the right proportions. The house is well-aired. It has a garden. I believe that they will do justice to my patriotism and all that I have done for the Republic. The only sorrow therefore is to be far from you, my other children, and my fields." Hagley, W2-418, letter from Du Pont to Victor, 25 July 1794.
[123] Saricks, *Du Pont*, p. 227.
[124] Ibid., p. 233.

*de politique*. Mystical reliance on divine Providence and hopes for reconciliation of all Frenchmen in the aftermath of the Revolution drew him to a new cult, Theophilanthropy, which offered an ecumenical alternative to Christianity in the ways of *La Philosophie de l'univers*.[125]

The aftershocks of the Terror, the association of the cults of Reason and the Supreme Being with the worst excesses of the Jacobin regime, left few options to those moderates who hoped to guide the social and spiritual recovery of the Republic in the aftermath of Thermidor. Theophilanthropy sought to reawaken civic virtue in rituals that brought together the public and private spheres. Besides a love of nature, their approach was deist, tolerant, sentimental, and patriarchal.[126] The fundamental tenets consisted in belief in the existence of God and the immortality of the soul. Devotees must respect natural laws (which God had instituted), and to acknowledge that everything happened for a reason, linked in an infinite chain of causation.

Albert Mathiez, historian of revolutionary cults, treated Du Pont's support of Theophilanthropy as a sign that it was "the religion of the enlightened bourgeoisie."[127] Du Pont actively promoted the cult in his journal *L'historien*, and recommended it to his friends, although without much success. The appeal for Du Pont rested, actually, in the cult's stress on family rituals and the moral preaching that took place in the home, in order, presumably, to prevent the demagogic manipulations that had led the Revolution astray. "To create a national church, to pave the path to a universal church, every family must be its own church led by its pontiff, the father, in whom God rests his authority, assisted by his charming and beloved vicar, the mother."[128] The paterfamilias led his household in daily prayers (which Du Pont gleefully composed). He must perform these rites with gravitas and assiduity, he insisted, in order to impress the young and further their education.[129]

Under the stewardship of La Reveillière-Lépeaux, the cult expanded to massive public festivals.[130] Du Pont detached himself from

---

[125] See Albert Mathiez, *La Théophilanthropie et le culte décadaire. Essai sur l'histoire religieuse de la Révolution, 1796–1801* (Paris, 1904).

[126] Ibid., pp. 38–9, 57.

[127] Ibid., pp.120, 123–4.

[128] Hagley, W2-5027, n.d. He also composed very short daily prayers to the Roman deities on whose names they were based, W-5025.

[129] Mathiez, *Théophilanthropie*, p. 113. It is interesting to note that if Du Pont had taken part in the planning of the "fête de la loi" of 3 June 1793, that Olympe de Gouges had insisted on women's presence in the parade.

[130] See Mathiez, *Théophilanthropie*, and Henri Grange, "La Reveillière-Lépeaux, théoricien de la fête nationale (1797)," p. 496, and Nicolas Wargnier, "Fête et dissolution sociale, à

Theophilanthropy at that point, especially once it became clearly tied to a Jacobin revival, and he left Paris, once more for the countryside.[131]

Mathiez and others have argued that the religious cults of the mid-1790s arose in response to the revolutionaries' disappointment that laws did not alter men's nature and their new conviction that moral and civic education would be necessary before people would accept a new social order. Du Pont (and fellow physiocrats) had conceded this point decades earlier and he had carried this creed to his association with Turgot: Educate and legislate he had advised the minister. Educational reform had been mooted during the Constituent Assembly, but continually put off.[132] Gabriel de Mirabeau had called for education through "public festivals" and Robespierre took it to an extreme, although the civic virtues they vaunted were open to different interpretations.[133] The Revolution taught Du Pont that education began at home, developed in the classroom (and he tried repeatedly to have the National Assembly endorse physiocratic manuals), and, at best, reinforced in public celebrations.

Quesnay believed his system allowed states to procure endlessly renewable resources based on nature's fecundity, man's labor, capital infusions, and rational consumer spending. The formula was impersonal but presumed that man's greatest wish was for stability, not the satisfaction of urges or the accumulation of goods. Men could therefore be brought to sacrifice their desires especially once they understood that nature could satisfy the needs of an entire society but only afford individuals a modest contentment. Of course, men's conjoined efforts would improve conditions by small, regular increments, through improvements in productivity, but the overall conception was essentially static. The system provided the greatest happiness for the greater number as long as one agreed with the definition of happiness. Unfortunately, Quesnay's "laws of the natural order" only worked properly if *everyone* fulfilled his or her function – which placed a heavy burden on humanity. One could not "opt out." Physiocrats argued that the alternative was worse, because unbridled pursuit of self-interest eventually backfired

---

propos de quelques notices du 'Journal de Paris' (1797)," pp. 526–7, in Jean Ehrard and Paul Viallaneix, eds., *Les fêtes de la Révolution, Colloque de Clermont-Ferrand (juin 1974)* (Paris, 1977).

[131] He continued to hope that love would spread since it offered the only relief in this vale of tears. Thus, the poem "Le Colin-Maillard" at the Hagley in manuscript, W2-4812, concludes that man is caught between Fortune and Love. It was published in 1801 in *L'Almanach des Muses*.

[132] M. J. Guillaume, ed., *Procès-verbaux du Comité d'instruction publique de l'assemblée législative* (Paris, 1889), "Introduction," pp. i–iii.

[133] Ozouf, *La fête révolutionnaire*, p. 103.

both at the individual and societal levels, whereas the natural order reconciled the two.

In the early 1770s Du Pont embroidered on the joys of physiocratic society, emphasizing its domestic bliss and communal harmony, and the sense of purpose it conferred. This still entailed repressing desires and orienting them toward simpler satisfactions. As the *Tableau* in disequilibrium demonstrated, there were dire consequences to not doing so. Individual happiness was thus fitted within the provisions for societal welfare. Yet individuals expected more, Du Pont came to realize, and wanted to know how the laws of nature would improve their own lives. Unable to offer more solid reassurance, Du Pont ended up with the delayed gratifications of the afterlife. Passivity, however, would not do. Individuals must continue to strive and hope for recognition by a higher power by obeying the material and moral laws he had set. This was a religious, not an economic, program.

Du Pont, he, his wife, his children and their families left France in 1799 for the United States to found a powerful dynasty in Delaware. America beckoned as the land of opportunity. In 1798 Du Pont's elder son Victor had been named French Consul General to the United States but, before he could take up his post in Philadelphia, relations between the two countries had so deteriorated that he was forced to return to Paris. Du Pont Senior, meanwhile, had concocted a project to establish a model agricultural community in Virginia (close to his friend Jefferson).[134] Victor opposed the plan but Du Pont could not be dissuaded. He sold shares to friends in the hopes of raising two million francs for the enterprise and amazingly collected 214,347 francs.[135] This was nowhere near enough to fund an agrarian community so Du Pont came up with a new scheme to act as overseas agent for French merchants on a commission basis. He chose the wrong moment: Commercial relations between France and the United States, complicated by Napoleon's rise and war with England, remained at a standstill. Luckily, through a French contact, his second son Irénée learned that the American government was looking for gunpowder. Investigating their methods, he realized that Lavoisier had taught him techniques as yet unknown in the United States.[136] After searching for months for a site he could afford, Irénée settled on a property on the

---

[134] For details see Mack Thompson, "Causes and Circumstances of the Du Pont Family Emigration," *French Historical Studies*, 6:1 (1969), 59–77.
[135] Saricks, *Du Pont de Nemours*, p. 273.
[136] Ibid., pp. 284–6.

shores of the Brandywine river on the outskirts of Wilmington, Delaware, where he set up his powder works.

Life in America disappointed Du Pont and he was back in Paris in spring 1802, helping Jefferson negotiate the Louisiana transfer in 1803. Napoleon did not appoint him to the Senate as he had hoped and repeatedly refused to grant him the Legion of Honor. He had to wait for the Bourbon Restoration to secure the ribbon.[137] Du Pont spent the next decade in France, writing articles, attending Institut meetings, and publishing a complete edition of Turgot's works. He also served on the Paris Chamber of Commerce, supervised Paris charities for five years, and through the recommendations of a friend, obtained the post of assistant librarian at the Arsenal in 1807. Napoleon's escape from Elba convinced him it was time to return to the United States, and he reached its shores on 20 March 1815, just as Napoleon marched into Paris.[138] Mme Du Pont had opted not to accompany him although she hoped to join him later. Du Pont meant to visit her in summer 1817, but he caught a chill after helping to extinguish a fire at the powder mill, in the middle of the night, and died on 7 August 1817.[139]

Du Pont never renounced his faith in physiocracy but economics, meanwhile, moved on to factor in desires as well as needs in the demand for goods, to appreciate the role of labor, and to seek the holy grail of a natural equilibrium. But fear of irrational drives, whose power the Revolution displayed in terrifying fashion, would continue to haunt the "science of economics."

---

[137] Ibid., pp. 293, 301.
[138] Ibid., p. 344.
[139] Ibid., p. 357.

# Acknowledgments

This book has been long in the making, and in the process I have benefited from the support of friends, colleagues, and institutions. I began the research initially as part of the project on the harvest in which I was engaged. I was curious about the cultural world that had stimulated Jacques Turgot to translate *The Georgics* and, more significantly, Gessner and Ossian, and decided to follow that trail. Working my way through eighteenth-century theories of language, poetry, and the arts, I discovered to my stupefaction that Jacques Derrida's *De la grammatologie* could hold my attention. A semester teaching at Yale allowed me to burrow into its extensive collections and pay visits to the Benjamin Franklin collection where I read the entire run of the *Éphémérides du citoyen*. Thus began my love-hate relationship with the Physiocrats, and I would still be at it had I not realized that I could explore new avenues to my dying days. One question led to another, and I moved from language and culture, to political economy, history of medicine, philosophy of science, and philosophy *tout court*, endlessly drawn to the complex world of the Enlightenment.

This switch from the social history and cultural history that I had worked on previously was unexpected and raised quite a few skeptical eyebrows. I would therefore like to thank those who encouraged me, especially by believing that I had discovered an interesting way of thinking about political economy. They include David Bell, Rafe Blaufarb, Tom and Katherine Brennan, Yves Citton, Jim Collins, Fanny Cosandey, Dan Edelstein, Paul Freedman, Alain Guéry, Michèle Hannoosh, Colin Jones, Tom Kaiser, Michael Kwass, Deidre Lynch, Claude Maire, Harriet Ritvo, Rob Schneider, Bob Schwartz, Jim Scott, Jay Smith, Michael

Sonenscher, Tim Tackett, and Dror Wahrman. Particular thanks go to Howard Brown, Emma Rothschild, and Michael Sibalis.

I also wish to thank Eric Crahan of Cambridge University Press for his faith in the project and for waiting while I worked my way through various drafts, and also the readers of the manuscript for their extremely useful suggestions. I am grateful to Peter Paret of the Institute for Advanced Study at Princeton for sponsoring my stay there in 2000–2001. At the Hagley Museum and Library, Roger Horowitz and Carol Lockman, and the devoted staff of the Soda House were endlessly helpful both during my two-week stay and subsequent visits. My time in Paris would not have been the same without the friendship of Françoise and Louis Levioux. In New Haven, I benefited from the warm hospitality of John and Carol Merriman, and in Princeton from the welcome by Harold and Vivian Shapiro. I thank Loïc Charles, Christine Théré, and Jean-Claude Perrot for sharing their encyclopedic knowledge of Quesnay. The interlibrary loans service at the University of Buffalo went beyond the call of duty to provide me with every book I asked for and put up with my occasional irritation at the library's purchasing priorities.

Years ago, Stuart Juzda purchased the complete set of *L'Ami des hommes* for me at a time when no one gave the physiocrats a thought. My daughter Elise has stuck to me through thick and thin and has become an historian in her own right. I dedicate this book to her with all my heart. Lastly, I recognize that this book could not have been completed without my cat-sitters and sometime-students, James Bonnano, Morgan Denton, Nathan Hefinstine, Carlton Hickok, Jon Markle, and Alex Yarbrough, who allowed me to leave Buffalo knowing that Zoe and Bertie were in good hands.

# Bibliography

### Primary Sources

#### Archives nationales, Paris

K1219 item 9, n.d. in "Recueil et mémoires aux Etats de Provence" [Mirabeau 1758–60].

Mirabeau Papers in M 780, 783, 784, 785, 790, 791.

M 806 item 2: 187-page notebook, correspondence between Mirabeau and various Provençal notables from March to August 1768.

P2736, Plumitif de la chambre des comptes, 20 February 1772.

P2594, Registre des Chartes, "annoblissement a François Quesnay, l'un des médecins consultans du Roy," folio 29–31, registered 5 April 1754.

V3 192, Prévôté de l'hostel, folio 138, 1727.

Z1a 603, No139. "Arrêt d'enregistrement des lettres de noblessse du Sr. Quesnay, médecin, 5 mars 1755."

Z1a 604, "enquête de noblesse," 25 février 1755.

#### Bibliothèque nationale, Paris

Manuscrits occidentaux, nouvelles acquisitions françaises, No. 3348, folios 218–46, dossier on "Théorie de l'impôt par M. de Mirabeau."

#### Bibliothèque de l'Arsenal, Paris

Fonds Rondel, "Notice biographique sur Antoine Le Blanc de Guillet 1730–1799" par M. Claude Perroud, in *Annales de la Société d'Agriculture, Sciences, Arts et Commerce du Puy*, XXV (Le Puy, 1864).

#### Bibliothèque de l'Institut, Paris

**Condorcet papers**

MS 880–882, include Letters to Turgot.

## Fonds Hennin

MS 1259, Hennin correspondance with Forbonnais.
MS 1266, Hennin Correspondence with Lefebvre de Beauvaray and Butel du Mont.
MS 1268, Hennin correspondance with miscellaneous.
MS 1274, Hennin correspondance with miscellaneous.

*Pierpont Morgan Library, New York*

### Misc. French manuscripts

Quesnay, letter to unidentified physician, 16 January 1755, 4 pages,

*Hagley Museum and Library, Wilmington, Delaware*

### Winterthur Manuscripts, Group 2: Pierre Samuel Du Pont de Nemours papers

W2-5, Letter from Du Pont to Le Trosne, 24 July 1766.
W2-6, Du Pont to Trudaine de Montigny, 20 October 1766.
W2-10, Du Pont letter to Méliand of spring 1767.
W2-17, Du Pont to Abeille n.d. [1768].
W2-18, Du Pont to Voltaire, 10 September 1769.
W2-35, Du Pont, "Fragment d'une lettre à Mr. Turgot du 7 octobre 1774."
W2-36, "Fragment d'une lettre à M. Turgot en date de Varsovie, le 12 octobre 1774."
W2-37, Du Pont to Turgot, 29 October 1774.
W2-38, Du Pont to Quesnay, 18 December 1774.
W2-49, Du Pont to Baudeau, 12 March 1776.
W2-50, Du Pont to the Marquis de Pezay, 12 March 1776.
W2-60, letter from Du Pont to Necker of 25 December 1778.
W2-74, Du Pont to the Marquise de Monnier, 27 October 1779.
W2-101, Du Pont to Malesherbes, 7 April 1781.
W2-122, Du Pont to the Marquis de Saint-Lambert, 8 August 1782.
W2-235, Du Pont, "L'empereur Joseph Second" manuscript.
W2-272, Du Pont to Mirabeau, Paris, 30 January 1787.
W2-288, Du Pont to the comte d'Angiviller, Paris, 13 April 1787.
W2-386, Du Pont to his son Victor, 22 May 1790.
W2-399, Draft of letter to Pétion de Villeneuve, mayor of Paris, Paris, 13 April 1792.
W2-409, Du Pont to his son Victor, 8 January 1794.
W2-418, Du Pont to Victor, 25 July 1794.
W2-425, Du Pont to the marquis de Saint-Lambert, 17 December 1794.
W2-1516, Voltaire to Du Pont, 16 August 1763.
W2-1621, Turgot to Du Pont, 12 February 1771.
W2-1624, Turgot to Du Pont, 13 March 1771.
W2-1626, Turgot to Du Pont, 12 April 1771.
W2-1639, Turgot to Du Pont, Limoges, 29 October 1771.

W2-1642, Turgot to Du Pont, Limoges, 14 July 1772.
W2-1655, Mirabeau to Du Pont, 21 September 1773.
W2-1667, Turgot to Du Pont, 14 March 1774.
W2-1672, Turgot to Du Pont, 21 September 1774.
W2-1928, Du Pont to Mirabeau, 1786.
W2-4571, "Stances irrégulières au sujet de l'Ordonnance qui établit trente-deux régiments de recrues pour tenir lieu de milice" [written for Choiseul 1763].
W2-4579, Du Pont, *Éléments de philosophie économique*, 120-page manuscript [1771–74].
W2-4582, Du Pont to Carl Ludwig of Baden, Paris, 22 January 1772.
W2-4585, Du Pont, "Sallons" in manuscript.
W2-4589, "Projet d'une académie et des universités en Pologne par Du Pont de Nemours" [1774].
W2-4796, Mémoires de Pierre Samuel Du Pont adressés à ses Enfans.
W2-4812, Du Pont poem "Le Colin-Maillard."
W2-5025, Theophilanthropic prayers by Du Pont.
W2-5027, n.d. Du Pont on Theophilanthropy.
W2-5036, Agricultural society memberships, Soissons (4 September 1763).
W2-5037, Orléans (16 November 1754).
W2-5038, from London Society for the Encouragement of the Artss (18 November 1766).
W2-5045, Du Pont passport, 1774.
W2-5046, permission to travel to Poland by the King on 8 July 1774.
W2-5050, letter recalling Du Pont from Poland 19 September 1774.
W2-5075 and W2-5076, first-sword ceremonies for Victor and Irénée Du Pont.
W2-5095, Du Pont "epitaph" written by himself (1778).
W2-5097, Letter from Du Pont to his father.
W2-5098, Du Pont 1814 letter on his "accomplishments."
W2-5678, manuscript of François Quesnay, *Despotisme de la Chine*.
W2-5694, Turgot, "Canevas pour la déclaration du 13 septembre 1774 sur le commerce des grains," 4 pages.

**Winterthur Manuscrpts, Series E (Eleutheria Du Pont Smith transcripts of Du Pont family correspondence)**

Vol. 3, Du Pont correspondance with the Margrave of Baden, p. 119, letter from Carolina Luisa, Margravine of Baden to Du Pont, 22 September 1772 (not in Knies).
Vol. 13, pp. 26–31 Letter from Irénée Du Pont to his brother Victor, from Nemours, dated 18 March 1789 on election to Tiers of Nemours.
Vol. 13, p. 109 Du Pont and son on 10 August 1792.

### Printed Primary Sources

Alembert, Jean Le Rond d', "Eloge de M. Quesnay par M. d'Alembert," *Mercure de France*, XXX (15 November 1778), 145–57.

*Preliminary Discourse to the Encyclopedia of Diderot* (Chicago and London, 1995).
Angiviller, *Mémoires de Charles-Claude Flahaut Comte de la Billarderie d'Angiviller. Notes sur les Mémoires de Marmontel* (Copenhagen, 1933).
Argenson, René Louis de Voyer de Paulmy, marquis d', *Considérations sur le gouvernement ancien et présent de la France* (Amsterdam, 1764).
*Mémoires et Journal inédit du Marquis d'Argenson, Ministre des affaires étrangères sous Louis XV*, 5 vols. (Paris, 1857–1858).
Aulard, François-Alphonse, *La Société des Jacobins, Recueil de documents pour l'histoire du club des Jacobins de Paris*, 6 vols. (Paris, 1889–1897).
Basan, François, *Dictionnaire des graveurs anciens et modernes*, vol. II (Paris, 1789).
Batteux, Charles, *Les beaux-arts réduits à un même principe* (Paris, 1746).
Baudeau, Nicolas, "Chronique secrète de Paris sous le règne de Louis XVI (1774)" in *Revue rétrospective ou Bibliothèque historique*, vol. III (Paris, 1834), I, pp. 29–96, II, pp. 262–96, III, pp. 375–415.
Boerhaave, Hermann, *Boerhaave's Aphorisms: Concerning the Knowledge and Cure of Diseases*, translated from the last edition printed in Latin at Leiden, 1722 (London, 1724).
Boileau-Despréaux, Nicolas, *Traité du sublime ou du merveilleux dans le discours traduit du Grec de Longin* in *Oeuvres diverses du Sieur D\*\*\** (Paris, 1674).
Bonnet, Charles, *La Palingénésie philsophique* (Geneva, 1769).
Bosse, Abraham, *De la manière de graver à l'eau-forte et au burin et de la gravûre en manière noire* (Paris, 1745), edition revised by Charles-Antoine Cochin.
Boulanger, Nicolas-Antoine, *L'Antiquité dévoilée par ses usages*, 3 vols. (Amsterdam, 1766).
Buchez, P. J. B., and P.-C. Roux, *Histoire parlementaire de la Révolution francaise*, 40 vols. (Paris, 1834–1838).
Buffon, Georges Louis Leclerc, comte de, *Correspondance générale*, ed., H. Nadault de Buffon, 2 vols. (Paris, 1885).
Burke, Edmund, *A Philosophical Enquiry into the Origins of our Ideas of the Sublime and Beautiful* (London, 1757).
*Reflections on the Revolution in France* (London, 1790).
Burton, John Hill, *Life and Correspondence of David Hume*, 2 vols. (Edinburgh, 1846).
Chastellux, François-Jean, marquis de, *De la félicité publique ou Considérations sur le sort des hommes dans les différentes époques historiques*, 2 vols. (Amsterdam, 1772).
Condillac, Etienne Bonnot de, *Essai sur l'origine des connaissances humaines* (1746).
*Traité des sensations* (1754).
Condorcet, Marie Jean Antoine Nicolas de Caritat, marquis de, *Esquisse d'un tableau historique des progrès de l'esprit humain* (Paris, 1988).
*Vie de M. Turgot*, in A. Condorcet-O'Connor and M. F. Arago, eds., *Oeuvres de Condorcet*, 12 vols. (Paris, 1847–1849), vol. 5 (Paris, 1847), and *Essai sur la constitution et les fonctions des assemblées provinciales* (1847), vol. 8, pp. 117–659.

Cottin, Paul, *Un Protégé de Bachaumont, Correspondance du marquis d'Eguilles (1745–1748)* (Paris, 1887).
Coudray, Alexandre-Jacques, Chevalier du, *Anecdotes intéressantes et historiques de l'illustre voyageur pendant son séjour à Paris* (Paris, 1777).
Court de Gébelin, Antoine, *Monde Primitif analysé et comparé avec le monde moderne*, 9 vols. (Paris, 1773–1782).
*Plan général et raisonné du Monde Primitif analysé et comparé avec le monde moderne* (Paris, 1773).
Croÿ, Emmanuel, duc de, *Journal inédit du duc de Croÿ, 1718–1784*, 3 vols. (Paris, 1906).
Diderot, Denis, *Salons* in Laurent Versini, ed., Diderot, *Oeuvres*, vol. IV, *Esthétique-Théâtre* (Paris, 1996).
Du Bos, Jean Baptiste, abbé, *Réflexions critiques sur la poësie et sur la peinture* (Paris, 1770 edition).
Du Hausset, Madame, *Mémoires sur Louis XV et Madame de Pompadour* (Paris, 1985).
Du Pont de Nemours, Pierre Samuel, *The Autobiography of Du Pont de Nemours*, translated by Elizabeth Fox-Genovese (Wilmington, Del., 1984).
*De l'origine et des progrès d'une science nouvelle* (London, 1768).
*Lettre de M. Du Pont à M. Pétion, 13 avril 1792* (reprinted in 1796), *Réponse de M. Pétion à M. Dupont*, followed by *Seconde lettre de M. Du Pont à M. Pétion, 27 avril 1792*. In French Revolutionary Pamphlets, Kroch Rare Book Room, Cornell University.
"Lettres sur les salons de 1773, 1777 et 1779 adressées par Du Pont de Nemours à la Margrave Caroline-Louise de Bade," *Archives de l'art français*, nouvelle période, Tome II (1908), pp. 1–123.
*Mémoires sur la vie et les ouvrages de M. Turgot, Ministre d'Etat* (Philadelphia, 1782).
ed., *Oeuvres de M. Turgot, ministre d'état*, 9 vols. (Paris, 1808–11).
*Philosophie de l'univers* (Paris, 1796).
*La Physiocratie ou constitution essentielle du gouvernement le plus avantageux au genre humain* (1767).
*Sur l'exportation et l'importation des grains* (Paris, 1764).
"Sur les assertions du Docteur Gall," from *Publiciste*, 8 pages (1805) in Collection of Pamphlets by Du Pont, Hagley, N* B2019. D815.02.
"Vues sur l'éducation nationale par un cultivateur," 48 pages (Paris, 1794).
*Éphémérides du citoyen ou chronique de l'esprit national* (1765–1766) renamed *Éphémérides du citoyen ou bibliothèque raisonnée des sciences morales et politiques* (1767–1772).
Ermannsdoerffer, B. et al., eds., *Politische Correspondenz Karl Friedrichs von Baden, 1783–1806*, 6 vols. (Heidelberg, 1888).
Fénelon, François de Salignac de la Motte, "Sur l'éloquence" in M. Saucier, ed., *Oeuvres choisies de Fénelon* (Tours, 1859).
*Les aventures de Télémaque* (Paris, 1968).
Forbonnais, François Véron de, *Principes et observations oeconomiques* (Amsterdam, 1767).
Galiani, Ferdinando, *Dialogues sur le commerce des blés* (London, 1770).

Gessner, Salomon, *La mort d'Abel*, translated by Michel Huber [and Jacques Turgot] (Paris, 1760).
Grimm, Melchior, Diderot, Raynal, Meister etc., *Correspondance littéraire, philosophique et critique*, ed., Maurice Tourneux, 16 vols. (Paris, 1877–1882).
Guillaume, M.J. ed., *Procès-verbaux du Comité d'instruction publique de l'assemblée législative* (Paris, 1889).
Haller, Albrecht von, *The correspondence between Albrecht von Haller and Charles Bonnet*, ed., Otto Sonntag (Bern, Stuttgart, Vienna, 1983).
  *Deux mémoires sur la circulation du sang et sur les effets de la saignée fondés sur des expériences faites sur des animaux* (Lausanne, 1756).
Hutcheson, Francis, *An Inquiry into the Original of Our Ideas of Beauty and Virtue* (London, 1725).
Knies, Carl, *Carl Friedrichs von Baden, Brieflicher Verkher mit Mirabeau und Du Pont*, 2 vols. (Heidelberg, 1892).
Lanjuinais, Joseph, *Le Monarque accompli ou prodiges de Bonté, de Savoir et de Sagesse qui font l'éloge de Sa Majesté impériale Joseph II et qui rendent cet Auguste monarque si précieux à l'humanité*, 3 vols. (Lausanne, 1774).
Le Blanc de Guillet Antoine, *Albert Premier ou Adeline, comédie héroique en trois actes, en vers de dix syllabes* (Paris, 1775).
Le Mercier de la Rivière, Pierre-Paul, *L'Heureuse nation ou gouvernement des Féliciens*, 2 vols. (Paris, 1792).
  *L'Intérêt général de l'Etat, ou la liberté du commerce des blés* (Amsterdam, 1770).
  *L'Ordre naturel et essentiel des sociétés politiques* (London, 1767).
Le Trosne, Guillaume-François, *De l'ordre social* (Paris, 1777).
  *De l'administration provinciale et de la réforme de l'impôt* (Basel, 1788).
Linguet, Simon-Nicolas-Henri, *Réponse aux Docteurs modernes ou Apologie pour l'auteur de la théorie des loix et des lettres sur cette théorie, avec la réfutation du système des philosophes économistes*, 3 vols. (Paris, 1771).
Locke, John, *An Essay Concerning Human Understanding* (London, 1690).
Louis, A., ed., *Eloges lus dans les séances publiques de l'Académie royale de chirurgie de 1750 à 1792* (Paris, 1859).
Luynes, Charles Philippe d'Albert de, *Mémoires du duc de Luynes sur la cour de Louis XV (1735–1758)*, edited by L. Dussieux and E. Soulié, 17 vols. (Paris, 1860–1865).
Mably, Gabriel Bonnot de, *Doutes proposés aux philosophes économistes sur l'ordre naturel et essentiel des société politiques* in *Collection Complète des Oeuvres de l'Abbé de Mably*, 15 vols. (Paris, 1794–1795), XI (1795).
Malebranche, Nicolas de, *Oeuvres*, 2 vols. (Paris, 1979).
Marmontel, Jean-François, *Mémoires* (Paris, 1999).
Mercier, Louis Sébastien, *Du Théâtre ou Nouvel Essai sur l'Art dramatique* (Amsterdam, 1773).
Mirabeau, Victor Riquetti, marquis de, *L'Ami des hommes*, 7 vols. (Paris, 1759–1760).
  *Les Devoirs* (Milan, 1780).
  *Les Économiques* (Amsterdam, 1770).
  *Examen des poésies sacrées de M. Lefranc de Pompignan* (Paris, 1755).

*Leçons économiques* (Amsterdam, 1769).
*Lettres sur la législation ou l'ordre dépravé rétablit et perpétué* (Bern, 1775).
*Mémoire concernant l'utilité des Etats provinciaux* (Rome, 1750), in *Objets proposés à l'assemblée des notables par de zélés citoyens. Premier Objet: administrations provinciales* (Paris, 1787).
*Philosophie rurale ou Economie générale de l'agriculture* (Paris, 1763).
*Précis sur l'organisation ou mémoire sur les états provinciaux* in *L'Ami des hommes*, vol. IV (Paris, 1757).
*Théorie de l'impôt* (Paris, 1760).
and François Quesnay, *Traité de la monarchie*, ed., Gino Longhitano (Paris, 1999).

Montesquieu, Charles-Louis de Secondat, baron de, *De l'esprit des lois*, 2 vols. (Paris, 1995).
*Essai sur le goût* (Paris, 1993).
*Lettres persanes* (Paris, 1989).

Nivernais, Louis Jules Mancini-Mazarini, duc de, *Oeuvres posthumes du duc de Nivernois*, ed., François de Neufchâteau, 10 vols. (Paris, 1807).

Oncken, Auguste, *Oeuvres économiques et philosophiques de F. Quesnay fondateur du système physiocratique accompagnées des éloges et d'autres travaux biographiques sur Quesnay par différents auteurs*, 2 vols. (Paris, 1888).

Pitra, "Lettre à Meister sur la fête civique de 1792 en l'honneur de Simonneau, juin 1792" in "Corpus historique étampois," available online. Also in Grimm, Meister, et al., *Correspondence littéraire, philosophique et critique*, ed., Maurice Tourneux (Paris, 1882), XVI, pp. 139–45.

Pompignan, Jean-Jacques Le Franc, marquis de, *Dissertation sur les biens nobles avec des observations sur le vingtième* (Paris, 1758).
*Oeuvres complètes de Jean-Georges Lefranc de Pompignan suivies des Oeuvres religieuses de J.-J. Lefranc marquis de Pompignan*, ed., M. Emery, 2 vols. (Paris, 1855).

Prieur, Jean-Louis, *Tableaux historiques de la Révolution française*, Number 61, 3 June 1792, Musée Carnavalet, Paris.

Prudhomme, Louis-Marie, *Révolutions de Paris*, Douzieme Trimestre, Numéro 152, 2–9 June 1792, "Procession en mémoire du maire d'Etampes," pp. 450–5.

Quesnay, François, *L'art de guérir par la saignée* (Paris, 1736).
*Aspect de la psychologie: l'âme est une substance qui a la propriété de sentir*, 4 pages, [Versailles], 1760. Kress Collection # 9648.
*Despotisme de la Chine* (1767).
*Essai physique sur l'oeconomie animale*, 2 vols. (Paris, 1736), expanded edition, 3 vols. (Paris, 1747).
"Evidence," "Fermiers," "Grains" in d'Alembert and Diderot, eds., *Encyclopédie ou Dictionnaire Raisonné des Sciences, des Arts et des Métiers*, 17 vols. (1751–1772).
"Lettre de M. Alpha, maître-ès-arts, à l'auteur des *Ephémérides* sur le langage de la science économique" in *Ephémérides du citoyen* (October 1767).
*Lettres sur les disputes qui se sont élevées entre les médecins et chirurgiens sur le droit qu'a M. Astruc d'entrer dans ces disputes* (Paris, 1737–1738).

ed., *Mémoires de l'Académie royale de chirurgie*, vol. 1 (Paris, 1743).

"Observations sur le droit naturel des hommes réunis en société," first published in *Journal de l'Agriculture, du Commerce, et des Finances* in September, 1765, republished in *Physiocratie* (1768), I, pp. 1–38.

*Observations sur les effets de la saignée* (Paris, 1730).

*Oeuvres économiques complètes et autres textes*, ed., Christine Théré, Loïc Charles, and Jean-Claude Perrot, 2 vols. (Paris, 2005).

*Recherches critiques et historiques sur les divers états et sur les progrès de la chirurgie en France* (Paris, 1744).

*Traité de la gangrène* (Paris, 1749).

*Traité de la suppuration* (Paris, 1749).

*Traité des effets et de l'usage de la saignée* (Paris, 1750).

*Traité des fièvres continues* (Paris, 1753).

Rousseau, Jean-Jacques, *Correspondance complète de Jean-Jacques Rousseau*, ed., R. A. Leigh 257, vol. XXXIII (Oxford, 1979); vol. XXXV (Oxford, 1980).

*Considérations sur le gouvernement de Pologne et sur sa réformation projetée en avril 1772* in *Du contrat social* (Paris, 1962), pp. 337–417.

*Discours sur l'origine et les fondements de l'inégalité parmi les hommes* (1755) in *Du contrat social* (Paris, 1962), pp. 25–122.

*Essai sur l'origine des langues* (Paris, 1990).

*Lettre à M. D'Alembert*, in *Du contrat social* (Paris, 1962), pp. 123–234.

Say, Jean-Baptiste, *Cours d'économie politique pratique*, vol. V (Brussels, 1833).

Schelle, Gustave ed., *Oeuvres de Turgot et documents le concernant*, 5 vols. (Paris, 1913–1923).

Shaftsbury, Anthony Ashley-Cooper, 3rd earl of, *An Inquiry into Virtue or Merit* in *Characteristics of Men, Manners, Opinions, Times* (London, 1711).

Silhouette, Etienne de, *Mélanges de littérature et de philosophie*, 2 vols. (London, 1742).

Smith, Adam, *An Inquiry into the Nature and Causes of the Wealth of Nations*, ed., Kathryn Sutherland (Oxford, 1993).

Turgot, Anne Robert Jacques, "Eloge de Vincent de Gournay" (1759), in Joel-Thomas Roux and Paul-Marie Romani, eds., *Turgot, Réflexions sur la formation et distribution des richesses* (Paris, 1997), pp. 123–53.

"Lettre de M. Turgot aux Auteurs du *Journal étranger* sur les poésies Erses," *Journal étranger* (September, 1760), 3–16.

*Réflexions sur la formation et la distribution des richesses*, *Ephémérides du citoyen*, vols. XI and XII (1769) and vol. I (1770).

"Tableau philosophique des progrès successifs de l'esprit humain" in Joel-Thomas Ravix and Paul-Marie Romani, Turgot, *Formation et distribution des richesses* (Paris, 1997), pp. 70–94.

Vauvernargues, Luc de Clapier, marquis de, *Oeuvres posthumes et oeuvres inédites de Vauvenargues*, ed., D.-L. Gilbert (Paris, 1857).

*Oeuvres complètes*, Jean-Pierre Jackson, ed. (Paris, 1999).

Véri, Joseph-Alphonse de, *Journal de l'abbé de Véri*, 2 vols. (Mâcon, 1930).

Wille, Johann Georg, *Mémoires et Journal de J.G. Wille, graveur du roi*, ed., Georges Duplessis, 2 vols. (Paris, 1857).

## Secondary Sources

Acke, Daniel, "Les moralistes européens entre 1680 et 1780" in Peter-Eckhard Knabe, Roland Mortier, and François Moureau, eds., *L'aube de la modernité 1680–1760* (Amsterdam and Philadelphia, 2002), pp. 441–69.

*Vauvenargues moraliste, la synthèse impossible de l'idée de nature et de la pensée de la diversité* (Cologne, 1993).

Albertone, Manuela, "Du Pont de Nemours et l'instruction publique pendant la révolution, de la science économique à la formation du citoyen," *Revue française d'histoire des idées politiques*, 20:2 (2004), pp. 353–71.

"Fondements économiques de la réflexion du XVIIIe siècle, Autour de l'homme porteur de droits," *Clio@Themis*, 3 (2010), 25 pages.

Alimento, Antonella, *Réformes fiscales et crises politiques dans la France de Louis XV, de la taille tarifiée au cadastre général* (Brussels, 2008).

"Tra fronda e fisiocrazia: il pensiero di Mirabeau sulle municipalità (1750–1757)," *Annali della Fondazione Luigi Enaudi*, XXII (1986), 97–141.

Ambrosoli, Mauro, *The Wild and the Sown, Botany and Agriculture in Western Europe: 1350–1850* (Cambridge, 1997).

Anderson-Riedel, Susanne, *Creativity and Reproduction: Nineteenth-Century Engraving and the Academy* (Newcastle upon Tyne, 2010).

Antoine, Michel, *Louis XV* (Paris, 1989).

Antognazza, Maria Rosa, *Leibniz, An Intellectual Biography* (Cambridge, 2009).

Arendt, Hannah, *The Origins of Totalitarianism* (New York, 1951).

Azouvi, François, Michel Baridon, and Christine Rolland, "Mouvement des sciences et esthétique(s)," special issue of *Dix-huitième siècle* 31 (1999).

Badinter, Elisabeth, and Robert Badinter, *Condorcet, un intellectuel en politique* (Paris, 1988).

*Les Passions intellectuelles*, vol. I, *Désirs de gloire (1735–1751)* (Paris, 1999).

*Les "Remontrances" de Malesherbes* (Paris, 1978).

Bailey, Colin C., *Patriotic Taste, Collecting Modern Art in Pre-Revolutionary Paris* (New Haven, 2002).

Baker, Keith Michael, *Condorcet, From Natural Philosophy to Social Mathematics* (Chicago, 1975).

"Representation" in Keith Baker, ed., *The French Revolution and the Creation of Modern Political Culture*, vol. I: *The Political Culture of the Old Regime* (Oxford and New York, 1987), pp. 469–92.

Banzhaf, Spencer H., "Productive Nature and the Net Product: Quesnay's Economies Animal and Political," *History of Political Economy* 32:3 (2000), 517–51.

Barrell, John, *The Political Theory of Painting from Reynolds to Hazlitt* (New Haven, 1986).

Barroux, Gilles, *Philosophie, maladie, et médecine au XVIIIe siècle* (Paris, 2008).

Barthes, Roland, *Sur Racine* in *Oeuvres complètes*, 5 vols. (Paris, 2002), II, pp. 53–194.

Barton, H. Arnold, "Gustav III of Sweden and the Enlightenment," *Eighteenth-Century Studies* 6:1 (1972), 1–34.
Beauchamp, Chantal, *Le sang et l'imaginaire médical, histoire de la saignée aux XVIIIe et XIXe siècles* (Paris, 2000).
Beales, Derek, *Enlightenment and Reform in Eighteenth-Century Europe* (London and New York, 2005).
  *Joseph II*, vol. I: *In the Shadow of Maria Theresa, 1741–1780* (Cambridge, 1987).
Becq, Annie, *Genèse de l'esthétique moderne, 1680–1814* (Paris, 1994).
Beer, M., *An Inquiry into Physiocracy* (London, 1939).
Beik, Paul H., *A Judgment of the Old Regime* (New York, 1944)
Belaval, Yvon, *Leibniz critique de Descartes* (Paris, 1960).
Bell, David A., *The Cult of the Nation in France, Inventing Nationalism, 1680–1800* (Cambridge, Mass., 2001).
  *Lawyers and Citizens: The Making of a Political Elite in Old Regime France* (Oxford, 1994).
Bender, John, and Michael Marrinan, *The Culture of Diagram* (Stanford, 2010).
Bénézit, E., *Dictionnaire critique et documentaire des Peintres, Sculpteurs, Dessinateurs, et Graveurs*, vol. VII (Librairie Grund, 1966).
Bénichou, Paul, *Morales du grand siècle* (Paris, 1948).
  *Le sacre de l'écrivain, 1750–1830* (Paris, 1973).
Béraud Alain, and Gilbert Faccarello eds., *Nouvelle histoire de la pensée économique*, vol. I (Paris, 1992).
Bertrand, Aliénor, ed., *Condillac, l'origine du langage* (Paris, 2002).
Billington, James H., *Fire in the Minds of Men* (New Brunswick, N.J., 1999).
Biver, Marie-Louise, *Fêtes révolutionnaires à Paris* (Paris, 1979).
Blanchard, Anne, Henri Michel, and Elie Pélaquier, eds., *Les assemblées d'Etats dans la France méridionale à l'époque moderne* (Montpellier, 1995).
Blaufarb, Rafe, "Noble Tax Exemption and the Long-Term Origins of the French Revolution: The Example of Provence, 1530s to 1789" in Jay M. Smith, ed., *The French Nobility in the Eighteenth Century* (University Park, 2006), pp. 141–65.
Blaug, Mark, "Is There Really Progress in Economics?" in Stephan Boehm, Christian Gehrke, Heinz D. Kurtz et al., eds., *Is There Progress in Economics? Knowledge, Truth and the History of Economic Thought* (Cheltenham, UK, and Northampton, Mass., 2002), pp. 21–41.
Blondel, Nicole, and Tamara Préaud, *La manufacture royale de Sèvres, parcours du blanc à l'or* (Charenton, 1996).
Bolton, Martha Brandt, "The Taxonomy of Ideas in Locke's *Essay*" in Lex Newman, ed., *The Cambridge Companion to Locke's* Essay *Concerning Human Understanding* (Cambridge, 2007), pp. 67–100.
Bonnet, Jean-Claude, "La mort de Simonneau" in Jean Nicolas, ed., *Mouvements populaires et conscience sociale* (Paris, 1985), pp. 671–6.
  *Naissance du Panthéon, Essai sur le culte des grands hommes* (Paris, 1998).
Bouloiseau, Marc, *Bourgeoisie et Révolution, Les Du Pont de Nemours (1788–1799)* (Paris, 1972).
Bourde, André J., *Agronomie et agronomes en France au XVIIIe siècle*, 3 vols. (Paris, 1967).

Bouveresse, Jacques, *Essais V: Descartes, Leibniz, Kant* (Paris, 2005).
Boylan, Thomas A., and Paschal F. O'Gorman, *Beyond Rhetoric and Realism in Economics: Towards a Reformulation of Economic Methodology* (London and New York, 1995).
Braun, Theodore E. D., *Un ennemi de Voltaire, Le Franc de Pompignan* (Paris, 1972).
Braun, Theodore E. D., and Guillaume Robichez, eds., *Lumières voilées. Oeuvres choisies d'un magistrat chrétien du XVIIIe siècle* (Saint-Etienne, 2007).
Brewer, Anthony, "Cantillon, Quesnay, and the *Tableau Economique*," Discussion Paper No. 05/577, October 2005, Department of Economics, University of Bristol.
Brewer, David, *The Enlightenment Past, Reconstructing Eighteenth-Century French Thought* (Cambridge, 2008).
Brewer, John, *The Pleasures of the Imagination: English Culture in the Eighteenth Century* (Chicago, 2000).
Brian, Eric, *La mesure de l'Etat, administrateurs et géomètres au XVIIIe siècle* (Paris, 1994).
Broadie, Alexander, "Art and Aesthetic Theory" in Alexander Broadie, ed., *The Cambridge Companion to the Scottish Enlightenment* (Cambridge, 2003), pp. 280–97.
  "The Human Mind and Its Powers" in Alexander Broadie, ed., *The Cambridge Companion to the Scottish Enlightenment* (Cambridge, 2003), pp. 60–78.
Brockliss, Laurence, *French Higher Education in the Seventeenth and Eighteenth Centuries, A Cultural History* (Oxford, 1987).
Brockliss, Laurence, and Colin Jones, *The Medical World of Early Modern France* (Oxford, 1997).
Broman, Thomas H., "The Medical Sciences" in Roy Porter, ed., *The Cambridge History of Science*, vol. 4, *The Eighteenth Century* (Cambridge, 2003), pp. 463–84.
Brown, Gregory, *A Field of Honor: Writers, Court Culture, and Public Theater in French Literary Life from Racine to the Revolution* (New York, 2005).
Brunet, Marcelle, and Tamara Préaud, *Sèvres des origines à nos jours* (Fribourg, 1978).
Bryan, Michael, *Dictionary of Painters and Engravers*, vol. II (London, 1889).
Bryson, Norman, *Word and Image, French Painting of the Ancien Régime* (Cambridge, 1981).
Calhoun, Craig J., ed., *Habermas and the Public Sphere* (Cambridge, Mass., 1993).
Caradonna, Jeremy L, *The Enlightenment in Question, Academic Prize Competitions* (concours académiques) *and the Francophone Republic of Letters, 1670–1794* (PhD diss. Johns Hopkins, 2007).
Cartelier, Jean, ed., *Quesnay, Physiocratie, Droit naturel, Tableau économique et autres textes* (Paris, 1991).
Carthart, Michael C., *The Science of Culture in Enlightenment Germany* (Cambridge, Mass., 2007).
Cassirer, Ernst, *The Philosophy of the Enlightenment* (Princeton, 1951).
Chanier, P., "Le Dilemme de Mirabeau: Cantillon ou Quesnay?" in Albert Soboul, ed., *Les Mirabeau et leur temps, Actes du Colloque d'Aix-en-Provence* (Paris, 1968), pp. 23–35.

Charles, Loïc, "The Tableau économique as Rational Recreation," *History of Political Economy*, 36:3 (2004), 445–74.
  "The Visual History of the Tableau économique," *The European Journal of the History of Economic Thought*, 10:4 (2003), 527–50.
Charles, Loïc, and Philippe Steiner, "Entre Montesquieu et Rousseau. La Physiocratie parmi les origines intellectuelles de la Révolution française," *Études Jean-Jacques Rousseau*, 11 (1999), 83–159.
Charlton, Donald G., *New Images of the Natural in France* (Cambridge, 1984).
Charrak, André, *Contingence et nécessité des lois de la nature au XVIIIe siècle* (Paris, 2006).
  *Empirisme et métaphysique, L'Essai sur les Origines des connaissances humaines de Condillac* (Paris, 2003).
Chartier, Roger, *The Cultural Origins of the French Revolution* (Durham and London, 1991).
Chassagne, Anne, *La bibliothèque de l'Académie royale des sciences au XVIIIe siècle* (Paris, 2007).
Chaussinand-Nogaret, Guy, *Comment peut-on être intellectuel au siècle des lumières?* (Paris, 2011).
Cheney, Paul, *Revolutionary Commerce, Globalization and the French Monarchy* (Cambridge, Mass., 2010).
Chevalier, Claire, *L'Invention d'une origine, Traduire Eschyle en France de Lefranc de Pompignan à Mazon: le Prométhée enchaîné* (Paris, 2007).
Chevallier, Pierre, *Journal de l'Assemblée des Notables de 1787* (Paris, 1960).
Christenten, Paul, "Fire, Motion and Productivity: The Proto-energetics of Nature and Economy in François Quesnay" in Philip Mirowsky, ed., *Natural Images in Economic Thought, Markets Read in Tooth and Claw* (Cambridge, 1994), pp. 249–88.
Citton, Yves, *Portrait de l'économiste en physiocrate: Critique littéraire de l'économie politique* (Paris, 2000).
Clayton, Timothy, *The English Print 1688–1802* (New Haven and London, 1997).
Collins, James B., *The State in Early Modern France* (Cambridge, 1995).
Culoma, Michel, *La Religion civile de Rousseau à Robespierre* (Paris, 2010).
Courboin, François, and Marcel Roux, *La Gravure française, Essai de bibliographie* (Paris, 1927).
Courtine, Jean-Jacques, and Claudine Haroche, *Histoire du visage* (Paris, 1988).
Crombie, A. C., *Styles in Scientific Thinking in the European Tradition*, 3 vols. (London, 1994).
Crow, Thomas E., *Painters and Public Life in Eighteenth-Century Paris* (New Haven and London, 1985).
Cubells, Monique, *La Provence des Lumières, Les parlementaires d'Aix au 18ème siècle* (Paris, 1984).
Daire, Eugène, ed., *Economistes financiers du XVIIIe siècle* (Paris, 1843).
  ed., *Physiocrates*, 2 vols. (Paris, 1846).
  ed., *Oeuvres de Turgot*, 2 vols. (Paris, 1844).
Darnton, Robert, "An Early Information Society: News and the Media in Eighteenth-Century France," *The American Historical Review* 105:1 (2000), 1–35.

*The Great Cat Massacre and Other Episodes in French Cultural History* (New York, 1985).
  "The High Enlightenment and the Low-Life of Literature in Pre-Revolutionary France," *Past and Present* 51 (1971), 81–115.
  *Mesmerism and the End of Enlightenment in France* (New York, 1970).
Daston, Lorraine, ed., *Biographies of Scientific Objects* (Chicago and London, 2000).
  "Fear and Loathing of the Imagination in Science" in Peter Galison, Stephen R. Graubard, and Everett Mendelsohn, eds., *Science in Culture* (New Brunswick, 2001), pp. 73–95.
  "On Scientific Observation," *Isis* 99 (2008), 97–110.
Daumas, Maurice, and René Tresse, "La description des arts et métiers de l'académie des sciences et le sort de ses planches gravées en taille-douce," *Revue d'histoire des sciences et de leurs applications*, 7 (1954), 163–71.
Declercq, Gilles, "La rhétorique classique entre évidence et sublime (1650–1675)" in Marc Fumaroli, ed., *Histoire de la rhétorique moderne 1450–1950* (Paris, 1999), pp. 629–706.
de Dijn, Annelien, *French Political Thought From Montesquieu to Tocqueville, Liberty in a Levelled Society?* (Cambridge, 2008).
Dear, Peter, *Discipline and Experience, The Mathematical Way in the Scientific Revolution* (Chicago, 1995).
Delmas, Bernard, Thierry Demals, and Philippe Steiner, *La diffusion internationale de la physiocratie (XVIIIe–XIXe)* (Grenoble, 1995).
Demeulenaere-Douyère, Christiane, and David J. Sturdy, *L'enquête du Régent, 1716–1718, Sciences, techniques et politique dans la France pré-industrielle* (Paris, 2008).
Didier, Béatrice, "La fête champêtre dans quelques romans de la fin du XVIIIe siècle (de Rousseau à Senancour)" in Jean Ehrard and Paul Viallaneix, eds., *Les Fêtes de la Révolution, Colloque de Clermont-Ferrand (juin 1974)* (Paris, 1977), pp. 63–72.
Diom, Marie-Pierre, *Emmanuel de Croÿ (1718–1784) itinéraire intellectuel et réussite nobiliaire au siècle des lumières* (Brussels, 1987).
Dowd, David Lloyd, *Pageant-Master of the Republic, Jacques-Louis David and the French Revolution* (Lincoln, Neb., 1948).
Doyle, William, *The Oxford History of the French Revolution*, 2nd edition (Oxford, 2002).
Droixhe, Daniel, *La linguistique et l'appel de l'histoire (1600–1800), Rationalisme et révolutions positivistes* (Geneva and Paris, 1978).
Duffo, Fr.-Albert, *J-J Lefranc, marquis de Pompignan, poète et magistrat (1709–1784)* (Paris, 1913).
Dumouchel, Daniel, "Le problème de Du Bos et l'affect compatissant: l'esthétique du XVIIIe siècle à l'épreuve du paradoxe tragique" in Thierry Belleguic et al., ed., *Les Discours de la sympathie, Enquête sur une notion de l'âge classique à la modernité* (Quebec, 2007), pp. 473–95.
Duscheneau, François, *Leibniz et la méthode de la science* (Paris, 1993).
Edelstein, Dan, *The Enlightenment: A Genealogy* (Chicago, 2010).
  *The Terror of Natural Right, Republicanism, the Cult of Nature, & the French Revolution* (Chicago, 2009).

Egret, Jean, *The French Prerevolution 1787–1788*, trans. Wesley D. Camp (Chicago and London, 1977).
Ehrard, Jean, "'L'Ami des hommes,' Paris et la capitale du royaume," in Albert Soboul, ed., *Les Mirabeau et leur temps, Actes du Colloque d'Aix-en-Provence* (Paris, 1968), pp. 37–43.
*L'Idée de nature en France dans la première partie du XVIIIe siècle* (Paris, 1963).
"Les Lumières et la fête" in Jean Ehrard and Paul Viallaneix, eds., *Les Fêtes de la Révolution, Colloque de Clermont-Ferrand (juin 1974)* (Paris, 1977), pp. 27–44.
Eltis, Walter, "Le rejet de Condillac par les physiocrates: une occasion manquée" in B. Delmas, T. Demals, and Ph. Steiner, eds., *La diffusion internationale de la physiocratie (XVIIIe–XIXe siècles)* (Grenoble, 1995), pp. 177–93.
Emmanuelli, François-Xavier, "Les assemblées provinciales en Provence et en comtat venaissin aux XVIIe et XVIIIe siècles" in Anne Blanchard, Henri Michel, and Elie Pélaquier, eds., *Les assemblées d'Etats dans la France méridionale à l'époque moderne* (Montpellier, 1995), pp. 91–105.
"Réflexion sur les Etats Provinciaux au XVIIIe siècle: Provence, Comtat Venaissin, Corse" in *Parliaments, Estates and Representation* 16 (1996), 131–9.
Eriksen, Sven, and Geoffrey de Bellaigue, *Sèvres Porcelain. Vincennes and Sèvres 1740–1800* (London, 1987).
[Association Etampes-Histoire], *Étampes en Révolution, 1789–1799* (Le-Mée-sur-Seine, 1989).
Faccarello, Gilbert, "Le legs de Turgot. Aspects de l'économie sensualiste de Condorcet à Roederer" in Faccarello and Ph. Steiner, eds., *La pensée économique pendant la Révolution française* (Grenoble, 1991), pp. 67–107.
Farge, Arlette, and Michel Foucault, *Le désordre des familles. Lettres de cachet des archives de la Bastille au XVIIIe siècle* (Paris, 1982).
Faure, Edgar, *La disgrâce de Turgot* (Paris, 1961).
Félix, Joël, *Finances et politique au siècle des Lumières, Le ministère L'Averdy 1763–1768* (Paris, 1999).
Ferguson, Kitty, *The Music of Pythagoras* (New York, 2008).
Ferret, Olivier, *La Fureur de nuire: échanges pamphlétaires entre philosophes et antiphilosophes (1750–1770)* (Oxford, 2007).
Fitzsimmons, Michael, *The Night the Old Regime Ended: August 4, 1789, and the French Revolution* (University Park, 2003).
Fleury, Cynthia, *Métaphysique de l'imagination* (Paris, 2000).
Fontaine, André, *Les doctrines d'art en France, peintres, amateurs, critiques de Poussin à Diderot* (Geneva, 1989).
Ford, Brian J., "Scientific Illustration in the Eighteenth Century" in Roy Porter, ed., *Eighteenth-Century Science*, vol. 4 (Cambridge, 2003), pp. 561–83.
Foucault, Michel, *Les mots et les choses, une archéologie des sciences humaines* (Paris, 1966).
Fox-Genovese, Elizabeth, *The Origins of Physiocracy* (Ithaca, 1976).
Fox-Genovese, Elizabeth, trans., *The Autobiography of Pierre Samuel Du Pont de Nemours* with introduction and notes (Wilmington, 1984).

France, Peter, "Lumières, politesse, et énergie (1750–1775)" in Marc Fumaroli, ed., *Histoire de la rhétorique dans l'Europe moderne 1450–1950* (Paris, 1999), pp. 945–99.
*The French Renaissance in Prints from the Bibliothèque nationale de France* (Los Angeles and London, 1994).
Fumaroli, Marc, *Héros et orateurs: Rhétorique et dramaturgie cornélienne* (Paris, 1996).
*La Querelle des Anciens et des Modernes* (Paris, 2001).
Furet, François, "L'Ancien régime et la Révolution" in Pierre Nora, ed., *Lieux de mémoires*, III (Paris, 1992), reproduced in *La Révolution française* (Paris, 2007), pp. 828–54.
*La Révolution de Turgot à Jules Ferry* (Paris, 1988).
*Penser la Révolution française* (Paris, 1978).
Furet, François, and Jacques Ozouf, *Lire et écrire: l'alphabétisation des Français de Calvin à Jules Ferry*, 2 vols. (Paris, 1977).
Galison, Peter, Stephen R. Graubard, and Everett Mendelsohm, *Science in Culture* (New Brunswick and London, 2001).
Gardey, F., "Quelques planches des Descriptions des Arts et Métiers de l'Académie royale des sciences au Cabinet des Estampes," *Nouvelles de l'estampe* 5–6 (1964), 166–9.
Garrigues, Frédéric, "Trois mille bouches à nourrir" in Joël Cornette, ed., *Versailles, le pouvoir de la pierre* (Paris, 2006), pp. 207–15.
Gaukroger, Stephen, *Descartes' System of Natural Philosophy* (Cambridge, 2002).
Gauthier, Florence, "Le Mercier de la Rivière et les colonies d'Amérique," *Revue française d'histoire des idées politiques*, 20:2 (2004), 261–83.
Gelfand, Toby, *Professionalizing Modern Medicine, Paris Surgeons and Medical Science and Institutions in the 18th Century* (Westport, Conn. and London, 1980).
Gérome, Noëlle, "La tradition politique des fêtes: interprétation et appropriation" in Alain Corbin, Noëlle Gérome, and Danielle Tartakowsky, eds., *Les Usages politiques des fêtes aux XIXe–XXe siècles* (Paris, 1994), pp. 15–23.
Gherke, Christian, and Heinz D. Kurz, "Karl Marx on Physiocracy," *The European Journal of the History of Economic Thought* 2:1 (1995), 53–90.
Gillespie, Stuart, "Translation and Canon-Formation" in Stuart Gillespie and David Hopkins, eds., *The Oxford History of Literary Translation in English*, vol. 3: *1660–1790* (Oxford, 2005), pp. 9–20.
Gillespie, Stuart, and Robin Sowerby, "Translation and Literary Innovation" in Stuart Gillespie and David Hopkins, eds., *The Oxford History of Literary Translation in English*, vol. 3: *1660–1790* (Oxford, 2005), pp. 21–37.
Gillispie, Charles, *Science and Polity in France at the End of the Old Regime* (Princeton, 1980).
Gojosso, Eric, "Le Mercier de la Rivière et l'établissement d'une hiérarchie normative. Entre droit nature et droit positif," *Revue Française d'histoire des idées politiques*, 20:2 (2004), 285–305.
Goldstein, Jan, *The Post-Revolutionary Self, Politics and Psyche in France, 1750–1850* (Cambridge, Mass., 2005).

Goodman, Dena, *The Republic of Letters, A Cultural History of the French Enlightenment* (Ithaca, 1994).
Goulemot, Jean-Marie, *Le Règne de l'histoire, Discours historiques et révolutions XVIIe et XVIIIe siècles* (Paris, 1996).
Grange, Henri, "La Reveillière-Lépeaux, théoricien de la fête nationale (1797)" in Jean Ehrard and Paul Viallaneix eds., *Les Fêtes de la Révolution, Colloque de Clermont-Ferrand (juin 1974)* (Paris, 1977), pp. 493–502.
Gregory, Richard L., *Eye and Brain, The Psychology of Seeing*, 5th edition (Princeton, 1997).
Grell, Chantal, and Christian Michel, eds., *Primitivisme et mythes des origines dans la France des Lumières 1680–1820* (Paris, 1989).
Grenier, Jean-Yves, Claude Grignon, and Pierre-Michel Menger, *Le Modèle et le récit* (Paris, 2001).
Grmek, Mirko D., ed., *Histoire de la pensée médicale en Occident*, vol. 2: *De la Renaissance aux Lumières* (Paris, 1997).
Groenewengen, Peter D., "From Prominent Physician to Major Economist. Some Reflections on Quesnay's Switch to Economics in the 1750s" in Peter D. Groenewengen, ed., *Physicians and Political Economy: Six Studies of the Work of Doctor-Economists* (London and New York, 2001), pp. 93–115.
Graver, Margaret R., *Stoicism and Emotion* (Chicago, 2007).
Gruder, Vivian, *The Notables and the Nation: The Political Schooling of the French, 1787–1788* (Cambridge, Mass., 2007).
Guardiola, Pascal Torres, "Remarques sur la suite d'estampes gravées par madame la marquise de Pompadour d'après les pièces gravées par Jacques Guay" in Xavier Salmon, ed., *Madame de Pompadour et les arts* (Paris, 2002), pp. 215–36.
Gueniffey, Patrice, *La politique de la Terreur, Essai sur la violence révolutionnaire 1789–1794* (Paris, 2000).
Guéry, Alain, "Principe monarchique ou roi très chrétien? Les funérailles des rois de France," *Revue de Synthèse*, CXII: 3–4 (1991), 443–54.
Guibal, Georges, *Mirabeau et la Provence*, 2 vols. (Paris, 1901).
Guichard, Charlotte, *Les Amateurs d'art à Paris au XVIIIe siècle* (Paris, 2008).
Guyer, Paul, "The Origins of Modern Aesthetics: 1711–35" in Peter Kivy, ed., *Blackwell Guide to Aesthetics* (Oxford, 2004), pp. 15–44.
Habermas, Jürgen, *The Structural Transformation of the Public Sphere* (Cambridge, Mass., 1991).
Hacking, Ian, *The Emergence of Probability* (Cambridge, 1975).
  "Leibniz and Descartes: Proof and Eternal Truths" in *Historical Ontology* (Cambridge, Mass., 2002), pp. 200–13.
  *The Taming of Chance* (Cambridge, 1966).
Hahn, Roger, *The Anatomy of a Scientific Institution, The Paris Academy of Sciences, 1666–1803* (Berkeley and Los Angeles, 1971).
Hallyn, Fernand, "Dialectique et rhétorique devant la 'nouvelle science' du XVIIe siècle" in Marc Fumaroli, ed., *Histoire de la rhétorique dans l'Europe moderne 1450–1950* (Paris, 1999), pp. 601–28.
Hamon, Philippe, "Descartes, Newton et l'intelligibilité de la nature" in Pierre Wagner, ed., *Les philosophes et la science* (Paris, 2002), pp. 110–65.

Hardman, John, *Overture to Revolution, The 1787 Assembly of Notables and the Crisis of France's Old Regime* (Oxford, 2010).
Harris, Robert D., *Necker and the Revolution of 1789* (Lanham, Md., 1986).
Havelange, Carl, *De l'oeil et du monde: Une histoire du regard au seuil de la modernité* (Fayard, 1998).
Hecht, Jacqueline, "La Vie de François Quesnay" in Jacqueline Hecht, ed., *François Quesnay et la Physiocratie* 2 vols. (Paris, 1958), I, pp. 211–94, reproduced in Christine Théré, Loïc Charles and Jean-Claude Perrot, eds., *François Quesnay, Oeuvres économiques complètes et autres textes* (Paris, 2005), II, pp. 1331–420.
Henry, Gilles, *Mirabeau père, 5 octobre 1715–11 juillet 1789* (Paris, 1989).
Hirschmann, Albert O., *The Passions and the Interests* (Princeton, 1977).
Hobson, Marian, *The Object of Art. The Theory of Illusion in Eighteenth-Century France* (Cambridge, 1982).
Hochstrasser, T. J., "Physiocracy and the Politics of *Laissez-Faire*" in Mark Goldie and Robert Wokler, eds., *The Cambridge History of Eighteenth-Century Political Thought* (Cambridge, 2006), pp. 419–42.
Holmes, Richard, *The Age of Wonder: The Romantic Generation and the Discovery of the Beauty and Terror in Science* (New York, 2010).
Hont, Istvan, *Jealousy of Trade, International Competition and the Nation-State in Historical Perspective* (Cambridge, Mass., 2005).
Hours, Bernard, *Louis XV et sa cour* (Paris, 1995).
Huard, Georges, "Les planches de l'Encyclopédie et celles de la Description des arts et métiers de l'académie des sciences," *Revue d'histoire des sciences et de leur applications*, 4 (1951), 238–49.
Hudson, Nicholas, "Theories of Language" in H. B. Nisbet and Claude Rawson, eds., *The Cambridge History of Literary Criticism*, vol. IV: *The Eighteenth Century* (Cambridge, 2005), pp. 335–64.
Hunt, Lynn, *Politics, Culture, and Class in the French Revolution* (Berkeley, 1984).
Israel, Jonathan, *A Revolution of the Mind: Radical Enlightenment and the Intellectual Origins of Modern Democracy* (Princeton, 2009).
Jacob, Margaret C., "The Mental Landscape of the Public Sphere: A European Perspective," *Eighteenth-Century Studies* 28 (1994), 95–113.
Jacques, Catherine, "Pratiques mondaines au travers de textes inédits" les "Assemblées économiques du Marquis de Mirabeau (1770–1777)," paper presented at the international conference on Quesnay, Versailles, 1994.
James, Susan, *Passion and Action: The Emotions in Seventeenth-Century Philosophy* (Oxford, 1997).
Johnstone, Paul H., "The Rural Socrates," *Journal of the History of Ideas* 5 (1944), 151–75.
Jolley, Nicholas, *Leibniz and Locke: A Study of the New Essays on Human Understanding* (Oxford, 1984).
Jolley, Nicholas, ed., *The Cambridge Companion to Leibniz* (Cambridge, 1995).
Jones, Colin, *Madame de Pompadour, Images of a Mistress* (London, 2002).
Jones, Peter, *Liberty and Locality in Revolutionary France, Six Villages Compared, 1760–1820* (Cambridge, 2003).

Kaiser, Thomas E., "The Abbé de Saint-Pierre, Public Opinion, and the Reconstitution of the French Monarchy," *Journal of Modern History*, 55 (1983), 618-43.
  "Louis *le Bien-Aimé* and the Rhetoric of the Royal Body" in Sara E. Melzer and Kathryn Norberg, eds., *From the Royal to the Republican Body* (Berkeley, Los Angeles, London, 1998), pp. 131-61.
  "Rhetoric in the Service of the King: The abbé Du Bos and the Concept of Public Judgment," *Eighteenth-Century Studies*, 23:2 (1989-90), 182-99.
  and Dale K. Van Kley, eds., *From Deficit to Deluge, the Origins of the French Revolution* (Stanford, 2011).
Kaplan, Steven L., *La Bagarre, Galiani's "Lost" Parody* (The Hague, 1979).
  *Bread, Politics and Political Economy in the Reign of Louis XV*, 2 vols. (The Hague, 1976).
  *Farewell Revolution: The Historians' Feud, France, 1789/1989* (Ithaca, 1996).
  *La fin des corporations* (Paris, 2001).
Kerslake, Lawrence, *Essays on the Sublime: Analyses of French Writings on the Sublime from Boileau to La Harpe* (Bern and New York, 2000).
Kertzer, Richard I., *Ritual, Politics, and Power* (New Haven, 1988).
Kessler, Amalia D., *A Revolution in Commerce, The Parisian Merchant Court and the Rise of Commercial Society on Eighteenth-Century France* (New Haven, 2007).
Koselleck, Reinhart, *Critique and Crisis: Enlightenment and the Pathogenesis of Modern Society* (Cambridge, Mass., 1988).
Kubota, Akiteru, "Quesnay, disciple de Malebranche" in Jacqueline Hecht, ed., *François Quesnay et la Physiocratie*, 2 vols. (Paris, 1958), I, pp. 69-96.
Kwass, Michael, "Consumption and the World of Ideas: Consumer Revolution and the Moral Economy of the Marquis de Mirabeau," *Eighteenth-Century Studies* 37:2 (2004), 187-213.
  "Economies of Consumption: Political Economy and Noble Display in Eighteenth-Century France" in Jay M. Smith, ed., *The French Nobility in the Eighteenth Century, Reassessments and New Approaches* (University Park, Pa., 2006), pp. 19-41.
  *Privilege and the Politics of Taxation in Eighteenth-Century France. Liberté, Egalité, Fiscalité* (Cambridge, 2000).
Lambert, Susan, *The Image Multiplied, Five Centuries of Printed Reproductions of Paintings and Drawings* (New York, 1987).
Larguier, Gilbert, "Normes, production et évolution des compoix terriens en Languedoc XVIe-XVIIIe siècles" in Mireille Touzery, ed., *De l'estime au cadastre en Europe, L'époque moderne* (Paris, 2007), pp. 339-72.
Larrère, Catherine, "L'arithmétique des physiocrates: la mesure de l'évidence," *Histoire et mesure* 7:1 (1992), 5-24.
  *L'invention de l'économie au XVIIIe siècle. Du droit naturel à la physiocratie* (Paris, 1992).
  "Montesquieu's Paradoxical Economics," The Gimon Conference on French Political Economy 1650-1848, Stanford University, April 2004.
Laurent, Ch., *Les voyages en Bretagne du Chevalier de Mirabeau, 1758-1760* (Mayenne, 1983).

Lebem, Ulrich, *Object Design in the Age of Enlightenment: The History of the Royal Free Drawing School in Paris* (Los Angeles, 2004).
Le Blanc, Charles, *Manuel de l'amateur d'estampes* (Paris, 1971).
Ledbury, Mark, "Imagining the *Salon*: Mapping Art Criticism in the Eighteenth Century" in Jonathan Mallison, ed., *The Eighteenth Century Now: Boundaries and Perspectives*, in *Studies on Voltaire and the Eighteenth Century* (Oxford, 2005), 10, pp. 205–19.
Legay, Marie-Laure, "L'état, les pouvoirs intermédiaires et la réforme cadastrale dans la France du XVIIIe siècle" in Mireille Touzery, ed., *De l'estime au cadastre en Europe: l'époque moderne* (Paris, 2007), pp. 373–89.
  *Les états provinciaux dans la construction de l'état moderne* (Geneva, 2001).
Lennon, Thomas M., "Locke on Ideas and Representation" in Lex Newman, ed., *The Cambridge Companion to Locke's* Essay Concerning Human Understanding (Cambridge, 2007), pp. 231–57.
  "Malebranche and Method" in Steven Nadler, ed., *The Cambridge Companion to Malebranche* (Cambridge, 2000), pp. 8–30.
Leroy, Christian, *La poésie en prose française du XVIIe siècle à nos jours* (Paris, 2001).
Lever, Evelyn, *Madame de Pompadour* (Paris, 2000).
Lever, Maurice, *Théâtre et Lumières: Les Spectacles de Paris au XVIIIe siècle* (Paris, 2001).
Lilti, Antoine, *Le monde des salons, sociabilité et mondanité à Paris au XVIIIe siècle* (Paris, 2005).
Linton, Marisa, *The Politics of Virtue in Enlightenment France* (New York, 2001).
Loménie, Louis de, *La comtesse de Rochefort et ses amis. Etude sur les moeurs en France au XVIIIe siècle* (Paris, 1870).
  *Les Mirabeau, nouvelles études sur la société française au XVIIIe siècle*, 2 vols. (Paris, 1889).
Lorin, P., "François Quesnay" in *Mémoires de la Société archéologique de Rambouillet*, XIV (Versailles, 1900), pp. 63–236.
Losonsky, Michael, "Language, Meaning, and Mind in Locke's *Essay*" in Lex Newman, ed., *The Cambridge Companion to Locke's* Essay Concerning Human Understanding (Cambridge, 2007), pp. 286–312.
Lothe, José, "Les livres illustrés par Abraham Bosse" in Sophie Join-Lambert and Maxime Préaud, *Abraham Bosse, savant graveur, Tours vers 1604–1676* (Paris, 2004), pp. 46–7.
Lucas de Montigny, Gabriel, ed., *Mémoires biographiques, littéraires et politiques de Mirabeau écrits par lui-même, par son père, son oncle et son fils adoptif*, 8 vols. (Paris, 1834–1835).
Lunel, Alexandre, *La Maison médicale du roi, XVIe–XVIIIe siècles, le pouvoir royal et les professions de santé* (Paris, 2008).
Marion, Marcel, *Histoire financière de la France depuis 1715*, 2 vols. (Paris, 1914).
  *Machault d'Arnouville, Etude sur l'histoire du contrôle général des finances de 1749 à 1754* (Paris, 1891).

Mariot, Nicolas, "Qu'est-ce qu'un 'enthousiasme civique'? Sur l'historiographie des fêtes politiques en France après 1789," *Annales Histoire, Sciences Sociales* 63:1 (2008), 113–39.

Martin, Henri-Jacques, *The History and Power of Printing* (Chicago, 1994).

Martin, Thierry, ed., *Arithmétique politique dans la France du XVIIIe siècle* (Paris, 2003).

Marx, Karl, *Theories of Surplus Value* in *Economic Manuscript of 1861–63, Karl Marx and Frederick Engels, Collected Works*, vol. 31 (New York, 1989).

Mathiez, Albert, *La Théophilanthropie et le culte décadaire. Essai sur l'histoire religieuse de la Révolution, 1796–1801* (Paris, 1904).

Maurion de Laroche, "Notice sur François Quesnay" in *Mémoires et documents publiés par la société archéologique de Rambouillet*, vol. 18 (1887–1888), 93–102.

Mauzi, Robert, *L'Idée du bonheur dans la littérature et la pensée française au XVIIIe siècle* (Paris, 1994).

Mayr, Otto, *Authority, Liberty, and Automatic Machinery in Early Modern Europe* (Baltimore, 1986).

McClellan III, James E., *Specialist Control: The Publications Committee of the Académie Royale des Sciences (Paris) 1700–1793* (Philadelphia, 2003).

McCloskey, Deirdre N., *The Rhetoric of Economics* (Madison, 1998).

McCorrmick, Ted, *William Petty and the Ambitions of Political Arithmetic* (Oxford, 2010).

McMahon, Darrin M., *Happiness, A History* (New York, 2006).

Meek, Ronald L., *The Economics of Physiocracy* (London, 1962).

"The Interpretation of the Tableau économique," *Economica* NS XXVII (November, 1960), 322–47.

Mercer, Christa, and R. C. Sleigh, Jr., "Metaphysics: The Early Period to the Discourse on Metaphysics" in Nicholas Jolley, ed., *The Cambridge Companion to Leibniz* (Cambridge, 1995), pp. 67–123.

Meyer, Michel, *Questionnement et historicité* (Paris, 2000).

Mercier-Faivre, Anne-Marie, *Un supplément à "L'Encyclopédie": Le "Monde primitif" d'Antoine Court de Gébelin, suivi d'une édition du "Génie allégorique et symbolique de l'Antiquité" extrait du "Monde primitif"* (Paris, 1999).

Meuvret, Jean, *Le Problème des subsistances à l'époque de Louis XIV*, 6 vols. (Paris, 1987–1995).

Meyssonier, Simone, *La Balance et l'horloge, la genèse de la pensée libérale en France au XVIIIe siècle* (Montreuil, 1989).

Michaud, Claude, "L'assemblée provinciale du Berry, 1778–1789" in Anne Blanchard, Henri Michel, and Elie Pélaquier, eds., *Les assemblées d'Etats dans la France méridionale à l'époque moderne* (Montpellier, 1995), pp. 215–38.

Michel, Patrick, "Caroline Louise de Bade 'La Minerve de Hesse,' collectionneur exemplaire" in Pierre Rosenberg, ed., *Peintures françaises dans les collections allemandes XVIIe–XVIIIe siècles* (Paris, 2005), pp. 65–74.

Michon, Georges, *Histoire du parti feuillant, Adrien Duport (1789–1792)* (Paris, 1924).

Mille, Jérôme, G.-F. *Le Trosne (1728–1780) Etude économique, fiscale et politique* (Paris, 1905).
Minard, Philippe, *La Fortune du Colbertisme: état et industrie dans la France des Lumières* (Paris, 1998).
Montlaur, Hubert de, *Mirabeau. "L'Ami des hommes"* (Paris, 1992).
Moriceau, Jean-Marc, *Les Fermiers de l'Île-de France* (Paris, 1994).
Morilhat, Claude, *La Prise de conscience du capitalisme, Economie et philosophie chez Turgot* (Paris, 1988).
Mornet, Daniel, *Le sentiment de la nature en France de J.-J. Rousseau à Bernardin de Saint-Pierre* (Paris, 1907).
  *Les origines intellectuelles de la Révolution française* (Paris, 1933).
Mortoer, Roland, "Prélude à la fête révolutionnaire: la 'fête bocagère' dans la poésie descriptive de la fin du XVIIIe siècle" in Jean Ehrard and Paul Viallaneix, eds., *Les Fêtes de la Révolution, Colloque de Clermont-Ferrand (juin 1974)* (Paris, 1977), pp. 73–84.
Nadler, Steven, *The Best of All Possible Worlds: A Story of Philosophers, God, and Evil* (New York, 2009).
Nadler, Steven, ed., *The Cambridge Companion to Malebranche* (Cambridge, 2000).
Nagle, Jean, *La Civilisation du coeur, histoire du sentiment politique en France du XIIe au XIXe siècle* (Paris, 1998).
Newman, Lex, "Locke on Knowledge" in Lex Newman, ed., *The Cambridge Companion to Locke's Essay Concerning Human Understanding* (Cambridge, 2007), pp. 313–51.
Newton, William R., *Derrière la façade, Vivre au château de Versailles au XVIIIe siècle* (Paris, 2008).
  *L'Espace du roi, La Cour de France au château de Versailles 1682–1789* (Paris, 2000).
  *La Petite Cour: services et serviteurs à la Cour de Versailles au XVIIIe siècle* (Paris, 2006).
Olson, Richard, "The Human Sciences" in Roy Porter, ed., *Cambridge History of Science*, IV (Cambridge, 2003), pp. 436–62.
O'Malley, Therese, and Amy R. W. Meyers, eds., *The Art of Natural History: Illustrated Treatises and Botanical Paintings, 1400–1850* (New Haven and London, 2008).
O'Neal, John C., *The Authority of Experience, Sensationist Theory in the French Enlightenment* (University Park, Pa., 1996).
Own, David, "Locke on Judgment" in Lex Newman, ed., *The Cambridge Companion to Locke's Essay Concerning Human Understanding* (Cambridge, 2007), pp. 406–37.
Ozouf, Mona, *La Fête révolutionnaire, 1789–1799* (Paris, 1976).
Passeron, Irène, "La Société des arts, espace provisoire de reformulation des rapports entre théories scientifiques et pratiques instrumentales" in Christiane Demeulenaere-Douyère and Eric Brian, eds., *Réglement, usages et science dans la France de l'absolutisme à l'occasion du troisième centenaire du réglement instituant l'Académie royale des sciences (26 janvier 1699)* (London, Paris, New York, 2002), pp. 109–32.

Patey, Dougald Lane, "Ancients and Moderns" in H. B. Nisbet and Claude Rawson, eds., *The Cambridge History of Literary Criticism*, vol. IV, *The Eighteenth Century* (Cambridge, 1997), pp. 32–71.
"The Institutions of Criticism in the Eighteenth Century" in H. B. Nisbet and Claude Rawson, eds., *The Cambridge History of Literary Criticism*, vol. IV: *The Eighteenth Century* (Cambridge, 1997), pp. 3–31.
Peronnet, Michel, "Réflexions sur les Etats de Languedoc: une histoire intermédiaire à l'époque moderne" in Anne Blanchard, Henri Michel, and Elie Pélaquier, eds., *Les assemblées d'Etats dans la France France méridionale à l'époque moderne* (Montpellier, 1995), pp. 107–28.
Perrin, Jean-François, "Métempsychose: soi-même comme multitude: Le cas du récit à métempsychose au 18e siècle," *Dix-huitième siècle* 41 (2009), 169–86.
Perrot, Jean-Claude, *Une histoire intellectuelle de l'économie politique, XVIIe–XVIIIe siècle* (Paris, 1992).
Pichot, André, *Histoire de la notion de vie* (Paris, 1993).
Pinault-Sorensen, Madeleine, "La Description des arts et métiers et le rôle de Duhamel du Monceau" in Académie d'Orléans, ed., *Duhamel du Monceau 1700–2000, un Européen du siècle des Lumières* (Orléans, 2001), pp. 133–55.
"Les dessinateurs de l'Académie royale des sciences" in Christiane Demeulenaere-Douyère and Eric Brian, eds., *Réglement, usages et science dans la France de l'absolutisme à l'occasion du troisième centenaire du réglement instituant l'Académie royale des sciences (26 janvier 1699)* (London, Paris, New York, 2002), pp. 147–67.
Pocock, J. G. A., *The Machiavellian Moment: Florentine Political Thought and the Atlantic Republican Tradition* (Princeton, 1975).
*Virtue, Commerce, and History: Essays on Political Thought and History, Chiefly in the Eighteenth Century* (Cambridge, 1985).
Polino, Marie-Noelle, "Quatremère de Quincy et la fête de la loi en l'honneur de Simoneau, maire d'Etampes (juin 1792)" in R. Chevallier, ed., *La Révolution française et l'antiquité* (Tours, 1991), pp. 285–309.
Pomian, Krysztof, "Vision and Cognition" in Caroline A. Jones and Peter Galison, eds., *Picturing Science, Producing Art* (London and New York, 1998), pp. 211–31.
Pommier, Edouard, *Winckelmann, inventeur de l'histoire de l'art* (Paris, 2003).
Poitrineau, Abel, "La Fête traditionnelle" in Jean Ehrard and Paul Viallaneix, eds., *Les Fêtes de la Révolution, Colloque de Clermont-Ferrand (juin 1974)* (Paris, 1977), pp. 11–26.
Poovey, Mary, *Genres of the Credit Economy: Mediating Value in Eighteenth- and Nineteenth-Century Britain* (Chicago, 2008).
Porée, Jérôme, *Le Mal, homme coupable, homme souffrant* (Paris, 2000).
Porter, Roy, ed., *The Cambridge History of Science*, vol. 4: *Eighteenth-Century Science* (Cambridge, 2003).
Porter, Theodore, *Trust in Numbers, the Pursuit of Objectivity in Science and Public Life* (Princeton, 1995).
Pottinger, David T., *The French Book Trade in the Ancien Régime, 1500–1791* (Cambridge, Mass., 1958).

Proust, Jacques, *Diderot et l'Encyclopédie* (Paris, 1967).
Quétel, Claude, *Escape from the Bastille, The Life and Legend of Latude*, trans. Christopher Sharp (Cambridge, 1990).
Rahe, Paul A., *Soft Despotism, Democracy's Drift. Montesquieu, Rousseau, Tocqueville, and the Modern Prospect* (New Haven and London, 2009).
Ravel, Jeffrey S., *The Contested Parterre: Public Theater and French Political Culture, 1680–1791* (Ithaca, 1999).
Reddy, William R., *The Navigation of Feeling, A Framework for the History of Emotions* (Cambridge, 2001).
Reill, Peter Hanns, "The Legacy of the 'Scientific Revolution' Science and the Enlightenment" in Roy Porter, ed., *The Cambridge History of Science*, vol. 4: *The Eighteenth Century* (Cambridge, 2003), pp. 23–43.
  *Vitalizing Nature in the Enlightenment* (Berkeley and Los Angeles, 2005).
Renouvin, Pierre, *Les Assemblées provinciales de 1787. Origines, développement, résutlats* (Paris, 1921).
Reuss, Rodolphe, *Charles de Butré 1724–1805, Un physiocrate Tourangeau en Aslace et dans le Margraviat de Bade* (Paris, 1887).
Rey, Roselyne, *Naissance et développement du vitalisme en France dans la deuxième moitié du 18e siècle à la fin du Premier Empire* (Oxford, 2000).
Rickless, Samuel C., "Locke's Polemic Against Nativism" in Lex Newman, ed., *The Cambridge Companion to Locke's* Essay Concerning Human Understanding (Cambridge, 2007), pp. 33–66.
Riley, James C., *The Seven Years War and the Old Régime in France: The Economic and Financial Toll* (Princeton, 1986).
Riley, Patrick, "Malebranche's Moral Philosophy" in Steven Nadler, ed., *The Cambridge Companion to Malebranche* (Cambridge, 2000), pp. 220–61.
Ripert, Henri, *Le marquis de Mirabeau (L'Ami des hommes), ses théories politiques et économiques* (Paris, 1901).
Riskin, Jessica, *Science in the Age of Sensibility, The Sentimental Empiricists of the French Enlightenment* (Chicago, 2002).
  "The 'Spirit of System' and the Fortunes of Physiocracy," *History of Political Theory*, 43 (annual supplement 2003), pp. 42–73.
Roberts, Warren, *Jacques-Louis David and Jean-Louis Prieur, Revolutionary Artists, The Public, the Populace, and Images of the French Revolution* (Albany, 2000).
Robertson, John, *The Case for the Enlightenment, Scotland and Naples 1680–1760* (Cambridge, 2005).
Roche, Daniel, *La France des Lumières* (Paris, 1993).
  *Les Républicains des lettres, gens de culture et lumières au XVIIIe siècle* (Paris, 1988).
Roe, Shirley, *Matter, Life, and Generation: Eighteenth-Century Embryology and the Haller-Wolff Debate* (Cambridge, 1981).
Roger, Jacques, *The Life Sciences in Eighteenth-Century French Thought* (Stanford, 1998, orig. French ed., 1963).
Rogers, G. A. J., "The Intellectual Setting and the Aims of the *Essay*" in Lex Newman, ed., *The Cambridge Companion to Locke's* Essay Concerning Human Understanding (Cambridge, 2007), pp. 7–32.

Romani, Roberto, *National Character and Public Spirit in Britain and France, 1750–1914* (Cambridge, 2002).
Rosanvallon, Pierre, *Le libéralisme économique, Histoire de l'idée de marché* (Paris, 1989, orig. ed., Le capitalisme utopique, 1979).
Rothkrug, Lionel, *Opposition to Louis XIV, The Political and Social Origins of the French Enlightenment* (Princeton, 1970).
Rothschild, Emma, *Economic Sentiments, Adam Smith, Condorcet, and the Enlightenment*, (Cambridge, Mass., 2001).
Rubin, James H., "The Politics of Quatremère de Quincy's Romantic Classicism" in George Levitine, ed., *Culture and Revolution, Cultural Ramification of the French Revolution* (College Park, Md., 1989), pp. 230–44.
Russo, Elena, *La cour et la ville de la littérature classique aux Lumières* (Paris, 2002).
   *Styles of Enlightenment, Taste, Politics, and Authorship in Eighteenth-Century France* (Baltimore, 2007).
Rutherford, Donald, *Leibniz and the Rational Order of Nature* (Cambridge, 1995).
Salmon, Xavier, ed., *Madame de Pompadour et les arts* (Paris, Réunion des Musées nationaux, 2002).
Salomon-Bayet, Claire, *L'Institution de la science et l'expérience du vivant* (Paris, 2008).
Sanyal, Sukla, "The 1792 Food Riot at Étampes and the French Revolution," *Studies in History*, 18:1 (2002), an. 3–50.
Saricks, Ambrose, *Pierre Samuel Du Pont de Nemours* (Lawrence, Kan., 1965).
Schabas, Margaret, *The Natural Origins of Economics* (Chicago, 2005).
Schelle, Gustave, *Le Docteur Quesnay, Chirurgien, Médecin de Madame de Pompadour et de Louis XV, Physiocrate* (Paris, 1907).
   *Du Pont de Nemours et l'école physiocratique* (Paris, 1888).
Schmaltz, Tad M., "Malebranche on Ideas and the Vision in God" in Steven Nadler, ed., *The Cambridge Companion to Malebranche* (Cambridge, 2000), pp. 59–86.
Schmitt, Carl, *Political Theology: Four Chapters on the Concept of Sovereignty* (Chicago, 2006).
   *The Concept of the Political*, expanded edition (Chicago, 2007).
   *The Leviathan in the State Theory of Thomas Hobbes* (Chicago, 2008).
Schneerman, Peter J., "Lire et parler. La réception de l'*exemplum virtutis*" in Thomas W. Gaehtens et al., eds., *L'art et les normes sociales au XVIIIe siècle* (Paris, 2001), pp. 443–57.
Scholar, Richard, *The Je-Ne-Sais-Quoi in Early Modern Europe: Encounters with a Certain Something* (Oxford, 2005).
Schumpeter, Joseph A., *History of Economic Analysis* (Oxford, 1954, reprint 1994).
Sermain, Jean-Paul, "Le code du bon goût (1725–1759)" in Marc Fumaroli, ed., *Histoire de la rhétorique moderne 1450–1950* (Paris, 1999), pp. 879–943.
Sgard, Jean, ed., *Condillac et les problèms du langage* (Paris, 1982).
Shovlin, John, *The Political Economy of Virtue, Luxury, Patriotism, and the Origins of the French Revolution* (Ithaca and London, 2006).

Sirven, Oswald, "Ur Markis de Mirabeau's Brev Till Greve Carl Fridrik Scheffer," *Lychnos* 9 (1948), 51–84.
Skinner, Quentin, *Hobbes and Republican Liberty* (Cambridge, 2008).
  *Reason and Rhetoric in the Philosophy of Hobbes* (Cambridge, 1996).
Smith, Jay M., *Nobility Reimagined: The Patriotic Nation in Eighteenth-Century France* (Ithaca and London, 2005).
  *The Culture of Merit: Nobility, Royal Service, and the Making of Absolute Monarchy in France, 1600–1789* (Ann Arbor, 1996).
Smith, Jay M., ed., *The French Nobility in the Eighteenth Century: Reassessments and New Approaches* (College Park, 2006).
Smyth, Orla, "La sympathie des belles âmes: réflexion sur la théorie des Belles-Lettres au début du XVIIIe siècle" in Thierry Belleguic et al., eds., *Les Discours de la sympathie, Enquête sur une notion de l'âge classique à la modernité* (Quebec, 2007), pp. 131–48.
Soler, Lena, *Introduction à l'épistémologie* (Paris, 2002).
Sonenscher, Michael, *Before the Deluge: Public Debt, Inequality, and the Intellectual Origins of the French Revolution* (Princeton, 2007).
  "The Nation's Debt and the Birth of the Modern Republic: The French Fiscal Deficit and the Politics of the Revolution of 1789," Parts I and II, *History of Political Thought* XVIII (1997).
  "Physiocracy as Theodicy" in *History of Political Thought* XXIII:2 (2002), 326–39.
  *Sans-Culottes, An Eighteenth-Century Emblem in the French Revolution* (Princeton, 2008).
Sparry, E. C., "Rococo Readings of the Book of Nature" in Marina Frasca-Spada and Nick Jardine, eds., *Books and the Sciences in History* (Cambridge, 2000), pp. 255–75.
Stafford, Barbara Maria, *Body Criticism, Imaging the Unseen in Enlightenment Art and Medicine* (Cambridge, Mass., MIT Press, 1993).
Starobinsky, Jean, *1789, Les emblèmes de la raison* (Paris, 1973).
  *L'Oeil vivant*, revised edition (Paris, 1999).
  *L'Oeil Vivant II: La relation critique* (Paris, 1970).
  *Le remède dans le mal* (Paris, 1989).
Stasavage, David, *Public Debt and the Birth of the Democratic State: France and Great Britain 1688–1789* (Cambridge, 2003).
Steenage, Albert E., and Richard Van Den Berg, "Transcribing the Tableau Économique: Input-Output Analysis a la Quesnay," *Journal of the History of Economic Thought* 29:3 (2007), 331–58.
Steiner, Philippe, "Introduction," special issue on physiocrats of *Revue française d'histoire des idées politiques*, 20:2 (2004).
  *La "science nouvelle" de l'économie politique* (Paris, 1998).
Stewart, Matthew, *The Courtier and the Heretic: Leibniz, Spinoza, and the Fate of God in the Modern World* (New York, 2007).
Stewart, Philip, *L'invention du sentiment: roman et économie affective au XVIIIe siècle* (Oxford, 2010).
Stroup, Alice, *A Company of Scientists, Botany, Patronage, and Community at the Seventeenth-Century Parisian Royal Academy of Sciences* (Berkeley and Los Angeles, 1990).

*Royal Funding of the Parisian Académie Royale des Sciences during the 1690s* (Philadelphia, 1987).

Sturdy, David J., "L'Académie royale des sciences et l'enquête du Régent de 1716–1718," in Christiane Demeulenaere-Douyère and Eric Brian, eds., *Réglement, usages et science dans la France de l'absolutisme (Actes du colloque international, Paris, 8–10 juin 1999)* (London, Paris, New York, 2002), pp. 133–46.

Sureau, R., *Les représentations figurées des physiocrates* (Paris, 1958).

Swann, Julian, *Provincial Power and Absolute Monarchy: The Estates General of Burgundy, 1666–1790* (Cambridge, 2003).

Tackett, Timothy, *Becoming a Revolutionary: The Deputies of the French National Assembly and the Emergence of a Revolutionary Culture (1789–1790)* (Princeton, 1996).

Taillefer, Michel, *Une Académie interprète des Lumières, L'Académie des sciences, inscriptions, et belles-lettres de Toulouse au XVIIIe siècle* (Paris, 1984).

Talmon, J. L., *The Origins of Totalitarian Democracy* (London, 1952).

Théré, Christine, and Loïc Charles, "François Quesnay: A 'Rural Socrates' in Versailles?" in E. Roy Weintraub and Evelyn L. Forget, eds., *Economists' Lives: Biography and Autobiography in the History of Economics* (Annual Supplement to Volume 39 of *History of Political Economy*) (Durham and London, 2007), pp. 195–214.

"From Versailles to Paris: The Creative Communities of the Physiocratic Movement," *History of Political Economy*, 43:1 (2011), 25–58.

"The Writing Workshop of François Quesnay and the Making of Physiocracy," *History of Political Economy* 40:1 (2008), 1–42.

Thomson, Ann, *Bodies of Thought, Science, Religion, and the Soul in the Early Enlightenment* (Oxford, 2008).

Thompson, Mack, "Causes and Circumstances of the Du Pont Family Emigration," *French Historical Studies*, 6:1 (1969), 59–77.

Tocqueville, Alexis de, *L'ancien régime et la révolution*, in François Furet, ed., [Tocqueville] *Oeuvres* (Paris, 2004).

Tornare, Alain-Jacques, *Vaudois et Confédérés au service de France (1789–1798)* (Yens, 1998).

Tribe, Keith, *Governing Economy: The Reformation of German Economic Discourse, 1750–1840* (Cambridge, 1988).

Trotthein, Serge, ed., *L'Esthétique naît-elle au XVIIIe siècle?* (Paris, 2000).

Tronchin, Henry, *Un médecin du XVIIIe siècle: Théodore Tronchin (1709–1781) d'après des documents inédits* (Paris and Geneva, 1906).

Turco, Luigi, "Moral Sense and the Foundations of Morals" in Alexander Broadie, ed., *The Cambridge Companion to the Scottish Enlightenment* (Cambridge, 2003), pp. 136–56.

Van Den Berg, Richard, "Contemporary Responses to the Tableau économique" in Stephan Boehm, Christian Gehrke, Heinz D. Kurtz et al., eds., *Is There Progress in Economics? Knowledge, Truth and the History of Economic Thought* (Cheltenham, UK, and Northampton, Mass., 2002), pp. 259–316.

Van Kley, Dale K., *The Religious Origins of the French Revolution from Calvin to the Civil Constitution, 1560–1791* (New Haven, 1999).

Van Thiegen, Paul, *Ossian en France*, 2 vols. (Paris, 1920).
*Le Préromantisme*, 3 vols. (Paris, 1929–1947).
Vardi, Liana, "Du Pont's Autobiographical Writings" in *2009 Selected Papers from the Consortium on the Revolutionary Era* (2012).
  "Imagining the Harvest in Early Modern Europe," *The American Historical Review*, 101 (1996), 1357–97.
  "Writing the Lives of Eighteenth-Century Economists," *The American Historical Review*, 114:3 (2009), 652–61.
Vardi, Liana, and Jonathan Dewald, "The French Peasants, 1400–1789" in Tom Scott, ed., *The Peasantries of Europe* (London, 1998), pp. 20–47.
Venturi, Lionello, *Histoire de la critique d'art* (Paris, 1969).
Vergonjeanne, Hélène, *Un Laboureur à Versailles* (Paris, 2008).
Viala Alain, *La France galante* (Paris, 2008).
  *Naissance de l'écrivain* (Paris, 1985).
Vidal, Fernando, *Les sciences de l'âme: XVIe–XVIIIe siècles* (Paris, 2006).
Vigarello, Georges, ed., *Histoire du corps*, vol. 1: *De la Renaissance aux Lumières* (Paris, 2005).
Vila, Anne C., *Enlightenment and Pathology, Sensibility in the Literature and Medicine of Eighteenth-Century France* (Baltimore, 1998).
Vincent-Munnia, Nathalie, *Les premiers poèmes en prose: généalogie d'un genre dans la première moitié du dix-neuvième siècle français* (Paris, 1996).
Vovelle, Michel, *1793, La Révolution contre l'Église: de la Raison à l'Être suprême* (Lausanne, 1988).
Wahnich, Sophie, "Un avocat sensible dans l'émotion de l'évènement: le curé Dolivier face au meurtre du maire d'Étampes, printemps 1792," *Journée d'histoire des sensibilités*, EHESS, Paris, 6 March 2006, in *Mundos Novos*, online publication, 16 March 2006.
Wargnier, Nicolas, "Fête et dissolution sociale, à propos de quelques notices du "Journal de Paris" (1797)" in Jean Ehrard and Paul Viallaneix eds., *Les Fêtes de la Révolution, Colloque de Clermont-Ferrand (juin 1974)* (Paris, 1977), pp. 525–36.
Weber, Dominique, ed., *Hobbes, Descartes et la métaphysique* (Paris, 2005).
Weintraub, E. Roy, *How Economics Became a Mathematical Science* (Durham, 2002).
Wellman, Kathleen, *La Mettrie: Medicine, Philosophy and Enlightenment* (Durham and London, 1992).
Weulersse, Georges, *La physiocratie à la fin du règne de Louis XV* (Paris, 1959).
  *La physiocratie à l'aube de la Révolution* (Paris, 1985).
  *La physiocratie sous les ministères de Turgot et de Necker* (Paris, 1950).
  *Le mouvement physiocratique en France (de 1756 à 1770)*, 2 vols. (Paris, 1910).
  *Les manuscrits économiques de François Quesnay et du marquis de Mirabeau aux Archives nationales (M. 778 à M. 785)* (Paris, 1910).
Whatmore, Richard, *Republicanism and the French Revolution: An Intellectual History of Jean-Baptiste Say's Political Economy* (Oxford, 2000).
Williams, Raymond, *The Country and the City* (Oxford, 1975).
Winch, Donald, "Does Progress Matter" in Stephan Boehm, Christian Gehrke, Heinz D. Kurtz et al., eds., *Is There Progress in Economics? Knowledge, Truth*

*and the History of Economic Thought* (Cheltenham, UK, and Northampton, Mass., 2002), pp. 3–20.

Wise, M. Norton, "Mediations: Enlightenment Balancing Acts, or the Technologies of Rationalism" in Paul Horwich, ed., *World Changes, Thomas Kuhn and the Nature of Science* (Cambridge, Mass., 1993), pp. 207–56.

Wood, Paul, "Science, Philosophy, and the Mind" in Roy Porter ed., *Cambridge History of Science*, vol. 4: *Eighteenth-Century Science* (Cambridge, 2003), pp. 800–24.

Worvill, Romira M., *"Seeing" Speech: Illusion and Transformation of Dramatic Writing in Diderot and Lessing* (Oxford, 2005).

Wright, Johnson Kent, *A Classical Republican in Eighteenth-Century France, The Political Thought of Mably* (Stanford, 1997).

Zaretsky, Robert, *The Philosophers' Quarrel: Rousseau, Hume, and the Limits of Human Understanding* (New Haven, 2010).

# Index

Abeille, Louis-Paul (1719–1807), 5, 191
Académie française, 91, 104
Academy of Painting, 29, 75, 196, 202
Academy of Sciences, 25–31, 33, 76, 128
Academy of Surgery, 34, 40, 58–61, 185
*Albert Premier ou Adeline*, 223–4
Aesthetics, 29–30, 65, 75, 107–10, 128, 192–210
Aggregation, 4, 53, 67, 116, 209, 268
Agriculture, 3, 9, 12, 47, 67, 79–81, 114–8, 121, 130, 141, 143, 145, 150, 166, 184, 186, 199–200, 206, 208, 214, 216–8, 229–32, 235, 238–9
Agronomy, 8–9, 22, 31, 110, 115–8, 185
Albertone, Manuela, 151
Alimento, Antonella, 151, 180
Analogy, 36, 55, 59, 66, 211, 214, 220, 270
Antoine, Michel, 43–5
Arts, 21, 71, 95, 97, 100, 105–9, 126, 192–210, 230
Assembly of Notables, 190, 243, 256–9

Baden, Carl-Ludwig, heredetary prince of (1755–1801), 188, 194, 200, 226–7, 229, 237–8, 264, 267
Baden, Margrave of, Carl-Friedrich (1728–1811), 8, 121, 172, 175, 188–9, 194, 222, 228, 234, 237, 249, 251, 259
Baden, Margravine Caroline-Louisa (1723–1783), 188, 201–2, 222
Baker, Keith Michael, 151–2, 181
Banzhaf, Spencer, 63–4

Batteux, Charles (1713–1780), 197
Baudeau, Nicolas, abbé, 7, 48, 147, 187, 224, 246, 254
Baumgarten, Alexander Gottlieb (1714–1762), 197
Beauty, 196–8, 201–4, 270
Becq, Annie, 107
*Belle-nature*, 30, 107, 195, 207–8
Blaufarb, Rafe, 162
Boerhaave, Hermann (1668–1738), 32, 38, 61
Boileau-Despréaux, Nicolas (1636–1711), 196
Bonnet, Charles (1720–1793), 231–2
Bonnet, Jean-Claude, 266
Bosse, Abraham (ca.1604–1676), 28–9
Bouillé, François Claude Amour, marquis de (1739–1800), 261
Boulainvilliers, Henri de (1658–1722), 100, 119
Boulanger, Nicolas-Antoine (1722–1759), 232
Bourde, André, 9
Bourgogne, duc de, circle, 149, 155
Brewer, Daniel, 57
Brienne, Étienne-Charles de Loménie de (1727–1794), 259
Broman, Thomas, 39
Buffon, Georges-Louis Leclerc, comte de (1707–1788), 42, 61, 204, 208
Burke, Edmund (1729–1797), 10
Butré, Charles de (1724–1805), 123–4, 140, 168, 175, 232

Calonne, Charles Alexandre de (1734–1802), 190, 256–8
Certainty, 3, 53, 72–3, 270
Charles, Loic, 63, 68, 147
Chartier, Roger, 17
Chastellux, François-Jean, marquis de (1734–1788), 229–30
Châteauvieux regiment, 260–6
China, 130, 137, 151, 170, 232, 235, 237, 270
Choiseul, Étienne-François, duc de (1719–1785), 40, 185–6
Christensen, Paul, 63
Circulation, 4, 12–14, 40, 53, 66, 117, 120–1, 201, 216
Citton, Yves, 115, 178
Civic spirit, 156, 158, 171, 180, 198, 233, 237, 243, 263, 267, 274
Civilization, 106, 109, 112, 167, 176, 192, 230
Clear and distinct ideas, 55, 70, 72–4
Cognition 2–3, 21, 68–78, 81–2, 122–3, 126–8, 132, 138–9, 175, 180, 197, 210, 238, 249
Colbert, Jean-Baptiste (1619–1683), 5, 116
Collot d'Herbois, Jean-Marie (1749–1796), 261
Committee of Thirty, 190
Condillac, Étienne Bonnot de, abbé (1715–1780), 5, 15, 74, 77, 142
Condorcet, Marie Jean Antoine Nicolas de Caritat, marquis de (1743–1794), 4, 10, 15, 58, 151, 190, 241, 248, 251, 253–4, 267
Contingent 40, 56, 59, 66–7, 116, 143–5
Corneille, Pierre (1606–1684) 95, 105, 212
*Cour des aides*, 103, 154, 242
Court, courtiers 40–6, 49–50, 91, 97–8, 130, 159–61, 168, 189, 208–9
Court de Gébelin, Antoine (1725–1784), 228, 231–4

Daire, Eugène (1798–1847), 10–12
d'Alembert, Jean le Rond (1717–1783), 37, 42, 57, 76, 78, 127
d'Angiviller, Charles-Claude Flahaut de la Billarderie, comte (1730–1810), 45, 49, 79, 204
d'Argenson, René Louis de Voyer de Paulmy, marquis de (1694–1757), 149–50, 243–4, 250

David, Jacques-Louis (1748–1825), 261, 264–5
Deregulation 7, 21, 115, 241, 247
Descartes, René (1596–1650), 3, 38, 54–7, 62, 68–70, 74–5, 77, 126
*Despotisme de la Chine*, 137, 151
Diderot, Denis (1713–1784), 35, 37, 42, 139, 142, 199, 202–4, 209, 219
Divine authority, 3, 53, 55, 62, 64, 68, 70, 73–7, 82, 107, 110, 134, 143, 165, 217, 268–72
Du Bos, Jean-Baptiste, abbé (1670–1742) 107–8, 197
Du Hausset, Madame (c.1720–?), 43–5, 48–9, 105, 212
Du Pont (de Nemours), Pierre Samuel (1739–1817), chapters 6–8, and pages 2, 7–10, 42, 49, 62, 65, 67, 123, 136, 150, 171, 181

Economics, 3–4, 14, 18, 21, 49, 53, 61–6, 81, 112, 121, 180, 194, 277
Edelstein, Dan, 58
Education, 22, 25–6, 32–5, 72, 107, 152, 166, 176, 179, 188, 194, 196–9, 211, 220–1, 226–40, 244–7, 250, 263–4, 267, 274–5
Ehrard, Jean, 233
Emotions, 65, 91, 95, 99–103, 108, 112, 127–8, 139–40, 167, 198, 209, 211, 234
*L'Empereur Joseph Second*, pp.213–21
Encyclopedia 37, 41, 57, 76, 114, 127, 184, 186, 208, 232
Engraving, 25–31, 34
Enlightened despotism, 200, 213–24, 228, 240, 242–5
*Éphémérides du citoyen*, 7–8, 48, 137, 139, 146, 148, 151, 167, 187–8, 192, 194, 213, 220, 222
Estates General, 174, 190, 193, 259
Evidence, 50, 52–4, 68, 71–3, 76–8, 81, 123–4, 132, 136–8, 143, 169, 221, 245, 247
Exchange 3–4, 18, 21, 56, 63, 66, 145, 194

Factionalism, 260–7
*Farmers, Grains*, 114–7
Favart, Charles-Simon (1710–1792) 111–2
Félix, Joel, 173, 242

# Index

Fénélon, François de Salignac de la Mothe (1651–1715), 107–8, 120, 149, 155–6, 165, 204–5
Festival of Liberty, 15 April 1792, 261–4
Festival of the Law, 3 June 1792, 264–7
Festivals, 226, 228–9, 231–8, 252, 260–7, 274–5
Feuillants, 260–7
Finances, 21–2, 41, 45–8, *see also* Taxation
Forbonnais, François Véron Duverger de (1722–1800), 141, 145–6
Foucault, Michel (1926–1984), 13–4, 30, 126
Fox-Genovese, Elizabeth (1941–2007), 62
Franklin, Benjamin (1705–1790), 65, 207
Freedom, 200, 246, 261–3, 267
Free trade in grains, 5–6, 115, 117–8, 141, 145, 172, 185–7, 228, 241, 264–6
Free will, will, 71, 78, 95
Freemasonry, 37, 104
Furet, François (1927–1997), 18–9

Galen (131–201) 38, 61, 66
Galiani, Ferdinando (1728–1787), 139, 141, 144–5, 218–9, 221
Gender, 46, 96, 105, 109, 131, 184, 192, 204, 206–7, 209, 216, 218, 224–7, 235, 250, 267, 274
Genres in art and literature, 93, 111, 129, 195–6, 212, 220
Gournay, Jean Claude Marie Vincent de (1712–1759), 7
Grace, 78, 107, 178, 271
Greuze, Jean-Baptiste (1725–1805), 26, 194, 202–3, 205–6
Grimm, Melchior (1723–1807), 87, 112, 126, 129–30, 137, 141, 146, 156, 202, 212, 223–5

Habermas, Jurgen, 133
Haller, Albrecht von (1708–1777), 32, 37–8, 56, 60, 231–2
Happiness, 199–200, 213–4, 218, 229–30, 245, 275–6
Harmony, 76, 157, 179, 233, 237–9, 245, 250–1, 263–4, 271, 276
Hennin, Pierre-Michel (1728–1807), 101, 256
Hévin, Prudent (1715–1789), 23, 34, 47
Hippocrates (c.450–c.380 BC), 38–9, 61, 66

Hirschman, Albert O., 15–16
Hirzel, Hans-Caspar (1725–1803), 110–1
History, 19, 130, 167–8, 227–32, 235
Hobbes, Thomas (1588–1679), 19, 74
Hutchison, Francis (1660–1739), 197

Image, 13, 30, 53, 69, 73–5, 81, 128, 200, 209
Imagination, 3, 21, 36, 58, 67, 71, 74, 81, 93–5, 97, 107, 116, 127–8, 140, 146, 169, 176, 197, 210–1, 217, 240, 269–72
Innate ideas, 3, 68, 70–1, 77, 131
Inequality, 66, 97, 119, 130–1, 143, 158, 168, 176, 239
Institut de France, 273, 277
Intuition, 3, 21, 54, 77–8, 132

Jacobins, 260–7
*Je-ne-sais-quoi*, 146, 195, 201, 209, 238
Joseph II (1741–1790), 8, 213, 218, 220, 222–8

Kant, Immanuel (1724–1804), 197
Kaplan, Steven, 116, 142, 170, 241
Koselleck, Rheinart, 19
Kwass, Michael, 154

*L'Ami des hommes*, 47, 79, 87, 90, 109, 117–24, 134, 152–3, 161, 176
L'Averdy, Clément Charles François (1724–1783), 168, 172–4, 186–7, 242–3
La Chalotais, Louis-René de Caradeux de (1701–1785), 45
La Fayette, Gilbert du Motier, marquis de (1757–1834), 190, 261
La Peyronie, François Gigot de (1678–1747), 34–5
Laissez-faire, 6, 8, 66, 190, 214, 216, 227, 241, 243, 246
Landowners 12–3, 18, 115, 119–21, 135, 151–2, 156–8, 168–9, 173, 175, 177–9, 185, 243, 247–50, 255
Language, 74–5, 81–2, 95–8, 106, 126–9, 133, 141–3, 146
Larrère, Catherine, 38–9
Law, John (1671–1729), 6
Law 3, 55, 131–2, 157, 166, 170, 174, 178–9, 196, 198, 215, 228, 238, 261, 264–7
Law of nature, 4–5, 53, 55, 64, 109, 136–9

Le Blanc de Guillet, Antoine (1730–1799), 199, 223–4
Le Franc de Pompignan, Jean-Jacques (1709–1784), 85–7, 91–2, 96, 102, 103–9, 154–6
Le Mercier de la Rivière, Pierre-Paul (1719–1801), 7, 45, 130, 137–9, 142–4, 149–52, 169–71, 178, 180–1, 201, 210, 244
Le Trosne, Guillaume-François (1728–1780), 12, 130, 150, 178–80, 230, 244, 251
*Leçons économiques*, 132
Legal despotism, 137–9, 143, 149–50, 152, 166, 170–1, 179, 181, 244
Leibniz, Gottfried (1646–1716), 76–7, 268, 271
Leiden, 32, 38
*Les Devoirs*, 140, 152, 176–7
*Lettres sur la législation*, 167–9
Linguet, Simon-Nicolas-Henri (1736–1794), 143, 145
Locke, John (1632–1704), 3, 69–70, 72, 74–7, 196
Longhitano, Gino, 124
Longo, Marquis, 102, 133–4, 152, 176
Louis XV (1710–1774), 34, 41–9, 68, 104–5, 167, 219, 222
Louis XVI (1754–1793), 8, 49, 88, 188, 190, 224, 239, 241–2, 245–7, 252, 256, 260
Luxury, 41, 43, 50, 76, 115–20, 125, 168
Lyons, 37

Mably, Gabriel Bonnot abbé de (1709–1785), 141–2, 145, 237
Machault d'Arnouville, Jean-Baptiste de (1701–1794), 153–6
Magistrates, 121, 139, 143, 154, 157, 170, 174, 180
Malebranche, Nicolas (1638–1715), 62, 69, 74–8, 107
Malesherbes, Guillaume-Chrétien de Lamoignon de (1721–1794), 134, 242, 255
Mantes, 25–6, 34–5
Marat, Jean-Paul (1743–1793), 261, 270
Maria-Theresa of Austria (1717–1780), 222–8
Marie-Antoinette (1755–1793), 8, 222

Marmontel, Jean-François (1723–1799), 42, 79, 212
Marseilles, 83, 85, 173–5
Marx, Karl (1818–1883), 12–3, 17–8
Mathematics, 3, 53–4, 62, 75, 112, 121–4, 127, 131, 135–6, 180
Mathiez, Albert (1874–1932), 274–5
McCloskey, Deirdre, 55
Mechanics, 36, 54, 56, 63–5, 67
Medicine, 23, 26, 30–6, 56, 59, 61–7, 185, 208
Meek, Ronald, 53
*Memoir on Municipalities*, 242–60
Mercier, Louis-Sébastien (1740–1814), 209
Merit, 158, 164–5, 177
Metempsychosis, 232, 267–72
Mind, 57–8, 73, 81, 108, 112, 122, 140, 175, 209, 234, 270, see also Cognition, Soul
Mirabeau, Honoré Gabriel, comte de (1749–1791), 86, 88–9, 152–3, 233, 256–7, 275
Mirabeau, Jean-Antoine-Joseph-Charles-Elzéar, chevalier and *Bailli* of Malta (1717–1794), 46, 50, 84, 88, 121, 159–62
Mirabeau, Victor de Riquetti, marquis de (1715–1789), chapters 3–5, and pages 3, 12, 16, 17, 20, 46–51, 53, 65, 79–82, 186, 190–1, 209, 211–2, 225, 228, 230–3, 239, 250–1, 256–8, 272
Mirabeau's Economic Tuesdays, 49, 53, 93, 112, 140, 147–8, 228
Model, 29, 50, 53, 63, 78–82, 116, 136–7, 146, 148
Monarchy, 124–5, 131, 137–9, 200, 213–25, 249–50, see also Enlightened despotism
Montesquieu, Charles-Louis de Secondat, baron de (1689–1755), 15–6, 85–6, 120, 152–3, 158, 164, 233
Morality, moral order, mores, 4, 16, 19, 51–2, 79, 83, 100, 110, 118–21, 131–2, 166, 176, 192–5, 198, 200, 204–8, 211, 263, 269
Morellet, André, abbé (1727–1819) 104
Mornet, Daniel (1878–1954), 17

Nadler, Steven, 268
Napoleon, Bonaparte (1769–1821), 277

# Index

Nation, 159, 247, 262–4
National Assembly, 260–4, 267, 275
National debt, 6, 150, 190, 245–6
Natural law 4, 14, 21, 67, 130, 136–7, 143, 165, 187, 217, 274
Natural order, 4, 21, 52, 57, 109–10, 116, 124, 132, 136–40, 142–4, 147–8, 151, 167–71, 179, 192, 198–200, 225, 230–1, 234, 238, 275
Natural rights, 130, 136, 200, 267
Nature, 4, 6, 52, 55–6, 63–4, 75, 106, 114–7, 128–9, 130, 144, 152, 171, 195, 198, 201–2, 205–6, 210, 213, 216, 229, 269, 272
Necessity, 3, 67, 152, 230–1
Necker, Jacques (1732–1804), 189, 248, 257–8
Net product, 12, 42, 51, 76, 79, 121, 123, 144, 152, 171, 245, 272
Newton, Isaac (1642–1727), 4, 54–5, 62
Nivernais, Louis-Jules Mancini-Mazarini, duc de (1716–1798), 48, 85, 88, 91, 134, 167
Nobility, chapter 5 and pages 16, 83, 87–100, 118–9, 129–31, 230, 243

*Ordre naturel et essentiel des sociétés politiques*, 137–9, 143, 151, 169–70
Ozouf, Mona, 233, 261

Pain and pleasure, 70–1, 137, 196
Paris, 25–6, 31, 34–5, 41, 85, 87–8, 90, 92, 94, 120, 147, 184, 190, 239, 260–2, 267, 273
Parlement, 20, 45, 88, 104–5, 244
Passions, 4, 15, 94, 98–100, 133, 143–4, 167, 179, 209, 267
Pastoral, 111–2, 206
People (the), 233–8, 262–7
Perfectibility, 120, 229–32, 245, 271
Perrot, Jean-Claude, 147
Pétion, Jérôme (1756–1794), 260–4
Petit, Jean-Louis (1674–1750), 32, 60
*Philosophie de l'univers*, 267–73
*Philosophie rurale*, 87, 132, 167
Physiocracy, 2–5, 7, 54, 56, 62–7, 78, 83, 114–7, 120–32, 134–9, 143–4, 148, 150, 170–2, 176–80, 191–4, 198, 209–10, 227–9, 234, 238–9, 244–5, 249, 266, 275
Physiognomy, 205–9

Poetry, 91, 95–8, 101–2, 110–1, 130, 184, 193, 198–9, 211–2, 220–1, 231–2, 268–9
Poland, 85, 188, 222, 227, 233, 239, 241, 246
Political arithmetic, 62, 115
Political economy, 10, 47, 57, 115, 161, 175, 180, 194, 232, 244, 254
Political theory, 14, 17–20, 124, 133, 137–8, 151–3, 165–6, 179, 229–30, 245–50
Pompadour, Jeanne-Antoinette Poisson, marquise de (1721–1764), 40–9, 79, 160, 186
Population, 47, 113–4, 116–8, 168
Prieur, Jean-Louis (1756–1827), 261, 265
Primitivism, 106, 109–11, 130, 167, 228–32, 269
Probability, 4, 56, 72, 127
Production, productivity, 12, 21–2, 52, 129, 145, 166
Progress, 57–8, 130, 177, 230, 253, 267–73
Proof, 53, 55, 114, 134, 136, 145, 172, 238
Property, 128, 132, 136–8, 151, 155, 157, 171, 181, 217, 266
Provence, 86–7, 92, 113, 159, 161–3, 171–5, 268
Providence, 3, 66, 77, 110, 117, 124, 129, 152, 165, 170, 217, 231, 238–9, 274
Provincial Estates, 86–7, 121, 131, 149–50, 152–9, 162, 164, 166, 242, 247, 250, 257
Public, 3, 9, 17–8, 22, 92, 97, 136, 143, 159, 179, 194–9, 201, 212–3, 220–2, 226, 239, 241, 245–6, 249–50, 254, 264, 275

Quarrel of the Ancients and Moderns, 57–8, 94–5, 100, 196, 200–1, 230
Quatremère de Quincy, Antoine-Chrysostome (1755–1849), 264–6
Quesnay, François (1694–1774), chapters 1–2, 4–5, and pages 3, 6, 10, 12–4, 16, 20–1, 83, 87, 95, 99, 108–11, 182, 185, 189, 191, 193, 209, 211–2, 221, 230–1, 239, 244, 268, 270–2, 275
Quesnay's medical treatises, 34, 37–8, 40, 59–61, 68, 87

Racine, Jean (1639-1699), 94-5
Reason, 3, 11, 18, 21, 58, 67, 71, 95, 99, 103, 108, 116, 132-3, 140, 143, 167, 169, 176, 194, 196, 211, 215, 221, 240, 246, 253-4, 264, 270
Reform, 6, 14-5, 19, 22, 136, 149, 160-1, 166, 188-9, 216, 228, 241-60
Regularities, 54-6, 66
Religion, 4, 65, 105-8, 131-2, 139, 165, 176, 199, 203, 230, 238, 269, 273-6
Rent, 12-3, 121
Representative assemblies, chapter 5, also pages 20, 242-60
Republic of Letters, 9, 21, 92-3, 104, 133, 142
Revolution, 2, 10-11, 14-9, 88, 177, 190-1, 201, 209, 233, 260-9, 272-7
*Révolutions de Paris*, 265-6
Riley, James, 172
Riskin, Jessica, 65-6
Robertson, John, 57
Robespierre, Maximilien (1758-1794), 261, 265, 270, 273, 275
Rochefort, Marie Thérèse de Larlan de Kercadio, comtesse de (1716-1782), 88, 90
Rochefort, Pierre de (c.1673-1728), 25-7, 30-1
Rothschild, Emma, 58
Rousseau, Jean-Jacques (1712-1778), 20, 50, 109, 111, 120, 122, 128, 130, 143-5, 152, 170-1, 184, 207, 226, 233, 239

Saint-Lambert, Jean-François, marquis de (1716-1803), 199-200
Salon (art), 188, 201, 202-8
Say, Jean-Baptiste (1767-1832), 10
Schelle, Gustave (1845-1927), 26-7, 249
Schmitt, Carl (1888-1985), 19
Science, 30, 40, 53, 56-7, 112, 126, 134, 146, 152, 180
Scientific method, 4, 40, 52-4, 59, 61-2, 121-2, 127, 134-5, 140, 146, 272
Sculpture, 203-5, 207
Self, 4, 67, 99-102, 131, 133, 144, 160, 174-6, 178, 182, 204, 209, 240, 268-9, 272, 275, 276
Self-evidence, 52, 70, 73, 76, 79, 128, 132, 136, 139, 148
Self-interest, 4, 14-6, 52, 70, 131-3, 136-7, 157, 162, 168, 176, 249, 269, 275

Sensations, sensationalism, 3, 21, 54, 62, 68-72, 75, 77, 108, 139, 167, 196, 203, 235, 238-40, 270
Sensibility, 65, 140, 184, 196-8, 201, 206, 215, 226, 231-2, 238-40, 272
Seven Years War, 5-6, 43, 154
Shaftsbury, Anthony Ashley Cooper, third earl of (1671-1713), 197
Silhouette, Étienne de (1709-1767) 105, 161
Simonneau, Jacques-Guillaume (1740-1792), 264-6
Sixth sense, 108, 197, 269
Smith, Adam (1723-1790), 5, 10, 14, 58
Sociability, 16, 106, 118-20, 140, 175-6, 197, 238, 269
Société des arts, 33, 37
Sonenscher, Michael, 121, 177, 181, 268
Soul, 68, 76-7, 112, 148, 201, 204, 238, 268, 271-4
Sovereignty, 19, 131, 138, 165, 171, 177, 263
Steiner, Philippe, 62-3
Style, 48, 95-7, 100, 106, 114, 120, 125, 128-9, 133-4, 136, 141-3, 146-7, 178, 219-20
Sublime, 21, 75, 78, 95-6, 105-8, 133, 139, 194, 196, 272
Surgery, 25-6, 31-7, 39-40, 59-61
Surplus value, 3, 14, 238

Tableau économique, 3, 12-4, 44, 48, 53-6, 63, 65-6, 78-82, 117, 122-4, 132-6, 144-6, 175, 178, 180, 201, 209, 229, 276
Taxation, 8, 48, 86, 115, 121, 150, 153-63, 165-75, 185, 190, 214-8, 243-60
Text, 17, 30, 94, 126, 129, 193, 210
Theater, 94-5, 104-5, 199, 212-24
Theodicy, 268, 271-2
Theophilanthropy, 274-5
*Théorie de l'impôt*, 87, 125, 131, 134, 136, 140, 162, 166, 175, 251
Tier of assemblies, 166, 175, 179, 258
Tocqueville, Alexis de (1805-1859), 11-2, 14, 18, 171
*Traité de la monarchie*, 164-6
Translation, 104-7, 189, 193
Tree of knowledge, 126-7
Truth, 55, 70-3, 76-7, 79, 82, 127-8, 130, 132, 138, 141, 211, 220-1

Turgot, Anne-Robert-Jacques (1727–1781), 7–20, 42, 49, 58, 65, 101, 111, 146, 181–2, 186–90, 193–4, 203–5, 211, 219–23, 231–2, 239–40, 241–60, 267, 277

Uncertainty, 58–9, 66
Universalism, 121, 144, 170, 177, 197, 215, 269
Utopianism, 11–2, 19–20, 144, 201–2, 226, 233, 255
Utility, 14, 199, 201–2, 204, 206, 238, 250

Value, 12–3
Vauvenargues, Luc de Clapiers, marquis de (1715–1747), 85, 87–100, 103, 119
Vergennes, Charles Gravier, comte de (1717–1787), 190, 253

Véri, Joseph-Alphonse, abbé de (1724–1799), 248
Versailles, 34, 40–51, 79, 97–8, 147, 159–61, 173
Vien, Joseph-Marie (1716–1809), 203
Virtue, 16, 90, 98, 100, 108–10, 121, 130–1, 158, 164–5, 169, 177, 193, 198, 201–3, 207, 209, 226–7, 229, 267
Vision, 13, 28, 30, 39, 58, 69, 78, 80–2, 123, 128, 204
Vitalism, 36, 59–61, 63–5, 68, 98, 109, 208
Voltaire, François-Marie Arouet (1694–1778), 44, 74, 92, 101, 104–5, 142, 154, 186–7, 201, 207, 223

Weulersse, Georges (1874–1950), 6, 14, 52, 61
Wille, Johann-Georg (1715–1808), 26

Printed in Great Britain
by Amazon